THE SHADOW OF
THE ANTICHRIST

THE SHADOW OF THE ANTICHRIST

NIETZSCHE'S CRITIQUE OF CHRISTIANITY

STEPHEN N. WILLIAMS

BakerAcademic
Grand Rapids, Michigan

Paternoster:
thinking faith

©2006 by Stephen N. Williams

Published by Baker Academic
a division of Baker Publishing Group
P.O. Box 6287, Grand Rapids, MI 49516-6287
www.bakeracademic.com

and

Paternoster
9 Holdom Avenue
Bletchley
Milton Keynes MK1 1QR
United Kingdom

Printed in the United States of America

Library of Congress Cataloging-in-Publication Data
Williams, Stephen N. (Stephen Nantlais)
    The shadow of the antichrist : Nietzsche's critique of Christianity / Stephen N. Williams.
        p.   cm.
    Includes bibliographical references and index.
    ISBN 10: 0-8010-2702-0 (pbk.)
    ISBN 978-0-8010-2702-4 (pbk.)
    1. Nietzsche, Friedrich Wilhelm, 1844–1900—Influence. 2. Christianity—Philosophy—History—19th century. 3. Christianity—Controversial literature. I. Title.
B3318.C35W55 2006
230.092—dc22   2006002006

British Library Cataloguing-in-Publication Data
A catalogue record for this book is available from the British Library.

UK ISBN 10: 1-84227-476-7
UK ISBN 978-1-84227-476-7

To the memory of Rheinallt Nantlais Williams (1911–1993), witness and minister, theologian and philosopher

CONTENTS

Acknowledgments

THANKS ARE DUE to three people in particular. First, I am grateful to the anonymous reader of an earlier draft of this manuscript for a number of helpful suggestions. My thanks, second, to Robert Hosack of Baker Academic for a good dose of graciousness, patience, and encouragement. Finally, special thanks to my wife, Susan, for support too easily taken for granted. At one stage, Nietzsche hoped that he could set up a household of three (I avoid using the French) consisting of himself, one male friend, and one female friend. Over the years, my wife must have occasionally felt that he had achieved a measure of posthumous success.

ABBREVIATIONS

A *The Anti-christ*, in *Twilight of the Idols and The Anti-christ*, trans. R. J. Hollingdale (New York and London: Penguin, 1990)

AOM *Assorted Opinions and Maxims*, in *Human, All Too Human*, trans. R. J. Hollingdale (Cambridge: Cambridge University Press, 1996)

BGE *Beyond Good and Evil*, trans. Judith Norman (Cambridge: Cambridge University Press, 2002)

BT *The Birth of Tragedy and Other Writings*, trans. Ronald Speirs (Cambridge: Cambridge University Press, 1999)

CW *The Case of Wagner*, in *The Birth of Tragedy and the Case of Wagner*, trans. Walter Kaufmann (New York: Random House, 1967)

D *Daybreak*, trans. R. J. Hollingdale (Cambridge: Cambridge University Press, 1997)

DD *Dithyrambs of Dionysus*, trans. R. J. Hollingdale (London: Anvil, 2001)

EH *Ecce Homo*, trans. R. J. Hollingdale (New York and London: Penguin, 1979)

GS *The Gay Science*, trans. Josefine Nauckoff (Cambridge: Cambridge University Press, 2001)

HH *Human, All Too Human*, trans. R. J. Hollingdale (Cambridge: Cambridge University Press, 1996)

NCW *Nietzsche contra Wagner*, in *The Portable Nietzsche*, trans. Walter Kaufmann (New York: Viking, 1954)

OGM *On the Genealogy of Morality*, trans. Carol Diethe (Cambridge: Cambridge University Press, 1994)

PT   *Philosophy and Truth: Selections from Nietzsche's Notebooks of the Early 1870's*, trans. Daniel Breazeale (Atlantic Highlands, NJ: Humanities, 1990)

PTA   *Philosophy in the Tragic Age of the Greeks*, trans. Marianne Cowan (South Bend, IN: Gateway, 1962)

SL   *Selected Letters of Friedrich Nietzsche*, trans. Christopher Middleton (Chicago and London: University of Chicago Press, 1969)

TI   *Twilight of the Idols*, trans. Duncan Large (Oxford: Oxford University Press, 1998)

UO   *Unfashionable Observations*, trans. Richard T. Gray (Stanford, CA: Stanford University Press, 1995)

WP   *The Will to Power*, trans. Walter Kaufmann and R. J. Hollingdale (New York: Viking, 1967)

WS   *The Wanderer and His Shadow*, in *Human, All Too Human*, trans. R. J. Hollingdale (Cambridge: Cambridge University Press, 1996)

Z   *Thus Spoke Zarathustra*, trans. R. J. Hollingdale (New York and London: Penguin, 1969)

PREFACE

BOOKS ON NIETZSCHE, wrote John Neville Figgis, "crystallise into death the flaming soul, which speaks in them."[1] Perhaps it is because authors of studies on Nietzsche are aware of this that not only books but also chapters and articles on Nietzsche commonly place at their head one of his sayings. These sayings are often either gnomic or portentous or, to put it less pompously, either catchy or scary. I follow this convention, though with something better described as shrill and sobering:

> Wherever there are walls I shall inscribe this eternal accusation against Christianity upon them—I can write in letters which make even the blind see. . . . I call Christianity the *one* great curse, the *one* great intrinsic depravity, the one great instinct for revenge for which no expedient is sufficiently poisonous, secret, subterranean, *petty*—I call it the one immortal blemish of mankind.

So, more or less, concludes *The Anti-christ*. Nietzsche was a subtle author, and we all want to think of ourselves as subtle readers. Nevertheless, he gives it to us pretty straight here, and we should take it as given. What was it about Christianity that caused his agitation?

This book aims to answer that question and provide an occasional, rather than systematic, response. Many people know that Nietzsche was and is an extremely influential foe and have a general notion of what he was up to without knowing in detail what he said or why he said it. Over the years, I have often tried to convey Nietzsche's ideas to academic and nonacademic audiences plus those that hover somewhere in between.

1. John Neville Figgis, *The Will to Freedom, or The Gospel of Nietzsche and the Gospel of Christ* (London: Longmans, Green, 1917), 159.

Whether or not this has been well done, I have often been told that what has been presented in the name of Nietzsche is identifiable as a depiction of attitudes commonly encountered at a whole range of cultural and social levels, at least in the West. Karl Jaspers observed that "in the end one cannot help but ask how a man who is by no means representative can still become as overwhelmingly significant as though he spoke for humanity itself."[2] One reason is that Nietzsche was a powerful writer; *that* quality is surely hard to deny, whatever our judgments on the philosophical strength of his work. What follows tries to convey something of this power, as well as the substance.

My account is definitely tailored for a strictly academic and not a nonacademic readership. It is not, first and foremost, an attempt to supplement the voluminous scholarly material on Nietzsche for the benefit of Nietzsche scholars. If they find in it the occasional morsel in the form of something freshly thought or said, I shall be glad enough. I am less interested in making an original contribution than in offering the best description that I can, within inevitable limits, of Nietzsche on Christianity. I have tried not to presuppose knowledge of Nietzsche's thought, and in this sense the book is introductory. But it is not a very gentle introduction, and it is pitched to those who have an academic interest in intellectual history.

My own craft is that of the common or garden theologian, of whom Nietzsche more or less rightly asked: "But who still bothers about theologians—except other theologians?" (*HH* 28).[3] Yet both Nietzsche and the state of scholarship on Nietzsche present an obvious dilemma even— perhaps especially—for an undertaking such as the present one, where a theologian tries to come to grips with Nietzsche. Nietzsche himself is rich and complex. A phenomenal amount of stuff has been produced on him over the last years, and there is huge diversity in interpretation. It is altogether daunting, if sometimes exhilarating, for any creature of tender intellectual conscience with relatively modest ambitions in exposition. The scale of the problem is unpretentiously indicated by the remarks of a well-known Nietzsche scholar and translator, the late Reginald Hollingdale, in the Postscript to the second edition of his biography of Nietzsche. Not only had he not read all that had been written on Nietzsche—an impossible task for anyone—but he also had not understood all that he

---

2. Karl Jaspers, *Nietzsche: An Introduction to the Understanding of His Philosophical Activity* (Tucson: University of Arizona Press, 1965), 16.

3. With the exception of *SL*, unless otherwise stated, in Nietzsche's texts the numbering is of sections, not pages. References keyed to the abbreviations listed in the front of the book will usually be incorporated into the main text of the present work.

had read.[4] Biser said twenty years ago that there is a "pressing need for a Nietzschean hermeneutic."[5] If so, we are not close to achieving it.

What, then, remains for the relative amateur? One might plead insanity, but instead I plead compulsion. Having done so, the author should either take his own line in the interpretation of Nietzsche, thus risking conveying to the readership that this simply is *the* correct reading, or state everything with such an admixture of blandness and qualification, in the cause of disinterested caution, that readers who have not died of boredom en route reach the journey's end none the wiser, even if somewhat better informed. From the paranoid point of view, it would be easy to worry about indictment on either the charge of misrepresentation or the charge of superficiality. There comes a time, however, when we just have to get on with the job as we see it.

The author of a quite short study of Nietzsche announced that "the reader will meet only the shadow of Nietzsche."[6] This sometimes turns out to be the case in longer studies too. Does the title of the present volume announce that this is the case here? No, I think I am more ambitious than that, though I certainly do not claim to accomplish something where others have failed. The "shadow" in the title signifies, rather, my desire to look beyond Nietzsche while concentrating on Nietzsche, and it has an interesting warrant in Nietzsche's own usage (*GS* 108). What follows includes an invitation to follow various trails further. The volume could have been written differently. Richard Schacht, for example, has written an admirably detailed volume on Nietzsche's philosophy that cuts its own exegetical and analytical philosophical path through Nietzsche and avoids much reference to secondary sources or any deviation off the main track.[7] From a theological point of view, there is ample room for such a study.[8] But I have approached things differently. Fairly copious reference and quotation has its drawbacks and can be criticized on several scores: it is sophomoric; it betrays lack of mastery of material; it is motivated by the desire to display, for example. Perhaps I shall be accused of all three things, but my hope is that, from the reader's point of view, it is all gain. Furthermore, I have benefited greatly

4. Reginald J. Hollingdale, *Nietzsche: The Man and His Philosophy*, rev. ed. (Cambridge: Cambridge University Press, 1999), 259.

5. Eugen Biser, "Nietzsche: Critic in the Grand Style," in *Studies in Nietzsche and the Judaeo-Christian Tradition*, ed. James C. O'Flaherty, Timothy F. Sellner, and Robert M. Helm (Chapel Hill: University of North Carolina Press, 1985), 17.

6. H. van Reissen, *Nietzsche* (Philadelphia: Presbyterian & Reformed Publishers, 1960), 9.

7. Richard Schacht, *Nietzsche* (London: Routledge & Kegan Paul, 1983).

8. It is unfortunate that an editor described the second part of an article on Nietzsche that I wrote some years ago as "an analytic response to Nietzsche," which it designedly was not: Stephen N. Williams, "Dionysus against the Crucified: Nietzsche *contra* Christianity," part 2, *Tyndale Bulletin* 49, no. 1 (1998): 131–53.

from considering Nietzsche in light of Dostoyevsky, Hesse, Thomas Wolfe, Barth, and Bonhoeffer, and Nietzsche's comments on Pascal and Laurence Sterne have sent me back to the primary texts. Much is well said by all these, not to mention commentators on Nietzsche's work, and we should benefit from their wisdom. I am persuaded that casting a net way beyond Nietzsche's own text does better justice to that text for my purposes than something more restrictive. Nevertheless, if these various figures have enriched the treatment, they have not governed the line of thought.

A specific comment is in order about what is included and what is excluded in what follows. For reasons that I try to make clear in the text, I believe that Nietzsche's early encounters with the Greeks, Schopenhauer, and Wagner—prior to his anti-Christian writing—need to be given a reasonable amount of exposure if we want to understand his hostility to Christianity. We should not immediately seize on what Nietzsche says about Christianity in order to understand his position. So in the first two chapters, I have tried to both describe and muse on these wider considerations. However, I have not allotted space to the discussion of Nietzsche, Christianity, and postmodernity, although I do touch a little on the question, especially in the final chapter. There are two reasons for this omission. The first is simply that it would substantially add to the length of the volume. The second is that, reading Nietzsche, I am not persuaded that the things in his literature that have fueled postmodern interest in him are the things that most illuminate his attack on Christianity in particular. The term "postmodern" is used in different ways, and readers may feel that much of what is said in this volume actually impinges on postmodernity, even if it is given little formal consideration. That would be to the good. But it is fair to warn the reader on this score.

Each chapter begins with a quotation from Lord Byron's *Manfred*. This does not signify an insistent hermeneutical move in relation to Nietzsche, as though this is the single most appropriate rubric under which to discuss Nietzsche on Christianity. However, certainly in his youth Nietzsche knew, appreciated, and was influenced by Byron and *Manfred*, and lines from it provide a suitable backdrop to the different scenes that we shall view.[9] Reflecting on himself and on his authorship at the end of his life, Nietzsche said: "I must be profoundly related to Byron's *Manfred*: I discovered all these abysses in myself."[10] What abysses these were! Beyond Faust, beyond the hope of reconciliation, Manfred toys

9. Here some interesting connections may be chased down. In his youth, Nietzsche wrote a story featuring two chamois hunters: Rüdiger Safranski, *Nietzsche: A Philosophical Biography* (New York and London: Norton, 2002), 33. Is it coincidence that a chamois hunter comes into *Manfred* too? The "forces of nature" and "storm" themes (31–33) are also among those that are interesting when we try to connect Nietzsche and *Manfred*.

10. *EH*, "Why I Am So Clever," 4.

with dark wraiths and communes with self within and spirits without, to compose a soul that is locked in on itself, an agent that has affirmed its acts and itself in its acts.[11]

But is this persistent return to *Manfred* designed to (literally) demonize Nietzsche in line with the title of the present volume? No. I merely take Manfred and Nietzsche, and Nietzsche on *Manfred*, at their own word. "The Antichrist," a title Nietzsche accords to himself and to a volume, is usually so translated but can also be rendered as "The Anti-Christian."[12] There may be good reasons for preferring the standard translation, but nothing whatsoever hangs on this as far as I am concerned, so from the outset readers should exorcize from their minds the notion that *Antichrist* in the title of my work and *Manfred* in its chapters are signs of a campaign to demonize Nietzsche.

It is universally recognized that Nietzschean scholarship owes an immense amount to Walter Kaufmann, not just for his translations of Nietzsche's work but also for rescuing him from misrepresentation; this is acknowledged even by those who quarrel both with Kaufmann's own interpretations and, occasionally, with his translations. The title of his work that became something of a landmark in Nietzsche studies in the English-speaking world was *Nietzsche: Philosopher, Psychologist, Antichrist*.[13] In it, Nietzsche is de-demonized as much as he can possibly be and perhaps domesticated more than he plausibly can be.

Yet, ultimate questions are at stake in Nietzsche's work, and it is by no means just the religious who wonder about the nature, dimension, or reality of the demonic when they ponder those ultimate questions.[14] "I

11. See Michael Allen Gillespie, *Nihilism before Nietzsche* (Chicago and London: University of Chicago Press, 1996), 121–25. I borrow the phrase "composing the soul" from Graham Parkes (*Composing the Soul: Reaches of Nietzsche's Psychology* [Chicago and London: University of Chicago Press, 1994]), who handles the influence of Byron on Nietzsche but frequently orders his own exposition by using Emerson's words rather than Byron's. In his play *Arms and the Man* (in *The Complete Plays* [London: Oldhams, 1934], 103), George Bernard Shaw has a delightful description of the Byronic character that invites psychological comparison with Nietzsche. Shaw also has an explicit reference to Nietzsche at the close of the scene on Don Juan in hell in *Man and Superman*, in *Complete Plays*, 389. Cf. Nietzsche, *WP* 871.

12. It seems to me that a remark in *EH* is among those that warrant translating *Der Antichrist* as "The Antichrist": "I am, in Greek and not only in Greek, the *Anti-Christ*" (*EH*, "Why I Write Such Excellent Books," 2). But the text and not just the title of Nietzsche's work often offers more than one possibility in translation. Some declare from the outset their unwillingness to be committed on the title; see, e.g., Weaver Santaniello, ed., *Nietzsche and the Gods* (New York: State University of New York Press, 2001), xix.

13. Walter Kaufmann, *Nietzsche: Philosopher, Psychologist, Antichrist*, 4th ed. (New York: Vintage, 1974).

14. Paul Tillich's work still repays study here, even on the part of those who take a very different line than Tillich does on symbol and ontology. I am thinking especially of *The*

know the Devil and all his visions of God," Nietzsche said.[15] "In Manfred," says Gillespie, "[William] Blake's tiger and the mysterious creator of the tiger have become one; they have become the chimera," and W. B. Yeats, who was deeply and actively interested in the occult, viewed Nietzsche as the "completion" of Blake, with whom he was familiar as the author of *The Marriage of Heaven and Hell*.[16] The question of good and evil has never been more important than it is today. Nietzsche wrote about it eloquently, and it is impossible to grapple with him without grappling with the question of their ultimate unity or distinction. Blake and Byron both, in their way, help us to locate Nietzsche, in some respects, in his wider modern context.

Lest this look like a return to demonization by the back door, let me finally comment that the spirit of my personal reaction to Nietzsche is as well captured in words from Thomas Wolfe's sprawling novel *Of Time and the River* as it is by a consideration of *Manfred*. Intense and fatiguing, spectacular and exaggerated in his prose, Wolfe builds up to this sentiment, if he builds up to anything. Perhaps the reader would care to reread these words after the end of the fifth chapter of this book, which attempts to describe Nietzsche's magnum opus, *Thus Spoke Zarathustra*. Wolfe's words are quoted here with no comment.

> For what are we, my brother? We are a phantom flare of grieved desire, the ghostling and phosphoric flicker of immortal time, a brevity of days haunted by the eternity of the earth. We are an unspeakable utterance, an insatiable hunger, an unquenchable thirst; a lust that bursts our sinews, explodes our brains, sickens and rots our insides, and rips our hearts asunder. We are a twist of passion, a moment's flame of love and ecstasy, a sinew of bright blood and agony, a lost cry, a music of pain and joy, a haunting of brief, sharp hours, an almost captured beauty, a demon's whisper of unbodied memory. We are the dupes of time.[17]

Courage to Be (London: Fount, 1962), which has a discussion of Nietzsche (34–49) but is more widely useful, for example, on "Vitality and Courage," 81–88. Tillich also includes an account in his *Perspectives on Nineteenth and Twentieth Century Protestant Theology* (London: SCM, 1967), 191–207.

15. Erich Heller, *The Importance of Nietzsche* (Chicago: University of Chicago Press, 1988), 3.

16. Gillespie, *Nihilism before Nietzsche*, 125. Yeats told Lady Gregory that "Nietzsche completes Blake and has the same roots" (Terence Brown, *The Life of W. B. Yeats: A Critical Biography* [Oxford: Blackwell, 1999], 151). A sentence from Nietzsche appears on the title page of Brown's volume. How close to the surface of Yeats's mind was the connection between Nietzsche and Blake is suggested by his introduction to Rabindranath Tagore, *Gitanjali* (New York: Macmillan, 1971). I do not endorse Yeats's description, but see Blake, "Proverbs of Hell," in *The Marriage of Heaven and Hell* (Oxford: Oxford University Press, 1975), esp. 77.2–3. When C. S. Lewis spoke of *The Great Divorce* (London: Fount, 1977), he had Blake in mind (7).

17. Thomas Wolfe, *Of Time and the River* (New York: Scribner, 1999), 852–53.

1

DIFFERENT WORLDS

Forgetfulness
. . . Of that which is within me; read it there—
Ye know it, and I cannot utter it.
. . . Oblivion, self-oblivion—.

Byron, *Manfred*, act 1, scene 1

Early Days

It has long been something of a truism that "the modern consciousness of history is a consciousness of crisis."[1] So to say that Nietzsche
was born in critical times is not to say much. Still, we should recognize
that the years of his life (1844–1900) encompassed the revolutions of
1848, which took place in the year when the *Communist Manifesto* was
published, the unification of Germany under Bismarck in 1871, and the
ominous buildup toward the First World War, in 1914–18. Nietzsche's
thought and even his life are sometimes described in relative detachment from the political story of his times. When the scope of an account
requires such detachment, as it does in the present case, at least we must
keep in mind that there is a price for omission.

It is impossible to say how the bigger scene might have impacted
Friedrich Wilhelm Nietzsche, born in a quiet village in Prussian Saxony,

1. Jürgen Moltmann, *Theology of Hope* (London: SCM, 1967), 230.

not far from Leipzig, had his childhood in a Lutheran parsonage been happy and uneventful. It was not. He was not yet five years old when his father died.[2] This was shattering for little Friedrich, or "Fritz." What is particularly sad and striking is not just his immediate and natural experience of grief. It is also the impression still left on his mind and soul years later. Looking back, at the age of fourteen, Nietzsche wrote: "The thought [that] I was forever parted from my beloved father seized hold of me and I wept bitterly. . . . The ceremony began at one o'clock, accompanied by the tolling of the bells. Oh, I shall always have the hollow clangour of those bells in my ears, I shall never forget the gloomy melody of the hymn 'Jesu, meine Zuversicht.'"[3] This death was on August 2, 1849. Nietzsche later wrote: "The sight of the surroundings of our childhood moves us deeply: the garden-house, the church with the graveyard, the pond and the wood—we see all these with a sense of suffering. We are seized with pity for ourselves, for what have we not gone through since those days!" (*HH* 277).

Admittedly, he ended this paragraph with a contrast between what these things can represent, namely, somewhat unthinking contentment and the path that he would himself tread, leading to the acquisition of "a higher culture."[4] But the suffering sensibility is manifest. "That which we call 'Nietzsche' is an extraordinarily, almost incredibly sensitive substance, whose endeavor from beginning to end is to bind the flood of painful stimuli called 'life' by becoming the 'most powerful and tremendous nature' who could absorb it all."[5] Much can be made of Nietzsche's eventual emotional reaction to religion in connection with the early loss of his father. A good portion of Nietzsche's greatest work, *Thus Spoke Zarathustra*, was drafted in 1883, the year when the author turned thirty-nine. At what is perhaps its highest moment of drama, as a perplexed and burdened Zarathustra advances toward insight into the eternal recurrence of all things, we read the following:

2. Because Nietzsche was born late in 1844 (October), even standard accounts will often say that Nietzsche's age was one year more than it actually was at the time when various things happened. For the basic facts about Nietzsche's life, see especially Reginald J. Hollingdale, *Nietzsche: The Man and His Philosophy* (Cambridge: Cambridge University Press, 1999); and Ronald Hayman, *Nietzsche: A Critical Life* (London: Phoenix, 1995). See also Rüdiger Safranski, *Nietzsche: A Philosophical Biography* (New York: Norton, 2002); and Curtis Cate, *Friedrich Nietzsche* (London: Hutchinson, 2002).

3. Hollingdale, *Nietzsche*, 9–10.

4. Shortly after this section, Nietzsche writes of the "double face" of "religion, . . . according to whether a man gazes up to it so that it may take from him his burdens and distress, or looks down on it as on the fetters fastened to him so that he may not rise too high into the air" (*HH* 280). In early childhood, he seems to have looked up.

5. Henry Staten, *Nietzsche's Voice* (Ithaca, NY: Cornell University Press, 1990), 82. This is a particularly rewarding study of Nietzsche.

Thus I spoke more and more softly: for I was afraid of my own thoughts and reservations. Then, suddenly, I heard a dog *howling* nearby. Had I ever heard a dog howling in that way? My thoughts ran back. Yes! When I was a child, in my most distant childhood. . . . Had I been dreaming? Had I awoken? All at once I was standing between wild cliffs alone, desolate in the most desolate moonlight. *But there a man was lying!*[6]

In a commonly used English translation of this text, Hollingdale glosses this passage as "a memory from Nietzsche's childhood. Nietzsche's father died following a fall, and it seems that Nietzsche was attracted to the scene by the frightened barking of a dog."[7] He tacitly dropped this reference in both the first and second editions of his biography of Nietzsche, and we cannot presume on its accuracy, but there is plenty of fodder in Nietzsche's literature for psychoanalysts, who highlight the impact of the death of a beloved father on an extremely sensitive child. And *Z* apparently contains allusions to Nietzsche's childhood experience of mortality.[8]

A psychological account of the formation of Nietzsche's views on God and on Christian belief is both possible in principle and instructive in the attempt. It is surely hard to become seriously interested in Nietzsche's thought without becoming seriously interested in Nietzsche's personality, and it is not only hard but also wrong to resist the temptation to read his literary output as a biography or autobiography of the soul. "It has gradually become clear to me," Nietzsche once remarked, "what every great philosophy has hitherto been: a confession on the part of its author and a kind of involuntary and unconscious memoir" (*BGE* 6). Still, in the pages that follow, little is offered in the way of psychological interpretation. The way by which someone comes by a philosophy of life does not of itself tell us to what extent that philosophy has something to be said for it. Many have been influenced by Nietzsche's teachings without the presence of the same or similar psychological factors. However interesting we find the man Nietzsche and however much interest in him is spiced by an observation Freud somewhere makes—to the effect that Nietzsche knew himself better than any man who had ever lived—it is not with the man himself that we are principally concerned in this study. Yet, it is difficult to block out things like his thirty-eight-year-old

6. "Of the Vision and the Riddle," *Z* 3.46.

7. Ibid., p. 341n25.

8. See Robert Gooding-Williams, *Zarathustra's Dionysian Modernism* (Stanford, CA: Stanford University Press, 2002), 369n119, though the dream to which he refers is surely the one he had *before* the death of Nietzsche's baby brother, not afterward. Away from the scene of death, see Jung's intriguing discovery in connection with *Z* in Carl G. Jung, *Man and His Symbols* (New York: Doubleday, 1964), 37.

disclosure that he had "not for a moment been able to forget . . . that my mother called me a disgrace to my dead father."[9] A little over a year before his eventual mental breakdown in 1889, he wrote to that mother: "Never since childhood to have heard anything deep and understanding said about me—that's all part of my *fate*; also I do not remember having complained about it."[10]

As in the case of neglecting the political context, so also there is a price to pay for relatively ignoring the "psychological" trajectory of interpretation. Just what this might amount to is indicated by Joachim Köhler's recently translated psychobiography of Nietzsche.[11] In this sad and oppressive, moving and memorable account, Köhler purports to lay bare Zarathustra's secret, which is Nietzsche's own. It lies buried not just in the bleak agony of nightmares and visions that succeeded his father's death but also in homoeroticism, forbidden homosexuality, and intense attachment to the culture of the naked Greek. Here is the ground of the profound suffering and profound spiritual and psychological disturbance that constitute Nietzsche's inner reality. Read aright, *Thus Spoke Zarathustra* discloses it. So Köhler argues. In the nature of the case, the argument is often suppositious, and the author frequently guesses at various matters with unjustifiable confidence, thus disposing the critical reader to be suspicious of the main line of the argument.[12] However, too much in Köhler's presentation of Nietzsche's erotic melancholy is persuasive and illuminating for us to dismiss hastily his basic contention.[13] The nature of my treatment makes it impossible to take such factors into account, but ignoring them does not mean passing judgment one way or the other. Staten is right: when Nietzsche remarks that the "degree and type of a person's sexuality reaches up into the furthermost peaks of their spirit" (*BGE* 75), this "authorizes us, invites us, to look for the trace of his erotic economy in all of his thoughts, to find the system of displacements, conversions, defenses, and sublimations by which his

9. To Overbeck, *SL*, received on February 11, 1883.

10. Ibid., October 18, 1887.

11. Joachim Köhler, *Zarathustra's Secret: The Interior Life of Friedrich Nietzsche* (New Haven and London: Yale University Press, 2002).

12. A careful reading shows that our suspicion should apply to statements made about others, not just about Nietzsche. How, for instance, can Köhler possibly know that Wagner's assumptions and information were "*nothing but . . . vague*" in relation to the relevant issues surrounding Nietzsche's condition (ibid., 101, my italics)?

13. Graham Parkes in *Composing the Soul: Reaches of Nietzsche's Psychology* (Chicago: University of Chicago Press, 1994), 429n2, is wrong to say, in relation to Köhler, that "the 'evidence' for his subject's homosexuality does not consist of any revelatory new materials but rather in a distinctly quirky reading of selected passages in *Zarathustra*." There may be little in the way of "revelatory new materials," but the evidence adduced goes beyond a reading of Z.

relation to Eros drives the unfolding of the intellectual structures he generates."[14] We are more concerned with those structures than their underlying economy, but Nietzsche himself observed that sexual interest was a potent driving force in modern culture.[15]

In principle, things of causally decisive importance in Nietzsche's rejection of Christianity might never come to light even in a meticulously detailed biographical account. Consider his childhood nightmares. Those acquainted with religious households may venture the informed surmise that Nietzsche cried out to the God of his childhood faith for deliverance from the terrors of the night. Apparently there was no deliverance. Why not? Did Nietzsche conclude that it was because the theistic account of the world is false and illusory that his cry was vainly raised on a wind of false presupposition? The question is hypothetical; Nietzsche may neither have asked nor answered questions along these lines. Even if he had, would they have been religiously decisive? I merely illustrate the difficulty in principle of expounding Nietzsche's interior life and its bearing on his thought. His writing might be a biography of the soul, but this does not mean that it was crafted to bare his soul for all to see. "Every philosophy also *conceals* a philosophy; every opinion is also a hiding-place, every word also a mask" (*BGE* 289). Yet, plenty in Nietzsche's work is rather plain speaking, sincere and direct persuasion. We do not always need to know what exactly goes *into* it to get *out of* it much of what Nietzsche intends us to get, at least at one level. It is both interesting and rewarding to ponder the connection between philosophy and sexual experience, or philosophy and the experience of mortality, especially where antiquity and Christianity have vied for the soul of modern Europe. However, the scope of my account, not to mention the competence of its author, does not permit exploration along these lines.

Nevertheless, proceeding as I am within the parameters of a broad biographical framework, Nietzsche's early experiences of death deserve more than merely casual mention. Apart from his father, three members of his household died in Nietzsche's early years. A brother, three years younger, died in infancy; an aunt when he was ten; a grandmother when he was eleven. So by the time he went off to school in Pforta in 1858, Nietzsche's life had been engulfed by the shadow of death. Once in Pforta, it was not long before he lost a grandfather and a school chaplain; he was fond of both. On at least two out of all these occasions, Nietzsche apparently had some premonition of the deaths. Little wonder that a sense of homelessness pervades both his youthful poetic writing and also the

14. Staten, *Nietzsche's Voice*, 140.
15. See the whole section in which the claim is made that "all the higher culture and literature of *classical* France, too, grew up on the soil of sexual interest" (*TI* 9.21).

personal experience of the later years. If there is something Romantic in that sense, it was forged in the furnace of most unromantic affliction.

Experience of mortality does differ from culture to culture. Thomas Mann describes the fictional Hans Castorp's experience of death as follows: "Thus in so short a space in such young years did death play upon the spirit and the senses—but chiefly the senses—of the lad."[16] In Nietzsche's case, it is hard to prioritize.[17] At any rate, the time at Pforta was unsurprisingly a formative period in Nietzsche's life, as he came to terms with grief and loss. Nietzsche regarded it as decisive: "I absolutely cannot see how one can later make up for having failed to go to a *good school* at the proper time. Such a man does not know himself; he walks through life without having learned to walk; his flabby muscles reveal themselves with every step" (*WP* 912). He remained in Pforta until 1864. There followed a brief period of theological and philological study at Bonn before he proceeded to Leipzig to read classical philology. During his teenage years, he began to lose or relinquish his childhood faith and apparently strong piety. Why?

There is no single or uniform answer to this question. But then there is no single or uniform question. Attempting a precise dating makes sense only when we know what we are trying to date. Is it religious doubt or distancing, skepticism or rejection, and do these distinctions obtain in Nietzsche's case? There are shades of unbelief and varieties of atheism with which to reckon.[18] Perhaps Nietzsche's early and rather stereotyped religious sentiments quite soon became a cloak for breaking with them. Perhaps we should delay a date for the final relinquishment of faith until a year or two after Nietzsche had exited his teens. Both the intrinsic and the voluntary limits we have ascribed to psychological analysis obviously apply here. In a literary swan song, composed on the verge of collapse into insanity, Nietzsche wrote that he had "absolutely no knowledge of atheism as an outcome of reasoning, still less as an event: with me it is obvious by instinct."[19] His self-assessment is contentious.[20] It is hard

16. Despite its generally notorious quality, I am here using the older H. T. Lowe-Porter translation of Thomas Mann's *The Magic Mountain* (New York: Heritage, 1962), though John E. Woods in *The Magic Mountain* (New York: Vintage, 1995), 26, renders *Geist* as "mind" rather than "spirit," which perhaps better picks up the contrast with *die Sinne* (senses).

17. Comparison between Castorp and Nietzsche can profitably be extended by reflection on how experiencing death relates to their respective capacities for friendship. As George Santayana put it: friendship "where nature has made minds isolated and bodies mortal, is rich also in melancholy," in *Three Philosophical Poets: Lucretius, Dante, Goethe* (Cambridge, MA: Harvard University Press, 1910), 66.

18. See, e.g., Thomas Brobjer, "Nietzsche's Atheism," in *Nietzsche and the Divine*, ed. John Lippitt and Jim Urpeth (Manchester, UK: Clinamen, 2000).

19. *EH*, "Why I Am So Clever," 1.

20. It is accepted too uncritically by, e.g., Helmut Thielicke, *The Evangelical Faith*, vol. 1 (Edinburgh: T&T Clark, 1974), 249. I mention this volume because it offers an account

to decide how authentic or how conventional are the expressions of piety well into Nietzsche's teens and whether it is fair to contrast the authentic and the conventional. In school, Nietzsche certainly pondered the big questions about the divine providential governance of life, fate and freedom, destiny and suffering. In connection with what we have said thus far, it should be observed that something like the traditional conundrum of God, evil, and suffering may be nearer the bottom of Nietzsche's departure from Christianity than readily appears on the surface of much of the later work. Certainly, his first major publication, *The Birth of Tragedy*, contains the telling averment that "only as an *aesthetic phenomenon* is existence and the world eternally *justified*," after we have read that the "gods justify the life of men by living it themselves—the only satisfactory theodicy" (*BT* 5, 3).

However the story should exactly be told, there are a number of influences that must be reckoned with in any brief report. Historical criticism of the Bible has a fair claim to head up the list. Nietzsche lived in a century of liberal or radical approaches to Scripture, and among the celebrated doyens of the more radical type, none was more celebrated or notorious than David Friedrich Strauss. In 1835 Strauss had published his *Life of Jesus Critically Examined*, identifying and analyzing what he perceived as the mythological elements in the New Testament accounts. His production embroiled him in severe public and professional difficulties. Nietzsche had felt the impact of historical criticism before encountering Strauss; before hitting his sixteenth birthday, he was reading and recommending that his sister read radical approaches to Jesus. But a remark he made about Strauss in 1865 is particularly illuminating. If Strauss's identification of mythology is valid, "that can have serious consequences; if you give up Christ you will have to give up God as well."[21] Strauss showed how we cannot be gently weaned out of theological conservatism into genial religious breadth. Things are much more serious than that. Later, Nietzsche would argue that if you give up God, you have to give up morality as well. Meanwhile, once historical criticism had done its work on the text of the New Testament, Nietzsche was not disposed to allow some variant of theism or Deism to fill the

---

of Nietzsche on the death of God, written by a theologian who has carefully studied modern thought. Also see idem, *Modern Faith and Thought* (Grand Rapids: Eerdmans, 1990), which also contains some discussion of Nietzsche.

21. Hollingdale, *Nietzsche*, 33. Nietzsche had just read a new edition of Strauss's work. The standard English translation, however, is from a different German edition, and editions of Strauss's work vary significantly. See Peter Hodgson's introduction to David F. Strauss, *The Life of Jesus Critically Examined* (London: SCM, 1973). For Nietzsche's earlier reading, see Hayman, *Nietzsche*, 39.

spot vacated by Christianity.[22] This is not surprising, because Strauss was part of something bigger and radically further reaching than the purely historical-critical investigation of the New Testament.

This was all about Hegel and what happened after him.[23] Hegel could be, was, and is read in many ways, including as a relatively orthodox and conservative Lutheran. But in and after his day, an influential coterie spied not only the bloom of serious radicalism in Hegel's philosophy but also the seed of still more thoroughgoing radicalism, and they steered the principles of his system in the direction of atheism. Ludwig Feuerbach, in particular, offered his interpretation of *The Essence of Christianity* in 1841, and Nietzsche read it in his formative years.[24] Broadly, Feuerbach interpreted standard Christian belief as a projection onto a mythical reality (God) of characteristics of our own (human) being. There are affinities between Feuerbach's and Nietzsche's critiques of religion. "Religion," Feuerbach announced, "is the disuniting of man from himself; he sets God before him as the antithesis of himself. . . . God is the absolutely positive, the sum of all realities; man the absolutely negative, comprehending all negations."[25] Succinctly and anthropologically, according to Feuerbach, "in religion, man separates himself from himself."[26] When Nietzsche comes to sound a quite similar note, speaking of "this division of oneself, this mockery of one's own nature . . . of which the religions have made so much," he is expressing something fundamental in his analysis of religion (*HH* 137). And when Nietzsche, aged seventeen, contrasted faith and knowledge, the former being essentially a matter of the heart in a way that the latter is not, he might have been echoing Feuerbach: "God, as the object of religion, . . . is essentially an object only of religion, not of philosophy,—of feeling, not of intellect,—of the heart's necessity, not of the mind's freedom."[27] Nietzsche later wrote of "this pathological excess of feeling" in Christianity (*HH* 114).

22. Whether we are justified in ascribing pantheism to Nietzsche at any stage is more controversial. See, e.g., Graham Parkes on Nietzsche's "dionysian pantheism" in "Nature and the Human 'Redivinised': Mahayana Buddhist Themes in *Thus Spoke Zarathustra*," in Lippitt and Urpeth, *Nietzsche and the Divine*. In *HH* 272, does Nietzsche hint at the presence of pantheism in his own development?

23. Karl Lowith's study *From Hegel to Nietzsche: The Revolution in Nineteenth Century Thought* (London: Constable, 1965) remains an illuminating introduction.

24. Thomas H. Brobjer, "Nietzsche's Changing Relation with Christianity: Nietzsche as Christian, Atheist, and Antichrist," in *Nietzsche and the Gods*, ed. Weaver Santaniello (New York: State University of New York Press, 2001), 140.

25. Ludwig Feuerbach, *The Essence of Christianity* (New York: Prometheus, 1989), 33.

26. Ibid., 181.

27. Ibid., 186. He continues: "But that which I do not trust myself to doubt, which I cannot doubt without feeling disturbed in soul, without incurring guilt; that is no matter of theory but a matter of conscience, no being of the intellect, but of the heart" (cf. 140).

It would be easy to press on to further positive comparison, for example, with respect to prayer and miracle. And readers of Nietzsche will certainly prick up their ears on hearing Feuerbach declare: "Only he who has the courage to be absolutely negative has the strength to create something new."[28] Where there is no direct influence, there can yet be a significant measure of affinity. Although he does not often refer to Feuerbach, Nietzsche may well have owed him more than he indicated.[29] He was not given to crediting others with ideas that he himself firmly maintained. Nevertheless, in tone and atmosphere, quite apart from some points of content, Feuerbach's work differs from what Nietzsche would later produce. After remarking that in post-Hegelian radicalisms "everyone seeks to point out a remnant of Christianity in everyone else," Lowith quotes Stirner: Feuerbach did not discard Christianity but rather tried "to drag it from its heaven and keep it forever."[30] We are reminded of the "death of God" movement in the theology of the 1960s, in which Nietzsche's name featured: Feuerbach's humanism somewhat cushions the atheistic blow just as the humanism of the sixties' theologians severely cushioned the Nietzschean blow. I have been quoting from Nietzsche's work *Human, All Too Human* to illustrate the parallels with Feuerbach, since this work contains Nietzsche's first major direct assault on Christianity. But this volume testifies to contrast as well. Nietzsche subtitled it *A Book for Free Spirits* and anything but endorsed Feuerbach's contrasting evaluation of Hebrew and Christian religions, expressed in Feuerbach's comment that "in relation to the Israelite, the Christian is an *esprit fort*, a free-thinker."[31] As his own work proceeded, Nietzsche rather reversed the evaluation. The difference between the two becomes especially evident when we study Feuerbach's various comments on love, brought to their summation in the closing chapter of *The Essence of Christianity*.

I anticipate. Feuerbach and the post-Hegelian context of German philosophy of religion provided soil for Nietzsche's early growth away from Christianity, though what in this tradition made its impact and when are not easily charted in detail. If we enter into the worlds of the early and the later Hegel; the radical reaction to the later Hegel and its intellectual relation to the early Hegel; Bauer and Stirner; Proudhon and Kierkegaard;

28. Quoted by Lowith, *From Hegel to Nietzsche*, 75.
29. Tyler T. Roberts, *Contesting Spirit: Nietzsche, Affirmation, Religion* (Princeton, NJ: Princeton University Press, 1998), 58n9.
30. Feuerbach, *Essence of Christianity*, 340, 357. Nietzsche himself eventually pointed out remnants of Christianity in the atheistic Schopenhauer, and John Neville Figgis in *Will to Freedom, or The Gospel of Nietzsche and the Gospel of Christ* (London: Longmans, Green, 1917), 210–12, imagines Stirner doing the same with Nietzsche. The influence of Stirner himself on Nietzsche is controverted now, as it was a century and more ago.
31. Feuerbach, *Essence of Christianity*, 32.

Marx and Engels—a wealth of conceptual relationships are presented for consideration as we plot Nietzsche's move away from Christianity. But alongside historical criticism and early-nineteenth-century philosophy of religion, we must mention the influence of scientific materialism on Nietzsche's early thinking. To the names of Strauss and Feuerbach as reference points on the intellectual scene, we add that of Friedrich A. Lange.

When Lange's lengthy *History of Materialism* appeared in 1866 (in German), it profoundly influenced Nietzsche, who had struck out in a countertheistic direction.[32] Lange expounded the historical course of materialism from its atomistic roots in Democritus, Epicurus, and then Lucretius through to its post-Kantian manifestations. He carefully considered not only the contemporary form of materialism but also its intellectual justification. Lange did not actually commit himself to it, maintaining that it could not satisfactorily explain the phenomenon of consciousness. He judged as "insoluble" the riddle of the connection between brain and soul.[33] So Lange joined in the conclusion that "Herbert Spencer favors—thus approaching our own standpoint—a Materialism of the phenomenon whose relative justification in natural science finds its limitation in the idea of an unknowable absolute."[34] He sympathized with Kant's postulation of an unknowable metaphysical entity in relation to the phenomenal world, having early announced that Kant has thrown light on the question: Where is sensation?[35] This was not to be Nietzsche's developed position, however he may have been drawn to it when he first encountered it. But Lange's examination lent rigor and weight to the metaphysical claims of a materialism that Nietzsche would own in its materialist principle, if not in its atomistic form. As a student, Nietzsche worked purposefully on Democritus (with whom Marx had also dealt in his doctoral thesis). Whatever Lange's reservations about materialism, rejection of a philosophically ill-grounded theism was essential to his weighty enterprise.

Reading Nietzsche from *HH* onward impresses on us the sense that early-nineteenth-century metaphysics of a Hegelian stamp is, as far as he is concerned, an unwelcome detour from eighteenth-century materialism. Lange himself looks to be more in continuity with it. Yet

32. Friedrich A. Lange, *The History of Materialism*, trans. Ernest Chester Thomas, 3rd ed., 3 vols. in 1 (London: Kegan Paul, 1925). Because of the awkward way in which this is paginated, I refer to "First Book" as 1.1; "First Book (continued)" as 1.2; "Second Book" as 2.1; and "Second Book (continued)" as 2.2. Nietzsche was influenced by the first edition and then reread Lange over the years.

33. Ibid., 2.2.213; cf. 2.2.111.

34. Ibid., 2.2.189–90. Also see Lange's declaration of affinity with John Stuart Mill in his "Preface to the Second Book [as Postscript]" (2.2.363–65).

35. Ibid., 2.1, chap. 1, deals particularly with Kant.

Lange's final attitude to the Social Question differs from that of Nietzsche in a way not dissimilar to the Feuerbach-Nietzsche difference on love.[36] If we cannot alliteratively linger longer with Lange, we cannot even start on other influences on Nietzsche. Ralph Waldo Emerson, for example, is very interesting here.[37] However, Lange's exposition of the Greek materialists beckons us to consider something with which we certainly must linger. Nietzsche did not just experience a "push" factor away from Christianity. He also experienced the powerful pull of the Greek world. Doubtless in Nietzsche's day, as in Kant's, "classical antiquity provided escape from the harsh realities of life, school and church."[38] Escape or not, Pforta, stronghold of classical study and education, gave Nietzsche access to that world. Something emotionally much richer than strict Greek or Roman scientific materialism was in store for him there.

"The Tyranny of Greece over Germany"

It is January 1882—"Sanctus Januarius," "Holy Januarius"—and Nietzsche publicizes a New Year's resolution: "I do not want to wage war against ugliness. I do not want to accuse; I do not even want to accuse the accusers. Let *looking away* be my only negation! And all in all and on the whole: some day I wish only to be a Yes-sayer" (*GS* 276). By the end of his literary career, Nietzsche's "yes-saying" had taken such an idiosyncratic form that many have preferred his "no-saying," his "no" to Christianity in particular. Yet, as Christianity set out on the road to exile during Nietzsche's teenage years, so the force of an alternative attraction made itself felt. In fact, we might put it the other way around: it was surely the possibility of a new world that caused the clouds to darken over the terrain of conventional religion. The new world was the world of the Greeks. It was a delightfully "yes-saying world," exalting not just humanity but also the human individual. If we do not pause with the Greeks, we shall get a badly distorted view of Nietzsche's response to Christianity.

To capture the spirit of excitement over Greece in Germany, there is hardly a better way than poring over a study published by Eliza Marian

36. Ibid., 2.2.361–62.

37. Although Ralph Waldo Emerson has an essay "The Over-Soul" (1841), a designation that rings so reminiscent of the later Nietzschean *Übermensch*, his essay "Fate," which seems to have had an early influence on Nietzsche, brings the two into closer alignment. See Emerson's *Selected Essays* (New York and Harmondsworth, UK: Penguin, 1982).

38. Manfred Kuehn, *Kant: A Biography* (Cambridge: Cambridge University Press, 2001), 59.

Butler in the interwar years: *The Tyranny of Greece over Germany*.[39] It is written in a style that today many will find indulgent, and it doubtless invokes critical dissent on a number of issues. But it superbly exegetes the simple words of Santayana, who himself mused over Germany and over Greece, that Greece "was a remote, fascinating vision, the most romantic thing in the history of mankind" for the Germans of the period in question.[40] Butler peerlessly introduces us to this world of thought and sensibility as appropriated in Germany, and if we indwell her world, we shall experience something of the allure of Greece.

It is only fair to apostrophize that her thesis, announced on the first page, was that the

> Germans cherish a hopeless passion for the absolute, under whatever name
> and in whatever guise they imagine it. . . . The Germans are unique perhaps
> in the ardour with which they pursue ideas and attempt to transform them
> into realities. . . . If most of us are the victims of circumstances, it may truly
> be said of the Germans as a whole that they are at the mercy of ideas.

She took it to be an axiom that, for Germans, "ideals are more potent than realities."[41] However, it is neither Greece nor the German mind per se that detains us here but Greece as it concerned Germany, or Greece and its ethos as it appeared to thinkers who shaped the intellectual and cultural world that Nietzsche accessed at Pforta. The curriculum at Pforta was not typical of German schools in introducing pupils to this world, but it did push Nietzsche into it. Hegel (not included in Butler's roll call of prominent German Grecophiles) at one stage was head of a high school in Nuremberg and made a speech at the end of the school year in which he urged upon his pupils and hearers that

> if we agree that excellence should be our starting-point, then the founda-
> tion of higher study must be and remain Greek literature in the first place,
> Roman in the second. The perfection and glory of those masterpieces must
> be the spiritual bath, the secular baptism that first and indelibly attunes
> and tinctures the soul in respect of taste and knowledge. . . . A general,
> perfunctory acquaintance with the ancients is not sufficient; we must take
> up our lodging with them so that we can breathe their air, absorb their

39. Eliza M. Butler, *The Tyranny of Greece over Germany: A Study of the Influence Exercised by Greek Art and Poetry over the Great German Writers of the Eighteenth, Nineteenth and Twentieth Centuries* (Cambridge: Cambridge University Press, 1935).

40. Ibid., 175. George Santayana's musings on Germany are recorded in his well-written and scathing study *Egotism in German Philosophy* (London: Dent, 1939), which includes discussion of Nietzsche. He thought that the Germans had misappropriated the Greeks.

41. Butler, *Tyranny of Greece*, 306. In her analysis, "ideas" and "ideals" are closely related, if not synonymous.

ideas, their manners, . . . and become at home in this world—the fairest that ever has been, . . . where the human spirit emerges like a bride from her chamber, endowed with a fairer naturalness, with freedom, depth and serenity. . . . He who has never known the works of the ancients has lived without knowing what beauty is. . . . The works of the ancients contain the most noble food in the most noble form: golden apples in silver bowls. They are incomparably richer than all the works of any other nation and of any other time.[42]

Butler's story starts with Winckelmann, who opened the portals to German exhilaration with the Greeks. Lessing follows, whom Heine was to call "the living critique of his period" and whom Nietzsche was to call the "most honest of theoretical men."[43] Then there was Johann Herder, who went beyond Greece and increased the scope of intellectual interest in nations and cultures but whose words about Greece in particular merit quotation:

Where have you vanished, childhood of the ancient world, sweet, beloved simplicity, in pictures, works and words? Where are you now, beloved Greece . . . ? . . . We . . . have, as it were, nothing but a shadowy outline left of the object of our wishes, but that very indistinctness only awakens a more earnest longing for what we lost, and we study the copies of the originals more attentively than we should have studied the originals themselves, if we had been in full possession of them.[44]

And then there is the great Goethe himself, "who expressed a wish to live and sleep in a hall of statues, that he might wake up in the mornings among the images of the gods."[45] Then there is Schiller. Taking leave of Butler, let us hear Schiller's lament in "The Gods of Greece":

Art thou, fair world, no more?
Return, thou virgin-bloom on Nature's face.
Ah, only on the Minstrel's magic shore,
Can we the footstep of sweet Fable trace!
The meadows mourn for the old hallowing life;

42. Georg W. F. Hegel, "On Classical Studies," in his *Early Theological Writings* (Chicago: University of Chicago Press, 1948), 325–36.

43. Heinrich Heine, *Religion and Philosophy in Germany* (Boston: Beacon, 1959), 96, with a memorable portrayal of Lessing. Nietzsche's comment is found in *BT* 15. In its context, it is a studiously qualified compliment to Lessing.

44. Quoted in Butler, *Tyranny of Greece*, 77. Herder is referring specifically to works of art.

45. Ibid., 140. Johann Wolfgang von Goethe's influence was so massive in Germany that one hesitates to mention him just as a name in a list. Nietzsche's admiration for Goethe is a study in itself.

Vainly we search the earth of gods bereft;
And where the image with such warmth was rife,
A shade alone is left!

Cold, from the North, has gone
Over the flowers the blast that kill'd their May;
And, to enrich the worship of the One,
A universe of Gods must pass away!
Mourning, I search on yonder starry steeps,
But thee no more, Selene, there I see!
And through the woods I call, and o'er the deeps,
No voice replies to me![46]

This is just a small portion of the poem; the whole should be read to get its author's sense of Greece. Schiller's controversial early play *The Robbers* impressed Nietzsche in his school days. He read of independence, heroism, and daring, features that generally but markedly attracted him to the Greeks. Further, he was at least as young as fourteen when he took it all in; at the same time as he was imploring a loving heavenly God to lead by his hand a weak and willing child (Nietzsche himself), he was simultaneously being drawn to the titanic challenge to religion and virtue that informed the spirit of Schiller's work.[47] For indeed, "a man must keep his footing. . . . Be what you will, you nameless Beyond—as long as this self of mine stays true to me. . . . Be what you will, as long as I can take my Self with me. Externals are only the varnish on a man: I am my own Heaven and Hell. . . ."[48] So announces the play's hero, Karl Moor.

This play brings into alignment the questions of Greece and of Nietzsche's experience of death. On any account, it exhibits a sustained intensity, and it does not take much imagination to taste the strong and acrid brew that cascaded onto Nietzsche's palate when he drank in the lines: "Let me die a hero's death, since I have no father any more" (2.2). Most poignantly of all, perhaps: "There was a time, when my tears flowed too freely, oh those days of peace! My father's castle! Green, dreaming valleys! Elysian fields of my childhood! Will you never return, to cool my burning breast with rustling sweetness?" (3.2). What, then, is to be done? "Am I going to die because I fear a life of torment? Am I going to concede victory to my misery? No, I shall bear it. . . . Suffering yields to my pride! I go on to the end!" (4.5). So let heroism take all: "My eyes are

---

46. Friedrich von Schiller, *Poems and Ballads*, ed. E. B. Lytton (Edinburgh and London: Blackwood, 1852). Selene is the Greek goddess of the moon.

47. On this period, see Safranski, *Nietzsche*, 33–34.

48. Friedrich von Schiller, *The Robbers* (London: Oberon, 1998), act 4, scene 5; text references are to act and scene of this edition.

open at last. I was a fool to want to return to prison—my spirit longs for action, I want to breathe the air of freedom—with that word I trod the law underfoot. . . . I have no father, no love, and blood and death will teach me to forget I ever held anything dear" (1.2).

Schiller knows that the world of the Greeks has gone, but he will evoke a world that is inspired by it. It is true that Nietzsche would later read in Lange that the gulf between Schiller and the Christian world should not be exaggerated, at least not if we discriminate carefully the various items in Schiller's corpus.[49] Meanwhile, Nietzsche could view Schiller's characters as *Übermenschen*, an attractive breed; *Übermensch* is the word often translated "Superman" in Nietzsche's Z. We cannot assume a strict identity between Nietzsche's earlier and largely inherited use of the term *Übermensch* and his studied later usage.[50] But young Nietzsche was in pursuit of a new kind of humanity, at least once he was inducted into its possibilities. Ancient Greeks and modern artists, *Übermenschen* in general and his own *Übermensch* in particular, will help shape his conception.[51] At this juncture it is Greece that principally concerns us, and its pull is nowhere better experienced than when we turn to the character who comes next, after Schiller, on Butler's roster: Friedrich Hölderlin.

Hölderlin

That great historian of medieval philosophy, Étienne Gilson, thought that anyone who had once stepped into Thomas Aquinas's enchanted world would never want to step out of it again. A cognate sentiment may be applied to Hölderlin too.[52] If ever a man could be defined as a poet, surely it was Hölderlin. He was a poetic genius in whom spiritual

49. Lange, *History of Materialism*, 2.2.345.

50. Johann Gottfried von Herder's *Letters for the Advancement of Humanity* (1793–97) gives us an example of its earlier use: see Robert T. Clark, *Herder: His Life and Thought* (Berkeley: University of California Press, 1955), 370. The idea of the *Übermensch* as the highest human being justifying his (masculine) own existence and the goal of our striving, according to Brobjer, was "relatively common in the nineteenth century"; see Thomas H. Brobjer, "A Discussion and Source of Hölderlin's Influence on Nietzsche: Nietzsche's Use of William Neumann's Hölderlin," *Nietzsche-Studien* 30 (2001): 407. Brobjer reports that Schiller used the term three times. Walter Kaufmann (*Nietzsche: Philosopher, Psychologist, Antichrist*, 4th ed. [New York: Vintage, 1974], 307–8) and Lowith (*From Hegel to Nietzsche*, 182–83) remark on the nineteenth-century development of the notion.

51. Before he was seventeen, Nietzsche had described Lord Byron's *Manfred* as at least bordering on the *Übermensch* type (see Safranski, *Nietzsche*, 35). Parkes (*Composing the Soul*, 30) is a bit more tentative about this characterization.

52. I am heavily indebted to David Constantine's *Hölderlin* (Oxford: Clarendon, 1988) for my understanding and appreciation of him.

sensibility and artistic brilliance were apparently singularly blended.[53] Nietzsche felt his touch and entered his enchanted world at Pforta. Whether he stepped out of the world or became increasingly a stranger within it; whether, when he stepped into it, he penetrated a long way within its borders; whether, if he stepped out of it, he did so with misgiving—all this, one suspects, is for the gods to judge. Far from all this distracting us from an aim to understand Nietzsche on Christianity, we need to make more than a passing allusion to Hölderlin.

If we were trying to assess the exact influence of Hölderlin on Nietzsche, we would need to consider Hölderlin's *Empedocles* along with his *Hyperion*, but in following the Greek trail, it suffices to mention the latter work. Nietzsche said of it that "nowhere has the longing for Greece been revealed in purer tones."[54] Like Friedrich Nietzsche, Friedrich Hölderlin (1770–1843) experienced sorrow when he was young. Before he was nine years old, he had lost father and stepfather, and four of his siblings died at birth or in infancy. His mother wanted him to enter the Lutheran ministry, but there was an ongoing struggle between the two of them. This may be broadly comparable to Nietzsche's position up to a point, but the family dynamics were not quite the same, and this particular scenario was not unfamiliar in nineteenth-century Germany.

For the second half of his life, Hölderlin was insane, a point that has also invited obvious if rudimentary comparison with Nietzsche, who was himself insane for the last eleven years of his life. Further, Hölderlin's friend Sinclair initially suspected that his appearance of insanity masked a conscious flight from life, just as Nietzsche's friend Overbeck suspected that Nietzsche was somewhat faking it after his dramatic collapse.[55] In a letter of 1798, Hölderlin analyzed himself in terms of "having been more sensitively receptive than others to any destructive thing which befell me, ever since my youth," and he related his artistic production to this fact.[56] It is a piece of self-knowledge that surely illuminates Nietzsche's makeup as well, and Nietzsche somewhat echoes this sentiment when he remarks: "My nature is all too concentrated, and whatever strikes me

53. As far as I can judge, "singularity" defensibly denotes the peculiar quality of Hölderlin's work, however its excellence might be compared with that of others.

54. *SL*, October 9, 1861.

55. Another of Nietzsche's friends, Gast, seems to have thought the same; see Hayman, *Nietzsche*, 340–41; and Joseph P. Stern, *Nietzsche* (London: Fontana, 1985), 39. In light of our later discussion of Dostoyevsky's Prince Myshkin and Nietzsche's Christology, we note the connection between "idiot" and the "holy fools," in whose cases it can be hard to decide whether the madness is feigned or real; see P. Travis Kroeker and Bruce K. Ward, *Remembering the End: Dostoevsky as Prophet to Modernity* (Boulder, CO: Westview, 2001), 263n27.

56. Friedrich Hölderlin, *Hyperion and Selected Poems*, ed. E. L. Santner (New York: Continuum, 1994), xxix.

moves straight to my center."[57] Again, Hölderlin speaks from his own experience in terms that also capture Nietzsche's experience when he says that the "man who ascends his own unhappiness stands one step higher."[58] But what about Greece?

Nietzsche read "magnificent" Hölderlin's magnificently haunting *Hyperion*, which Hölderlin published just before the turn of the century (1797–99).[59] It profoundly impressed him. A lyrical novel, or whatever it is rightly called, it expressed a deep longing for Greece and the Greeks. It also climaxed with a denunciation of contemporary Germany in their light, a move and mood that connects Hölderlin with Nietzsche, who himself lambasted German culture, or what passed for culture in contemporary Germany. Still, Nietzsche judged Hölderlin to be patriotic.[60] As for Greece, Hölderlin's message was conveyed in a medium that defies prosaic account. Wandering through diverse friendships, Hyperion romantically commits himself to the cause of liberating the Greek nation, in a quest for the vanished glory of Greece. Along with his contemporaries, Hölderlin realized that the Greece that was had disappeared forever in the form of its pristine beauty and its historical and historic antiquity. Yet it could come to life again, transfigured, in the words of a poet. Its spirit may yet animate—truly animate—poetry. But Hölderlin did not just long for Greece; he also lived, felt, and responded to the reality of his time, which was supremely the loss of the God that was. The resonant notes of longing in his work gave it the ethos that the young Nietzsche absorbed. "The scale of longing in any Hölderlin poem is always potentially infinite. The poem moves up and down in it."[61] As the "dynamism . . . of insatiable longing" marks Hölderlin's poetry in general, so it is with the poetic novel *Hyperion*.[62] David Constantine's account of things might be summarized as follows. The Greeks were the medium through which divinity was realized. In their absence, the ideal poem, inspired with longing, would fulfill that function. It would re-create immanence, body forth God. Longing is the present manifestation of antique spirit rather than a line cast hopefully from the present in the direction of the past.

Jumping ahead for a moment, it is certainly instructive to read *Hyperion* alongside *Thus Spoke Zarathustra*, which Constantine calls a "hyper-*Hyperion*" in some respects.[63] In the former, we read: "Oh how I wished I

57. *SL*, Summer 1883, 215.

58. Constantine, *Hölderlin*, 207 (translation on 370).

59. Nietzsche calls Hölderlin "magnificent" in "David Strauss, the Confessor and the Writer," *UO* p. 17.

60. *SL*, October 6, 1861.

61. Constantine, *Hölderlin*, 128.

62. Ibid., 47.

63. Ibid., 131.

could flee to the stars with my happiness, that it might not be debased by
what was around me."[64] Is this so far from Zarathustra's reversal of the
movement: "Great star! What would your happiness be, if you had not
those for whom you shine! . . . I must descend into the depths" to a humanity that, Zarathustra knew, was a debasing influence (Z, "Prologue,"
1)? It might sound prosaic to our ears when Hyperion asks: "What is it
for which man so immeasurably longs? . . . What is eternity doing in his
breast? . . . Man wants more than he is capable of."[65] But Zarathustra
echoes and answers anyway: "All joy wants eternity . . .—wants deep,
deep, deep eternity!" (Z 3.59, "The Second Dance Song," 3).[66] We are
gliding along the textual surface here; an intellectually proper case can
be made for the influence of *Hyperion* on *Thus Spoke Zarathustra*.[67]

But a far profounder longing than the above words convey courses
through *Hyperion*. At its heart is the love between Hyperion and Diotima,
movingly portrayed and anything but hollow or trite. Hyperion loves Diotima, and their parting is a sorrowful sacrifice for both. He returns, but
by then she has left and no longer walks the earth. The figure of Diotima
appears in Plato's *Symposium*. There she is Socrates' instructor in the
truth about Love and Beauty, but her depiction as a dispassionate didact
is not what Hölderlin picks up in *Hyperion*.[68] Nevertheless, the theme of
Beauty, central in the *Symposium*, is central in Hölderlin's work too, and
in *Hyperion* in particular.[69] It is intimately connected with joy, though the
exact conceptual description of their relationship is a delicate business.

Perhaps Hölderlin's will-to-joy and Nietzsche's later will-to-power are
to be contrasted. Be that as it may, the differences with Nietzsche are
marked. Contrasting him with Hölderlin also indicates something of
Nietzsche's attitude toward Christianity, even in the early stages of his
break with it. We observed that Hölderlin's Grecophile longing is bound
up with a poignant sense of divine absence. His lament has a positive

64. Hölderlin, *Hyperion*, 7.

65. Ibid., 31.

66. "Love in absence . . . is the summary of Hölderlin's predicament and theme" (Constantine, *Hölderlin*, 63). By delineating in detail their respective loves, we should find what
most profoundly distinguishes Nietzsche from Hölderlin.

67. See Brobjer, "Hölderlin's Influence on Nietzsche."

68. Possibly, it is less the figure of Diotima than the sentiment she expresses in *Symposium* concerning "poetry" and "making" that connects it with *Hyperion*. We have to
be careful here with translation. Compare Benjamin Jowett's "All creation or passage of
non-being into being is poetry or making" (*The Dialogues of Plato* [Oxford: Clarendon,
1875], 2:56) with R. E. Allen's translation and comments (*The Dialogues of Plato*, vol. 2,
The Symposium [New Haven: Yale University Press, 1991], 205b–c). In Plato's *Symposium*,
poetry and philosophy appear to be reconciled.

69. A question concerning homosexuality arises out of the *Symposium*, and Köhler
(*Zarathustra's Secret*, 237ff.) weaves the question into his account of Nietzsche's reception
of *Hyperion*.

religious, christological, and social aspect. Religiously, it looks as though Greece, while loved by Hölderlin for its antique self, is also a symbol of what is longed for, a deity proximate to Hegel's Absolute Spirit. But, for Nietzsche, the Hegelian Absolute must, to all appearances, be expelled as a form of dreaded theism. Christologically, whatever the related ambiguities in Hölderlin's work, taken as a whole, and however Christ stands in conflictual tension with Greece, there remains a place for Christ, a place alongside Dionysus in the heavenly choir.[70] However, Nietzsche's public authorship, which virtually began with the celebration of Dionysus, virtually ended with a declaration of fixed, eschatological hostility between Dionysus and Christ.[71] Socially, Hölderlin did not cultivate a theoretic asocial isolationism; his ideal Germany would exhibit interhuman love. On his part, Nietzsche effectively comes to excoriate such love, along with morality, as a remnant of Christianity. And so even when the two appear similar, as in their partiality to Heraclitus and their belief in the forces of strife as constitutive of the world, Hölderlin joins his philosophy to a hope of eschatological harmony; Nietzsche does not. In the end, Hölderlin exhibits a religious and human gentleness; Nietzsche sets his face against it.[72] "Long now one power has prevailed, hostile to song," said Hölderlin; in *GS*, in which he announced the death of God, Nietzsche made sure that we would never dance to the Christian tune again.[73] "Here, among men, and even now there's a lack of those strong for / Joy's extremity," said Hölderlin again; in *Z*, literary successor to *GS*, Nietzsche made sure that there was one man strong enough.[74]

70. See Mark Ogden, *The Problem of Christ in the Work of Hölderlin* (London: Institute for Germanic Studies, 1991), esp. chap. 4 on Dionysus. See also Constantine, *Hölderlin*, e.g., 171–72, 248–59. Michael Allen Gillespie in *Nihilism before Nietzsche* (Chicago: University of Chicago Press, 1996), 241, observes that the symbolism of bread and wine is the medium for the identification of Christ and Dionysus in Novalis as well as Hölderlin. See the brief comment about Novalis, Hölderlin, and Nietzsche on Dionysus in Jürgen Habermas, *The Philosophical Discourse of Modernity* (Cambridge, UK: Polity, 1987), 92.

71. *EH*, "Why I Am a Destiny," 9: "—Have I been understood?—*Dionysos against the Crucified.*"

72. Differences with Nietzsche also emerge indirectly in Martin Heidegger's comments on the contrast to violence and domination in some of Hölderlin's work; see his *Elucidations of Hölderlin's Poetry* (Amherst, NY: Humanity, 2000), 147. But here I am viewing Nietzsche particularly in terms of his developed thought; his early work might have some features closer to Hölderlin than later work. See, e.g., Thomas Pfau's editorial remark on how the aesthetic via the tragic exposes the problems of a philosophical system, in *Friedrich Hölderlin: Essays and Letters on Theory* (Albany: State University of New York Press, 1988), 26. However, Philip Pothen in *Nietzsche and the Fate of Art* (Burlington, VT: Ashgate, 2002) forces us to reconsider this general area of Nietzsche's philosophy.

73. "The Only One" (second version) in Friedrich Hölderlin, *Poems and Fragments*, trans. M. Hamburger (London: Routledge & Kegan Paul, 1966).

74. "Bread and Wine," in Hölderlin, *Poems and Fragments*, 8.

Hölderlin's work illustrates the grip of Greece on post-Christian longing, and Nietzsche learned from Hölderlin in his youth. Years later, Nietzsche still expresses German homesickness for Greece (*WP* 419). But if Greece still holds us in its grip, it has become a Greece severed from any fusion, alliance, or friendship with Christianity. At its mildest, the contrast of worlds was, in Nietzsche's formative days, statable in terms of noble Greek and infantile Christian. Greek and Christian anthropologies evidence contrasting intellectual and spiritual maturities. Nietzsche's spirit was homeless at least as early as his Pforta days and onward. It wanted to savor freedom along with exploring homelessness and to launch out on the seas that separate us from Christianity. In the address "On Classical Studies," Hegel also said:

> The youth enjoys the prospect of leaving his native country and living like Robinson Crusoe on a distant island. It is a necessary illusion to begin by mistaking distance for profundity; in fact, the depth and strength to which we attain can be measured only by the distance between the point to which we were fleeing and the center in which we were engrossed at first and to which we shall finally return again. This centrifugal force of the soul must always be provided with the means of estranging itself from its natural condition and essence, and why in particular the young mind must be led into a remote and foreign world. Now, the screen best suited to perform this task of estrangement for the sake of education is the world and language of the ancients.[75]

For Nietzsche, the seas were rough and, from the beginning, promised to be far. That is to the good. Strife is food for the soul, as a Greek like Heraclitus well understood, even to the point of advancing strife as the ground of a cosmic metaphysic. "It is a wonderful idea," said Nietzsche regarding Heraclitus, "welling up from the purest springs of Hellenism, the idea that strife embodies the everlasting sovereignty of strict justice, bound to everlasting law."[76] Here, we are actually quite close to the heart of Nietzsche's mature philosophy, its seed well sown in his early years.[77] In these years, the Nietzschean seas were rough indeed. From at least the age of eleven, he struggled with sickness. The story of his ailments—of head and stomach, and the syphilitic paralysis of the insane (if that is the correct diagnosis)—is central to the story

75. Hegel, "On Classical Studies," 328.
76. *PTA* 55; for this text, I use page numbers rather than section numbers.
77. In this volume, I do scant justice to Nietzsche's indebtedness to Heraclitus. See his early account in *PTA* 50–68. For an especially strong and telling statement in the context of his overall thought, see Nietzsche's treatment of Heraclitus on innocence, play, and justice (*PTA* 62–63). For the connection between Schopenhauer and Heraclitus, see *PTA* 53ff. Schopenhauer's significance for Nietzsche is discussed below.

of Nietzsche's life.[78] The student who eventually resolved to give up theology—by Easter 1865—was well acquainted with debilitating strife in body as well as in soul. Those who have been spared ill health or proximity to it little appreciate how different is the world of the sick person from the world of the healthy.

Late in life, Nietzsche delighted in the discovery of Dostoyevsky. First he stumbled on *Notes from the Underground*, whose harrowing exposure of the soul begins with the words: "I am a sick man. . . . I am an angry man."[79] To Peter Gast, Nietzsche wrote on April 6, 1883: "You would not believe . . . what an abundance of suffering life has unloaded upon me, at all times, from *early* childhood on."[80] Nietzsche knew all about the sentiments of the underground man. By the time he came to read Dostoyevsky's work, he was Christianity's violent critic. Contrastingly, he had little quarrel with the Greeks, at least at their best, though he did quarrel with scholars who were pretentiously incapable of entering into their inheritance, and he did dissent from an important strand in the interpretation of the Greeks. He thought that when Greek culture was pictured as an exhibition of fundamentally serene grandeur, this was wrongheaded. The Greeks knew all about the dread of existence. Nevertheless, they produced all sorts of good things, "fair and bathed in sunlight" (*WS* 184). The draw of the Greeks was no evanescent schoolboy attraction. To the contrary, Nietzsche was still growing toward them in adulthood.[81] Karl Jaspers, musing on Nietzsche musing on world-historical realities, commented: "Existentially, Nietzsche is constantly connected with his subject-matter only at one single point in history: the golden age of Greece."[82] Not all in Greece, however, was gold or glitter. Nietzsche knew it, but what did he make of the dross?

The Other Side of the Coin

We needed to dwell on Nietzsche's predilection for the Greeks to grasp what goes into his nonpredilection for Christianity. It is equally important for Christians both to understand and appreciate the Greek world for

78. A great strength of Hayman's almost day-by-day and blow-by-blow account of Nietzsche's life (in *Nietzsche*) is that it constantly keeps all his ailments before us.

79. Fyodor Dostoyevsky, *Notes from the Underground/The Double* (London: Penguin, 1972), 15. The "underground man" had been like that for forty years.

80. To Peter Gast, *SL*, April 6, 1883. See Nietzsche's note on the *"Usefulness of sickliness,"* *AOM* 356.

81. See the letter to Mathilda Maier, *SL*, July 15, 1878: "I am so much closer to the Greeks than ever before. . . . I now *live* my aspiration to wisdom, down to the smallest detail."

82. Karl Jaspers, *Nietzsche: An Introduction to the Understanding of His Philosophical Activity* (Tucson: University of Arizona Press, 1965), 235.

themselves. The twin sources of Western civilization are classical culture
and Christianity. If by now Westerners are largely or entirely ignorant
of the inner nature of the latter, at least they may be acquainted with
some of its outward institutional and social expressions. However, the
former is practically a closed book, save for classical scholars or those
whose strictly scholarly concerns oblige them to become acquainted
with it. Certainly this is so in the English-speaking world, although for
rather different reasons in different parts of it.[83] But if we want to reckon
with Nietzsche, we must reckon with Greece. "Greek civilization," we
know, was not a monochrome monolith. But if generalization be permitted, there is no theological reason why delight in the aesthetic detail of
such things as Greek architecture and the literary detail of Greek drama
should not be poised for expansion into delight at the civilization and the
humanity that gave it birth. There is no reason why notions of the free
and the serene, the beautiful and the investigative, the courageous and
the democratic—notions of the idealized Greek in the abstract form—
should not appeal to Christian religious sensibility, whether or not our
imagination is tutored. Adam was meant to be free; serenity distantly
reflects messianic peace; beauty marks God's creation; investigation is
beneficent dominion over nature; courage stamps the Old Testament
hero; democracy reminds us of human equality qua image of God. All
this certainly needs to be teased out, nuanced, qualified, and defended.
Yet, even if we judge some of these Greco-Christian connections to be
specious, mature Christian sensibility can appreciate much about the
idealized Greek, as far as we have gone.

However, there is another side of the coin, and we are warned not to
visit Greece as intellectual tourists unconcerned, like the standard tourist,
about daily reality in the exotic location being visited. Nietzsche knew
all about the other side of the coin. In 1871–72, he wrote an essay, "The
Greek State,"[84] in which he protested against those who regard work
as something honorable and dignified. That, he retorted, makes sense
only if existence is itself worthwhile. Greeks did not see things like that.
Existence per se was not of value. A human being might be a "disgraceful and pathetic non-entity" and, while certain kinds of work—slaves'
labor—might be necessary, it was no less shameful and disgraceful for
that. Compare slavish work and artistic creation. It is the latter that
enhances culture. And culture always needs enhancement, which is
impossible without the worker. Nietzsche puts it like this:

83. George Grant apparently "explains American identity in terms of its rejection of one
of the two 'primals' of Western civilization," meaning Greece; see Robert Song, *Christianity
and Liberal Society* (Oxford: Clarendon, 1997), 90–91.
84. See in *OGM* pp. 176–86. All the quotations above are from this brief piece. It was
originally intended to be the first chapter of *BT*.

In order for there to be a broad, deep, fertile soil for the development of art, the overwhelming majority has to be slavishly subjected to life's necessity in the service of the minority, *beyond* the measure that is necessary for the individual. At their expense, through their extra work, that privileged class is to be removed from the struggle for existence, in order to produce and satisfy a new world of necessities.

"Slavery belongs to the essence of culture," Nietzsche concludes. He is not insensitive. To be suitably grim about it, "this truth is the vulture which gnaws at the liver of the Promethean promoter of culture. Still, the misery of men living a life of toil has to be increased to make the production of the world of art possible for a small number of Olympian men." It is rightly said that we should not miss the "tone of horrified fascination with which Nietzsche presents his observations."[85] It is a *decretum horribile*, to borrow Calvin's celebrated description of the divine decree of reprobation without analyzing the nuances of his phrase. To the end of his days, Nietzsche struggled with the "problem of how to stomach history as he imagines it, as the totality of effect of suffering humanity, how to keep from vomiting it back up when he tries to swallow it."[86] His essay "Homer in Competition" gives a similar impression.[87] But if you kept your eye on the misery and the need to alleviate it, you would feed egalitarianism, so that "the urge for justice, for equal sharing of the pain, would swamp all other ideas." Then where would you be, with "the cry of pity tearing down the walls of culture"?[88] The fact is that hardship, cruelty, and unequally distributed power and pain belong to life. Strife, as we have said, is fundamental to existence. Nietzsche does not shrink from a hoary conclusion: "Therefore, we have the right to compare the magnificent culture to a victor dripping with blood, who, in his triumphal procession, drags the vanquished along chained to his carriage as slaves."

Nietzsche's conviction was that justice, in the egalitarian sense beloved of contemporary social reformers, was historically not original.

85. Staten, *Nietzsche's Voice*, 83.

86. Ibid., 86, where textuality is under discussion. In considering another, yet ultimately related, aspect of Greek culture, Michel Foucault finds the "ethic of pleasure . . . quite disgusting"; see his "On the Genealogy of Ethics: An Overview of Work in Progress," in *The Foucault Reader*, ed. Paul Rabinow (Harmondsworth, UK: Penguin, 1984), 346.

87. Published with *OGM* pp. 187–94. In *HH* 101, Nietzsche speaks of "much that is horrific and inhuman in history in which one can hardly bear to believe" and of how it is ameliorated.

88. This is the cry of compassion and not of pain, but the text is sometimes treated as though Nietzsche were speaking of a cry *by* and not *for* the oppressed. So Keith Ansell-Pearson, *An Introduction to Nietzsche as Political Thinker* (Cambridge: Cambridge University Press, 1994), 77. He frequently alludes to this passage.

Power was. Power makes right and assumes violence. States came into being that way. The Greek state came into being that way. Without all this, there would have been no Greek civilization; the existence of such a civilization therefore hallows a type of violence. Genius flourishes on the soil of concentrated strife. The state of nature is neither orderly nor peaceful. Since the slave is necessary for society, so war is for the state; or as war is necessary for the state, so is the slave for society. If you still want to talk about universal human dignity, let dignity reside in the fact that the slave cooperates with others in making the genius great. Although military genius is the type of genius Nietzsche mainly instantiates when he is making these points, he goes beyond the warrior and criticizes Plato for excluding the artistic genius from a privileged position in the state.

Christians are bound to see life on the Greek ground quite differently. It is not just slavery that is in question.[89] Hearing the cry of the exposed infant and sensitized to the pain of the pederast's prey, Christians might celebrate and try to preserve the works of Aeschylus, but they would rather rescue and preserve the weak. Toward such an attitude, Nietzsche would later express unfeigned, undisguised, and well-nigh unmitigated contempt and hostility. Later we shall hear him on the matter. But theoretically forced to choose between a society that elevates art at the expense of enduring human pain and a society that alleviates that pain at the expense of art, Christianity surely opts for the latter. Of course, clinical as it may sound, we must distinguish within pain, and elitist as it may sound, we must distinguish within art. "Theoretically," we said, because Christianity is implacably hostile toward a situation where it is forced to make a choice. Nietzsche's quarrel with nineteenth-century philanthropy was that it abjured nature and induced a barbarically egalitarian demolition of high culture. His protest should not simply be dismissed. But neither should Ivan Karamazov's protest be muted when he says that the whole worldly edifice of the divine creation is not worth the price of a child's agony.[90] Mutatis mutandis, we must balance the child's agony against the world's art in a way entirely antithetic to that of Nietzsche.

89. Nietzsche's attitude to the question of slavery can be usefully culled from unpublished work as well as the published; see, e.g., *WP* 69, 80, 464, 859. Safranski (*Nietzsche*, 148) mentions that Nietzsche was a proponent of child labor. Robert M. Adams (*Finite and Infinite Goods: A Framework for Ethics* [Oxford: Oxford University Press, 1999], 324) touches on the questions involved; also see Oliver O'Donovan, *The Desire of the Nations: The Roots of Political Theology* (Cambridge: Cambridge University Press, 1996), 184–86, 263–66.

90. In the celebrated account "The Rebellion," in Fyodor Dostoyevsky's *The Brothers Karamazov*.

Here, I affirm rather than argue. On the other hand, Nietzsche did argue for his way of seeing things. His point, made over the course of his authorship, was that Christian evaluations subject existence to the adjudication of a drummed-up moral perspective. Christians simply hate existence and promote a morality that does not belong to it. Yet, as Nietzsche reveled in Greece in those early days, he became captivated by a non-Christian whose own loathing of existence was expressed in the most captivating philosophical prose. Enter Arthur Schopenhauer. We cannot leave him out of our account any more than we could the Greeks.

Schopenhauer

In 1864, Nietzsche left Pforta to take up theology and philology at Bonn University, but before the end of the academic year he dismayed his family by making clear that he was dropping his Christianity along with his theology.[91] After the strict regimen at Pforta, this seems to have been a year of personal indiscipline. Possibly, Nietzsche contracted syphilis during that year and set foot on the road to his eventual breakdown. At any rate, resolved to give up musical composition—a resolution not well kept—he left at the end of the year to concentrate on philology at Leipzig.[92] He was a brilliant student. Exceptionally, he was awarded a doctorate from Leipzig in March 1869, on the basis of published articles, without fulfilling statutory examination requirements. Hence, he was able to take up an appointment at Basel in 1869 as associate professor in the field of classical philology, particularly Greek language and literature. He became full professor in the following year. Outwardly, the stage was set for a very promising career in the field. Inwardly, Nietzsche did not relish the prospect. Philosophy was beckoning, so when Gustav Teichmüller took off for Estonia in 1871, vacating one of two chairs in philosophy at Leipzig, Nietzsche applied for the position. He was unsuccessful.

By then, he had encountered *the* philosopher. While pursuing his classical studies at Leipzig and before he had to take time out for military service (a time cut short by injury and illness), Nietzsche came under the spell of a philosopher whose thought would become a permanently

91. What Nietzsche registered for in Bonn varies in different accounts. Sometimes it is just described as "theology," and in at least one account, it is "theology and philosophy," though perhaps "philology" is meant; see Brobjer, "Nietzsche's Atheism," 4, though he does not use the word "registered."

92. In an autobiographical fragment of 1868–69, Nietzsche displays interesting self-knowledge while commenting on the shift from music to classical philology (*SL* 47).

molding influence, first by attraction, then by reaction. "Spell" is perhaps a particularly advisable word, for in the fourth part of Z, Zarathustra meets a "trembling old man with staring eyes," a "sorcerer" or "magician" ("The Sorcerer," 4.65). Although this is probably Wagner, Schopenhauer may also be represented in the figure, especially if it is a type. Wagner was shortly to become the other man in Nietzsche's life; he, like Nietzsche, was enamored of Schopenhauer.

It is hard to convey an idea of Schopenhauer's authorship to anyone who has not been exposed to his literature. Draw us or repel us, he will not leave many unaffected, even if our reactions go to neither of those extremes. He is regarded as one of the greatest stylists in the history of philosophy, but one whose influence and prescience have arguably been overlooked for much of the twentieth century.[93] Born in 1788, Schopenhauer's constructive efforts to come to terms with Kant bore fruit before he was thirty years old, in *The World as Will and Representation*.[94] Whatever our philosophical verdict on the merits of this work, it exudes an extraordinary and bleak power, haunting, brooding, darkly enchanting. Devotees of Emily Brontë might conjure up the impression of Wuthering Heights in a gale under a chill and brilliant harvest moon. The lunar image gets us into Schopenhauer. "Life," he tells us, "is never beautiful, but only the picture of it, namely, in the transfiguring mirror of art and poetry." When the world is viewed thus, "the moon gradually becomes our bosom friend."[95] Hölderlin wrote of the moon as "our globe's shadowy image," a being "enthusiastic, rapt, scarcely concerned about us."[96] It follows its own course. Schopenhauer can conceptualize it, as he conceptualizes the whole world, under the aspect of detached necessity. But he also invites us to an aesthetic response and to a whole mode of aesthetic representation that frees us for tranquil enjoyment. Such enjoyment is parasitic on and wrung out of the strife that is at nature's heart, and it is quite poignant. Where Immanuel Kant had wondered at the starry heavens without (the realm of necessity) and the moral law within (the realm of freedom), Schopenhauer went on to advertise the beauty of those heavens (without) and the pain of compassionate fellow-feeling (within).

93. This is argued in a lively, though not uncritical, piece of advocacy by Bryan Magee in *The Philosophy of Schopenhauer* (Oxford: Clarendon, 1988). Helen Zimmern in *Schopenhauer: His Life and Philosophy* (London: Allen & Unwin, 1932) captures the spirit of the man and his work; Christopher Janaway in *Schopenhauer* (Oxford: Oxford University Press, 1994) provides a helpful introduction to his thought.

94. The second edition, which considerably expanded the first, was published in Nietzsche's year of birth. A third edition came out in 1859; see Arthur Schopenhauer, *The World as Will and Representation*, 2 vols. (New York: Dover, 1966).

95. Ibid., 2:374–75.

96. The first phrase is from "Bread and Wine," in Hölderlin, *Poems and Fragments*; the latter is quoted by Constantine, *Hölderlin*, 203 (trans. on 369).

In what he informs us was an uncharacteristic move, Nietzsche picked up this work at random, late in 1865, just after turning twenty-one. Nine years later, he testified:

> When in my younger days I used to indulge my wishes to my heart's content, I thought that fate would relieve me of the terrible effort and duty of educating myself: at exactly the right moment I would find a philosopher to be my educator, a true philosopher whom I could obey without further reflection because I could trust him more than myself.[97]

He goes on:

> It was truly a flight into wishful thinking when I imagined I would find a true philosopher as educator, one who would elevate me above my inadequacies, to the extent that they were products of the age, and would teach me once again to be *simple* and *honest* in thought as in life. . . . It was in such a state of need, distress and desire that I first encountered Schopenhauer. I am among those readers of Schopenhauer who after having read the first page know with certainty that they will read every page and pay attention to every word he ever uttered. My faith in him appeared immediately, and today is just as complete as it was nine years ago.[98]

What did Nietzsche read on that first page?

> This world is my representation: this is a truth valid with reference to every living and knowing being, although man alone can bring it into reflective, abstract consciousness. If he really does so, philosophical discernment has dawned on him. It then becomes clear and certain to him that he does not know a sun and an earth, but only an eye that sees a sun, a hand that feels an earth; that the world around him is there only as representation, in other words, only in reference to another thing, namely that which represents, and this is himself. . . . Therefore no truth is more certain, more independent of all others, and less in need of proof than this, namely that everything exists for knowledge, and hence the whole of this world, is only object in relation to the subject, perception of the perceiver, in a word, representation.[99]

Schopenhauer spins out his proposal. Kant had taken a vital and irreversible step forward in claiming that mind molded our world; things as they appear are not things as they are in themselves. What Kant did not do was to identify the "thing in itself," which he alleged to be unknowable. Schopenhauer did identify it, as "will." We know "will" not in

97. "Schopenhauer as Educator," *UO* p. 175.
98. Ibid., p. 179.
99. Schopenhauer, *World as Will and Representation*, 1:3.

itself but in and according to its phenomenal manifestation in the world. By "will" Schopenhauer did not mean a personal and conscious reality or deity. It is an impersonal force that blindly grounds and governs the universe, which is its representation. It is, in fact, just the "will to live" or "will-to-life."[100]

Schopenhauer tells us that the decisive term of his philosophical enterprise will be learned when we reach the sustained and culminating discussions that press beyond the metaphysical ontology of "will" and "representation."[101] By the time he has arrived here, Schopenhauer has already invoked the significance of art in our world, a world marked by and suffused with suffering, whether in futility or pain, frustration or death. Aesthetic contemplation has the potential to detach us from the striving that is our endless human lot. In aesthetic contemplation, as Schopenhauer puts it in an immortal line, "we celebrate the Sabbath of the penal servitude of willing; the wheel of Ixion stands still."[102] Ixion was the legendary king of Thessaly who foolishly incurred the wrath of Zeus. The latter consigned him to a sweet fate in Tartarus, a region located far below Hades, at least in the early myths, binding him to a fiery wheel, which illustrated the principle of perpetual motion. So, for Schopenhauer, aesthetic release is as momentarily glorious as life is perpetually grim. Profound aesthetic moments are comparatively rare and unsustained.

Intellectually and spiritually, Schopenhauer turned East to India as no major Western philosopher had done before. The Hindu and Buddhist traditions give religious or quasi-religious expression to the philosophical conclusion that, when we break through to a knowledge and realization of the way of the will and the world, we must practice resignation, denying ourselves in the course of our striving for fulfillment and satisfaction. Let us conquer self-seeking and let spontaneous compassion express itself in true love for others in their misery. We can thus be saved. The soul will possess inner tranquillity, the fruit of deeming all earthly things worthless, and express outgoing pity, the fruit of identifying with others who, like ourselves, suffer the ravages of the will to live. Christianity, Brahmanism, and Buddhism all know about this. While Schopenhauer will have nothing to do with theistic metaphysics, he finds value in the *agapē* ethic of Christianity, though the East realized the supremacy of compassionate love a few centuries before Christianity arrived.[103]

100. For a good description, see, e.g., ibid., 2:353–60.
101. See, e.g., ibid., 1:271, where the author says that this last part is "the most serious, for it concerns the actions of men."
102. Ibid., 1:196.
103. Here see the concluding supplemental discussion in Arthur Schopenhauer, *On the Basis of Morality* (New York: Bobbs-Merrill, 1965).

"I have lifted the veil of truth higher than any mortal before me. But I should like to see the man who could boast of a more miserable set of contemporaries than mine."[104] Thus spoke Schopenhauer, but it is equally the voice of Nietzsche. "The two men had a remarkable number of personal attributes in common: both were psychologists of genius, deeply musical, superb prose stylists, despisers of the generality of mankind and the world in which they found themselves, venerators of antiquity, atheists, unbalanced haters of women, animal lovers, racists, anti-socialists, despisers of Germany and Germans in spite of being themselves German."[105] It is impossible to give ten out of ten to Bryan Magee for this list, because he mentions eleven things, but he is either close to or right on maximum points. His list follows the identification of other obvious similarities in lifestyle, in isolation, and in contempt for the academic establishment and the initial contemporary reception of their work. The similarities are certainly impressive.

What Nietzsche gained from Schopenhauer is well captured in his account of the first reading: "I began to let that dynamic, dismal genius work on my mind. Each line cried out with renunciation, negation, resignation. I was looking into a mirror that reflected the world, my life and my own mind with hideous magnificence."[106] About three years later, Nietzsche told a friend that what drew him to Schopenhauer was "the ethical air, the Faustian odor, Cross, Death, Grave and so on."[107] This world has some affinity to the world of death and Titanism that helped draw Nietzsche to the Greeks, but in Schopenhauer there is a pessimism, a settled conviction that the color of the world is bleak gray. If Schopenhauer's world is not strictly monochrome, it is only because bleak gray comes in shades, and we catch the occasional aesthetic flash. It is not hard to see how this would appeal to one who had had Nietzsche's experience of life.

Sustained exposure to Schopenhauer's statements about the human condition, persistently offered in the course of a long work in philosophy, is calculated to knock the good cheer out of a sympathetic reader and leave us wondering how anyone can survive in this Slough of Despond that we call life. In one of his lighter moments, Schopenhauer compares life "to a circular path of red-hot coals, having a few cool places, a path we have to run over incessantly."[108] Or with equal levity: "If we knocked on the graves and asked the dead whether they would like to rise again, they would shake their heads."[109] Prosaically speaking:

104. Quoted in Magee, *Philosophy of Schopenhauer*, 16.
105. Ibid., 265.
106. Hayman, *Nietzsche*, 72.
107. To Rohde, *SL*, October 8, 1868.
108. Schopenhauer, *World as Will and Representation*, 1:380.
109. Ibid., 2:465.

> The will finds itself as an individual in an endless and boundless world, among innumerable individuals, all striving, suffering and erring. . . . Life bears so clearly the stamp of something which ought to disgust us, that it is difficult to conceive how anyone could fail to recognize this, and to be persuaded that life is here to be thankfully enjoyed, and that man exists in order to be happy.[110]

There is plenty more. Petrarch was right when he said that "a thousand pleasures do not compensate for one pain." Ivan Karamazov's "rebellion" comes to mind again when we encounter a judgment: "That thousands had lived in happiness and joy would never do away with the anguish and death-agony of one individual." If we lower the temperature a bit, the following summarizes things nicely: "The truth is that we ought to be wretched, and are so." Hence, is it not obvious that "it appears just as foolish to embalm corpses as it would be carefully to preserve our excreta"?[111] All this is expressed with a poetic (and philosophical?) force that the preceding quotations do not fully capture. Those who want something stronger might follow the exposition that culminates in Schopenhauer's comment on Dante.[112]

My flippancy in these comments is designed as a thinly ironic veiling of the acknowledgment that life looks precisely like this for many people. Some will warm to Schopenhauer's expression of things out of a purely emotional indulgence. For others, his words are direly true to what they have gone through or seen in life. We shall not begin to appreciate Nietzsche's reaction to Christianity until we see how profoundly in tune he was with Schopenhauer at this point: the misery of existence. Eventually, he broke with Schopenhauer on that point, but even then, Schopenhauer's ideas are often taken up into something different and so taken up in a different way. Meanwhile, what do you do if Schopenhauer is basically right? Some might conclude that suicide is the logical course of action, though Schopenhauer himself did not think that this solved the problem of existence.[113] Others might plunge into philanthropy. Schopenhauer preferred this, advocating in its pursuit the renunciation of striving, the stilling of our wills. We "are like entrapped elephants, which rage and struggle fearfully for many days, until they

---

110. Ibid., 2:573–74. For what follows, see 2:573–77.

111. Ibid., 1:277.

112. Ibid. Dante comes in at 1:325.

113. Referring to his discussion of this in *The World as Will and Representation*, Schopenhauer offers a summary of his claim that "the only valid reason against suicide . . . lies in the fact that suicide is opposed to the attainment of the highest moral goal since it substitutes for the real salvation of the world of woe and misery, one that is merely apparent"; see "On Suicide," in *Parerga and Paralipomena* (Oxford: Clarendon, 1974), 2:309.

see that it is fruitless, and then suddenly offer their necks calmly to the yoke, tamed for ever."[114]

Before he has quite reached that stage of the argument, or at least that expression of sentiment, Schopenhauer has made another proposal. I have mentioned his reference to art and the aesthetic. Schopenhauer judged that its highest form is music. Music not only liberates intellect from will in order to release mind into aesthetic enjoyment; it also has a deep metaphysical meaning, being a copy of the will itself, seen in a transfiguring mirror. To explain what this means in Schopenhauer's philosophy would take us too far away from Nietzsche and Christianity. In any case, what it meant for Nietzsche is more than we can convey through an interpretation of Schopenhauer himself. Liberation through music was not a merely theoretical possibility for Nietzsche. It was the most exhilarating of existential possibilities. The Savior himself has come and is alive just down the road. Schopenhauer shares the top of the bill with Richard Wagner.

114. Schopenhauer, *World as Will and Representation*, 1:306.

2

Launching Out

Can it be that thou
Art thus in love with life? the very life
Which made thee wretched?

Byron, *Manfred*, act 3, scene 4

Encounter with Wagner

"Nietzsche experienced music as authentic reality and colossal power.
Music penetrated the core of his being, and it meant everything to him."[1]
Nietzsche would like to have been a composer and was delighted when
Wagner told him that music was his "conductor."[2] In his classic novel
Doktor Faustus, Thomas Mann deliberately models the composer who
is its central character on Nietzsche. Although the original and the fictitious characters were not meant to be exactly alike, the novel gives us
the feeling that, had Nietzsche been as musically gifted as Mann's character Adrian Leverkühn, Leverkühn is plausible as one of the *personae*
into whom Nietzsche could have evolved. And although Mann's novel is
not just about an individual but about the tragedy of twentieth-century

---

1. So Rüdiger Safranski begins his philosophical biography, "Overture: The Drama
of Disillusionment," in *Nietzsche: A Philosophical Biography* (New York and London:
Norton, 2002), 19.
2. *SL*, May 21, 1870.

Germany, metaphorically represented in the story of the character, it one way or another is a rich resource for meditation on Nietzsche. Important Nietzschean resonances have also been detected in a second great German twentieth-century novel with a musical or largely musical theme, Hermann Hesse's *The Glass Bead Game*, which clinched for its author a Nobel Prize.[3] *The Glass Bead Game* actually captures elements of what Nietzsche was going through when he joined forces with Wagner.[4]

But what has all this to do with Nietzsche and Christianity? Just as we cannot appreciate how shabby Christianity looked to Nietzsche unless we attend to the Greeks, so also we shall not appreciate the abysmal poverty of Christianity's spiritual offering in his eyes unless we credit the wealth that was music and that was Wagner. Hesse, who was much influenced by Nietzsche, has a character in another novel observe: "I had reflected upon the significance of my relation to music, and not for the first time recognized this appealing and fatal relation as the destiny of the entire German spirit. In the German spirit the matriarchal link with nature rules in the form of the hegemony of music to an extent unknown in any other people."[5] What music meant in nineteenth-century Germany and what it meant to Nietzsche are bound up with the fate of Christianity and its relation to music since the time of the Reformation.[6] Music lavishly bestowed what Christianity neither did nor could.

Wagner was not Nietzsche's earliest love; Schumann, for example (who composed a *Manfred*), was more like it. But *Tristan and Isolde*, produced in 1865, did the trick. Nietzsche, relatively indifferent to Wagner's music when he first encountered it, heard and was captivated by it late in 1868. In a meditation on the relation of word and image to music and of individual to universal existence, Nietzsche says:

3. See Walter Kaufmann's introduction to his translation of *The Gay Science* (Vintage: New York, 1974), 14–15. I find myself unconvinced by Kaufmann's comparison between Knecht's and Zarathustra's *untergehen* (going down). In Hermann Hesse, *The Glass Bead Game* (Harmondsworth, UK: Penguin, 1972), Knecht affirms a cohumanity quite dissimilar to anything contemplated by Zarathustra. In light of the account of Nietzsche's *BT*, forthcoming in this chapter, see the remark that Knecht reflects Hesse's "substitution of Apollonian identity for Dionysian actuality," in Joseph Mileck, *Hermann Hesse: Life and Art* (Berkeley: University of California Press, 1978), 287.

4. I cannot fully document this claim here, but it ranges from reference to the general integration of music, mind, and culture in Hesse's novel to the description of a Purcell sonata that has resonances with Nietzsche's musical soul at the time, "so lonely and unworldly, and so brave and innocent also, both childlike and superior, as all good music must [sound] in the midst of the unredeemed muteness of the world" (Hesse, *Glass Bead Game*, 154).

5. Hermann Hesse, *Steppenwolf* (New York: Bantam, 1969), 154. For Hesse on music and the mother figure, see his novel *Demian* (London: Peter Owen, 2001).

6. On this, see the richly rewarding study by Daniel Chua, *Absolute Music and the Construction of Meaning* (Cambridge: Cambridge University Press, 1999).

> How could anyone fail to be shattered immediately, having once put their ear to the heart of the universal Will, so to speak, and felt the raging desire for existence pour forth into all the arteries of the world as a thundering torrent or as the finest spray of a stream? Is such a person, trapped within the miserable glass vessel of human individuality, supposed to be able to bear listening to countless calls of lust and woe re-echoing from the "wide space of the world's night," without fleeing, unstoppably, with the strains of this shepherd's dance of metaphysics in his ears, towards his first and original home? (*BT* 21)

Although I am broadening the context of these remarks, they capture something of what *Tristan and Isolde* must have done to their author. Not that Wagner had always composed music like this. In a career that we might understate as "eventful" and "colorful," Wagner had run around parts of Western Europe, making music, revolution, mischief, and love but not making much money or making quite the reputation that he wanted. Pausing to contemplate life and to write essays on art and on music in particular, Wagner had encountered Schopenhauer's work at first hand in 1854. It changed him. From then on, he was as much a Schopenhauerian as anyone could be.[7] The music also changed. So did the composer's fortunes. The patronage of Ludwig II, king of Bavaria, effected just as dramatic a development in Wagner's social being as did Schopenhauer in his intellectual being. Out of it came the establishment of one of the cultural monuments of modern European history, the Bayreuth Festival. Intense excitement surrounded the occasion, and Nietzsche became immersed in the prospect and the project.[8]

Just a few months before taking up his appointment in Basel, Nietzsche met the great man himself, who was then living not far from the city. The years of Wagner's residence in Tribschen, where he lived until moving to Bayreuth at the end of April 1872, were some of the great Wagner years, years of the *Meistersinger* and *Ring* compositions. For Nietzsche, life was transformed. He became devoted to Wagner, stayed with him, served him. It was not only that Wagner was a real man and an artist of genius or even that he was a disciple of Schopenhauer. It was much more than this: his music could save civilization. On top of this, Wagner was born in the same year as Nietzsche's father, whom he apparently resembled in appearance. After he met Wagner, Nietzsche seems to have referred less to his father. The days of friendship

7. For an interesting study, see Bryan Magee, *Wagner and Philosophy* (London: Penguin, 2000), although I am not competent to judge how well it stands up to rigorous critical scrutiny.

8. The politics of the festival has been lively for some time. Though things have moved on since then, see the riveting account of its background in Nike Wagner's work, *The Wagners: The Dramas of a Musical Dynasty* (London: Phoenix, 2001).

with Wagner and of familiar sojourns in the Wagner household were golden—so Nietzsche recalled them, and even allowing for a degree of idealization, there is no need to doubt the relative happiness along with the excitement of that epoch.[9]

Of *Tristan and Isolde*, it has been said that "its contemporary impact, its influence on the development of music, the powerful spell it exerted on literature and the visual arts, even its effects upon human thought and behaviour, were of an order achieved by few other single works in the history of art."[10] But Wagner was not just a composer; he was also the most philosophically interested and presumably the most philosophically minded of the great composers. He was a rarity. However soundly worked out and however badly rendered in prose, Wagner came up with a philosophy and a philosophy of art, the instruments and expression of his ambition to redeem and be the redeemer of culture. Around the time Nietzsche met Wagner, work written before Wagner's encounter with Schopenhauer was being reissued. It bears directly on our account of Nietzsche's attitude to Christianity. I approach it here with all the finesse of a scavenger.

In his essay "The Art-Work of the Future" (1849), Wagner had hailed the place of art in the following terms: "For as Man only then becomes free, when he gains glad consciousness of his oneness with Nature; so does Art only then gain freedom when she has no more to blush for her affinity with actual Life."[11] "Actual Life" became more or less Nietzsche's motto. For Wagner, art was exemplary in embodying the highest celebration of life. In a panegyric on Beethoven and in the course of remarks on "the Art of Tone," Wagner described the yearning expressed in the great art of music. The "most infinite capacity" of Nature consists in Desire and Love, Nature "in its insatiable longing . . . yet with nothing but itself."[12] In the case of Beethoven's work, "each letter of this speech was an infinitely soul-full element, and the measure of the joinery of these elements was utmost free commensuration, such as could be exercised by none but a tone-poet who longed for the unmeasured utterance of this unfathomed yearning."[13] Wagner tells us that what Beethoven achieved was hard-won in the teeth of Christianity. For Beethoven had to contend with a Christian culture that had directed its longing to something other than this life, under the tutelage of the Word and not of tone. Christian

9. See, e.g., the communication to sister Elisabeth, *SL*, February 3, 1882.

10. Derek Watson, *Richard Wagner: A Biography* (London: Dent, 1979), 235. See also chapter 11 in the illuminating account by Michael Tanner, *Wagner* (London: Harper-Collins, 1996).

11. Richard Wagner, *Prose Works*, vol. 1 (London: Kegan Paul, 1892), 71.

12. Ibid., 112–13.

13. Ibid., 121.

culture operated according to the impulse of faith and not out of a deep artistic and human sensibility.

The connection between Wagner's positive outlook and his hostility to Christianity emerges in a piece written a few months before that, called "Art and Revolution." Wagner began by lauding the Greek spirit and the tragic art that it spawned. But then the transition to philosophy took place, and the vivid impression of human strength and beauty expressed in tragedy faded. Rome degenerated into the cultivation of a monochrome culture of enslavement, attaining a sorry sensibility where no one was truly elevated over anyone else. Arriving on this scene, Christianity capitalized on this sensibility and brandished an attitude antithetical to art. "For Art is pleasure in itself, in existence, in community; but the condition of that period, at the close of the Romans' mastery of the world, was self-contempt, disgust with existence, horror of community."[14] The graying late-Roman world needed some apt expression of "manifest degradation and dishonour of all men; the consciousness of the complete corruption of all manly worth; the inevitably ensuing loathing of the material pleasures that alone were left." Wagner's words so strikingly prefigure Nietzsche's later work here that I quote them at length, though they may illustrate affinity as much as influence, for Wagner was neither alone nor original in so saying:[15]

> Christianity adjusts the ills of an honourless, useless and sorrowful existence of mankind on earth, by the miraculous love of God; who had not—as the noble Greek supposed—created man for a happy and self-conscious life upon this earth, but had imprisoned him in a loathsome dungeon; so as, in reward for the self-contempt that poisoned him therein, to prepare him for a posthumous state of endless comfort and inactive ecstasy. Man was therefore bound to remain in his deepest and unmanliest degradation, and no activity of the present life should he exercise; for this accursed life was, in truth, the world of the devil, i.e., of the senses; and by every action in it, he played into the devil's hands. Therefore the poor wretch who, in the enjoyment of his natural powers, made this life his own possession, must suffer after death the eternal torments of hell! Nought was required of mankind but Faith—that is to say, the confession of its miserable plight, and the giving up of all spontaneous attempts to escape from out this misery, for the *undeserved Grace* of God was alone to set it free.[16]

14. "Art and Revolution," in ibid., 36. The quotations that follow come from this segment of the work.

15. Wagner, for instance, apparently read Edward Gibbon's *Decline and Fall of the Roman Empire* (1782), which contains some similar sentiments.

16. In 1884, Nietzsche was observing that the "degeneration of the rulers and the ruling classes has been the cause of the greatest mischief in history! Without the Roman

The Schopenhauerian Wagner that Nietzsche encountered in person and the literary Wagner that Nietzsche encountered in print might not have all things in common. Wagner here contrasts Greek joy and nobility to Christian contempt for life and for self. Schopenhauer, however, far from repudiating relevant features in the Christian contribution at this point, actually applauded them, however they might compare with the Greeks.[17] We are not concerned here with changes in Wagner's thinking over time or with the relation of Nietzsche's thought to tributary waters that flowed into it from his direct exposure to the Greeks, to Schopenhauer, and to the earlier or the later Wagner. What is noteworthy is that Nietzsche became involved in the most magnificent of all crusades to produce Olympian culture and that for Wagner, who owned the crusade, Christianity was no ally. Schopenhauer's concessions to Christianity may have led Wagner to modify his view that the Christian way was weary and miserable. But when it came to the ideal of *Gesamtkunstwerk*—the holistic artistic task of cultural renewal—Christianity was not even lodging at the foothills of the Olympian venture.

Wagner and Nietzsche were on to nothing less than the grandest cultural and historical enterprise imaginable. Nietzsche became so enthusiastic that, at the start of the 1870s, he contemplated leaving his Basel professorship to devote his time to raising funds for and generally promoting the Bayreuth project, which Wagner was trying to get off the ground in earnest when Nietzsche took up his position. Regarding hope for cultural renewal, his friendship with and faith in Wagner placed him on the inside track. What better to devote one's time to after reading Schopenhauer? Professionally, there is something else: writing one's own book. So, against the background of all this, Nietzsche ventured his first full-length effort: *The Birth of Tragedy from the Spirit of Music*. Obviously, it is not just the product of Schopenhauerian and Wagnerian influences. In fact, at some points it challenges Schopenhauer.[18] And Nietzsche had for many years plowed his classical furrow without Wagner in sight. But the book is the product of those heady early years, when the world was spread out before a brilliant professor of classical studies and a standard-bearer of the exhilarating hope of a new cultural era. It was

Caesars and Roman society, the insanity of Christianity would never have come to power" (*WP* 874).

17. Arthur Schopenhauer remarked that the "power by virtue of which Christianity was able to overcome first Judaism, and then the paganism of Greece and Rome, is to be found solely in its pessimism"; see *The World as Will and Representation*, 2 vols. (New York: Dover, 1966), 2:170.

18. See, e.g., Martha C. Nussbaum, "Nietzsche, Schopenhauer, and Dionysus," in *The Cambridge Companion to Schopenhauer*, ed. Christopher Janaway (Cambridge: Cambridge University Press, 1999).

all a world removed from Christianity, one that we must enter. Could anyone in his or her right mind prefer Christianity to it?

The Birth of Tragedy

BT was published just as 1871 swung into 1872. In 1870, the Franco-Prussian War had broken out and, at one stage, Nietzsche served as a medical orderly. Yet again he was hit by illness. In the midst of sickness and war, he was preoccupied with the question of culture. Questions of conflict and of culture could be associated; if this war were to lead to the enhancement of culture, good for the war: "You say it is the good cause that hallows even war? I tell you: it is the good war that hallows every cause" ("Of War and Warriors," Z 1.10). Life is strife, so we should be neither pacifists nor squeamish. However, Nietzsche decided that this particular war accomplished nothing for culture. Crude or plebeian militaristic jingoism did not serve German culture even when Prussian victory was the outcome of the fray. Nietzsche's opening salvo, in his broadside against Strauss, makes the point.[19] *BT* set out what Nietzsche really wanted and hoped for.

Looking back on this work, Nietzsche in *Ecce Homo* rather wished that he had called it "Hellenism and Pessimism," a subtitle he actually deployed in a further edition many years later.[20] This was because people had been apt to think that it was a book about Wagner, a tendency betrayed by the fact that some people mistook the title as "The Rebirth of Tragedy out of the Spirit of Music." Nietzsche protested that he was writing not about the rebirth of tragedy in the work of Wagner but about its birth as the achievement of the Greeks. In fact, he insisted, the book was not about Wagner at all. It was about Nietzsche or Zarathustra, the fictitious figure that became Nietzsche's mouthpiece in that eponymous work, though his relation to Nietzsche is complex.[21] Yet in so describing or redescribing his work, Nietzsche glossed over, sidelined, or denied some of the book's attributes. *The Birth of Tragedy* was indeed the title, but after a vivid account and evocation of that birth, the work goes on to speak about the hope of rebirth in terms so passionately lyrical that, at the end of the work, readers are drawn to think as much about the

19. "David Strauss the Confessor and the Writer," in *UO*.

20. In *EH* Nietzsche's comments on his own books are usually easy to find because he works through his authorship in historical sequence, heading up the relevant sections of his discussion with the titles of those books. The exception is *Z*, to which reference is ubiquitous in *EH*.

21. There certainly is a nonfictitious, historical Zarathushtra (Old Iranian spelling), whom we normally know as Zoroaster.

cultural possibilities of contemporary Germany as about the historical
actualities of ancient Greece. Wagner himself looms even larger than a
great white hope that shimmers into the picture; he practically incarnates
the god Apollo himself.

A new preface to *BT*, written in 1886, went considerably further in
self-criticism than would the later account in *EH*, which was embedded
in a piece of literary choreography designed to expound the authorship
as a whole.[22] Indeed, in his new preface, Nietzsche practically castigates
his own work: "I repeat: I find it an impossible book today" (preface,
3). In this preface, he emphasizes the book's anti-Christian stance. In
EH, in the same section of the essay that contains the above disclaimer
about Wagner, Nietzsche simply remarks that there is a "profound hostile
silence with regard to Christianity throughout the book," though this
is mildly qualified a couple of sentences later.[23] The 1886 preface had
gone further. Here he had called his *BT* "anti-moral," a characteristic
signaled by "its consistently cautious and hostile silence about Christianity—Christianity as the most excessive, elaborately figured development
of the moral theme that humanity has ever had to listen to" (preface,
5). As far as Nietzsche is concerned, to oppose Christianity is to oppose
morality, and morality is here pitted against sheer, raw life. Whether or
not this view of things gives us the best clue to what was going on in *BT*
at the time of its composition, we shall find that it gives us more than
just a clue to what had become the heart of Nietzsche's opposition to
Christianity by the time the new preface was written.

With regard to the text of *BT* itself, discounting any evidences in unpublished notes or essays before and around that time, it is tempting to
say that, whatever Nietzsche's retrospective judgments, the work is not
obviously on a collision course with Christianity in just any conceivable
form. Plotting its relation to Christianity is no simple matter. Would
the author have committed a manifest breach of the logic of his argument, if he had allowed that we might square the thesis argued in *BT*
with permission to adhere to a radical reinterpretation of Christianity
in radically mythological form? What is said about Luther's chorale, for
instance, while emphasizing its Germanness rather than its Christianity,
surely portends the possibility of Nietzsche's ending up where Wagner
arguably ended up at the end of his day: with some positive use of or

22. The implication is not necessarily that, in *EH*, Nietzsche generally and idealistically
misrepresented things in *BT*. But in *EH* as a whole, he certainly offers a peculiarly studied
account of things, maximally unifying his authorship. For some retractive moments in
relation to his early work, see *WP* 91, 417.

23. I agree with Thomas Brobjer that this is not a convincing qualification; see his
essay "Nietzsche's Changing Relation with Christianity," in *Nietzsche and the Gods*, ed.
Weaver Santaniello (New York: State University of New York Press, 2001), 155n28.

gesture toward Christianity, in mythological guise. But we are in peril of deploying the word "Christianity" here as though it had a huge wax nose.[24] Appealing to the presence of an "ancient strength" lying concealed beneath the miserable externals of contemporary German culture, Nietzsche commented that the

> German Reformation grew up out of the depths of this abyss, and in its chorale there could be heard for the first time the future melody of German music. This chorale of Luther's sounded so profound, courageous, and soulful, so joyously good and tender, the first, enticing call of the Dionysiac, breaking forth from a tangled thicket at the approach of spring. It was answered by competing echoes from that consecrated yet exuberant procession of Dionysiac enthusiasts to whom we owe German music—and to which we shall owe the *rebirth of the German myth*! (*BT* 23)

So it is tempting to allow or to claim that in *BT* something might be salvaged for Christianity, even at the risk of stretching to the limits of credibility our idea of what constitutes compatibility with Christianity. That said, the temptation is probably best resisted. Christianity can survive *BT* only under the patronship of the god Dionysus, who is a central figure in *BT*, and perhaps it is silly even to contemplate such a possibility.[25] In any case, it is not my aim to salvage morsels of (Christian) religious comfort from *BT* or indeed to follow up everything in it that is implicitly critical of Christianity.[26] It is of more importance to understand what Nietzsche is saying and to appreciate how removed he conceived it to be from the world of Christianity.

Whatever Nietzsche came to think of *BT*, and however it measured up to the scholarly criteria by which contemporaries judged it, Nietzsche is well able in its pages to draw us into the world of Greek tragedy as he perceives it. There are at least two qualifications for latching on to the wavelength of *BT*. The first is the capacity to believe passionately that the world should be represented as a theater of both joy and pain and to feel their intensity. The second is the capacity to revel in the thought of Greece and of Greek tragedy in a circular open-air theater on an antique afternoon. We do not have to prefer Greek tragedy to Wagner

24. As for Wagner, he bowed out with *Parsifal*, but Magee regards this work as more Buddhist than Christian (*Wagner and Philosophy*, 276–85). There is, anyway, a difference between a work being "Christian" and a work containing elements inspired by Christianity.

25. Argument about who exactly Nietzsche's Dionysus is does not affect this question. See, e.g., Christian Kerslake, "Nietzsche and the Doctrine of Metempsychosis," in *Nietzsche and the Divine*, ed. John Lippitt and Jim Urpeth (Manchester, UK: Clinamen, 2000).

26. E.g., Nietzsche's contrast of Promethean myth to the Semitic myth of the fall (*BT* 9).

and Bayreuth or to Shakespeare and Stratford. We do not even have to pretend to know anything at all about it. It is true that a romantic and ignorant idealization of Greek tragedy on an imaginative level will not adequately engage the world that captivated Nietzsche. To engage it aright, we need to know that world as he knew it, not by unleashing romantic arrows back through time in the direction of the eastern Mediterranean. Nonetheless, for those of us who lack the competence to adjudicate great stretches of the argument, imaginative empathy will enable us to feel something of its emotional force.

The thesis of the work is announced in its title. Tragedy was born out of the spirit of music. Arrayed alongside Nietzsche's own scholarship and life experience are Schopenhauer, with his bleak world, strong Will, and connected theses about music, and Wagner, who believed Schopenhauer and also believed that Greek tragedy was Greek culture's supreme creative achievement. Nietzsche proposed a scholarly revision of existing notions of the birth of Greek tragedy. He argued that the key to getting it right is the identification of two drives that have a physiological basis. One is toward illusion, exemplified by the dream. Art orders illusion, a process symbolically represented by the god Apollo, beautiful in form. The other drive is exemplified by the state of intoxication, which produces ecstasy. This is symbolized by the god Dionysus, and we especially need to understand this underlying drive and force aright to penetrate the genesis of tragic drama. Apollonian art veils a world whose reality is tragic. The Greeks knew the horror of existence and dealt with it in tragedy. They harnessed the Apollonian drive to the Dionysiac instinct. The state of intoxication is fundamentally driven by tragic awareness. The tragic musical chorus is Dionysian and guides us to the manger where tragedy is laid. Now what exactly is meant by the "Dionysian" instinct or "Dionysian" nature?

We must skim the surface here, as with much else in Nietzsche; in connection with Dionysus, there are several issues in Nietzschean scholarship. If we turn to an unpublished essay written in 1870, just after the start of the Franco-Prussian War, Nietzsche offers us a succinct account of the "Dionysiac [or "Dionysian"] Outlook."[27]

> There are two principal forces which bring naive, natural man to the self-oblivion of intense intoxication: the drive of spring and narcotic drink.

27. Appended to *BT* under the literally accurate title "The Dionysiac World-View." Ronald Hayman in *Nietzsche: A Critical Life* (London: Phoenix, 1995), 127, however, renders *Weltanschauung* as "attitude" rather than "worldview," presumably to avoid the theory-laden Kantian and post-Kantian connotations of *Weltanschauung*. There are alternatives: Christopher Middleton renders it "The Dionysiac View of Life" (*SL* 70). The quotations that follow are found on pages 120 and 125 of *BT*.

Their effects are symbolized in the figure of Dionysos. In both states the
principium individuationis is disrupted, subjectivity disappears entirely
before the erupting force of the general element in human life, indeed of
the general element in nature.

The question of individuation plunges us deep into a philosophical
background that features the Schopenhauerian reaction to Kant. Its
importance surfaces in *BT*, but we simply recognize here that Dionysus
symbolizes ecstatic and tragic union with nature. Although reality has
pain at its heart, you can behold it in a transfiguring mirror. Art, including drama, is such a mirror, the product of Apollonian craftsmanship.
Underlying its representation is the pulsating Dionysian response to
existence, joining spiritual with physical intoxication. Prosaically speaking, the Dionysian response embraces suffering in the mode of tragic
joy, and so we are deeply reconciled to that reality that binds man and
nature, man and woman, man and beast—all existence—into one. Summing up a basic contention in his statement of the Dionysiac outlook,
Nietzsche points to the Greeks:

> For how else could that infinitely sensitive people with such brilliant talent
> for *suffering* have been able to bear life, if *that self-same life* had not been
> revealed to them in their gods, suffused with a higher glory! The same drive
> which summons art into being in order to perfect existence, to augment
> it and seduce men into continuing to live, also led to the creation of the
> Olympian world, a world of beauty, calm and pleasure.

In *BT* Nietzsche is constrained to explain, from a historical point of
view, the progress of the cultural Greek ages from pre-Homeric Titanism through Homer himself and down to the advent of tragedy and the
great tragedians. He insists that it be told as the story of the two drives
symbolized by Apollo and Dionysus. We need to grasp correctly the relation of music to poetry. Tragic drama is born out of the spirit of music.
Whereas a sculptor or an epic poet contemplates images, lyrical music
expresses what is more basic, "nothing but the primal pain and primal
echo" of the reality that lies behind and precedes artistic illusion (*BT*
5). Lyrical poetry depends on this musical base. From here, Nietzsche
proceeds to argue that it is the chorus that supports the tragedy. The
satyr, the meaning of the chorus, is a Dionysian figure who revels and
suffers. Nietzsche builds up to a powerful crescendo in this part of *BT*,
arguing that tragic drama expresses a response to the primitive state of
affairs, enabling us to live with it, not by inducing resignation, but by
rapturous and tragic acceptance.

Nietzsche actually wraps up this argument fairly quickly and then proceeds to two matters as crucial to his book as is the account of tragedy's

birth. First, what about the demise of tragedy? Euripides is on the death slope, but the dark-gray eminence is Socrates. Old Socrates casts the net of reason over everything. It is a net woven with intertwining strands of virtue. The texts on which basis we should interpret Socrates are the following: "In order to be beautiful, everything must be reasonable." "Only he who knows is virtuous." Canons of rationality and of morality are here used to judge everything, art and tragedy included. The tragedy born out of the spirit of music is not going to survive that kind of thing for long. With the demise of dramatic tragedy, the music that bore it fades away as well. But see the implications of this. Tragedy is rooted in existence and is, we might say, its measure. Therefore, Socrates is presuming to pass correcting and reproving judgment on existence. Doesn't he know that life is neither moral nor rational? It is to be appropriated, suffered, and celebrated in the train of Dionysus. Nietzsche persists in his engagement with Socrates throughout his authorship, though his relationship to Socrates is many-sided. On this point, however, he holds the line to the end: "Reason became = virtue = happiness" (*WP* 433).

Of the important strands simply ignored in the above account, we in a later chapter shall briefly revisit Nietzsche's treatment of justice and the significance of his conviction that "there is nothing more terrible than a class of barbaric slaves which has learned to regard its existence as an injustice and which sets out to take revenge, not just for itself but for all future generations" (*BT* 18). For now, we observe that, from Nietzsche's point of view, the damage done by the rationalizing, moralizing Socrates is not confined to closing the door on the past. In his analysis of the cultural upshot of this fateful intervention, Nietzsche derives from the phenomenon of "aesthetic Socratism" the course of future science, which is the product of the "theoretical man." Nietzsche is not knocking just any kind of scientific knowledge. The problem lies with posttragic scientific culture rather than with knowledge as such.

This leads us to the second concern that he presents after describing the birth of tragedy, one that is continuous with his interest in the Socratic assassination of tragedy. That is the question of contemporary culture. Nietzsche views European culture as the issue of Socratism. However, there is hope of rejuvenation. Nietzsche becomes lyrical at this point, and although his actual name is not much in evidence, he is speaking of Wagner. The Dionysiac spirit is again awakening with Wagner. The German spirit is Dionysian in its depths. As we have learned about Greece, we now learn about Germany. The rebirth of tragedy is as exciting in prospect as its birth is in retrospect.

> Yes, my friends, believe as I do in Dionysiac life and in the rebirth of trag-
> edy. The time of Socratic man is past. Put on wreaths of ivy, take up the

thyrsus and do not be surprised if tigers and panthers lie down, purring and curling around your legs. Now you must only dare to be tragic human beings, for you will be released and redeemed. You will accompany the festive procession of Dionysos from India to Greece! Put on your armour for a hard fight, but believe in the miracles of your god! (*BT* 20)

Then Nietzsche clips his thesis to the reiterated claim that the "Dionysiac, with the primal pleasure it perceives even in pain, is the common womb from which both music and the tragic myth are born." He pictures the German knight dreaming his Dionysiac dreams, now awakening and stirring as if toward resuscitation or resurrection (*BT* 24).

BT is indeed "the most 'nostalgic' of his works," and we must leave it there.[28] But what if things go wrong? What is left for Nietzsche if a German renaissance is aborted early? Only when we understand the strength of his cultural expectations do we understand the crashing disappointment at their nonrealization. Only when we ask how Christianity should be plotted in relation first to this hopeful scenario and then to its hopeless disappearance do we understand a whole deep dimension of Nietzsche's hostility to it. As he builds up to his crescendo in *The Antichrist*, almost seventeen years later, weeks away from his collapse into insanity, Nietzsche lashes, thrashes, and rages:

The Germans have robbed Europe of the last great cultural harvest Europe had to bring home—the harvest of Renaissance. . . . The Renaissance—an event without meaning, a great in vain!—Oh these Germans, what they have already cost us! In vain—that has always been the work of Germans. (*A* 61)

"Has a nation ever changed its gods?" God asks, in what is surely the most poignant chapter on sin in the whole of the Bible. "'But my people have exchanged their Glory for worthless idols. Be appalled at this, O heavens, and shudder with great horror,' declares the Lord" (Jer. 2:11–12 NIV). Nietzsche grimly understands how "Jehovah" (Yahweh) felt. What *did* seduce the German people into infidelity to the Renaissance? Answer: "Christianity." Christianity "robbed us [all] of the harvest of the culture of the ancient world" (*A* 60).[29] Christianity versus the ancient world; Luther versus the Renaissance; victory to Christianity and to Luther—that is how things have come to be in the state they are in. "If we never get rid

28. Alexander Nehamas, "Nietzsche, Modernity, Aestheticism," in *The Cambridge Companion to Nietzsche*, ed. Bernd Magnus and Kathleen M. Higgins (Cambridge: Cambridge University Press, 1996), 229.

29. The words that continue that line are noteworthy in our present global context: "It [Christianity] later went on to rob us of the harvest of the culture of *Islam*."

of Christianity, the *Germans* will be to blame" (*A* 61). Nietzsche's thought
developed in the years following *BT*, but the issue of culture remained
very much at the center of his concerns. Christianity has destroyed culture and, in destroying culture, destroyed highest humanity.

The Tragic Sense of Life

Two matters invite our reflection in connection with *BT* and that whole
epoch in Nietzsche's life. In this section we glance at the first. In theological perspective, what should we make of the tragic sense of life?

The problem of reconciling a theistic worldview with the realities of
suffering and evil saps the intellectual confidence of many Christians
who, nevertheless, cling to belief in a personal God. Schopenhauer offers an alternative that some will find attractive, an attraction born not
necessarily of brooding emotional sadomasochism but of the apparent
fittingness of Schopenhauer's response to the world. Schopenhauer aspired to be deeply empirical and offered philosophical argumentation
in support of his conclusions, albeit within roughly Kantian constraints.
It is not hard to see how he could lure the religious believer to his side.
Under his influence, attachment to the Christian God can transmute
into acknowledgment of the huge vital impulse that animates the world.
Both are big forces. Once we thought that *agapē* reigned in interhuman relationships, extending to the world the flow of the inner life of
a personal God; in a new day we might as a substitute switch over to
a resigned if sincere Schopenhauerian compassion. We receive from
Schopenhauer a heightened impetus to lose ourselves in art, with the
promise of a heightened pleasure in occasional release from the bondage
of existence, through aesthetic engagement. Schopenhauer presents us
with a "romantic pessimism," as Nietzsche later described it, comparing
it to his own "Dionysian pessimism" (*GS* 370). While writing *The World
as Will and Representation*, Schopenhauer averred that the "outcome
of this knowledge is sad and depressing, but the *state* of knowing, the
acquisition of insight, the penetration of truth, are thoroughly pleasur-
able—and . . . add a mixture of sweetness to my bitterness."[30] Nietzsche
effectively responds: "There are heights of the soul from whose vantage-
point even tragedy stops having tragic effects" (*BGE* 30). He later radi-
calized Schopenhauer to the point of reversal: the pleasure of knowing
is enhanced by the pleasure of willing, which conquers pessimism. But
Nietzsche has not yet reached that formulation.

30. Quoted in Magee, *Philosophy of Schopenhauer*, 25.

The Christian believer obviously cannot resolutely embrace Schopenhauer's outlook on life and remain committed to belief in a personal Creator and expectation of an eschatological Redeemer. In Christianity, creation and *eschaton* frame the temporal story of humanity, created and fallen, and that of Jesus, crucified and risen. What Schopenhauer believed to be absolutely and cosmically determinate the Christian interprets as temporally bounded, so that creation is not doomed to perpetual futility. Since it was made good, it will be restored to greater goodness, however the processes are conceived and however eschatological reality is related to the empirical actuality about us. Biblical eschatological hope includes the transformation of the created order. Both inside and outside the churches, Christian hope is often taken to be otherworldly, despite a sustained campaign against this in theology for a long time. "Otherworldly" and "this-worldly" are certainly more slippery terms than immediately appear and require careful definition. Yet the terms of Christian belief in and hope for creation entail a rejection of Schopenhauer's outlook.

So much is obvious enough, but study of Nietzsche's reaction to Schopenhauer and, indeed, of the critique of Christianity that animates Nietzsche's later work shows how little attention Nietzsche gives to the Christian understanding of creation, whether primal or eschatological. He found it intellectually incredible. But at least a critic needs to get a proper grip on the Christian understanding of the world. While Christians may not know how present creation is related to its eschatological future, they are constrained to love the earth. Love is the instinctive foe of pessimism, though it is not thereby the ally of optimism. Pessimism tends to sap the energy, if not stymie the motive, for what we might call a properly comprehensive philanthropy toward human creatures and a positive cultivation of nonhuman creation.

If embracing Dionysus reveals a kind of Nietzschean love for the earth that is already estranged from Schopenhauer, it may appear that our observing the power of Schopenhauer's pessimism and its contrast to Christianity does not connect with Nietzsche's criticisms of Christianity. But a move away from Schopenhauer's pessimism does not entail either that Nietzsche was thereby less alienated from Christianity or that he was less subject to an involuted kind of despair. Figgis reckoned that "pessimism, the nay-saying to life, is ten thousand times more wicked than all the variegated blasphemies of Nietzsche."[31] Is it? Schopenhauer tempered and allied pessimism with the spirit of true compassion, while Nietzsche's appropriation of Dionysus was conceivably allied to a pro-

31. John Neville Figgis, *The Will to Freedom, or The Gospel of Nietzsche and the Gospel of Christ* (London: Longmans, Green, 1917), 144.

founder misanthropy and so perhaps expressive of a deeper despair than Schopenhauer knew. Nietzsche's "blasphemies" actually came later in his life than the time at which we have arrived, and we must remember that Figgis well understood post-Schopenhauerian European pessimism, for he lived through it.[32] Yet, up to a point, Christians should join with Nietzsche, as with Schopenhauer, in finding a certain kind of "optimism" distasteful. If the "rationality" of the world is supposed to mean that its objectively existing structure is in principle grasped by reason, virtually without remainder, and that subjective rationality is in fact capable of figuring tragedy into a rational framework of explanation, we can sympathize with Nietzsche's repudiation of rationality on the ground that it does not give tragedy its due.

Nietzsche's Dionysiac response to pessimism invites theological attention. For our purposes it does not matter whether or not his account of Greek tragedy was a good one. What should we make of music and tragedy? Barth, whose response to Nietzsche will occupy us later, commends Mozart to us in this connection.[33] Mozart personally had never been happy; "what he translated into music was real life in all its discord." Like and yet unlike Dionysus (Barth does not make the comparison), Mozart expresses unity: "One marvels again and again how everything comes to expression in him: heaven and earth, nature and man, comedy and tragedy." Light and dark, weeping and joy, go together. Although Mozart "on one occasion . . . called death man's true best friend, and he thought daily of death," he is a great theologian of freedom and avoids Titanism. "Heaven arches over the earth, but it does not weigh it down, it does not crush or devour it. Hence earth remains earth, with no need to maintain itself in a titanic revolt against heaven." On this account of things, Christianity substitutes earth and heaven, joy and sorrow before God for Dionysian excess and despair. Obviously, this is all better heard than said.

Does Barth's Mozart provide a Christian countertheme to a Dionysian tragic sense of life? Nietzsche later came to pit Mozart favorably against Wagner. He refers to the "cheerful, enthusiastic, tender, enamored spirit of Mozart" in contrast to Wagner, and to our need for "the south, sun-

---

32. James Orr, *The Christian View of God and the World* (Vancouver: Regent, 2002), 454–55, is among those who bear witness to how strong it was. It is quite surprising that Emmanuel Mounier said of the late nineteenth century: "Never was optimism more joyous or indifference more serene than at this time," though the statement does not logically contradict claims for the massive influences of pessimism. He is quoted by Yves Ledure, "Nietzsche's Critique of Christianity," in *Nietzsche and Christianity*, ed. Claude Geffré and Jean-Pierre Jossua (Edinburgh: T&T Clark; New York: Seabury, 1981), 48.

33. Karl Barth, *Wolfgang Amadeus Mozart* (Grand Rapids: Eerdmans, 1986). My quotations are taken from 32–54.

shine 'at any price,' bright, harmless innocent Mozartian happiness and delicacy of tones."[34] But he never abandons the tragic sense of life. Barth places Mozart in opposition to it.[35] In *Church Dogmatics*, he wrote:

> In face of the problem of theodicy [particularly in wake of the Lisbon earthquake], Mozart had the peace of God which far transcends all the critical or speculative reason that praises and reproves. This problem lay behind him. Why then concern himself with it? He had heard, and causes those who have ears to hear, even today, what we shall not see until the end of time—the whole context of providence. As thought in the light of this end, he heard the harmony of creation to which the shadow also belongs but in which the shadow is not darkness, deficiency is not defeat, sadness cannot become despair, trouble cannot degenerate into tragedy and infinite melancholy is not ultimately forced to claim undisputed sway. Thus the cheerfulness in this harmony is not without its limits. But the light shines all the more brightly because it breaks forth from this shadow.[36]

"Not darkness"? "Trouble cannot degenerate into tragedy"? Admittedly, Barth formulates things a bit differently in the Mozart essays, but at this point we dangerously approximate a cavalier attitude toward evil and suffering.[37] It is unfair to make categorical judgments about Barth here; to do him justice, for example, we would need to take his eschatology into account. But if we have doubts about Barth on tragedy, it may entail either that we hear Mozart a little differently from the way Barth does or that we insist on listening to music other than Mozart's with the same insistence as Barth insisted on the "incomparable" nature of Mozart's music.[38] In other words, we may think that Nietzsche has not

---

34. "Wagner as Danger," in *NCW*; see *SL*, February 23, 1886. Cf. the climax of Hesse's *Steppenwolf* (232–48).

35. Hans W. Frei remarked that the "one form of imagination of [*sic*] which he [Barth] really had little sympathy was the tragic. . . . 'Titanism' he used to call it depreciatingly and wince whenever he saw it raising its classical or romanticized head"; see his "Karl Barth: Theologian," in *Theology and Narrative: Selected Essays*, by Hans W. Frei, ed. George Hunsinger and William C. Placher (New York and Oxford: Oxford University Press, 1993), 175.

36. Karl Barth, *Church Dogmatics*, vol. III/3 (Edinburgh: T&T Clark, 1960), 298.

37. But see G. C. Berkouwer, *A Half Century of Theology: Motives and Methods* (Grand Rapids: Eerdmans, 1977), 30–31 and 68ff. We might pit Leibniz and Mozart on the side of Barth, against Schopenhauer and Wagner on the side of Nietzsche. Barth's positive use of Leibniz is well brought out at various points in Timothy J. Gorringe, *Karl Barth against Hegemony* (Oxford: Oxford University Press, 1999). Chapter 5, in particular, is part of his buildup to a climactic exposition of Barth's theology as a theology of joy; it gives us a good idea of how we might oppose Barth to Nietzsche. But the picture of Barth on Leibniz that we see in Gorringe's volume should be balanced against what we read in Karl Barth's *Protestant Theology in the Nineteenth Century* (London: SCM, 1972), e.g., 77–79.

38. See Karl Barth, *Church Dogmatics*, vol. III/1 (Edinburgh: T&T Clark, 1958), 404; see also 335–40, where Barth offers a balanced treatment of Schopenhauer.

been disposed of; Dionysian pessimism captures something in the tragic sense of life that Barth on Mozart has elided.

In reflecting on Nietzsche's Dionysianism, another possibility is to plunder C. S. Lewis. In one of his Narnia stories, *Prince Caspian*, there is a scene whose mood is hard to capture without narrating the story to that point. It features the sojourners, the animals, and the land of Narnia rejoicing in Aslan's presence after he has acted in deliverance. As they join together to celebrate their happiness, with Aslan looking on, things develop into an abandoned, riotous dance. Among the dancers, the bemused and fascinated Lucy notices "a youth, dressed only in fawn-skin, with vine leaves wreathed in his curly hair. His face would have been almost too pretty for a boy's, if it had not looked so extremely wild. You felt, Edmund said when he saw him a few days later, 'There's a chap who might do anything—absolutely anything.'"[39]

Inquiry about his identity reveals him to be Bacchus. Bacchus was a Lydian name for Dionysus, and much of the mythological symbolism associated with Dionysus turns up in Lewis's account. The whole sequence is a memorable one even amid the plethora of memorable sequences that course through the seven volumes of Narnia stories. Lewis makes a suggestion here that, I think, is strictly unparalleled in any of the other Narnia volumes: the Dionysian is allowed its place—in the presence of Aslan. Aslan does not join in the romp. The vocational and emotional path carved out for him does not permit that, at least at that moment. But far from forbidding the gyrations, he presides over them, neither intrusively nor anxiously in the foreground, yet approving the riot and restraining no rioter. He does not need to direct or choreograph it. Dionysus is under no visible restraint. Lucy confides in Susan: "'I wouldn't have felt safe with Bacchus and all his wild girls if we'd met them without Aslan.' 'I should think not.' said Lucy." There the episode ends.

It might or might not be in order to identify a tragic element in all this revelry. Presumably, it anticipates eschatological deliverance beyond all tragedy, the deliverance of all creation. So it is a far cry from Nietzschean Dionysian pessimism. However, Lewis dares to propose that the Dionysian has its place in the presence of Christ. Dionysian vitality, exuberance, and abandonment are expressive of instincts that must be allowed, perhaps even fostered. We are entitled to seek ways of channeling them. But are we not elaborating a desperate gesture here in order to accommodate Nietzschean Dionysianism to Christian thought? From Nietzsche's standpoint, there can be no authentic concessionary theological gesture in the Dionysian direction while Christ rules in the

39. C. S. Lewis, *Prince Caspian* (London: Lion, 1980), 136–37.

pantheon. As we have observed, lacking eschatological belief, his own Dionysianism can express only the tragic present, although we shall later encounter the teaching of eternal recurrence. The substance of life is here and now; there is no shadow anticipating eschatological perfection.[40] In *BT*, Nietzsche is not alerting us to Dionysian moments in life. He is inducting us into a Dionysian worldview. Its significance, we may think, is not remotely paralleled by or consistent with anything Christians may dredge up from their worldview. Looking back at the amoral instinct for life that threaded its way through *BT*, Nietzsche asked: "What was it to be called? As a philologist and man of words I baptized it, not without a certain liberty—for who can know the true name of the Antichrist?—by the name of a Greek god: I called it *Dionysiac*."[41] The Dionysian as the antithesis of the Christian not only survived in Nietzsche's literature; it actually developed in significance. A few months before his final breakdown, Nietzsche wrote the following note:

> One will see that the problem is that of the meaning of suffering: whether a Christian meaning or a tragic meaning. In the former case, it is supposed to be the path to a holy existence; in the latter case, being is counted as *holy enough* to justify even a monstrous amount of suffering. The tragic man affirms even the harshest suffering: he is sufficiently strong, rich, and capable of deifying [himself] to do so. The Christian denies even the happiest lot on earth: he is sufficiently weak, poor, disinherited to suffer from life in whatever form he meets it. The god on the cross is a curse on life, a signpost to seek redemption from life; Dionysus cut to pieces is a *promise* of life. (*WP* 1052)

Coursing its way through this is the supposition that the Christian does nothing with creation: the path to holy existence is away from creation; the redemption of the cross is redemption from creation. Lewis's Dionysianism is parasitic on a Redeemer and a redemption, which become the nub of Nietzsche's criticism of Christianity. So what is the point of invoking it?

I am certainly not trying to fuse Nietzsche with Christianity via C. S. Lewis. But Lewis does draw our attention to the possibilities of purification rather than rejection of the Dionysian instinct.[42] The felt force

40. This form of words is not meant to prejudge the question of whether Lewis is a Platonist at this point.

41. "Attempt at Self-Criticism," *BT* 5.

42. His shifting of Dionysus in the direction of innocence, as it were, reverses Goya's Bacchic move in relation to Velazquez in what appears to be an eloquent disclosure of pre-Nietzschean modernity: see Janis Tomlinson, *Francisco Goya y Lucientes, 1746–1828* (London: Phaidon, 1994), 40–41. C. S. Lewis's *Pilgrim's Regress* (London: Fount, 1998) is broadly suggestive on the point under consideration.

of sheer vitality, the exuberance of an affirmation of life ungrounded in metaphysical religious consolation—this is easily lost on our Christian consciousness. Yet, in terms of Christian consciousness, we must insist that the erotic and energetic forces that surge through creation are to be celebrated because their Creator pronounced them "good." They are not relatively disembodied entities but animate person and beast, meadow and river. Against Schopenhauer, vital forces do not have unilinear, strictly determined historical effects that reveal those very energies to be the restless source of evil. Against Nietzsche, the commingling of good and evil in intertwining strife is for a season, not for material perpetuity. Creation, which Barth celebrates via Mozart, and eschatological anticipation, which Lewis appears to celebrate with Dionysus on board, frame the Christian approach to the tragic sense of life. Ultimately, we must view the irrational frenzy of Dionysus as a shadow of infinite delight in God, a delight to be released in untrammeled power of expression, when evil is finally destroyed. At least that is one important perspective.

The grip of sheer vitality on human consciousness can be enormous. Henri Blocher, in an attempt to set out a modified version of the traditional notion of hell as unending punishment, records the supposition that ancient Greeks would have feared annihilation far more than they feared conscious endless punishment.[43] In the early twentieth century, Miguel de Unamuno instructively claimed that he would prefer endless suffering to annihilation.[44] We may find this perspective at best unexpected, extreme, implausible, or idiosyncratic, conjured up by people totally removed from a certain kind of suffering. Yet, Christians should not be surprised to encounter the will to affirm the permanently indissoluble connection between body, life, and selfhood. The instinct behind it should scarcely be squashed. "I believe in the resurrection of the body." But Nietzsche's Dionysian instinct is not only about exuberance in the midst of tragedy. It is also at the service of grounding practically the only culture worthy of the name, and it is an instinct most magnificently discharged in the generation of culture. This brings us to the second matter for reflection. What are we to make of such enthusiasm for culture?[45]

43. Henri Blocher, "Everlasting Punishment and the Problem of Evil," in *Universalism and the Doctrine of Hell,* ed. Nigel M. de S. Cameron (Grand Rapids: Baker; Carlisle, UK: Paternoster, 1992), 311.

44. Miguel de Unamuno, *The Tragic Sense of Life* (London: Macmillan, 1931). In his novella, *Abel Sanchez,* Unamuno alerts us to the psychological possibility, though not logical necessity, of a link between passionately embracing life, tragic as it is, and a passionate longing to live forever under any conditions; see *Abel Sanchez and Other Stories* (Chicago: Gateway, 1956). Nietzsche apparently exhibits the first passion in *BT* and the second in *Z.*

45. The questions that have arisen in this discussion deserve broadest reflection. "The Western tradition," writes Michael Tanner, "has been inimical to tragedy, thanks to

The Wagnerian Pulse

"In the main, I agree more with the artists than with any philosopher hitherto: they have not lost the scent of life, they have loved the things of 'this world'—they have loved their senses" (*WP* 820). If this were the length and breadth of Nietzsche's sentiments on the matter, we might settle down to a rather relaxed if demanding discussion on art and artists. It is not. "All those things which we now call culture, education, civilization must some day appear before the judge Dionysus whom no man can deceive" (*BT* 19). What is at issue is not just art; it is the crisis of culture, "crisis" both in the ordinary-language sense of the word and "crisis" as in "judgment," *krisis*. Should we pay attention to such hyperbolic talk? Among those with any knowledge of or interest in it, many will find it difficult today to look back in a spirit of enthusiastic endorsement on Wagner's project of cultural renewal, the mighty *Gesamtkunstwerk* designed to bring out the fullest potential for expression in every art, each art helping along the other. Perhaps it is the more difficult for those who are not enamored of his music or, hearing it, cannot ignore the ominous associations of Wagner, anti-Semitism, and Hitler. Others will simply find it difficult to transpose out of its context the sense of intense excitement at counting Bayreuth as the mecca of cultural renaissance, in order to reflect more generally on art and cultural rejuvenation. Even if we overcome these obstacles and have some sympathy for or appreciation of Wagnerian ambitions for cultural renewal under the aesthetic aegis, is it theologically important to reflect on it? If we are drawn back to Nietzsche, Wagner, and cultural renewal in late-nineteenth-century Germany, are we not being sidetracked from an attempt to come to grips with Nietzsche on Christianity?

Far from it. There are two reasons for a quick sortie into the land spread out before us. First, we may or may not like, be interested in, or know much about Wagner—and I am a complete amateur here—but he has been very influential. Second, and more pertinently, the broader question facing the sympathetic or unsympathetic observer of Nietzsche's ambitions in the early 1870s concerns the Christian stake in "culture." We are not going to try to adumbrate a complete theology of culture here. The kind of culture that Nietzsche desiderates is high culture, and the first theological move that many will be disposed to make is to register a determined worry about Nietzsche as a despiser of the masses, Nietzsche as doyen of a "high culture" purchased at the price of unconcern for the

---

the co-operation of Platonism and Christianity, and its great tragedies, above all those of Shakespeare and Racine, are either removed from a theological context or in uneasy relation to it"; see his *Nietzsche* (Oxford: Oxford University Press, 1994), 15.

masses, with a disdain worse than unconcern. His "Schopenhauer as Educator" (1874) makes a comprehensive statement on state and education, philosophy and culture, as Nietzsche presses for a philosophy of education that will serve a philosophy of culture, which itself serves the culture whose aim is to serve the philosopher. Nietzsche's philosopher, if he understands his task aright, is the exemplar of true man.[46] Culture, whose foe is the culture vulture of the day, must foster *the production of the philosophers, artists and saints within us and around us, and thereby to work towards the perfection of nature*."[47] Although we cannot sketch a theology of culture, we should still ask whether cultural intoxication of the Wagnerian and Nietzschean kind, even if we abstract from their detailed proposals, already distances Nietzsche from Christianity.[48]

If we turn to the work of Roger Scruton, one of the ablest and most articulate defenders of high culture in our generation, we shall find an ideal way into the question before us.[49] Scruton has tried to show how high culture historically fulfills a role previously filled by religious belief and essentially aims at the same thing. The traditional common culture out of which modern high culture sprang has religion at its core. Religious belief is essentially about an ethical vision of humanity and of human community. It cannot be completely reduced to this, but its vital social function is to provide such a vision. The presentation of such a vision is also the job of high culture. Aesthetic experience is required to grasp what poetry, art, and music can deliver. In a world that has passed beyond religious belief, "maybe this is the importance of high culture, that it continues to provide, in a heightened and imaginative form, the ethical vision that religion made so easily available." Common culture, historically informed by religion, and high culture, usually alienated from religion in its traditional form, "perhaps stem from the same psychic need—the need for an ethical community into which the self can be absorbed, its transgressions overcome and forgiven, and its emotions re-made in uncorrupted form."[50]

This argument is presented less tentatively than the qualifiers "maybe" and "perhaps" suggest. "When a common culture declines, the ethical life can be sustained and renewed only by a work of the imagination. And that, in a nutshell, is why high culture matters."[51] Scruton is not

46. I use "man" as a noninclusive masculine when treating Nietzsche's thought.

47. *UO* p. 213.

48. Not that Wagner and Nietzsche were altogether the same; Wagner had at least previously stated positive views on the connection between culture and the people, the *Volk*.

49. See Roger Scruton, *An Intelligent Person's Guide to Modern Culture* (London: Duckworth, 1998); idem, *The Aesthetics of Music* (Oxford: Clarendon, 1997).

50. Scruton, *Intelligent Person's Guide*, 16–17.

51. Ibid., 42–43.

content to trade in abstractions; we encounter strong remarks about the moral effects of Beethoven's Ninth and Brahms's Fourth Symphonies.[52] Much is made of sympathy.[53] The structuring elements of true, authentic music—melody, harmony, and rhythm—instill into social life a human movement out of the self toward others; it orders human feeling. Decline in musical taste means decline in morals. "Education of taste is of primary moral significance."[54]

Scruton's views are intrinsically significant, but they are of particular concern to us because he also describes how the modern form of high culture is the product of the nineteenth century and a series of footnotes to Wagner, Nietzsche's captain. What matters here is Wagner's "as if." High culture teaches us to live *"as if* our lives mattered eternally."[55] Wagner led the way. He populated his works with gods and sprinkled them with redemptive motifs, knowing that the order of old religious (Christian) belief is gone and so knowing exactly what he was doing. "To understand the depth of the Wagnerian 'as if' is to understand the condition of the modern soul."[56] Underlying it is the Romantic longing for home. Religion and art both try to make sense of the world as home. In this respect aesthetic interest, like religious interest, is latent in human nature. "The 'point of high culture' is 'to recuperate by imaginative means the old experience of home.'"[57] If humanity is to survive as the bearer of moral knowledge in community, we need both religion and art. Traditional religious belief may have been superseded, but if we destroy its ritual, it will be the sign that we have abandoned the sphere that it opens for us and that ministers to our ennoblement. So a plea for the retention or renewal of art in high culture is not elitist. Rather, it offers an opportunity for moral regeneration and ethical perseverance. On this score, Scruton regards things as being in a bad way today, given the ascendancy of the banalities of popular culture. The Wagnerian "as if" is desperately needed, yet not along Wagnerian lines.[58] Scruton goes to the East, to Confucius. Confucius lived, as we do, in a world where moral order and respectful custom were collapsing, and "we too need the Confucian virtues of humanity, obedience,

52. Scruton, *Aesthetics of Music*, 359, 437.

53. "Classical harmony provides us with an archetype of human sympathy"; ibid., 501. On sympathy in fiction, see 355; and Scruton, *Intelligent Person's Guide*, 41–42.

54. Scruton, *Aesthetics of Music*, 386.

55. Scruton, *Intelligent Person's Guide*, 14.

56. Ibid., 68.

57. Scruton, *Intelligent Person's Guide*, 135. Cf. Hesse: "Our only guide is our homesickness" (*Steppenwolf*, 175).

58. Scruton consistently invokes the primary moral and community value of sexual fidelity and responsibility, plotting the relations of sex and love in a way different from Wagner, whom one tends not to associate with absolute chastity or unflinching monogamy.

and respect for custom and ceremony."[59] If Confucius did not give us religious faith, he does give us hope. So can the achievements of high culture.

Scruton works out a thesis along these lines both by contributing a technical study, moving from sound and tone to culture and ethics, and by offering a brief statement of the story of modern high culture.[60] On this account of matters, the Christian stake in high culture is moral. Contra Nietzsche, it is a morality for us all and not just for some; so on this account of matters, our proper cultural concerns are not elitist but communal. Scruton does not make this criticism of Nietzsche explicit.[61] His view is that religious ritual and the art of high culture are allies with an interest in mutual support and edification: they preserve an ethical vision of human community. Old religious belief is gone, and we might do better with Confucian philosophy, but regarding high culture, the preservation of religion is vital for moral reasons. Here, then, we have a vision that is in some respects alternative to Wagner's and Nietzsche's concerns but consonant in others. What are we to make of this in the context of an investigation into Nietzsche and Christianity? Many of us will quarrel with key features of Scruton's understanding of Christian religion. On sacrament, redemption, and liturgy, he takes a contentious position, to say the least.[62] I leave this aside, along with the case of Confucius.[63] So, what of his connection between the aesthetic and the moral? Is the moral enhancement of humanity at stake in the defense of high culture? Are Christians to welcome Nietzsche's early aesthetic passion, while alternatively tying it to a moral destiny?

59. Scruton, *Intelligent Person's Guide*, 137.

60. It should be recognized, however, that the Confucian option is not mentioned—and not relevant—in Scruton, *Aesthetics of Music*.

61. For his explicit criticisms, see Scruton, *Intelligent Person's Guide*, 64–65, 74–75. His claim that Nietzsche sought to "build a philosophy of life on the ruins of both science and religion, in the name of a purely aesthetic ideal" is contestable (75). It might apply to the period of *BT*, though even then we have to remember that Nietzsche was identifying drives rooted in the *physiological* phenomena of dream and intoxication, whose scientific explanation is potentially important in relation to the aesthetic impulse. In *Aesthetics of Music*, Scruton allows for "a grain of truth in Nietzsche's view, according to which high culture belongs to the 'pathos of distance' established by the aristocratic class," but he thinks that Nietzsche, like Marxism in this respect, "attaches culture to the wrong roots," to power relations rather than to first-person community (505).

62. Scruton, *Intelligent Person's Guide*, chaps. 2 and 4, e.g.; and see the remarks surrounding Durkheim in Scruton, *Aesthetics of Music*, 458.

63. Scruton sets his positive view of Confucius over against Søren Kierkegaard, but his interpretation of Kierkegaard collapsing truth and appearance is controversial if we interpret his observation on Kierkegaard in *Intelligent Person's Guide* (137) in light of his discussion of Kierkegaard in another work: Roger Scruton, *A Short History of Modern Philosophy: From Descartes to Wittgenstein* (London: Routledge, 1995), 190.

It is not clear from the works under consideration whether Scruton thinks that aesthetic experience has the moral tendency that it has independently of our maintenance of other grounds for moral conviction. It is hard to see how such a thing might be shown without bringing an empirical component into the demonstration and providing some inductive evidence that goes beyond a report of how some people feel or have felt on hearing music. Doubtless, art can promote a moral outlook, and aesthetic experience might well richly unite the beautiful and the good under the banner of the "as if true" and under rigorously specified conditions. But Scruton does not give an account of the connection between the aesthetic and the moral sufficient to bear the weight that he puts on it.

What morally renewing force does the "as if" really have if our moral impulses are heavily dependent on the exercise of imagination? Just how much can it ground and source moral power? Scruton comes down hard on Derrida, as a chapter title indicates: "The Devil's Work."[64] The chapter reveals how Scruton is tempted to despair over the fate of high culture. But there is no corresponding sign of despair about the moral capacities for regeneration that are intrinsic to humanity or about the power of aesthetic experience to stimulate them. From a theological point of view, Scruton appears to "lack the courage of despair" on this score.[65] From the same viewpoint, there is something about Nietzsche's Dionysian desperation that more profoundly reflects human reality than Scruton's relatively sanguine connections between art, morality, and human nature. Poussin's *Golden Calf* features on the cover of the paperback version of Scruton's *The Aesthetics of Music*. In *An Intelligent Person's Guide to Modern Culture*, Roger Scruton says of this painting:

> The emotional disorder involved in this [idolizing the mundane; profaning the sacred] has been beautifully conveyed by Poussin; . . . the people drunk, helpless and in the grip of collective delusion, dance like brainless animals around this thing less sacred than themselves. In focusing on the calf their emotions are also out of focus—bewildered, diseased, gyrating in a void. In the distance . . . is the figure of Moses, descending from Mount Sinai with the tables of the law: the abstract decrees of an abstract God, who can be understood through no earthly image but only through law. . . . The contrast here is between the active work of imagination, which points to a God beyond the sensory world, and the passive force of fantasy, which creates its own god out of sensory desires. Every idol is also a sacrilege, since it causes us to focus the worship that is due to higher

---

64. Scruton, *Intelligent Person's Guide*, chap. 11.
65. Karl Barth, *The Epistle to the Romans* (Oxford: Oxford University Press, 1968), 40. We might again invoke Paul Tillich here in *The Courage to Be* (London: Fount, 1962).

things on something lower than ourselves. Only by responding to what is higher than human, do we become truly human.[66]

In *The Aesthetics of Music*, Scruton makes some positive observations about dance, recognizing its culturally enhancing forms.[67] This is not the Nietzschean Dionysian dance, its circle defined by a sphere of tragedy. What Scruton says about dance may be well and wholesomely said. But Scruton's "active imagination" (see the quotation above) is not locked into any ontological order of the religious or any apparent morally transcendent kind such as Moses believed in. Nietzsche proposes the Apollonian "as if" as a deep artistic response to the deep ontological property of suffering, a property necessarily pertaining to existence as we experience it; Apollo deliberately and appropriately artistically veils reality. Scruton has a redemptive "as if"; Wagner and others deliberately and appropriately imaginatively project a reality. From a Nietzschean point of view, what Scruton is doing seems to be this: he is applying something like an Apollonian illusion, an "as if," to the malaise of modern culture, but he is turning a blind eye to Dionysus and tragedy. Here, we should sympathize with Nietzsche. For what can art do or what does it propose to do about sheer tragedy? And if art does not address tragedy, what scale and what kind of cultural renewal can art foster?

Poussin's painting reminds us that in the Old Testament Aaron's "Dionysian" deviancy is religiously unacceptable because it is objectively contrary to moral law, which is vested with the dignity of the revealed Lawgiver. Nietzschean Dionysianism might be an unimpeachably authentic emotional response to a cosmically godless, tragic state of affairs. There may be nothing illogical about it if the cosmic order does not proscribe a Dionysian response. Scruton's "as if" bears some resemblance to Nietzsche's Apollonian illusion in making human flourishing dependent on the projection of an imagined realm. But if there is no realm transcending the senses, pending a statement about morality that he does not give in the volumes discussed, Scruton's idea of what is moral may be built on a vast platform of social contingency, on the way the religious and social order have historically panned out. It is not built on anything more basic. Nietzsche came to think that the Wagnerian "as if" mistakenly sought to retain the permanence of the transcendent when, in fact, the disappearance of divine transcendence reveals that there is no immutable order whatsoever. By his consistent embrace of the tragic, Nietzsche commands our theological sympathy against Scruton

66. Scruton, *Intelligent Person's Guide*, 55–56.
67. Scruton, *Aesthetics of Music*, 359, 391, 498; see also idem, *Intelligent Person's Guide*, chap. 9.

and perhaps against Wagner, if it comes to that. It is scarcely addressed by Scruton's cultural hopes.

I do not wish to be unfair to Scruton or any who think like him. It certainly is possible to attempt a rigorous defense of the existence of a moral order in a godless world. I am not saying that Scruton categorically cannot establish the reality of something like a moral order in tandem with his "as if." But if he did establish it, we would nevertheless have to go over the question of how art generates moral *power*, even if moral *imperatives* come primarily or additionally from elsewhere. Again, perhaps Scruton can plausibly make intellectual room for the dimension disclosed in a tragi-Dionysian view of life. But if, in Christian perspective, creation and eschatological anticipation frame something akin to a tragic sense of life, what happens if you try to accommodate tragedy when the framework has disappeared? One answer emerges in Scruton's project: one can operate within a broad secularized version of the fall-redemption framework, where redemption is purely this-worldly, and where art takes on a redemptive function, just as long as art releases moral energy. Such a reductive move clearly signals that this is not the Christian route to addressing the question of culture as it surfaced in Wagner and Nietzsche.

Whether Christianity requires or endorses a connection between art and morality and whether that connection figures in a response to Nietzsche—such questions are too big for now. When Jesus joined the commandments to love God with heart, soul, strength, and mind and to love our neighbor as ourselves, he defined the life of the disciple without remainder. Nothing that cannot be subsumed under the one or the other has any place at all. Anything that can be subsumed under the one or the other conduces to both. The question of the Christian stake in culture must be addressed in light of these liberating imperatives, and art is not cut off from them. If we go beyond that point, we are into the business of suggesting theological and philosophical principles of aesthetics as well as probing the relation of the aesthetic to the moral spheres. We should find the question of creation kicking in here again. Any talk of the way art and morality are related must take into account the significance of the doctrine of creation for our philosophy of art. We might, for example, regard the aesthetic as a separate sphere from the moral, though always ministering to God and neighbor, a sphere in creation established in its own right, enjoining aesthetic delight upon us for the sake of aesthetic delight.[68] By thus hooking up art with creation, we might detach it from a

68. This is roughly in line, for example, with the thinking that takes its inspiration from the tradition shaped by Abraham Kuyper and Herman Dooyweerd. For Abraham Kuyper himself, see his *Lectures on Calvinism* (Grand Rapids: Eerdmans, 1931), esp. chap. 5; and

root connection with the sphere of moral good and evil, as it takes shape in our world in the train of the fall. This does not consign art to vacant space; it belongs, with God's creation, to what is good. Nor is it to pretend that art is not somehow implicated in the fallen order.[69] But however we think it through, Nietzsche's combination of aesthetic exuberance and tragic sensibility should evoke the sympathy of a Christian who both loves art and weeps for people. A renewed affirmation of a creational framework for thinking about art—incredible as this would have been for Nietzsche—provides a contribution to the profound enhancement of culture alternative to that proposed by Scruton.

Even if we leave it more or less at that, it is important to canvass such questions if we want to get to the guts of the conflict between Nietzsche and Christianity. Nevertheless, let us not miss the following dimension:

> The idea specifically derived from *The Birth of Tragedy* which has become perhaps most influential in the twentieth century is the conception of the "Dionysiac" and its role in human life, i.e., the view that destructive, primitively anarchic forces are a part of us (not to be projected into some diabolical Other), and that the pleasure we take in them is real and not to be denied. . . . In some sense higher culture rests on coming to terms with them.[70]

If that is what is really at stake here, should we quit what looks like an attempt to domesticate Dionysus and drag his heavily anesthetized and sanitized corpus into the kingdom of Christ? Well, no doubt there is enough about Dionysus to keep us worried. He will not discourage his followers from the lure of aesthetic immersion, bohemian individuality, and sexual indulgence. Jointly pursued, their ability to shape a lifestyle has been eminently attractive to many in the West for a long time. This is the surface style of things in much "higher culture," and Christians are bound to contend intelligently and spiritually with it. And we must connect what Raymond Geuss says about Dionysus, higher culture, and the twentieth century to this surface style of things. It is important to discern the nature of the Christian moral imperative in the sphere of artistic activity.

Nevertheless, if we quickly haul in talk of moral imperative and moral law when we are faced with the "Dionysian" challenge, this can look like

---

Peter S. Heslam, *Creating a Christian Worldview: Abraham Kuyper's Lectures on Calvinism* (Grand Rapids: Eerdmans; Carlisle: Paternoster, 1998), esp. chap. 8.

69. For a balanced perspective on art in relation to a created and a fallen world, see Hilary Brand and Adrienne Chaplin, *Art and Soul: Signposts for Christians in the Arts* (Carlisle, UK: Solway, 1999).

70. Raymond Geuss, in his introduction to *BT*, xxx.

an intrusive attempt to avoid dealing with "primitively anarchic forces." Are we simply avoiding the question of what we should be doing about the amoral forces that seethe and surge at the roots of our fleshly being? The terms of Geuss's proposition actually beg the moral question. He appears to assume that if anarchic forces are not to be "projected into some diabolical Other" but are instead "a part of us," then they cannot be denied. Precisely here we want debate. What constitutes the "us" of which these forces are a part is not just "created" energy; it is also "fallen" energy. This can be put more felicitously, for these are not two basic energies; the "fallen" is the "created" misdirected. Whatever is "primitive" in us, as Nietzsche or Geuss understands it, is compounded of the good and the fallen, as Christians understand it. In consequence of human sin, moral good and evil appear on earth.[71] Higher culture must come to terms with the derivatively moral as well as the primitively anarchic in our humanity. Nietzsche, as we shall see, came to appreciate that the Dionysiac program can be established only if morality is disestablished. This became the heart of the crusade against Christianity. Dionysus becomes the destroyer of Christian morality, and Christian morality becomes an impediment to culture.

To conclude: if we have doubts about Scruton's areligious moral commendation of high culture, can the Wagnerian and Nietzschean pulse of aesthetic excitement still throb in Christian veins? In 1882, Peter Taylor Forsyth made his first pilgrimage to the "temple-theater" in Bayreuth.[72] Years later, he testified as follows: "Nothing like *Parsifal*, upon the whole, has been seen, either in art or religion, since the Greek tragedians awed and melted Athens by lyric dramas which were at the same time religious functions."[73] Forsyth significantly specifies: "Nothing is more remarkable in *Parsifal* than the return to European culture of the sense of sin, the need for forgiveness, and the faith in its possibility."[74] This is what bothered Nietzsche about it. Coming from Forsyth, it is a significant statement because if any theologian was alive to the surpassing glory of the cross of Christ in its bearing on sin and forgiveness, he was. The last thing he would play down was the centrality of the atonement. Yet he could become immersed in Wagner's world. After Forsyth is through with describing *Parsifal*, we feel that we have sat alongside him. In the volume where he reports his reaction, he has been dealing with pre-

71. If any, for example in the tradition of Wittgenstein, are worried about collapsing the "moral" and "religious" at this juncture, the point can be appropriately reformulated.

72. William L. Bradley, *P. T. Forsyth: The Man and His Work* (London: Independent, 1952), 40; P. T. Forsyth, *Religion in Recent Art* (London: Hodder & Stoughton, 1901), 253.

73. Forsyth, *Religion in Recent Art*, 252. *Parsifal* was Wagner's last opera.

74. Ibid., 258–59.

Raphaelite artists in loving detail, tossing out the occasional apostrophe with reference to Robert Browning. His whole exposition is undergirded by theses about Greece and Christianity. And in a subsequent volume we get more of it, with some strong things said in favor of Greece.[75]

I am neither subscribing to nor dissenting from any of Forsyth's pertinent claims.[76] What matters here is not his aesthetics, replete with avowed Hegelian sympathies, but the example that a determined theologian of the cross gives of delight in and attention to art. Forsyth has a particular interpretation of art, but it would surely be impossible to write of it as he does without an aesthetic enthusiasm independent of the preferred interpretation. For those who do not agree with him, Forsyth can yet teach by enthusiastic example, if not by a theory of art, what it is to appreciate "high culture." There is no conflict between aesthetic enthusiasm and crucicentric theology. Nietzsche was hard pressed to see how they could be combined, for reasons that will be indicated when we document his break with Wagner. Anyone who doubts that the Christian has good reason to share aesthetic enthusiasm with Nietzsche, to the point of catching something of the infection of the Wagnerian project, has to demonstrate where and why Forsyth went wrong. I take Wagner here less according to his specific project than as a supreme example of heightened aesthetic excitement.

How, then, should we conclude on art and cultural renewal? Obviously, much depends on what ought to count as salutary renewal. Assume that we want to see the beautiful, the good, and the true flourishing under the kingship of Christ. Such is the power of good art that we might find it hard to believe that it plays anything but an important role in renewal. We might even understand, while resisting, the early Nietzschean temptation to enthrone it. But Scruton is surely right here: whatever theological reason is offered for a high view of the contribution of art, aesthetic sensibility, born of aesthetic experience, is a necessary, if not sufficient, condition for feeling the force of this outlook. If we do not enthrone art to the extent that Nietzsche and Wagner were doing at the time, it is because we regard it ultimately as the gift of an Other

75. P. T. Forsyth, *Christ on Parnassus: Lectures on Art, Ethic, and Theology* (London: Hodder & Stoughton, 1911).

76. Begbie reports the judgment that Forsyth's *Christ on Parnassus*, in particular, is an "aberrant work"; see Jeremy Begbie, "The Ambivalent Rainbow: Forsyth, Art and Creation," in *Justice the True and Only Mercy: Essays in the Legacy and Theology of Peter Taylor Forsyth*, ed. Trevor Hart (Edinburgh: T&T Clark, 1995), 206n32. My own difficulty with Forsyth is with his tendency to pitch Christianity somewhere between the Greeks and the Hebrews. He contrasts Greek religion, as the "apotheosis of natural joy," with that of the Hebrews: "The people of sorrow, like the Man of Sorrows, had no energy to spare for Art" (Forsyth, *Christ on Parnassus*, 67). In my judgment, this is worked out suggestively but not persuasively.

who is truly enthroned and who commands delight not only in himself but also in the work of his hands, the materials out of which artistic constructs are fabricated. His command may take the form of a verbal fiat, but the verbal fiat directs us to attend to the beauty of Creator and creation and sets us free for art, however we describe its relation to the beauty that we see. Thus do we come to live not by fiat but by wonder, under grace and not under law.

Nietzsche must not too swiftly slide out of theological favor on account of his temporary immersion in the Wagnerian project, for all the disputability of his presuppositions. Wagner, however, massively slid out of favor with Nietzsche. And with that process, the attack on Christianity began in earnest.[77]

77. Having referred briefly to him earlier, I should also allude to Jeremy Begbie's contribution to the questions of theology and music. I am generally persuaded by Adrienne Chaplin's criticisms of Begbie's specific volume *Theology, Music and Time* (Cambridge: Cambridge University Press, 2000), in the *Christian Scholar's Review* 33, no. 1 (Fall 2003): 135–41, but there is a helpful earlier and more general study—Jeremy Begbie, *Voicing Creation's Praise: Towards a Theology of the Arts* (New York and London: Continuum, 1991)—that also suggestively features Poussin's *The Golden Calf* on the cover of the paperback version.

3

BREAK, BREAK, BREAK

The mind, the spirit, the Promethean spark,
The lightning of my being, is as bright,
Pervading, and far-darting as your own. . . .

Byron, *Manfred*, act 1, scene 1

Wagner's Demise

Those who recognize the strains of Alfred Lord Tennyson in the title of this chapter may worry lest I am poised to savage the meaning of his poetry and catapult him into most unlikely company, causing him to turn several times in his grave.[1] Perhaps Nietzsche, however, would have been willing to commandeer two lines from this famous and beautiful piece. The first he would have publicly owned: "I would that my tongue could utter the thoughts that arise in me." However boldly Nietzsche uttered some of the thoughts in writing, he kept much to himself. The second he would have privately concealed: "But the tender grace of a day that is dead, will never come back to me." The thoughts that he uttered

---

1. Those who do not recognize them might care to consult the poem in Alfred Lord Tennyson, *The Poems of Tennyson*, ed. C. Hicks, vol. 2 (Harlow, UK: Longman, 1987). W. H. Auden thought that Nietzsche's description of Wagner applied, in lesser degree, to Tennyson as well; see Wystan H. Auden, "Tennyson," in *Forewords and Afterwords* (New York: Vintage, 1974), 226.

when he launched his public attack on Christianity were suffused with little tender grace, and the earliest days of childhood were truly dead and buried, as far as his public authorship was concerned.

During the decade of the 1870s, there was, indeed, a triple break. By the time he quit his position in Basel at the end of that time, Nietzsche had broken with Schopenhauer, broken with Wagner, and broken publicly with Christianity. These were physically and emotionally difficult and taxing years, as the years had been before and as they would, in increasing measure, be later. Nietzsche would not have allowed us to read the story of his constantly recurring ailments with pity—for which he had nothing but contempt—but it makes painful reading. He had to take sick leave from teaching and was finally pensioned off from his university position in 1879, during which year he counted 118 days of serious attacks plus milder ones. Thereafter, he led a roving existence, particularly favoring Switzerland and Italy, moving from boardinghouse to boardinghouse, occasional residence to occasional residence, in a pattern that basically remained until his final illness. He occasionally dipped into his family home but had no permanent base there, and his civic circumstances had rendered him technically stateless.

As a sick man battling through pain and suffering, Nietzsche often wondered when or whether death was at his door, welcoming the prospect of its arrival during many a long night and day. Migraine, eye problems, and a variety of stomach ailments accompanied him day and night. He wrote to Malwida von Meysenburg: "My life's terrible and almost unremitting martyrdom makes me thirst for the end."[2] There are other examples of communications along these lines.[3] "*Who*," he asked his friend Erwin Rohde, "has endured as much as I have?"[4] Concern for bodily welfare included worry about climatic conditions. The temperature both inside and outside Nietzsche's room was a matter for vigilant attention. And suffering was also of the soul, not just of the body. His was a nomad life from 1879, when he appears first to have called himself an atheist.[5]

Whereas the break with Schopenhauer can be described in terms of ideas, the break with Wagner was personal as well. Very much so. Wagner

2. *SL*, January 14, 1880. The letter should be read further; it includes a remark about the purification of the soul: "I no longer need religion and art as a means to that end." It ends with his self-description as "a young old man, who has no grievance against life, though he must still want it to end."

3. E.g., to Overbeck, *SL*, September 18, 1881.

4. *SL*, July 15, 1882.

5. Thomas Brobjer, "Nietzsche's Atheism," in *Nietzsche and the Divine*, ed. John Lippitt and Jim Urpeth (Manchester, UK: Clinamen, 2000), 8.

was nothing if not domineering. He was not of a markedly self-effacing and accommodating disposition in relation to friend or foe. Nietzsche, living in his shadow, could not endure his older friend forever. Independence must be gained. Wagner did little for Nietzsche's self-esteem. "My idea of myself is weak and pitiable," Nietzsche at the age of thirty wrote to Rohde, "and you have incessantly to guarantee me to myself."[6] At some stage after his break from Wagner, Nietzsche came to know of correspondence between Wagner and a medical practitioner who had treated Nietzsche. Quite apart from the breach of confidentiality involved, what Wagner said about Nietzsche's sexuality was extremely painful and sealed his emotional attitude toward Wagner, if it needed sealing after their personal friendship had ended.[7]

Some sort of turning point, even if it was in the form of a large last and public straw, came at the rehearsals for the Bayreuth Festival preparatory to the official opening of the Wagnerian opera house in the summer of 1876. There are indications that Nietzsche's symptoms were psychosomatically aggravated as the moment of his arrival at Bayreuth drew closer. He turned up there at the end of July. Nietzsche had expended a significant amount of physical, mental, emotional, and spiritual energy for some years in the service of the Bayreuth ideal, the harbinger of cultural renewal. We have observed that he had contemplated giving his entire time to advancing the Wagner cause, for this was to advance the cause of a true and worthy culture in Germany and for Europe, if not beyond. Nothing but Wagner's enterprise could do the trick. Only against the background of Nietzsche's intense and ambitious hope to witness its grand flourishing can we can grasp the dimensions of his opposition to Christianity; likewise, only against the same background can we appreciate the significance of his personal disillusionment with Wagner.

"Around 1876 I was terrified to see all I had desired hitherto *compromised*, as I grasped which way Wagner was going now" (*WP* 1005). Which way was that? It was one thing for Wagner to think himself the only major show in town, with the world as his parish. It was something more that this entailed Wagner's despising other artists of quality, such as Brahms. You might live with that kind of egotism, at least for a while, but it was a different matter when the launch of Bayreuth itself proved disastrous. For it brought into focus the difficulties with the

6. Ronald Hayman, *Nietzsche: A Critical Life* (London: Phoenix, 1995), 176.
7. Bryan Magee in *Wagner and Philosophy* (London: Penguin, 2000), 335–38, for example, indicates how painful things were. The trouble with Wagner started rather earlier than short accounts can sometimes convey; see Richard Gray, "Translator's Afterword," in *Unpublished Writings from the Period of Unfashionable Observations*, by Friedrich W. Nietzsche (Stanford, CA: Stanford University Press, 1999).

Wagnerian project both in practice and in principle. What was immediately disastrous was that those who turned up at Bayreuth, far from
constituting the culturally elite vanguard of a renewed Germany, were a
rather uncouth-looking rabble. "As it turned out," says Rüdiger Safranski,
"outrageous prices were being charged for food, lodgings, and carriage
rides between the city and the festival hill. Monarchs, princes, bankers,
diplomats, and women of ill repute were the center of attention. These
people typically languished during the performances, but perked up at
social events."[8] Nietzsche recorded his dismayed reaction to all this.
He lasted until the end of August and then hightailed out of town. At
the beginning of October 1876, he took a year's leave from university
teaching on medical grounds.

The personal break with Wagner was not yet complete. Wagner himself
was none too pleased with all that went on. They met again in Sorrento
later that year, and things seem to have been at least cordial. Nietzsche
had written to him in September about his leave of absence, pointing out
that he had "put up with torment after torment, as if I were born for that
and for nothing else."[9] But things between the two were not as they had
been. Intellectually, Nietzsche was on the move away from Wagner and
the Bayreuth ideal. When Wagner received his copy of the first volume
of *Human, All Too Human*, published in 1878, he was, to say the least,
displeased. After Sorrento, the two never met again. Wagner died in
February 1883. Nietzsche produced two short works on Wagner in 1888
and at the time published one of them, *The Case of Wagner*. The second,
not published until after his mental collapse in the following year, was
Nietzsche contra Wagner, in which he excerpted, with some editing, the
various critical things that he had said about Wagner over the previous
years. These were not the first comments devoted to Wagner that he
had put into print. An earlier effort said different things, but we first
need to take one step behind it and glance at an essay on Schopenhauer
published still earlier.

In 1874, Nietzsche had paid tribute to "Schopenhauer as Educator"
in the essay from which I quoted in the first chapter, where Nietzsche
describes his early reaction to Schopenhauer.[10] A true educator draws
forth what is in the student. "No one can build for you the bridge upon
which you alone must cross the stream of life, no one but you alone"
(*UO* 173). Nevertheless, you can be instructed to build. "Your true being
does not lie deeply hidden within you, but rather immeasurably high

8. Rüdiger Safranski, *Nietzsche: A Philosophical Biography* (New York and London:
Norton, 2002), 138.

9. *SL*, September 27, 1876.

10. In *UO*. In the text above, the reference numbers to both this and the essay on
Wagner are to pages rather than sections.

above you, or at least above what you commonly take to be your ego."[11] Nevertheless, your educator can chivvy you along. He can teach you how to unify and correlate the vital forces within. Morally speaking, this is an exemplary and exemplifying task. Schopenhauer executed it well and in style. Honest, cheerful, steadfast, Schopenhauer is or should be an example to us all. "I attach importance to a philosopher," Nietzsche tells us, "only to the extent that he is capable of setting an example" (183). Schopenhauer faced, fought, and vanquished the dangers of isolation, despair of the truth, and awareness of limitation. He valued existence anew, did it for himself, and was willing to suffer in so doing. Schopenhauer navigated both dangers common to all ages and those peculiar to his own. In so doing he enabled us to "educate ourselves *against* our age," an age of shallowest philosophy (196). Schopenhauer did not succumb to the malaise of our culture. Instead, he set before us a distinctive image of humanity: *"The Schopenhauerian human being voluntarily takes upon himself the suffering inherent in truthfulness"* (203). This is a truly educative ideal, and Nietzsche proceeds to analyze what is involved all the way through to remonstrations against both pecuniary greed and the political greed that enervates culture. Unfortunately, today it is a case of "Education: essentially the means of ruining the exceptions for the good of the rule. Higher education: essentially the means of directing taste against the exceptions for the good of the mediocre," to quote from a later note that makes the earlier point (*WP* 933).

That Nietzsche occupies himself with Schopenhauer as a philosophical educator, and not with Schopenhauer's philosophy, is a sign that he is on the move, a sign that we also find in unpublished notes that he was writing at and before that time. Some months before his mental collapse, he could write that this essay "contains the basic scheme according to which I have so far lived; it is a rigorous promise."[12] But how does Wagner fare at this stage? Is he the choice product of Schopenhauerian education, perhaps rising above the master in unrivaled accomplishment? Nietzsche published an essay on Wagner that appeared along with the one on Schopenhauer just before the rehearsals for the ill-fated Bayreuth festival.[13] Wagner seemed to love what he read there. And certainly we

---

11. *UO* 174; but Hollingdale's translation gives a slightly different meaning: "above that which you usually take yourself to be"; see Friedrich W. Nietzsche, *Untimely Meditations* (Cambridge: Cambridge University Press, 1983), 129. Gray's translation seems to bring out better the German "dein Ich"—"your 'I.'"

12. To Brandes, *SL*, April 10, 1888.

13. These make up two of the four essays in *UO*. The others are on Strauss and on "The Utility and Liability of History." This last-named essay was an influential piece that I must unfortunately ignore here. See Gianni Vattimo, *Nietzsche: An Introduction* (London: Athlone, 2002), 33, and the use made of it by Laurence Lampert, *Nietzsche and Modern Times: A Study of Bacon, Descartes, and Nietzsche* (New Haven and London: Yale Univer-

read nice things in it. We read that Wagner is a fecund personality and cultural force. We are informed that it is well worth pondering the musical, artistic, and philosophical streams that encircle his contribution. "The only ray of hope in the modern age" is provided by "the redemption of art," and Wagner finely hones his product (289). It is an interesting fact that Wagner became possessed of the notion "that theater had the potential to exert an incomparable influence, an influence greater than that exerted by any other art form" (297). As Beethoven discovered the musical language of pathos, so Wagner developed it. "All previous music, when measured against Wagner's seems stiff and timid, as if one should not look at it from all sides and as if it were ashamed. Wagner seizes every degree and every coloration of feeling with the greatest firmness and determination" (316). Nietzsche's philosophically significant partiality for Heraclitus lends gravitas to the tribute that "Wagner's music, taken as a whole is a likeness of the world in the sense in which it was conceived by the great Ephesian philosopher, as a harmony that discord produces out of itself, as the union of justice and strife" (316). In all of this, Wagner speaks as a man of the future.

Plenty of good things are indeed here, but I shall risk a moment of clumsy hindsight and base crudity in suggesting that the academic or professional reader might be forgiven a moment's sense that there is something vaguely familiar about this essay. And if the moment be forgiven, so might the thought that follows it, that the essay reads like a reference written for someone about whom one has reservations. What is said is true as far as it goes, and the writer takes some care to make the statements (occasionally) rather literally true. Still, what is unsaid is the more interesting portion of what is thought. If this description seems banal, the historical fact remains that Nietzsche's notes for earlier drafts of this essay indicate that, for quite some time before its publication, he was more critical of Wagner than he was letting on in the published product. "By the summer of 1876, during the time of the first *Festspiele*, I said farewell to Wagner in my heart," said Nietzsche just before offering an authentic description of his post-Wagnerian weariness.[14] To tune into the weariness is to tune into Nietzsche's anti-Christianity.

If the publication of the first volume of *HH* clarified some of the main intellectual grounds of separation from Schopenhauer and Wagner, by the time we come to the later writings on Wagner, the whole scene of those early days with Wagner has completely passed out of view. In *CW* Nietzsche declared that theatricality was not for him: "I am essentially

---

sity Press, 1993), part 3; also see Peter Berkowitz, *Nietzsche: The Ethics of an Immoralist* (Cambridge: Harvard University Press, 1995), chap. 1.

14. "How I Broke Away from Wagner," in *NCW*.

anti-theatrical," as he also put it in *NCW* ("Why I Offer Objections"). On the other hand, it defined Wagner. Wagner was "a first-rate actor" who actually "belongs elsewhere, not in the history of music. . . . What he wants is effect, nothing but effect" (*CW* 8). What is this but decadence, an attempt to create effect with the "sheer persuasion of the nerves"? (*CW* 7).[15] Its native element is life-denial. The Wagnerian product "hates everything that justifies itself solely out of abundance, out of the overflowing riches of strength" ("Epilogue"). There is an essential theoretical background to all this in Wagner's and Nietzsche's views on opera and drama, but the upshot is that Wagner's musical enterprise is a gloriously miserable flight from life. Wagner made music sick. It is sheer Schopenhauer. So who, now, is Schopenhauer for Nietzsche? The "old pessimistic counterfeiter." Once regarded by Nietzsche as the most honest of mortals, he is now "not a whit more 'honest'" than Hegel or Schelling, both of whom Schopenhauer, like Nietzsche, despised (10).

Nietzsche's *CW* is sometimes regarded as unbalanced and not up to his finest work. Nevertheless, in terms of its content, it is not unrepresentative of the intellectual critique developed over the years. In *NCW*, Nietzsche admitted that he had had to straighten himself out on the subject of Wagner.

> I interpreted Wagner's music as an expression of a Dionysian power of the soul; I believed I heard in it the earthquake with which a primordial force of life, dammed up from time immemorial, finally vents itself, indifferent to the possibility that everything that calls itself culture today might start tottering. It is plain what I misunderstood in, equally plain what I read into, Wagner and Schopenhauer—myself. ("We Antipodes")

Wagner now joined Schopenhauer as antipodal to Nietzsche because both "negate life, they slander it." Recognizing what he once promisingly detected in the lonely potential of art to redeem us, it is of great moment that Nietzsche added: "Regarding artists of all kinds, I now avail myself of this main distinction: is it the *hatred* against life or the excess of life which has here become creative?"

15. The Welsh writer Goronwy Rees heard Hitler speak and said of his oratory: "It is of the kind that speaks neither to the mind nor the heart of his audience, but plays upon its nerves until they are strung to such a pitch of intensity that they shriek for release in action." His religious upbringing helped him to understand: "It was the kind of oratory that in my childhood, was capable to transforming an incurable alcoholic into a life-long teetotaller in the twinkling of an eyelid. . . . Who knows, if I had not been inoculated in childhood against the tricks of oratory, I might have succumbed myself." I am grateful to the author for directing me to this quotation in his work in John Harris, *Goronwy Rees* (Cardiff, UK: University of Wales, 2001), 88. It is of particular interest in light of Nietzsche's identification of the religious sensibility that infused Wagner's music.

A complete account of Nietzsche's position as set out in this short essay would need to do justice to the strict demands that conclude *CW*, with reference to music and theater. For present purposes, what matters is not the nature of these demands but the fact that they are embedded in this wider claim about life-denial. This is precisely what the controversy with Christianity is about by now. When Nietzsche met Wagner, Wagner had behind him such works as *The Flying Dutchman, Tannhäuser, Lohengrin,* and *Tristan and Isolde* and before him the completion of the *Ring* cycle. There was still one piece to go after that: *Parsifal*. It was eventually completed in 1882 and performed in the same year. Nietzsche found its music haunting, but in terms of what art is about, it sealed Wagner's fate, from Nietzsche's viewpoint. He saw and heard it as a drama of Christian redemption, as others have since. Whether or not it should be so heard, nothing could be more sickening for Nietzsche than this. "Richard Wagner, apparently most triumphant, but in truth a decaying and despairing decadent, suddenly sank down, helpless and broken, before the Christian cross. Did no German have eyes in his head or pity in his conscience for this horrid spectacle?"[16] In his "Epilogue" after the "Second Postscript" to *CW*, Nietzsche sums things up. Wagner's adoption of a theology or psychology of redemption is a plunge into "declining life"; meanwhile, "ascending life," the real and noble thing, leaves the dregs of existence, captured in the phenomenon of Christianity, down in the pit. As in *EH* Nietzsche interpreted *BT* in the light of what he later thought about morality, decadence, and Christianity, so here in this "Epilogue" Nietzsche pulls into the Wagner-Christian equation his objections to Christian morality and his proposed alternative to it. It is easily done because the criticisms of Wagner and Christianity are deeply integrated. What he was saying about Wagner at the end of his authorship captures the heart of Nietzsche's critique of Christianity from its published beginning.

The denouement of Wagner is that he has dirtied his hands by association with a Christian view of life, one that regards life with hostility and proposes a way of redemption from it. "The case of Wagner" is in substantial measure also "the case of Christianity." For or against life? That is the question. Christianity, being against life, deserves the death sentence. Nietzsche's job is to execute it. As his own life ebbed away, Nietzsche brought down the lash in the repeated strokes that bring *The Anti-christ* to an end.

Parasitism as the *sole* practice of the Church; with its ideal of green-sickness, of "holiness" draining away all blood, all love, all hope for life; the Beyond as

16. "How I Broke Away from Wagner," in *NCW*.

the will to deny reality of every kind; the Cross as the badge of recognition for the most subterranean conspiracy that there has ever been—a conspiracy against health, beauty, well-constitutedness, bravery, intellect, *benevolence of soul, against life itself*. . . . Wherever there are walls I shall inscribe this eternal accusation against Christianity upon them—I can write in letters which make even the blind see. . . . I call Christianity the *one* great curse, the *one* great intrinsic depravity, the *one* great instinct for revenge for which no expedient is sufficiently poisonous, secret, subterranean, *petty*—I call it the *one* immortal blemish of mankind. . . . And one calculates *time* from the *dies nefastus* [ill-fated day] on which this fatality arose—from the *first* day of Christianity! *Why not rather from its last?—From today?* (A 62)

This encapsulates Nietzsche's case against Christianity, and I have jumped to the end of his authorship because it is so thoroughly true to what he began to say immediately after his break with Wagner. From now on, our job is to tease out this indictment. So first to *Human, All Too Human*.

Error

Nietzsche regarded Christianity as an intellectual error. In this respect, he was heir to the broadly rationalist tradition of the Enlightenment critique of Christianity and earlier nineteenth-century ideas of religion as projection. Religion originates in ignorant fear, attributing to the divine what we scientifically know to be natural causality. The fact that this line of criticism informs Nietzsche's attitude emerges clearly in *HH*. Nietzsche's similarities to Voltaire may not appear profound to those who know their respective philosophies, yet Nietzsche's desire to bring out *HH* on the one-hundredth anniversary of Voltaire's death was fitting in the limited but important respect of broad rationalist affinity.[17] What is distinctive in Nietzsche's thought is his view of what lies behind that error, what constitutes its deeper nature, and what kind of damage issues from it. Nietzsche was acutely concerned about the times in which he lived: the modernity that marked his epoch, the world-historical significance of the historical errors of Christianity, and the contemporary shortcomings of the current posttheistic era.

Nietzsche's direct critique of Christianity might be approached in a number of ways. It would be possible, for example, to distinguish three judgments on Christianity: it is intellectually impossible, it demeans

---

17. *HH* was followed by *AOM* and *WS*. They were subsequently united to make up the composite volume that goes under the overall published title of *HH*. I use the separate titles when citing Nietzsche.

humanity, and its morality is fatal to life. Nietzsche's announcement of the death of God contextualizes such a critique. I make some use of this thematic distinction in what follows. But these items are not neatly separable, and there is a danger of imposing artificial and misleading constraints on our reading of Nietzsche. Further, while the following biographical matter is quite thin, I still want to track the broad contours of Nietzsche's life. So I shall follow a modified form of a thematic treatment roughly but not fixedly integrated into an account of the historical movement of Nietzsche's thought. The idea is to bring his thinking about Christianity into optimal relief by following a loose but not rigid chronological account of his thinking, picking up its thematic threads as seems most natural in that framework. In all this, I am concerned to bring out Nietzsche's positive alternative to Christianity.

Nietzsche's explicit public, literary, direct, and focused campaign against Christian faith opens with his discussion of "The Religious Life" in *HH*. This discussion is preceded by two chapters that lay bare the intellectual roots of his anti-Christianity. Broadly speaking, he plumps for a naturalist over against an idealist philosophy. Something like a positivistic philosophy has now displaced Schopenhauer and Wagner. Metaphysics is a seduction, devising unreal worlds. Perhaps transitional modes of thought are needed in the nineteenth century, so where a change from a religious to a scientific outlook is mediated by philosophy, that is well and good, just so long as the philosophy tends to weaken and then to extirpate the religious instinct. Still, that last job is better done by art. As it is, nineteenth-century German philosophy unfortunately did not follow an edifying course and allowed Christianity too much oxygen. This is gravely disturbing because it is obviously the case that Christianity is an intellectual nonstarter, and anything that might favor its chances of being recalled to the starting line is rather woeful. "What thinker still has need of the hypothesis of God?" (*HH* 28).

Nietzsche rather assumes than argues the intellectual case against Christianity. He is more interested in examining the damage done by its content than in revisiting an intellectually familiar closed case against God. Schopenhauer, for example, rightly rejected the errors of reason that nest at the heart of Christianity, including the cardinal nonsense of a soteriological scheme of depravity and salvation. Unfortunately, however, his "metaphysics demonstrates that even now the scientific spirit is not yet sufficiently strong" for religiously rooted ideas to be expelled. Expelled they must be. To do this properly, we need to get behind idealistic metaphysics to the scientifically minded Enlightenment. But we need still more, which cannot be accomplished in a simple move. If we want to overcome the metaphysical remnant and residually religious view of life, we need to engage in both a historical and a psychological exercise to ferret out the putative justification people have offered for that metaphysics. Quite adamantly, that is the way forward, and Nietzsche, both here and in subsequent works, will study the Christian religion from historical and psychological angles.

At the start of *HH* Nietzsche announces what makes our intellectual operations tricky. We need to untie a knot.[18] "Error," Wagner had pronounced, "is the mother of knowledge; and the history of the birth of knowledge out of Error is the history of the human race. . . ."[19] Nietzsche asks: "How can something originate in its opposite, for example rationality in irrationality, the sentient in the dead, logic in unlogic, disinterested contemplation in covetous desire, living for others in egoism, truth in error?" (*HH* 1). That he sets great stock in this question is indicated by the way he opens both *D* and *GS*. The worlds of logic and of language, of mathematics and of morality, of religion and of art—all these have characteristically been built on the foundation of an idealizing mistake. A world has been constructed to give a causal explanation of an effect, the effect being the empirical world that we inhabit. But the world is not in fact caused by a transcendent reality. Although we should know that by now, untying the metaphysical knot that is at the heart of our intellectual culture will be a delicate operation for at least three reasons.[20] First, it is undeniably the case that, out of error, some noble movements of the human spirit and monuments to it have arisen. Second, you've got to give some shape to a society that finally learns to think aright about these things. What shape will it be? What will motivate society to build enduring edifices? What will bring them forth? And, third, these are tricky days for the labor of construction.

> The *contrast* between our agitated ephemeral existence and the slow-breathing response of metaphysical ages is still too strong, because the two ages are still too close together; the individual human being himself now runs through far too many inner and outer evolutions for him to venture to establish himself securely and once and for all even for so short a span as his own life-time.

In his essay on "Schopenhauer as Educator," Nietzsche declares: "Today . . . we still find ourselves in the ice-filled stream of the Mid-

18. Where I do not provide references for citations, it is because I am just following the sequence in the limited portion of text under discussion.

19. Richard Wagner, "The Art-Work of the Future," in *Prose Works*, vol. 1 (London: Kegan Paul, 1892), 70. It is instructive to read on beyond this point in Wagner in light of what Nietzsche now says in *HH*.

20. For a quick run-through of some of the intellectual problems, see "The Four Great Errors," *TI* 6.

dle Ages: it has begun to thaw and is rushing on with devastating power. Ice floe is piled upon ice floe, all shores are being flooded and threatened" (*UO* 200).[21] This is one of a number of earlier observations that find their dramatic conclusion, summation, and summary in the announcement of the death of God. In *HH* Nietzsche writes: "Our age gives the impression of being an interim state; the old ways of thinking, the old cultures are still partly with us. . . . It looks as though everything is becoming chaotic" (248). The title of this section is *"Words of consolation of a progress grown desperate."* In fact, "there will never again be a life and culture bounded by a religiously determined horizon" (*HH* 234).

Morality, aesthetics (or art), and religion are regularly connected in Nietzsche's opening observations in *HH*, and his subsequent chapters focus on particular areas. In sequence he deals with morality, art, and then religion, first specifically dwelling "On the History of the Moral Sensations." I shall concentrate on morality later; yet so pervasive and central is this theme in Nietzsche's literature, and so fundamental is his moral thought to the critique of Christianity, that we can never stray far from it. In *HH*, observations on morality not only immediately precede what he says about the religious life; they also strictly contextualize it. Nietzsche's critique of Christianity is not optimally approached simply by majoring on an exegesis of the passages in his work that specifically deal with it. It is not surprising that treatments of Nietzsche on Christianity seldom if ever rake over the whole range of particular statements that he makes on it. He hurls marked boulders, but there are smoother and sharper stones everywhere in his work. The quarry from which these missives are hewn is identified to a considerable extent from the very beginning of his remarks on morality in particular.

Nietzsche begins his account of moral sensations by lamenting the fact that no one reads "the great masters of the psychological maxim any more." La Rochefoucauld is his example here, but he provides a list of others in *WS* 214.[22] Appreciating this French *moraliste* tradition is important for a proper appreciation of Nietzsche himself. His entry into its inheritance has more than one explanation. Like these "moralists," Nietzsche wrote aphoristically. This suited the rhythm of his painful days

---

21. In this connection he is picking out the "age of the atom, the age of atomic chaos," but he integrates his thoughts on it into a wider view of modern life.

22. "When reading Montaigne, La Rochefoucauld, La Bruyère, Fontenelle, . . . Vauvenargues and Chamfort we are closer to antiquity than in the case of any other group of six authors of any other nation." Nietzsche is not uncritical of La Rochefoucauld (*WP* 362, 389, 772).

and weeks, when sustained thought could be difficult.[23] During the First World War, Figgis's comment on Nietzsche's writing nicely transports us back to Nietzsche's own day:

> Probably not a little of his attraction for many is owing to this [variety of landscapes finely described in his literature]. This is the day of flash-light and electric movement. Nietzsche is like a motor, whirling the occupant through many countries, giving at once the sense of rapid movement and of changeful beauty. His very inconsistencies and the aphoristic habit are a help in this respect.[24]

Nietzsche's writing conveys a sense of moral jauntiness, inculcating an unsettled frame of mind toward ponderous moral systems and moral law.[25] But there is more to aphorism than this. Nietzsche will not have us look to the *moraliste* tradition just to provide supplementary moral wisdom to the standard works of moral philosophers. It does better than supplement; his favored authors give you an alternative approach to morality. Psychological observation, conveyed in the form of maxims, can "hit the bullseye . . . of human nature" (*HH* 36). Nietzsche lauds those who are observant of the empirical, the human, the all too human, unconstrained by elaborate and artificial moral theory. This is a properly scientific approach to moral commentary. At the beginning of *HH* Nietzsche lauded the *"estimation of unpretentious truths"* (3). These are the little, the close at hand, the proper quarry in a moral investigation that we should undertake unencumbered by the errors of at least two European millennia. Psychological observation gives rise to what Foucault, albeit in a different context, called the *"insurrection of subjugated knowledges."*[26] It is a tool for discerning erroneous ways of thinking.[27] And you cannot become more errone-

23. This point is often made, but see, e.g., Karl Jaspers, *Nietzsche: An Introduction to the Understanding of His Philosophical Activity* (Tucson: University of Arizona Press, 1965), 400.

24. John Neville Figgis, *The Will to Freedom, or The Gospel of Nietzsche and the Gospel of Christ* (London: Longmans, Green, 1917), 226.

25. Although there may be a rigorous method behind Nietzsche's arrangements of his maxims, Hamann's comment on his own *Socratic Memorabilia* captures something of Nietzsche's enterprise: he tells us that it is comprehensible only to readers who can swim, with "many little ideas unconnected either by bridge or ferry in its method"; see Ronald Gregor Smith, *J. G. Hamann, 1730–1788: A Study in Christian Existence* (London: Collins, 1960), 53.

26. Michel Foucault, "Two Lectures," in *Power/Knowledge: Selected Interviews and Other Writings, 1972–1977*, ed. Colin Gordon (New York and London: Pantheon, 1980), 81.

27. Here too, Nietzsche was a disciple of the Greeks. Plato alludes to the Lacedaemonians' custom of expressing wisdom in "short memorable sentences, which individuals uttered"; see his *Protagoras*, in *The Dialogues of Plato*, trans. Benjamin Jowett (Oxford:

ous than this: that actions follow from the operations of free will and hence are not determined.

It is hard to exaggerate the significance of Nietzsche's conviction on this last point, either in his work as a whole or in his rejection of Christianity in particular. Kant wrestled with the questions of freedom and necessity, will and character, as did Schopenhauer in wrestling with Kant. Nietzsche came to think that Schopenhauer had gotten things significantly wrong. He mistook for moral truth something that had actually evolved out of nonmoral nature into the form of moral convictions. For nature is nonmoral. *"My chief proposition: there are no moral phenomena, there is only a moral interpretation of these phenomena. This interpretation itself is of extra-moral origin"* (*WP* 258; cf. *BGE* 108).

Here we have a prime, perhaps the prime, example of how Schopenhauer was trapped in older ways belonging to a religious age. In section 39 of *HH*, on *"The fable of intelligible freedom,"* Nietzsche lays matters out like this. First, actions become called "good" or "bad" on account of their consequences. Then people forget this and call them inherently "good" or "bad." Then people proceed to ascribe these qualities to motives more than to actions. When people have run through successive stages of accountability to the point that they are accountable for their motives, the last step is taken: we are accountable for our nature. But once we realize the mistake involved here and that our nature is the determinate product of all kinds of things, past and present, we should run back along the line to the point where we conclude that we cannot be accountable for consequences, the supposition with which people started out. If we so proceed, we have "thereby attained to the knowledge that the history of the moral sensations is the history of an error, the error of accountability, which rests on the freedom of the will." This becomes "clear as daylight": "No one is accountable for his deeds, no one for his nature." Schopenhauer, regrettably, wouldn't accept it. He was worried about the consequences of thinking that way. Yet the "strongest knowledge" is "that of the total unfreedom of the human will" (*AOM* 50).

This is bitter stuff indeed. But we've got to work through the pain of all this and face the future courageously. "It is true that everything in the domain of morality has become and is changeable, unsteady, everything is in flux: but *everything is also flooding forward, and towards one goal*." The goal is the "wise, innocent (conscious of innocence) man" (107). Here we are in Nietzsche's engine room, and the critique of Christianity is largely the intellectual efflux of what is going on here. Specific Christian errors are embedded within a general metaphysical scheme

---

Clarendon, 1875), 1:158. Psychological observations do not always require the aphorism, but aphorisms are often the literary form for their effective transmission.

that Nietzsche regards as radically wrong. Once we acknowledge this, we can look forward not to a metaphysical alternative but to a new type of human being.

At this point, we hit disagreements in Nietzsche interpretation that we cannot ignore. My account hitherto seems to imply that the root problem of Christianity is that it adopts a theistic metaphysic, either grounding or grafted on to a metaphysically mistaken philosophical anthropology. But is theistic metaphysics really the issue? On the one hand, Richard Schacht, for example, maintains that it "is profoundly mistaken" to deny Nietzsche's metaphysical concern for the existence of God.[28] Giles Fraser, on the contrary, believes that this philosophical reading of Nietzsche's approach to the question of God breeds "significant and disastrous consequences."[29] Why so? Because people have come to believe that Nietzsche's objections to Christianity are best understood as philosophical objections. They are not. In fact, they are not quite objections; they are attacks. There is no cool and philosophical neutrality about the issue. If there were, doubtless the first question under Nietzschean consideration would be whether God exists. It is not. "God is dead" is not a rhetorical way of saying "God does not exist." Nietzsche is relatively uninterested in the question of whether God exists. This is not to deny that he is an atheist but to ask what kind of atheism he is advancing. It is not philosophical atheism. In his previous chapter, Fraser has made much of Nietzsche's being against God rather than against theism. Nietzsche's concern is the business of salvation. What he denies is a Savior, not a philosophical proposition.[30]

This slant on things picks up a set of concerns in relation to the interpretation of Nietzsche that have occupied theological existentialists in the past.[31] Both sides of the argument have prima facie force. In prima facie support of an argument such as Fraser's, quite apart from what Fraser himself adduces, observe that in his discussion of *"Belief makes blessed and damns,"* Nietzsche combines the dogmatic statement that God does not exist with the assertion that "God, and a deputizing Lamb of God, . . . are . . . *superfluous* beings, even supposing they do exist,"

28. Richard Schacht, *Nietzsche* (London: Routledge & Kegan Paul, 1983), 119–30. The quotations from this work are all from these pages.

29. Giles Fraser, *Redeeming Nietzsche: On the Piety of Unbelief* (New York: Routledge, 2002), 26–31.

30. This last sentence is the only one where I am inferring a conclusion to Fraser's argument rather than reporting it, but it must be true to his philosophy/soteriology antithesis.

31. See Rudolf Bultmann's essay "The Idea of God and Modern Man," in *World Come of Age*, ed. R. Gregor Smith (London: Collins, 1967). Cf. Martin Heidegger, "The Word of Nietzsche: 'God Is Dead,'" in *The Question concerning Technology and Other Essays* (New York: Harper & Row, 1977).

because belief in their existence has the same effect whether or not they do exist.[32] There is an entry in *WS* titled *"Two means of consolation"* that begins: "Epicurus, the soul-soother of later antiquity, had that wonderful insight, which is still today so rarely to be discovered, that to quieten the heart it is absolutely not necessary to have solved the ultimate and outermost theoretical questions" (7). Nietzsche proceeds to characterize the mood of "the pure atheist" in these terms: "What do the gods matter to me anyway!" It is true that Nietzsche is generally concerned with the force of a belief more than its theoretical invincibility. To a large extent, Fraser both at this point and elsewhere admirably captures Nietzsche's soteriological concerns. Nietzsche is a passionate subject molded by soteriological sensitivity, not a detached philosopher inquiring into the objective existence of a divine agent. Nevertheless, for two reasons, I believe that Fraser draws mistaken conclusions from this.[33]

First, Fraser creates false antitheses. A passionate concern for salvation and refusal to offer a *detached* philosophical critique in relation to God are perfectly compatible both with an intellectual conviction that God does not exist and the persuasion that such a conviction matters. If Nietzsche is not *interested* in the question of God's existence or nonexistence, it is because the matter is settled for him, not because it is *intrinsically* unimportant, as far as he is concerned. There is no reason to deny that Nietzsche is well aware of the logical precedence of the assumption of divine existence behind the soteriological preoccupations of his youth. Fraser alludes to the Lutheran question "What shall I do to be saved?" which arose in the context of belief in God. It is true that spiritual and existential angst, grounded in a set of Christian soteriological presuppositions, can be passionately transposed into a practically atheistic frame of mind and reference so that the objectively detached question of God's existence is proclaimed an irrelevance. But the matter of whether God exists can and should be profoundly self-involving, and Nietzsche does not assume that it does not matter.

Second, Fraser overlooks pertinent distinctions. Schacht responds to the claim that Nietzsche is concerned with the "kind of morality and scale of values associated with belief in the existence of such a [theistic]

---

32. *AOM* 225. What I have reported as assertion takes the grammatical form of a rhetorical question in Nietzsche's text.

33. A more detailed study, out of place here, unearths problems in Fraser's handling of Nietzsche's texts. In the section to which I refer, he misquotes, gives a wrong citation, and omits vital words in the original. Compare his quotation purportedly from *A* 47 with the actual derivation of these words from *WP* 251. Relevant to our discussion, Fraser quotes Nietzsche as saying that the "question of the mere 'truth' of Christianity" (including on the existence of God) is "quite beside the point." What Nietzsche actually says is that this, among others, "is a matter of secondary importance *as long as the question of the value of Christian morality is not considered*" (my italics).

God," and not with the question of God's existence. According to Schacht, it is "both/and": "It should be observed that taking the position he does with respect to this morality and scale of values presupposes that one is prepared to answer this question [of the existence of God] in the negative." Fraser protests: "This last line is the give-away. Why must a concern for (or even attack upon) the kind of morality and scale of values associated with belief in the existence of God necessarily presuppose that one answers the question of God's existence in the negative? What, for instance, of Ivan Karamazov?" The point is that Ivan's best-known and highly effective attack on a God whose existence he does not deny has to do with the problem of suffering. But in response, we must say that this is Ivan Karamazov and not Nietzsche. An Ivan Karamazov might take his own approach, but Schacht is talking about the position that *Nietzsche* takes. More important, when discussing Nietzsche, we must be prepared, as occasion demands, to discriminate between "morality" and the "scale of values." This or that moral tenet proposed and adopted by Christianity might or might not be objectionable. What is consistently problematic about Christian values is that they posit another, transcendent realm of origin and impose an ideal artifice on life. To sustain that point, God's existence must be denied; as far as Schacht's *Nietzsche* is concerned, the abolition of that realm both requires and is required by the abolition of a scale of values putatively grounded in it.

Schacht, I think, is fundamentally right to insist on Nietzsche's metaphysical commitments regarding the question of God's existence, so I stand by my earlier characterization of the matter thus far.[34] On the other hand, Fraser is right to press the significance of the soteriological issue.[35] This brings to light the problem with responding theologically to Nietzsche on the question of God. On the face of it, an intellectual response is required. Schacht thinks that the logic of Nietzsche's position—which to all appearances he endorses—is that the theoretical possibility of the existence of God cannot be discounted but that this is because it is a merely logical possibility and not a plausible philosophical possibility. This way of putting things risks being an excessively formal rendering of Nietzsche's position (and one can understand why Fraser and others might start growling at this point). Nietzsche's naturalistic position is

34. In the context of this discussion, also see the conclusion that Berkowitz achieves (*Nietzsche*, 270–72), although one can endorse its broad outline without subscribing to all the arguments that have brought the author to this point.

35. Further, Schacht (*Nietzsche*), at one point at least, casually but significantly overstates his case. He claims that Nietzsche is "*also* intent upon establishing that . . . the supposition of the existence of a transcendent deity is philosophically unconscionable, and requires to be repudiated" (120). But Nietzsche has little to do with "establishing" that. He is presupposing it.

logically foundational to his enterprise. However passionate we may be and however implacably opposed to philosophical neutrality, naturalism is surely a core subject for debate in tackling Nietzsche's anti-Christianity. That is certainly so if we think that, for things that matter, their logical foundations themselves matter. So why not describe the issue between Nietzsche and Christians as fundamentally about the viability of a naturalistic worldview, and plunge into intellectual engagement?

I do not doubt that Christians need to respond intellectually to naturalism.[36] A broadly religious, generally theistic, or specifically Christian rebuttal of naturalism might be justified in the attempt and successful in the execution. If an atheist philosopher can now observe that "the justification of most contemporary naturalist views is defeated by contemporary theist arguments," we might at least seriously consider whether our response to Nietzsche should be to hammer away on these fronts and try to show that his critique of Christianity collapses on account of faulty intellectual presuppositions.[37] Nevertheless, argumentation along these lines will not take us to the heart of Nietzsche's anti-Christianity, even if they insistently expose its logical foundations. A text from *GS* tells us why: "What is now decisive against Christianity is our taste, no longer our reasons" (132). This is a text under which a great deal in Nietzsche's case against Christianity might be expounded. And it shows us why a narrowly intellectual response is problematic.

We have to tread carefully here. "No longer our reasons" is presumably a historical remark. Nietzsche is apparently taking for granted that the uprooting of Christianity began "in the *head*" in some cultures.[38] Jürgen Habermas's belief that Nietzsche "enthrones taste, 'the Yes and No of the palate,'" has come under fire.[39] Nietzsche surely presupposes the effectiveness of the rational assault on Christianity since at least the eighteenth century. But he refuses to join rational issue with Christianity in his own day on principally rational terms, in the narrow sense. As far as he is concerned, by now we really should be orbiting in an atmosphere where Christianity is plain tasteless. "All life is dispute over taste and

---

36. Different meanings and implications of "naturalism" are set out in the preface to William L. Craig and J. P. Moreland, eds., *Naturalism: A Critical Analysis* (London: Routledge, 2000), a volume of rigorously argued rebuttals of naturalism.

37. Douglas Groothuis has publicized this observation for a broad readership in "Defenders of the Faith," *Books & Culture* 9, no. 4 (2003): 12.

38. For example, in "the north" (see "On the Future of Christianity," *AOM* 97).

39. Alexander Nehamas, "Nietzsche, Modernity, Aestheticism," in *The Cambridge Companion to Nietzsche,* ed. Bernd Magnus and Kathleen M. Higgins (Cambridge: Cambridge University Press, 1996), 228. Jürgen Habermas actually says this twice in *The Philosophical Discourse of Modernity* (Cambridge, UK: Polity, 1987), on 123 as well as on the page cited by Nehamas.

tasting."[40] Christians might have a go at defeating every argument from before Hume to after Russell; they might try to show that, historically and intellectually, the anti-Christian case should never have come to where it did since the Enlightenment; they might argue a philosophically persuasive or respectable case for God. Nevertheless, Christianity will still not be to our taste. Nietzsche's authorship tells us why not. His contribution to late modernity or to postmodernity is more in this domain than in anything he inherited from the broadly rationalist Enlightenment.

What, then, is distasteful about Christianity? If we answer that question in a nutshell, with reference to the stage in Nietzsche's career heralded by *HH*, it would be as good an answer as any to say that Christianity is the antithesis of the free spirit. At the back of the original edition of *GS*, its author wrote: "This book marks the conclusion of a series of writings by Friedrich Nietzsche whose common goal is to erect *a new image and ideal of the free spirit.*" The first of these writings was *HH*, subtitled *A Book for Free Spirits*. Eventually *The Wanderer and His Shadow* (*WS*), like *Assorted Opinions and Maxims* (*AOM*), was attached to *HH* as its second part, under the overall title of *Human, All Too Human*, the title of the first part. In *WS* we encounter a key statement: "To test whether someone is one of us or not—I mean whether he is a free spirit or not—one should test his feelings towards Christianity" (182). *Daybreak*, which came between *WS* and *GS*, is also an expression of the free spirit. In contrast to Christians, Nietzsche and any worthy companions have a taste for the free spirit.

What is that like? It is hard precisely to pin it down in words and belongs to that considerable Wittgensteinian company of things rather shown than said. We really need to read everything Nietzsche has to say about various things in culture, about Greece and Germanness, music and literature, customs and nations, to gather an idea of what he thinks worth ruminating upon and exciting to ruminate upon. Those who turn to a specific consideration of Christianity, after strolling in such interesting groves, exit leafy richness in order to grub around for a few gnarled leaves in the undergrowth; or to change the metaphor, they are like folks who turn from an examination of assorted gems to probe around a dime store. Such is the impression we are given. Perhaps with these comparisons I am indulging in too much impressionism, but they may capture something that comes across in the literature and that sets off the contrast between free-spiritedness and Christianity in a way harder to capture in a more sober and concrete articulation of the contrast. Nietzsche is on a demanding, exacting, exciting, exhilarating, if costly

40. "Of the Sublime Men," *Z* 2.35; and *EH*, "Why I Am So Clever," 8. Here I suspend the question of different meanings and nuances of the English word "taste," which draws us into important post-Enlightenment philosophical currents.

and painful, intellectual and spiritual trail. Better than anything else, absorption in the whole range of his concerns, even when they seem at best indirectly or tangentially related to Christianity, helps us to understand why Christianity was so tasteless on his palate. What Nietzsche says about Christianity is basically hard to detach from what he has to say about everything else. The "spirit" of his enterprise is arresting.[41]

This being said, perhaps Nietzsche's literature brings to light at least three characteristics of the free spirit. In what follows, I give them unequal and selective but, I hope, purposeful treatment.

Curiosity

The free spirit is a spirit of inquiry. Christianity is allegedly sourced in revelation, but it is actually sourced in opinion (*D* 62). It is the opinion of a crude intellect at that (*D* 70). For it is interested in faith rather than reasons (*HH* 225). One who plots Christianity aright can plot the free spirit as its polar antithesis. For example, tradition is against reasons; Christianity is for tradition, and the Nietzschean free spirit is for reasons (*HH* 230). The free spirit is independent; it believes in itself (*WS* 319). Faith, its opposite number, comprises many things. It is deeply immersed in the religiously toned feelings, affects, and conscience that Nietzsche pits against reason (*AOM* 96; *WS* 48, 52; *D* 58). However, there is more to faith than innocent, unquestioning naïveté. Certainly, faith can be a matter of sheer habit, which is the hallmark of the "fettered spirit" (*HH* 226). But there also is hypocrisy: see, for instance, how Christianity is espoused for largely social reasons in contemporary Germany (*AOM* 299). This state of affairs provokes the free spirit in accordance with its individuality and individualism to resist the enfeeblement at which the State aims (*HH* 235). Whatever characterizes a given society, the free spirit searches for knowledge (*HH* 291). In *HH* Nietzsche's chapter "A Glance at the State" ends with the benignly gnomic "*And to repeat*.—Public opinions—private indolence." So we have a social critique of a thoughtless and not entirely innocent faith.

Lack of innocence is further displayed when we perceive that Christianity is antireason as a matter of epistemological principle. "Reason in school has

---

41. Should we not resist Laurence Lampert's recommendation that *Geist* be translated "mind" rather than "spirit" in this context? See his *Nietzsche and Modern Times: A Study of Bacon, Descartes, and Nietzsche* (New Haven and London: Yale University Press, 1993), 300. The exercise of choosing a translation runs the risk of reading distinctions into Nietzsche that are not there. "Mind" is certainly involved and included. I do not want to give the impression that Nietzsche is slack about the use of reason. Far from it. But his freedom is more than a matter of the intellect or the understanding; there is a spiritual bounce in his literary and intellectual step when Nietzsche goes about his explorations.

made Europe Europe" (*HH* 265), but how little "intellectual conscience" (*HH* 107) Christianity itself has is shown by the fact that contemporary Christians consciously cultivate rational skepticism in order to establish faith in the cross. "Christians today like to set up Pilate, with his question 'What is truth?,' as an advocate of Christ, so as to cast suspicion on everything known or knowable and to erect the Cross against the dreadful background of the impossibility of knowing" (*AOM* 8). Christianity dislikes the passion for knowledge (*D* 429). So the spirituality that underlies (Christian) religious epistemology is warped and rightly offends its antipode, the free spirit. In the light of this, Nietzsche dishes out a word for the wise: "Convictions are more dangerous enemies of truth than lies" (*HH* 483). In a series of sustained remarks on the nature of convictions, Nietzsche contrasts the religious with the scientific person (*HH* 630). For Christians, doubt is sin (*D* 89). Searching is distasteful, and Christians prefer the dogmatism of having arrived (*AOM* 98). The free spirit is searching for rather than dogmatically possessing the truth (*HH* 633). Hence, its spirit is the spirit of inquiry, an inquiry that matters even more than setting things intellectually right (*HH* 225). Make up your own mind; don't plump for conviction for plumping's sake and conviction's sake.[42]

These "free-spirited" works time and time again indicate Nietzsche's belief that Christianity is a tissue of intellectual errors. They are the first things that Nietzsche brings to our attention when embarking on the question of the death of God in *GS* (108–15). Christianity flies in the face of both actual reasons and the principle of reason, shunning fellowship with the spirit of rational inquiry. Much of what we might term a standardly rationalistic nature powders Nietzsche's literature as he makes observations on phenomena such as prayer or claims to private illumination. The section on "Christianity and Antiquity," which describes Christianity "in the context of our age" as "a piece of antiquity intruding out of distant ages past," eloquently expresses Nietzsche's disbelief and incredulity at anyone's belief in and credulity about the traditional christological and soteriological tenets of the church (*HH* 113). Religion developed in response to fear and need; our world is a place where people have little control, so would it not be a good thing if there were a controlling being to whom they could cozy up, if he were fearsome? So magicians and sorcerers do their thing, succeeded by priests, who learn power over the people and not just over the cosmos.

This is standard stuff in Western anti-Christianity, and we could give a standard response. But we need to go further in order to appreciate the nature or the mood of the free spirit. "For me," Nietzsche said,

42. This is not a full-blown account of Nietzsche's epistemological moves in relation to religion; I do not, for example, touch on perspectivism here.

"the Renaissance remains the climax of this millennium; and what has happened since then is the grand reaction of all kinds of herd instincts against the 'individualism' of that epoch."[43]

> The Italian Renaissance contained within it all the positive forces to which we owe modern culture: liberation of thought, disrespect for authorities, victory of education over the arrogance of ancestry, enthusiasm for science and the scientific past of mankind, unfettering of the individual, a passion for truthfulness and an aversion to appearance and mere effect. . . . The Renaissance possessed positive forces which have up to now never reappeared in our modern culture with such power as they had then. (*HH* 237)

This is the perspective that we have to take into account. Those who read Nietzsche's remarks on the question of Christianity and rational inquiry will sometimes want to substitute for the word "Christianity" the phrase "The Lutheran Christianity of my time" or "Christianity as I have experienced it" or "The bits about Christianity that I have read and have in mind" or "Christianity as it appears to one of my way of thinking." This would be an understandable and partly justified reaction. The shortcomings of Nietzsche's historical and philosophical grasp of "reason" and "rationality" in relation to the intellectual history of Christianity will be obvious to anyone well acquainted with the story. In company with someone like Freud, Nietzsche really does not come to grips at all with most of the components in a theologically and philosophically responsible Christian attitude toward reason.[44] But issues remain. For Christians who prize the degree of intellectual curiosity and rational interest that has characterized much of the Christian tradition and who are positive about the Renaissance and the scientific movement, a Nietzschean kind of criticism initially appears far wide of the mark. Yet elements of the critique can be effectively refined. Nietzsche might allow for a selective curiosity and restricted use of reason in the Christian tradition at its best but maintain that its subservience to faith wipes out its advantages. The free spirit will have none of that subservience. Faith may follow its own rational trajectories or welcome rational trajectories that lead to positions consistent with its own findings. But faith imposes boundaries and is thus opposed to the free spirit.

We can respond to this too. Suppose the exercise of curiosity and of reason, embedded in the minutest and most enthusiastic receptivity

43. To Overbeck, *SL*, October 1882.
44. See Sigmund Freud, *The Future of an Illusion* (London: Hogarth, 1952), esp. 22–25; and idem, *Civilization and Its Discontents* (New York: Norton, 1961), 58. Schopenhauer may have had some influence on Freud here, according to Sebastian Gardner, "Schopenhauer, Will, and the Unconscious," in *The Cambridge Companion to Schopenhauer*, ed. Christopher Janaway (Cambridge: Cambridge University Press, 1999), 375–421.

to life's experiences, should aid someone toward religious conviction, particularly to the conviction that the world is a created order. Or suppose that such conviction comes in some other way. We can still give free rein to intellectual exploration of this, our God-given domain: the world and all that is before us. A free spirit would be a perverse spirit, profoundly uninterested in truthfulness and as dogmatic as could be, if it insisted that a condition for the exercise of unfettered curiosity was the refusal to believe that a Creator had anything to do with it all. Nietzsche seems to treat faith as one monochrome entity, whether it is superstitious and untutored or offering to be tested in the furnace of rigorous intellectual interrogation. Yet Hans Blumenberg's detailed work suggests that the historical question of whether and how Christian hostility toward *curiositas* led, by reaction, to the modern age is both important and involved.[45] Blumenberg makes distinctions. He does not think that "Christian hostility" is a blanket that will cover all Christian attitudes: Augustine, Peter Damian, and Aquinas are not all of a kind.[46] Nevertheless, he instructs us in the importance of thinking theologically as well as historically about the Renaissance ideal as seen through Nietzsche's eyes.

Kant, who defined Enlightenment in terms of intellectual courage, dedicated his *Critique of Pure Reason* to Francis Bacon. What Nietzsche has to say about Bacon is tantalizingly brief and favorable.[47] In certain respects, there is a strong kinship between the two thinkers. Turning his back on the cloying metaphysics of scholastic Christian philosophy, the author of the *Novum organon* (1620) portrayed at its head a ship in full sail heading out to the ocean, passing freely between the Pillars of Hercules. In the *Advancement of Learning,* when Bacon says that he has made "as it were a small globe of the intellectual world," Blumenberg takes this as paradigmatic for the self-consciousness of the modern age.[48] Nietzsche often uses the image of a voyage.[49] He was no stranger to Bacon's spirit of global adventure, whatever the evolution of his opinions on Baconian scientific culture. Bacon initiated an epoch-making change in the way knowledge was mapped out, and Laurence

45. Hans Blumenberg, *The Legitimacy of the Modern Age* (Cambridge: Massachusetts Institute of Technology, 1983).

46. See, e.g., ibid., part 3, chaps. 5 and 6.

47. *EH*, "Why I Am So Clever," 4. This statement at least reflects what he says about the historical Bacon; Nietzsche was apparently one of those who suspected that "Shakespeare" was Bacon (*WP* 848).

48. Blumenberg, *Legitimacy of the Modern Age,* 340. Cf. Anthony Quinton, *Bacon* (Oxford: Oxford University Press, 1980), 53.

49. A volume on Nietzsche, edited by Michael Allen Gillespie and Tracy B. Strong, is aptly called *Nietzsche's New Seas: Explorations in Philosophy, Aesthetics, and Politics* (Chicago: University of Chicago Press, 1988).

Lampert has argued for a strong and historically momentous affinity between Bacon and Nietzsche. Investigating the apparently minor Baconian works, he claims that Bacon's esoteric style hid his true intention from many readers.[50] That intention was to clean up Europe by a holy war waged against Christianity, a religion whose repression of true philosophy and good science makes it a fit object for countercrusade. The "general world-view of inquiring science from Democritus to the present" is the alternative.[51] Scientifically informed philosophers are to be our legislators.

Is this, then, what it is to be a free-spirited man of the Renaissance? Whether or not Lampert's reading persuades (which I am not particularly competent to judge), his case is quite compellingly advanced. In any case, our sense of the sober importance and magnificent excitement of the scientific venture is well stimulated by his account. But it is dismaying when some of the most dynamic features of this Baconian spirit are deemed inimical to Christianity, or Christianity is deemed inimical to these features.[52] It is true that we might challenge a Bacon-style ambition for technological mastery over nature, that the religion of Christ is bound to be in conflict and not in harmony with anything that covertly or stridently sidelines or repudiates God, and that there may be motivating factors and substantive proposals essential to Bacon and his work that compel theological refusal. But what of the sheer spirit of scientific inquiry or the epistemological issues that surround the early modern turn against Christianized Aristotelian philosophy and crop up both in their own right and in Baconian ideas about the taxonomy of knowledge? What of this-worldly curious and beneficent interest, nearly to the point of absorption? About such things Christians may be cautious but not necessarily hostile.[53]

50. Lampert, *Nietzsche and Modern Times*, part 1. The works in question are Francis Bacon's *The New Atlantis* (1626) and *An Advertisement Touching a Holy War* (written 1622–23; published 1629).

51. Lampert, *Nietzsche and Modern Times*, 9. However, we must beware of assuming that Bacon saw Democritus as did a later era; see Stephen Gaukroger, *Francis Bacon and the Transformation of Early-Modern Philosophy* (Cambridge: Cambridge University Press, 2001), 108n20.

52. Laurence Lampert is way off the mark in thinking that cleverness is a vice in Christian eyes; see his *Nietzsche's Teaching: An Interpretation of "Thus Spoke Zarathustra"* (New Haven and London: Yale University Press, 1986), 29. Cf. idem, *Nietzsche and Modern Times*, 407. For the relevant significance of the difference between *Klugheit* and *listig*, see Robert Gooding-Williams, *Zarathustra's Dionysian Modernism* (Stanford, CA: Stanford University Press, 2002), 336n176, correcting Lampert.

53. We should also try to erase the impression that the "feast of thinking never takes place in Christianity"; thus Martin Heidegger, glossing Nietzsche in *WP* 916, quoted by Jacques Derrida, "Interpreting Signatures [of Nietzsche/Heidegger]: Two Questions," in *Dialogue and Deconstruction: The Gadamer-Derrida Encounter*, ed. D. P. Michelfelder and R. E. Palmer (Albany: State University of New York Press, 1989), 68.

In 1898, Abraham Kuyper delivered his remarkable series of lectures on Calvinism. Toward the end of them, he observed that "Nietzsche is the author whose works are being most eagerly devoured by the young *modern* Germany of our day."[54] By that time, Kuyper had established theses mandating Christian this-worldliness in the strongest terms.

> The Calvinistic preacher Peter Plancius of Amsterdam was an eloquent sermonizer, a pastor unrivalled in his consecration to his work, foremost in the ecclesiastical struggle of his days, but at the same time he was the oracle of shipowners and sea-captains on account of his extensive geographical knowledge. The investigation of the lines of longitude and latitude of the terrestrial globe formed in his estimation one whole with the investigation of the length and breadth of the love of Christ.[55]

In a later lecture, Kuyper proceeded to announce that "if Israel was chosen for the sake of Religion, this in no way prevented a parallel election of Greeks for the domain of philosophy and for the revelations of art, nor of the Romans for the classical development within the domain of Law and State."[56] Whether or not Kuyper overstepped the mark with some of these utterances, he was the influential advocate of a Christianity that mutes some of Nietzsche's criticisms, and he was certainly right to remind us—yet again—that a theology of creation warrants the most vivid possible interest in creation. If interest in God and cosmos, the spiritual and physical well-being of my neighbor, is rightly integrated, the boundaries of curiosity are established not by fearful faith or by faithless fear but by the concrete actuality of God and of others, the realities of a relational order. "Relationality" is a notion that now takes us to the second feature of the Nietzschean free spirit.

Nomad

In the course of a relatively solitary and wandering life, René Descartes made this eminently unquotable observation: "Three days ago, I met a learned man at an inn in Dordrecht, and I discussed the *Ars brevis* of Lull with him."[57] Why quote this inconsequential sentence? Because

54. Abraham Kuyper, *Lectures on Calvinism* (Grand Rapids: Eerdmans, 1931), 178. Kuyper was apparently one of the first thinkers in the Netherlands to pay attention to Nietzsche; see Peter S. Heslam, *Creating a Christian Worldview: Abraham Kuyper's Lectures on Calvinism* (Grand Rapids: Eerdmans; Carlisle, UK: Paternoster, 1998), 226.

55. Kuyper, *Lectures on Calvinism*, 120. On creation and salvation, see 118–21.

56. Ibid., 161–62.

57. Stephen Gaukroger, *Descartes: An Intellectual Biography* (Oxford: Clarendon, 1995), 102.

even those who, like myself, cannot intelligently follow everything in the account of Descartes's mathematical or scientific interests catch, in the scene at the Dordrecht inn, the whiff of vibrant excitement at the prospect of a wandering and intellectually exciting life. The cameo usefully evokes a distinction between individual curiosity, which is laudable, and curious individualism, which is different. The Nietzschean free spirit exhibits both. In addition to inhaling and exuding the air of intellectual curiosity, it revels in solitude and in nomadism, producing a "nomad philosophy" with all the appearance of deep, if lonely, joy accompanying indefatigable curiosity.

The times in which Nietzsche lived did not lend themselves to lonely reflectiveness (*HH* 282). Those who take for granted that the hustle and bustle of modern life is a curse of the twentieth and twenty-first centuries will sympathize with much that Nietzsche has to say on this score. A preface added to *D* some years after its first appearance captures the atmosphere both of this work and of those that flank it. "In this book you will discover a 'subterranean man' at work, . . . a solitary mole. . . . His path is *his alone*" (1–2). Nietzsche was later to describe *Z* as a work resonant with "*azure* solitude" (*EH*, "Thus Spoke Zarathustra," 6). It is a nomadic and not a stationary solitude; there is a lot of walking near the places where Nietzsche is staying, and he moves from place to place to stay. With consummate artistry, Nietzsche often ends chapters and books with a summary statement of what the foregoing was all about, though it is never mere summary and typically provides a spiritual spur. In a section titled "The Wanderer" (638), *HH* ends with reference to "all those free spirits who are at home in mountain, wood and solitude." Like Nietzsche, thoughtful and joyful, wanderers "seek the *philosophy of the morning*." In *AOM* Nietzsche writes: "What, however, we may call ourselves in all seriousness . . . is 'free-ranging spirits,' because we feel the tug toward freedom as the strongest drive of our spirit and, in antithesis to the fettered and firm-rooted intellects, see our ideal almost in a spiritual nomadism" (211). If Nietzsche's defense of spiritual nomadism does not require physical nomadism, his physical wandering was not just a contingent factor in his existence; it was more than just a sign and symbol of the perambulations of the mind.[58]

Nomadism is not for the fainthearted. It is a "highly perilous wandering on glaciers and polar seas" (*AOM* 21). It happens on mountains, too, where the path may now become "more solitary, and in any event more perilous" (*AOM* 237). Perhaps here, more than anywhere else in Nietzsche's work, we are transported back to another time and fraternity. We are in the company of the early-seventeenth-century *érudits*, the

---

58. For the interlocking elements, see *AOM* 237.

"wanderers, the irregulars, the independents," though we might not want to fit Descartes himself into that mold.[59] In all this, Nietzsche bids us be of good cheer. *"Forward,"* he hails at the end of his discussion of "Tokens of Higher and Lower Culture" in *HH*. Go your own way courageously; know yourself, and "perhaps you will also behold in its mirror [the mirror of your knowledge] the distant constellations of future cultures."

> Do you believe that such a life with such a goal is too laborious, too much lacking in everything pleasant? Then you have not learned that no honey is sweeter than that of knowledge, or that the clouds of affliction hovering over you will yet have to serve you as udders from which you will milk the milk of your refreshment. Only when you grow old will you come to realize how you have given ear to the voice of nature, that nature which rules the whole world through joy. . . . Towards the light—your last motion; a joyful shout of knowledge—your last sound. (292)

The "Epilogue" to the same work speaks of being "Among Friends":

> Fine to lie in quiet together,
> Finer still to join in laughing
> Underneath a silken heaven
> Lying back amid the grasses
> Join with friends in cheerful laughing,
> Showing our white teeth together.
>
> Am I right? let's lie in quiet;
> Am I wrong? let's join in laughing
> And in being aggravating,
> Aggravating, loudly laughing,
> Till we reach the grave together.

Solitude and nomadism, then, do not entail a resolute breach with all friendships. Like Augustine, Nietzsche could contemplate a little monastic enclave of like-minded philosophical thinkers, but it is the fraternity of those willing to go their own way in body and in mind. Writing of the free spirit, Nietzsche says it "is probable that even his love of other people will be prudent and somewhat short-breathed, for he wants to become involved with the world of affection and blindness only insofar as it is necessary for acquiring knowledge."[60] This collides

59. John S. Spink, *French Free-Thought from Gassendi to Voltaire* (London: Athlone, 1960), 12. For a timely distinction between *libertinage flamboyant* and *libertinage érudit*, see Gaukroger, *Descartes*, 135–39.

60. *HH* 291. See this whole section for remarks on the social and political role and responsibility of the prudent free spirit.

with Christianity. For Nietzsche, it is a matter of the individual against the herd. For Christianity, it is a matter of community against detachment. As it mandates intellectual curiosity, so Christianity will sanction the type of individualism entailed by such curiosity, with its intellectual and spiritual independence. But everything is geared to love and service and therefore to community and society. The independence fostered by genuine curiosity and the service fostered by interest in the community are joined together in the love of God. In our desire to understand God and our accountability to God, we are impelled to be alone as any free spirit is alone. The conviction that we are what we are on our knees and nothing else is a piece of sound Puritan wisdom.

This is not to denigrate the importance of ecclesial worship. However, to the worship of the assembly we must bring not just a life of service to others but also a life that has been exposed to God in the solitude of an unsubstitutably personal relationship. Ruminating on Heraclitus, Nietzsche said: "To walk alone along a lonely street is part of the philosopher's nature" (*PTA* 66). Christians who feel the force of this remark should do so precisely because of an individualism proper to Christianity.[61] Yet it is axiomatic for Christianity that we are constituted as selves in relationship; hence, nomadic solitude in body or in mind is not the ideal existence.

For all the importance of the features that I have picked out, neither curiosity nor nomadism per se takes us to the heart of Nietzsche's free-spiritedness. We shall get to this third feature of free-spiritedness rather unexpectedly by attending briefly to the rollicking burlesque that is Laurence Sterne's *Tristram Shandy*.

A Barrel of Shandy

"If we are sensible the only thing that need concern us is that we should have joy in our hearts.—Alas, someone added, if we are sensible the best thing we can do is to be wise" (*WS* 300). Nietzsche produced a "gay science" in the sense of a joyful wisdom.[62] This "most personal" of Nietzsche's works takes us back to twelfth-century Provençal, to the birth of European poetry and the day of the merry troubadours. To a second edition of *GS*, Nietzsche added a fifth book to the previous four books plus an appendix,

61. For the plea that "precisely as my life ceases to be solitary, it ceases to be distinct," made in the context of the collision between strict Christianity and mild free-thinking, see Edmund Gosse's moving *Father and Son: A Study of Two Temperaments* (London: Heinemann, 1907), 215.

62. Despite the fact that "gay" is now changed in meaning, I refer to the title of this work as *The Gay Science* because that is how the German is usually translated.

"Songs of Prince Vogelfrei" (one who is free as a bird).[63] Nietzsche tells us that the last of these poems is "an exuberant dance-song in which, if I may say so! I dance right over morality" (*EH*, "The Gay Science"). This constitutes "a perfect Provençalism." It is perfect free-spiritedness too. Christianity is a moral imposition mounted on an intellectual folly, and Nietzsche's attack on the fundamental moral philosophy in Christianity is of the first importance. But dancing over morality means more than taking up a substantive intellectual position on morality, as Nietzsche does. The dance begins with psychological observations of the close at hand, to which we have alluded. Observing the empirical, the human, and the unconstrained brings with it, whether by logic, tendency, or atmosphere, a whole attitude to morality that undercuts standard approaches and unwieldy, idealistic conceptual structures.

We have learned that if Nietzsche has "joy in the actual and active *of every kind*" (*AOM* 220), it is mingled with a sense of the tragic. It also has another dimension, which we encounter in the rambunctious and playful jocularity of the eighteenth-century novelist Laurence Sterne.

> *The most liberated writer.*—How, in a book for free spirits, should there be no mention of Laurence Sterne, whom Goethe honoured as the most liberated spirit of his century! Let us content ourselves here simply with calling him the most liberated spirit of all time, in comparison with whom all others seem stiff, intolerant and boorishly direct. (*AOM* 113)

Although Sterne's *Sentimental Journey* also enjoyed great vogue in the nineteenth century, Nietzsche has in mind the novel *Tristram Shandy*. In this supreme exemplification of the free spirit, we surely have a paradigm case of Nietzschean "dancing over morality." Surprising as it seems, in the field of literature perhaps only Shakespeare has had more influence outside the British Isles than Sterne, especially if we consider the eighteenth- and nineteenth-century reception of his work.[64] Yet, for all its international influence in the eighteenth and nineteenth centuries, *Tristram Shandy* is a novel that in certain respects comes into its own in the twentieth. The merry anarchy that superficially marks its literary arrangement is a crafty device for handling time and the association of ideas in a way particularly appealing to late-modern minds.

63. This is the literal translation and the emphasis in, e.g., Joachim Köhler's account, *Zarathustra's Secret: The Interior Life of Friedrich Nietzsche* (New Haven: Yale University Press, 2002), 169–76. But I am advised that *Vogelfrei* can bear the meaning "outlawed" and was used in this way in Nietzsche's time, so that Nietzsche may have had a double entendre in mind.

64. For the weighty Goethe on Sterne and Shakespeare, see W. R. R. Pinger, *Laurence Sterne and Goethe*, University of California Publications in Modern Philology 10.1 (Berkeley: University of California Press, 1920).

Yet again we encounter a work impossible to describe for those who have not read it and difficult enough for those who have; the *Critical Review* of January 1760 judged it "a humorous performance, of which we are unable to convey any distinct ideas to our readers."[65] As Elizabeth Bowen put it, "One does not attempt to 'follow' *Tristram Shandy*; one consigns oneself, dizzily, to it."[66] A reader "has to surrender unconditionally to Sterne's caprices," said Nietzsche. The novel has somewhat to do with the life, opinions, and events of interest to Tristram Shandy, starring also such figures as the conscientious parson Yorick and, above all, Uncle Toby, in whose case you get the sense that if you feel no warmth of affection toward him, the state of your soul needs serious examination. Nietzsche comments on both Sterne the writer and Sterne the man. The former draws forth his extraordinary commendation.

From the outset of the reception of *Tristram Shandy*, the question of Sterne and morality loomed large in public discussion. Leaving aside what was discussed about Sterne's person, many lamented the bawdy mockery of virtue and irreverent jesting at serious religion that they found in the work. Up to a point, the different responses to *Tristram Shandy* in both the eighteenth and the nineteenth centuries classically play out the "Puritan"-versus-"libertine" type of scenario. On one account, these responses reveal a dull, saturnine, moralistic, po-faced (solemn) piety, liberally laced with an intolerant hypocrisy opposed to the merry, knockabout, affable, harmless, humanly warm ribaldry of the book. On another account, at stake are serious and responsible concerns for what humanity owes its Maker, how humans edify one another versus an indulgent trifling in profound matters, and the culpable encouragement of attitudes that lead to dereliction of duty in the worship of God and cause human pain in the practices of life.[67] Where does Nietzsche stand?

Nietzsche's admiration for the literary quality of *Tristram Shandy* is largely on account of Sterne's capacity for psychological observation. But he expresses this somewhat indirectly, concentrating rather on literary manner than on substance. A key word in his account is "ambiguity." Sterne's stylistic mastery of ambiguity chimes in with the Janus-faced features of human life and reality that properly command our attention. Nietzsche apparently welcomes Sterne's work as

65. Alan B. Howes, *Sterne: The Critical Heritage* (Boston and London: Routledge & Kegan Paul, 1974), 52.

66. Ibid., 31.

67. However, trawling through the responses meticulously gathered in Howes, *Sterne*, there is a fair amount of quite impressive discrimination and balance in the responses; often critics do not see things in black or white.

an exhibition of what rightly and felicitously happens when we get onto the right wavelength for musing on morality.[68] "Because they dissect morality, moralists must now be content to be upbraided as immoralists" (*WS* 19). Sterne ranks as an immoralist in this sense, dissecting in incomparable fashion.

There is quite a dance in Sterne. Nietzsche says:

> Precisely because we are at bottom grave and serious human beings and more weights than human beings, nothing does us as much good as the *fool's cap*: we need it against ourselves—we need all exuberant, floating, dancing, mocking, childish and blissful art lest we lose that *freedom over things* that our ideal demands of us. It would be a *relapse* for us, with our irritable honesty, to get completely caught up in morality and, for the sake of the overly severe demands that we make on ourselves, to become virtuous monsters and scarecrows. We have also to *be able* to stand *above* morality. (*GS* 107)

Tristram Shandy in a nutshell, one is tempted to say. What literature better exhibits what Nietzsche is looking for here? It might be protested that there is a softness in Sterne where there is a hardness in Nietzsche, a benevolence toward others in the one where there is an isolated indifferentism in the other. But does this prevent our regarding *Tristram Shandy* as a paradigm case of Nietzschean free-spirited dancing over morality? Arguably, Sterne exudes sentimentality but sidelines morality.[69] The question of Sterne's humor, to which Nietzsche alludes, focuses the issue. Exposed to it, Sir Herbert Read found himself really struggling "to balance morality against art."[70] "There is nothing of a more ambiguous nature than strong humour, and Sterne found it to be so," said Isaac D'Israeli.[71] When Richard Hurd, bishop of Worcester, contended that author and reader "ought to be *laughing in such a manner, as that Virgins and Priests might laugh with him*," doubtless his solemn declara-

68. The question of Sterne's intellectual connection with the *moraliste* tradition is interesting. In *Tristram Shandy*, parson Yorick is explicitly La Rochefoucauldian on gravity; see Laurence Sterne, *The Life and Opinions of Tristram Shandy, Gentleman* (Oxford: Clarendon, 1983), 1:23. But Thomas McMahon contrasted Sterne with La Rochefoucauld (Howes, *Sterne*, 232).

69. Coleridge and Virginia Woolf are both suggestive on this point. See Samuel T. Coleridge, "On Sensibility," in *Aids to Reflection*, ed. John Beer (Princeton, NJ: Princeton University Press, 1993), 57–58; and idem, "Wit and Humour: Sterne," in *Coleridge's Miscellaneous Criticism*, ed. Thomas M. Raysor (Cambridge: Harvard University Press; London: Constable, 1936). See also Virginia Woolf's preface to *A Sentimental Journey* (London: Oxford University Press, 1928).

70. Herbert Read, "The Sense of Glory," in *Essays in Criticism* (Cambridge: Cambridge University Press, 1929), 127.

71. Howes, *Sterne*, 296.

tion itself raised a good old cackle.[72] This should not obscure the fact that we can ask moral questions about Sterne's humor. It is significant that even the *potential* moral issue arising from Sterne's humor does not remotely feature on Nietzsche's horizon. It is surely not unwarranted eisegesis to surmise that he regards the book as literary fun, moral time off. Surely its rhythms and cadences perfectly execute the celebrated dance over morality.[73]

Yet perhaps we should not be surprised that it is the dance of the classical clown, with seriousness and sadness underneath. Pierre-Simon Ballanche, writing early in the nineteenth century, inquired simply: "You who have read this remarkable book, haven't you felt the gaiety of heart which is so close to melancholy?"[74] Better, I think: we should sense the melancholy that is underneath the gaiety of heart. "What is the life of man!" we read, "Is it not to shift from side to side?—from sorrow to sorrow?—to button up one cause of vexation?—and unbutton another!"[75] It has been proposed that "two things are of fundamental importance to an understanding of Sterne; he was acutely self-conscious, and he was all his life a sick man."[76] So was Nietzsche. Gaiety and sadness in Sterne; joy and tragedy in Nietzsche; it is not always easy to say whether, between Sterne and Nietzsche, these things differ in degree, form, expression, or kind.

The Nietzschean free spirit is marked by curiosity, solitude, and dancing over morality. The question of morality is particularly important in the collision with Christianity. To the extent that he still cleaved to a God, morality, and philanthropy, Sterne had not come to where Nietzsche would arrive. But his merry capers will surely delight those learning the steps of the Nietzschean dance. And the bass note of his sadness will resonate with adherents of the tragic and of Dionysus. It is not for nothing that Nietzsche called Sterne the freest spirit of all time. He is for our postmodern time as well as Nietzsche's.[77] Since we shall come back to morality later, I shall not comment specifically on the dance here. Sterne never propelled his free spirit into an attack against Christianity; as a clergyman, he could not have, and I am not snidely suggesting that he wished to. Nietzsche

72. Ibid., 130–31.

73. In relation to specifically religious questions, there is a hilarious section on curses in Sterne, *Tristram Shandy*, 3:137–42. But how seriously can the question of damnation be taken after reading it? Sterne wants us to laugh off the question of any divine judgment on the obscenity of his own work (4:254–60).

74. Howes, *Sterne*, 406.

75. Sterne, *Tristram Shandy*, 4:268.

76. W. B. C. Watkins, *Perilous Balance: The Tragic Genius of Swift, Johnson, and Sterne* (Princeton, NJ: Princeton University Press, 1939), 101. This is a helpful essay.

77. Umberto Eco, "'I Love You Madly,' He Said Self-Consciously," in *The Fontana Post-modernism Reader*, ed. Walter Truett Anderson (London: Fontana, 1996), 33.

could, would, and wanted to. Nietzsche could be pathetically unrealistic about the morality of the future.[78] Still, he would regard its prospect as infinitely better than the otherworldly, menacing, and monochrome gray that backgrounds the moral landscape of Christianity. Christianity is the ultimate in abject religion, as we shall now see.

78. E.g.: "The wide regulation and disposal of death belongs to that morality of the future, at present quite ungraspable and immoral sounding, into the dawn of which it must be an indescribable joy to gaze" ("Of Rational Death," WS 185).

4

INDICTMENT

"I do know
My route full well, and need no further guidance."

Byron, *Manfred*, act 2, scene 1

The Death of God

After Hölderlin and before Nietzsche, E. M. Butler mentions just one name in the list that we skimmed through earlier, the name of Heinrich Heine. "It will one day be said," Nietzsche promised, "that Heine and I have been by far the first artists of the German language" (*EH*, "Why I Am So Clever," 4). The affinity extends beyond mastery in verbal artistry. In 1823 Heine wrote: "Every day I am more convinced that this final crash of Christianity is clearly coming."[1] That was ten years before the appearance of the first edition of his *Religion and Philosophy in Germany*.[2] The conclusion of the second part of the final German edition reads: "Hear ye not the bells resounding? Kneel down. They are bringing sacraments

---

1. Quoted in Henry Hatfield, *Clashing Myths in German Literature from Heine to Rilke* (Cambridge: Harvard University Press, 1974), 13.
2. The first edition was in French. A German edition was published in 1834 and another in 1852, which was translated into English: Heinrich Heine, *Religion and Philosophy in Germany: A Fragment*, trans. John Snodgrass (London: Trübner, 1882; repr., Boston: Beacon, 1959).

to a dying god."[3] Where Heine's god is dying, Nietzsche's is dead. Taken as a whole, Heine's volume is not likely to remind us of Nietzsche. By contrast with Nietzsche, Heine is relatively measured in his treatment of others; Luther does not come out of things badly, and the argument does not follow the same course. Heine was a subtle as well as brilliant author, and we certainly must not leap to take him at literal face value. Even so, this work *as a whole* does not strongly anticipate Nietzsche's presentation or conceptualization of the death of God.[4] Yet the words I have quoted appear to be directly reflected in Nietzsche's classic passage, which I now quote in full.[5]

> The madman.—Haven't you heard of that madman who in the bright morning lit a lantern and ran around the marketplace crying incessantly, "I'm looking for God! I'm looking for God!" Since many of those who did not believe in God were standing around together just then, he caused great laughter. "Has he been lost, then?" asked one. "Did he lose his way like a child?" asked another. "Or is he hiding? Is he afraid of us? Has he gone to sea? Emigrated?"—Thus they shouted and laughed, one interrupting the other. The madman jumped into their midst and pierced them with his eyes. "Where is God?" he cried; "I'll tell you! *We have killed him*—you and I! We are all his murderers. But how did we do this? How were we able to drink up the sea? Who gave us the sponge to wipe away the entire horizon? What were we doing when we unchained this earth from its sun? Where is it moving to now? Where are we moving to? Away from all suns? Are we not continually falling? And backwards, sidewards, forwards, in all directions? Is there still an up and a down? Aren't we straying as though through an infinite nothing? Isn't empty space breath-

3. Ibid., 103.

4. There are certainly points of contact with Nietzsche. Heine describes Christianity as the "annihilation of the life of the senses" (ibid., 38). The discussion of Lessing's honesty and "intellectual solitariness" makes the point that the "history of great men is always a martyrology"—a pleasing thought, on Nietzsche's view of things (99). For the affinity Heine felt for Laurence Sterne, see Ludwig Marcuse's introductory note (xxii); and Alan B. Howes, *Sterne: The Critical Heritage* (Boston and London: Routledge & Kegan Paul, 1974), 449–50. Heine apparently succumbed, as Nietzsche probably did, to syphilitic paralysis.

5. In Nietzsche studies, the question of Nietzsche's unacknowledged use of sources is sometimes raised. Reginald J. Hollingdale's appendix to the second edition of his biography, *Nietzsche: The Man and His Philosophy* (Cambridge: Cambridge University Press, 1999), takes us back to Nietzsche's early years. Max Stirner, author of *The Ego and Its Own* (*Der Einzige und sein Eigenthum* [Leipzig: Wigand, 1845]), is probably the most interesting case of such possible borrowing. John Glassford, who is cautious, knows "of no other example of two philosophers whose works bear such a strong similarity, but where no acknowledgement of debt took place" ("Did Friedrich Nietzsche [1844–1900] Plagiarize from Max Stirner [1806–1856]?" *Journal of Nietzsche Studies* 18 [1999]: 73–79). Also see Irving M. Zeitlin, *Nietzsche: A Re-examination* (Cambridge, UK: Polity, 1994), chap. 8.

ing at us? Hasn't it got colder? Isn't night and more night coming again and again? Don't lanterns have to be lit in the morning? Do we still hear nothing of the noise of the grave-diggers who are burying God? Do we still smell nothing of the divine decomposition?—gods, too, decompose! God is dead! God remains dead! And we have killed him! How can we console ourselves, the murderers of all murderers! The holiest and the mightiest thing the world has ever possessed has bled to death under our knives: who will wipe this blood from us? With what water could we clean ourselves? What festivals of atonement, what holy games will we have to invent for ourselves? Is the magnitude of this deed not too great for us? Do we not ourselves have to become gods merely to appear worthy of it? There was never a greater deed—and whoever is born after us will on account of this deed belong to a higher history than all history up to now!" (*GS* 125)

Greeted by the silent disconcert of the listeners, the madman throws his lantern to the ground, shattering it to pieces.

"I come too early," he then said; "my time is not yet. This tremendous event is still on its way, wandering; it has not yet reached the ears of men. . . . This deed is still more remote to them than the remotest stars—and yet they have done it themselves!" It is still recounted how on the same day the madman forced his way into several churches and there started singing his requiem *aeternam deo*. Led out and called to account, he is said always to have replied nothing but, "What then are these churches now if not the tombs and sepulchres of God?"

This is one of those purple passages whose impact is virtually deadened by comment. On the principle that we might as well be hanged for a sheep as for a lamb, let us bring it down to earth with a sixfold prosaic bump. It tells us, first, that God and theism are gone. Second, there are plenty of people around who know it. Third, there are not plenty of people around who understand it. Fourth, the demise of God and God's world is the product of human will and of human deed, not an accident. Fifth, it is more massively world-historical than anything imaginable. Sixth, it induces vertigo as we think about the future. And one could go on.[6]

From his lonely observation post, Nietzsche has witnessed cataclysm. The heraldic note in this passage, its sound as of one crying in the wil-

6. For a noteworthy anticipation of the proclamation of the death of God in Nietzsche's own writing, see *WS* 84. The idea of the death of God was around before Heine and Nietzsche, but it did not necessarily carry the same connotations. See Helmut Thielicke's discussion in *The Evangelical Faith*, trans. and ed. Geoffrey W. Bromiley (Grand Rapids: Eerdmans, 1974), vol. 1, chap. 14.

derness, might bring John the Baptist to mind. Nietzsche has actually been called "that unbalanced John the Baptist of the modern world."[7] He stands supreme and solitary among *"Weather prophets."*

> Just as the clouds tell us the direction of the wind high above our heads, so the lightest and freest spirits are in their tendencies foretellers of the weather that is coming. The wind in the valley and the opinions of the market-place of today indicate nothing of that which is coming but only of that which has been.[8]

Perhaps we need to go beyond John the Baptist. "My time is not yet come," says the madman. This might be an echo of John 2:4, where "Jesus replied, 'My time has not yet come'" (NIV), words spoken at the wedding in Cana of Galilee, portending further revelation. More interesting is John 7:6 (NIV): "Therefore Jesus told them, 'The time for me has not yet come; for you any time is right,'" words spoken shortly before an unexpected appearance and proclamation in the temple courts. It is more interesting because Nietzsche knew not only his New Testament but also his Schopenhauer. In *The World as Will and Representation*, Schopenhauer had written:

> Mere men of talent always come at the right time; for, as they are roused by the spirit of their age and are called into being by its needs, they are only just capable of satisfying them. . . . The genius, on the other hand, lights on his age like a comet into the paths of the planets, to whose well-regulated and comprehensible arrangement its wholly eccentric course is foreign. Accordingly, he cannot go hand in hand with the regular course of the culture of the times as found; on the contrary, he casts his works far out on the path in front. . . . His relation to the culminating men of talent during his time might be expressed in the words of the Evangelist: "My time is not yet come; but your time is always ready" (John vii, 6).[9]

The biblical text is quoted in the original Greek and not translated into German. It is hard to believe that Nietzsche is not echoing Schopenhauer here and so making some allusion to Jesus. Yet, if he wanted readers to recognize biblical language, he did not make it flat-footedly unambiguous. In the German translation of the Johannine text famil-

---

7. Evelyn Underhill, *Mysticism* (London: Methuen, 1914), 32.

8. *WS* 330. Observe the reference to the marketplace as in the parable of the madman. Cf. Z, "Prologue," 3.

9. Arthur Schopenhauer, *The World as Will and Representation*, 2 vols. (New York: Dover, 1966), 2:390–91.

iar to Nietzsche, we do not have the grammatical forms that Nietzsche used.[10] But whatever is going on, it is portentous.

The end of theism, the death of God, the end of Christianity—Nietzsche does not encourage us to make distinctions in relation to this passage. If there are distinctions, what counts against one really counts against all. Intellectually, it has all ended. What about socially and culturally? Even if belief will linger, we have arrived at the close of an epoch. To repeat: "There will never again be a life and culture bounded by a religiously determined horizon" (*HH* 234). Not in Europe, anyway, even if religion survives, say, in a Buddhist form.[11] This is a hugely momentous business. It sits well with the conviction that the free spirit of inquiry can be neither simply free nor simply merry. We cannot forget Dionysus. Innate cosmic tragedy is conjoined with historic cultural crisis. The responsible spirit should be extraordinarily burdened. It is burdened with the present and the future. It is also burdened by Christianity that is culturally alive and well, both in institutional glory and in the shape of a moral shadow, both in familiar ecclesial form and in ersatz products such as democratic, egalitarian socialism, which is really Christianity in a different key. "After Buddha was dead, they still showed his shadow in a cave for centuries—a tremendous, gruesome shadow. God is dead; but given the way people are, there may still for millennia be caves in which they show his shadow.—And we—we must still defeat his shadow as well!" (*GS* 108).

The death of God means that we are entering into a passage of time fraught with peril. Christianity has stirred everything up.

> The whole burden of culture . . . has become so great that an over-excitation of the nervous and thinking powers is now a universal danger; indeed, the cultivated classes of Europe have in fact become altogether neurotic, and almost every one of its great families has come close to lunacy in any rate [*sic*] one of its branches. . . . We have Christianity, the philosophers, poets, musicians to thank for an abundance of profound sensations. . . . It is principally through Christianity that this stream [of belief in ultimate definitive truths] has grown so turbulent. (*HH* 244)

In the preface to *BGE*, Nietzsche says:

> The struggle against Plato, or, to use a clear and "popular" idiom, the struggle against the Christian-ecclesiastical pressure of millennia—since

10. Nietzsche says: "*Ich bin noch nicht an der Zeit.*" The New Testament text that he would have used has the possessive (*meine*) in the German, though the word *Zeit* does appear in John 7:6.

11. Both *A* and the unpublished notes that go into *WP* are among the works that indicate Nietzsche's interest in Buddhism.

Christianity is Platonism for "the people"—has created a magnificent tension of spirit in Europe, the likes of which the earth has never known: with such a tension in our bow we can now shoot at the furthest goals.

Finely said, but is Nietzsche's gripe against Christianity predicated on his assumption that Christianity is basically Platonist, or is it a gripe against Christianity just at major but selected points where Christianity appears to him to be Platonist?

The double difficulty involved in adequately answering this question is that the task of interpreting Nietzsche is compounded by the requirement that we make a substantive judgment on the extent to which Christianity and Platonism are compatible. Certainly, Nietzsche closely links the two phenomena. There is a fragment in *TI* to which allusion is often made in the literature: "How the 'Real World' Finally Became a Fable," subtitled "History of an Error" (4). Christianity and Platonism are partners in crime. Both ascribe reality to the "unattainable, undemonstrable" transcendent world. In the wake of philosophical positivism, the abolition of this world fortunately terminates "the longest error." At the very time, then, when Nietzsche's authorship is progressing to its anti-Christian climax, Plato and Platonism are in the dock. In a letter of 1887, Nietzsche could echo what he said in the preface to *BGE* and call Plato "Europe's greatest misfortune."[12]

Those who want to distance Christianity from Plato and Platonism, regarding mutual concord or partial assimilation as theologically disastrous, might think that they can take something of the sting out of Nietzsche's criticism of Christianity by insisting on their dissociation. It is certainly not a negligible maneuver. There is quite a startling passage in one of Nietzsche's notes:

> Christianity has accustomed us to the superstitious concept of the "soul," the "immortal soul," soul-monads that really are at home somewhere else and have only by chance fallen, as it were into this or that condition, into the "earthly" and become "flesh"; but their essence is not held to be affected, to say nothing of being conditioned, by all this. Social, family, historical circumstances are for the soul only incidental, perhaps embarrassments. (*WP* 765)

At first blush, it may seem that Nietzsche is not committing himself to saying that this is Christian teaching, just that Christianity has "accustomed us" to this, perhaps by being responsible for the transmission of (Platonic? gnostic? Manichaean?) elements that may not have been native to its fundamental theology. However, the context in *WP* inclines

12. *SL*, January 1887. Plato is "the great viaduct of corruption" (*WP* 202).

one to believe that Nietzsche thinks he is describing Christianity here. Yet the evidence of *WP* has to be treated quite cautiously; it amounts to unpublished notes subsequently compiled and edited, about which more than one set of questions can be asked.[13]

Nevertheless, it is doubtful whether the dissociation of Christianity from Platonism, to the extent that it is judged desirable, and the identification of those elements in Nietzsche that appear to conflate Christianity and Platonism, would significantly modify Nietzsche's criticism of Christianity. In 1866, Nietzsche wrote: "If Christianity means 'Belief in an historical event or in an historical person' then I'll have nothing to do with Christianity. But if it means simply the need of redemption, then I can value it highly."[14] He certainly moved on from that outlook. For he found in the Christian understanding of sin and redemption the most noxious weed in world history, both undergirded by and, in turn, generating a lamentable view of humanity. But these words reveal that Platonism is not the problem. So it remains at the end of Nietzsche's days. "The Christian conception of God—God as God of the sick, God as spider, God as spirit—is one of the most corrupt conceptions of God arrived at on earth."[15] Here we are beyond Plato; as far as Nietzsche is concerned, it is not Platonic Christianity or Christianity understood as Platonism that should have withered away and absolutely must do so. If not the Platonic element, what induces such strong language in the assault on Christianity? The answer is this: the Christian understanding of humankind, which permits the doctrines of God, sin, and redemption that are peculiar to Christianity. From the very beginning, this is Nietzsche's big stumbling block.

Miserable Humanity

Christianity, on the other hand, crushed and shattered man completely and buried him as though in mud: into a feeling of total depravity it then

13. There is celebrated disagreement among Nietzsche scholars on the use to which this material should be put in an account of Nietzsche's thought. Even if we accord it a status equal to the published work, questions arise about the arrangement of the material. I have continued to use the Kaufmann and Hollingdale edition of *WP*, but I have sought to bear in mind the relevant issues. See Friedrich W. Nietzsche, *Writings from the Late Notebooks*, ed. Rüdiger Bittner (Cambridge: Cambridge University Press, 2003), ix–xxxiv.

14. *SL*, April 7, 1866.

15. *A* 18; cf. Michel Foucault, "Nietzsche, Genealogy and History," in *Language, Counter-memory, Practice: Selected Essays and Interviews*, ed. Donald F. Bouchard (Ithaca, NY: Cornell University Press, 1979), 155, on the "inverse of the Christian world, spun entirely by a divine spider, . . . without providence or final cause." In *WS* 46, Nietzsche speaks of God as the "cloaca of the soul," that is, the channel along which filthy soul-sewage is pumped out.

suddenly shone a beam of divine mercy, so that, surprised and stupefied by this act of grace, man gave vent to a cry of rapture and for a moment believed he bore all heaven within him. It is upon this pathological excess of feeling, upon the profound corruption of head and heart that was required for it, that all the psychological sensations of Christianity operate. (*HH* 114)

"On the other hand"—as opposed to what one finds in the Greeks, sponsors of the Homeric and Olympian gods. The contrast is all-important. The more we read Nietzsche, the more we should appreciate that the forcefulness of his anti-Christianity derives from the power of his alternative vision, something of which I shall present in the next chapter. The Greeks have already provided much of it, which is why we gave time to them in the first chapter. But in this chapter I explore the negative trail, the no-saying trail. The words quoted above follow a statement of the intellectual absurdity of Christian doctrine. They well capture Nietzsche's view of its soteriological misery and appear near the beginning of the discussion of Christianity in this, his first work to attack it directly. Here Nietzsche sets the tone for a great deal that follows in his literature in relation to Christianity. He picks out the bull's-eye of his target.

Sin is a central Christian preoccupation, and Plato cannot be blamed for that. "It was Christianity which first painted the Devil on the world's wall; it was Christianity which first brought sin into the world" (*WS* 78). If we study the principal passages where Nietzsche concentrates his observations on Christianity in these three free-spirited works, we shall find that the question of sin and redemption is the consistent major concern.[16] Nietzsche considered it "the presupposition of Christianity that all men are great sinners and do nothing whatever except sin" (*WS* 156). Christianity "invented the repellent flaunting of sin" (*D* 29). Judgment and damnation naturally follow. Think what this racket produces in us. From a historical point of view, in a wearied Roman Empire, Christianity "is the religion of antiquity grown old," promoting "a general uglification of man" (*AOM* 224; *HH* 247; cf. *D* 71–72). You name it, and Christianity has now produced it: profound self-dissatisfaction, guilt, soul torment, self-contempt, self-hatred, habitual shame, despair, and sickening submissive obeisance.[17]

As the whole business is, from an intellectual viewpoint, grounded in a colossal and grotesque error, so the corresponding need for redemption is obviously a fiction (*HH* 476). Anybody with half a brain should be able to see that Christ obviously did not redeem humanity (*AOM* 98).

16. *HH* 108–44; *D* 57–96; *GS* 122–51.

17. *D*, in particular, contains much along these lines (e.g., 60, 69, 75, 77–79, 94, 130, 321, 546).

As a matter of fact, Christian soteriology is so far removed from any kind of intellectual credibility that one cannot even intelligibly discuss such things as the Reformation position on justification (*AOM* 226). And so, from early on, Nietzsche seeks a psychological interpretation of why Christians embrace these doctrines (*HH* 132–37). It is probably not profitable to consider all Nietzsche's angles here; a variety of things are said with a variety of force. In good nineteenth-century style, Nietzsche makes remarks about the origin as well as the psychology of religion. Later we shall look at origins in relation to morality generally, rather than religion specifically, because this is the more important part of his critique. As for psychological factors, there is obviously no theological problem with admitting either that these can incline people to embrace certain doctrines or that they can be evaluated negatively.

If we identify the complaint about Christian anthropology as fundamental to Nietzsche, we do not imply that he was original here. Demeaned humanity plus subservience to the law of a Creator plus complicity in the grace of redemption equals the human worm: is this much more than an echo of attacks that go back at least to Celsus, who drew out of Origen the celebrated *Contra Celsum*? Celsus has been called the "first Nietzsche," and there are certainly noteworthy affinities.[18] Yet significant overlap should not lead us to exaggerate similarity.[19] Much of the time, Origen has to correct sheer misunderstanding, which is a major basis of Celsus's mockery. Celsus has to be enlightened all the time on the nature of Christian self-understanding; where Nietzsche caricatures one-sidedly, Celsus appears to be genuinely ignorant. Celsus and Nietzsche share revulsion at the Christian view of humanity, but Celsus appears to make much more of the intellectual absurdity of Christianity than of its demeaning view of humanity, or at least, the proportions of their respective critiques differ. However, if similarity should not be exaggerated, neither should difference.[20] Our present interest in Nietzsche is confined to the identification of what is central to him, not concerned with whether or how he is original.

18. Thomas F. Bertonneau, "Celsus, the First Nietzsche: Resentment and the Case against Christianity," *Anthropoetics: The Electronic Journal of Generative Anthropology* 3, no. 1 (Spring/Summer, 1997); online: http://www.humnet.ucla.edu/humnet/anthropoet ics/Ap0301/CELSUS.htm.

19. Bertonneau (ibid.) is heavily dependent on Joseph Hoffmann, who, working from Origen's *Contra Celsum*, extracted and translated the substance of Celsus's work *On the True Doctrine: A Discourse against the Christians* (New York and Oxford: Oxford University Press, 1987). Yet we gain a much better sense of where the weight of Celsus's criticism lay, at least as Origen reports it, if we concentrate on Origen's own *Contra Celsum*, trans. Henry Chadwick (Cambridge: Cambridge University Press, 1980). I am not suggesting that Bertonneau makes no serious use of this.

20. Bertonneau ("Celsus") makes some important points in this respect.

Nietzsche's distaste for the Christian scheme of things is underpinned by two related beliefs that form a bedrock of his analysis. The first is that we cannot legitimately bring to life criteria external to it in order to evaluate it. How can we? Life is here, here in its raw actuality, with its impulses and energies. To say that something is *wrong* with *life* as *such* is an absurd deployment of a fabricated scheme of moral evaluation. The second is that Christianity is antilife. If there is a nub to Nietzsche's objection to Christianity, it is that. Its scheme of sin and redemption clamps religious-moral evaluation upon life and proceeds to offer deliverance from it by proposing to us a saving reality. If we trace the line of treatment in *The Anti-christ*, we shall gather a good idea of Nietzsche's opposition, shrill as his language is.[21] From its beginning, *A* exudes the aura of discovery; millennia of error are being exposed. Without hesitation it launches into an attack on Christianity, which is a glorification of powerlessness, "active sympathy for the ill-constituted and weak" (2). Correspondingly, the Christian is "the domestic animal, the herd animal, the sick animal" (3). Opposed, as it is, to strong preservative instincts, Christianity has retarded human progress. Life, on the other hand, is will-to-power.[22]

"Will-to-power" is a key Nietzschean idea, but its interpretation is controversial. Just how much Nietzsche positively owed to Darwin is debatable, but where Darwin regards an organism according to its self-preserving quality, Nietzsche posits the maximization of its power.[23] Put baldly like this, Nietzsche seems to be propounding a form of metaphysical naturalism. On the other hand, what he says about epistemology and language, realism and perspectivism, appears to undercut any effort to adopt a positive metaphysic. Wherever we come down on the interpretation of Nietzsche, he clearly advocates that we *regard* life in terms of will-to-power in the biological sense, which identifies the inner dynamic and constitutional tendency of the living organism as the unfolding of living power. If Nietzsche is proposing that we *see* life this way without a metaphysically realistic commitment to claims about how life is, is he guilty of imposing on life an evaluation external to it, of the kind that he theoretically rejects? Possibly, but if so, it is an evaluation that goes with the grain of life as it manifests itself to us and not against it, as Christians advocate. However, perhaps a version of realistic positivism still lies at the bottom of all this.

21. In what follows, I am scurrying lightly but sequentially through selected portions of *A*.

22. Cf., e.g., *WP* 254, 619.

23. Nietzsche writes "Anti-Darwin" in *TI* 9.14, and some of his main protests against Darwin are gathered in *WP* 640–87. We are not concerned with what Darwin said, only with Nietzsche's take on Darwin.

However we interpret him, Nietzsche in *A* proceeds to castigate the guild of theologians who have revalued life against itself. They have infected the philosophers. Kant came down with a bad case of the disease. He took hold of the idea that life must be subject to moral law. As a matter of fact, an "action compelled by the instinct of life has in the joy of performing it the proof it is a *right* action"—properly, life itself is valuation—but Kant, "that nihilist with Christian-dogmatic bowels understands joy as an *objection.* . . . The erring instinct in all and everything, *anti-naturalness* as instinct, German *decadence* as philosophy—*that is Kant!*—" (11). Kant caught the bug from Christianity, which devised its own fictional world, starring God and the nexus of doctrines in his heavenly entourage, a world "which has its roots in *hatred* of the natural (—actuality!—), it is the expression of a profound discontent with the actual" (15). We are dealing here not only with the "hatred of *mind*, of pride, courage, freedom, *libertinage* of mind" but also "of *senses*, of the joy of the senses, of joy in general" (21). Christianity has only "*bad* ends: the poisoning, slandering, denying of life, contempt for the body, the denigration and self-violation of man through the concept of sin" (56).

It is this launching pad that catapults Nietzsche toward the crescendo with which I began the preface to this volume. Christianity is vampire and vermin. "Christianity was the vampire of the *Imperium Romanum*," and the Christian was "vermin" on top of vampire, "stealthy vermin," we might add, "which, shrouded in night, fog and ambiguity crept up to every individual and sucked seriousness for *real* things, the instinct for *realities* of any kind, out of him" (58). This is what the Renaissance failed to undo because it was throttled by the Reformation; this is what makes Germany a shame before humanity and Christianity a crime against it. "I call Christianity the *one* great curse, the *one* great intrinsic depravity, the *one* great instinct for revenge for which no expedient is sufficiently poisonous, secret, subterranean, *petty*—I call it the *one* immortal blemish of mankind" (62). Shrill as it is and unbalanced as it has seemed to many, *A* expresses what is essentially there as early as *HH* regarding the misery of Christianity.

More than once I have noted Nietzsche's neglect of the Christian attitude toward creation. We encounter much the same thing here again, for he treats Christian theological anthropology simply as the doctrine of the sinner and not of the creature. "If man is sinful through and through, then he ought only to hate himself" (*WP* 388). Nietzsche's inference might be justified, given the way he understands his premises, but the way he understands the premises is not the way Christianity understands humanity. We must respond either that (1) humans are not "sinful through and through," if what is meant by this is that they are sinful and only sinful through and through, or that (2) humans are indeed sinful through and through, if what we mean is that every part of our humanity is affected by sin but that they are both sinful through and through and good through and through according to their creatureliness.[24] Cut it as you will, the concept "sinner" in Christianity is parasitic on the concept "creature," and the concept "creature" entails goodness.

Nietzsche is not enamored of the idea of humanity as divine creation; creation and fall are ludicrous ideas (*WP* 224, 765). But at least let us be clear what Christians are saying or should be saying. On a theological account of things, the creation was created good, very good, in its reality, materiality, and sensuality. This is foundational biblical teaching, not some canonical aside. To fail to treat it is to fail to treat Christianity. In their own reality, materiality, and sensuality, humans differ from the good nonhuman creation not by being its opposite but by being its crown, its exemplar, its extreme case. God cannot clone himself, but he creates humanity in his image. Adam is the son of God (Luke 3:38). This may not be high enough for Nietzsche, but at least he ought to reckon with it. Everything but God was put under humanity; everything was permitted but the one tree whose fruit was self-division, a condition regarded by Nietzsche as lying at the monstrous heart of theological anthropology. Redemption is the restoration of creation, and more than restoration. It is creation recalled, rescued, restored, and remade; it is humanity reconstituted as its head. Hence, Jesus, its messianic heir, is constituted in his humanity as head of the new order on behalf of humanity and under God. Fall and sin mean the dispossession of creation and the forfeiture of the privileges of exalted humanity. Salvation is surplus repossession.

What Nietzsche apparently ignores, and what perhaps the church has often failed to emphasize enough at different times, is a major rubric under which the biblical narrative is offered: the dignity and goodness of creation. This has been emphasized by theologians for some decades, yet it bears repetition in a treatment of Nietzsche. Those who accuse Christianity of promulgating a life-denying ordinance that demeans humanity owe us an exposition of its doctrine of creation. But are we presupposing here the intellectual legitimacy of treating biblical theology as a whole, or at least using the beginning of the Hebrew Bible to interpret Christian doctrine? Yes, and rightly so, but Nietzsche effectively questions the presupposition. *BGE* is worth quoting at some length:

> In the Jewish "Old Testament," the book of divine justice, there are men, things and speeches of so grand a style that Greek and Indian literature

24. We could multiply considerations: if humans were sinful through and through in the way Nietzsche seems to have in mind—sinners and nothing but sinners, vile as can be—would they actually be able to hate themselves? An examination of self-hatred would be helpful in a more substantial study of Nietzsche.

have nothing to set beside it. One stands in reverence and trembling before these remnants of what man once was and has sorrowful thoughts about old Asia and its little jutting-out promontory Europe, which would like to signify as against Asia the "progress of man." To be sure: he who is only a measly tame domestic animal and knows only the needs of a domestic animal (like our cultured people of today, the Christians of "cultured" Christianity included—) has no reason to wonder, let alone to sorrow, among those ruins—the taste for the Old Testament is a touchstone in regard to "great" and "small"—: perhaps he will find the New Testament, the book of mercy, more after his own heart (there is in it a great deal of the genuine delicate, musty odour of devotee and petty soul). To have glued this New Testament, a species of rococo taste in every respect, on the Old Testament to form a single book, as "bible," as "the book of books": that is perhaps the greatest piece of temerity and "sin against the spirit" that literary Europe has on its conscience. (52)[25]

So the gulf is not just between Christianity and the Greeks but also between Old and New Testaments. Yet there is still plenty amiss with the Old. "The history of Israel," says Nietzsche in *A*, "is invaluable as a typical history of the *denaturalizing* of natural values" (25), and he takes us through the whole sorry story.[26] Originally, "Israel . . . stood in a *correct*, that is to say natural relationship to all things. Their Yahweh was the expression of their [Israelites'] consciousness of power, of their delight in themselves, their hopes in themselves." With the nonfulfillment of national hopes, following the captivity of the North, Israel should have given up Yahweh. He had had a good day, as long as it lasted. Unfortunately, the priests began operating. They interpreted misfortune in terms of sin, "altered the conception" of Yahweh, and thereby moralized God. Thus, a moral world order is substituted for a natural one. Although the concept of sin is actually the effect of misfortune, the cause of misfortune is theologically blamed on sin. Morality, a kind of hypostasized abstraction, is established as reality and becomes a normative and evaluative entity whereby the deepest and most natural instincts of a nation's life are measured. Under the Jewish priesthood that instigated this change in outlook, the entire history of Israel was worked over. The "Bible" emerged, produced to retell the story of Israel in terms of a "stupid salvation-mechanism of guilt towards Yahweh and punishment, piety towards Yahweh and reward." The great preexilic days were transformed into an epoch of decay, the exile into a type of eternal punishment. "On

25. Cf. *OGM* 3.12. See also *D* 84 on the "philological farce" of the Christian treatment of the Old Testament.

26. By the time Nietzsche has run this line through the New Testament, it has taken up a considerable portion of *A*, but I am taking only a segment of the argument from 25 onward.

a soil *falsified* in this way, where all nature, all natural value, all *reality* had the profoundest instincts of the ruling class against it, there arose *Christianity*, a form of mortal hostility to reality as yet unsurpassed." So it is not simply a case of Old versus New Testament; it is the earliest stratum of the Old versus the moralizing development, which is given its particular twist in the New. We have come a long way. "Christianity is a revolt of everything that crawls along the ground directed against that which is *elevated*" (*A* 43).

The evidence is that Nietzsche was particularly influenced by his reading of Julius Wellhausen. What bothers Nietzsche most of all about the moralizing process is the type of person thus produced, hence, the first sentence in the above quotation from *BGE*. Certainly, thought-provoking questions arise for Christians. Is it literally only the childish consciousness and imagination that can, without scenting inconsistency, simultaneously laud the heroism and heroics of the men of old, whose names stand out like mountain peaks on the Israelite landscape—Moses and Gideon, Joshua and Samson, Samuel and Saul, David and Jehu—and approvingly hear the New Testament injunctions to gentleness and forbearance? When the child's view of things is later modified and we begin to discriminate between the more and less godly individuals in the four pairs above, should we proceed to conclude that it is impossible to fuse an ideal humanity out of the mighty Israelite and humble New Testament canonical types?

Theological talk of "ideal humanity" is christological talk, and we come to that in chapter 6. Meanwhile, if we are taking the canon as a whole, we encounter types, models, or modes of humanity that have their significant differences, and all have their time. Adam is rather obscurely colorless, with little space afforded to his portrayal, but he is certainly not Joshua, a man after God's own heart under conditions of warfare and strife.[27] The New Testament convert is a person after God's own heart under conditions that advertise the eventual eschatological cessation of warfare and strife. The inhabitant of the new earth is God's person when messianic peace reigns. Different dispensations call forth a variety in the forms of human ideal.

This point is probably less important than the fact that Nietzsche simply misunderstands the portrayal of what we might call the New Testament type. The early church was full of rough diamonds called to rechannel their riotous energies by the strength of self-control in the Spirit; they were not natural wimps encouraged to turn pathetic necessity into the virtue of spiritual wimpery. One gets the impression that Nietz-

27. This description is drawn from the biblical designation of David (1 Sam. 13:14), but I am seeking a compromise candidate between one whose disposition perhaps gladdens the Nietzschean heart, but not the Christian heart (Samson), and vice versa (David).

sche sometimes thought in these latter terms. Nietzsche denies what he truly does find in the New Testament, but he also projects illusory light onto it. Although it is a mistake to interpret his anti-Christianity mainly in terms of the churches of his day, his own experience of contemporary Christianity must have played a part here. Nietzsche's overall verdict on the New Testament is sweeping:

> One does well to put gloves on when reading the New Testament. The proximity of so much uncleanliness almost forces one to do so. One would no more choose to associate with "first Christians" than one would with Polish Jews: not that one would need to prove so much as a single point against them. . . . Neither of them smell very pleasant.—I have looked in vain for so much as one sympathetic trait in the New Testament; there is nothing free, benevolent, open-hearted, honest in it. (*A* 46)

Compare Karl Barth on the eve of his theological breakthrough:

> During the work [on Paul's Epistle to the Romans] it was often as though I caught a breath from afar, from Asia Minor or Corinth, something primaeval, from the ancient East, indefinably sunny, wild, original, that somehow is hidden behind these sentences. Paul—what a man he must have been and what men also those for whom he could so sketch and hint at these pithy things in a few muddled fragments! . . . And then *behind* Paul: what realities those must have been that could excite the man in such a way! What a lot of far-fetched stuff we compile about his remarks, when perhaps ninety-nine per cent of their real content escapes us![28]

Nietzsche has some choice things to say about Paul. In *A*, Paul is credited with developing the theology of atonement and immortality to its canonically extreme point of antithesis to the natural and the vital.[29] Paul is a dishonest, vengeful powermonger. In *D* we have a fuller analysis under the rubric of "The first Christian" (68). The origins of Christianity come to light in Paul's writings: Saul of Tarsus's fanatical zeal for the law concealed a sin-laden conscience and "even more . . . lust for domination." Then it dawned on him that the cross might be interpreted as the fulfillment and abolition of the law, so he flipped over into antilaw mode. That nicely takes care of the torments of his soul, and more nicely still, "the intractable lust for power reveals itself as an anticipatory revelling in *divine* glories." In late unpublished notes "toward a psychology of *Paul*," Nietzsche mused:

28. As quoted in Eberhard Busch, *Karl Barth: His Life from Letters and Autobiographical Texts* (London: SCM, 1976), 98–99.
29. *A* 42–45. E.g.: "If one shifts the centre of the gravity of life *out* of life into the 'Beyond'—into *nothingness*—one has deprived life as such of its centre of gravity" (43).

The given fact is the death of Jesus. This has to be explained—That an explanation may be true or false has never entered the minds of such people as these: one day a sublime possibility comes into their heads: "this death *could* mean such and such"—and at once it does mean such and such! A hypothesis is proved true by the sublime impetus it imparts to its originator. (*WP* 171)

In contrast to all this from Nietzsche, if we care to heed Paul himself, moral dissolution was as far from him as could be when he encountered Christ. According to Nietzsche, however, "many things lay on his [Paul's] conscience—he hints at enmity, murder, sorcery, idolatry, uncleanliness, drunkenness and pleasure in debauch."[30] While, in fact, Paul gives all the appearance of having strenuously thought through the relation of Christ to the Judaism in which he had been reared, Nietzsche avers that he unthinkingly believes a notion that has popped into his head. It may well be wondered why anyone should take Nietzsche seriously on these points.[31]

But Paul is accorded an interesting title in *D* 68: he is "the Jewish Pascal." It is instructive to investigate Pascal in the light of what Nietzsche has to say about him.[32]

Pascal

That I do not read Pascal but *love* him, as the most instructive of all sacrifices to Christianity, slowly murdered first physically then psychologically, the whole logic of this most horrible form of inhuman cruelty; that I have something of Montaigne's wantonness in my spirit, who knows?[33]

30. Morgan H. Rempel in *"Daybreak* 68: Nietzsche's Psychohistory of the Pre-Damascus Paul," *Journal of Nietzsche Studies* 15 (1998): 58–59, fails to consider Phil. 3:6, though this fact need not undermine other things in his exposition. The Lutheran reading of Paul that doubtless influenced Nietzsche one way or another has been a lively and contentious topic of theological debate for some time.

31. Compare the humility of Ludwig Wittgenstein's tone when expressing his reservations about Paul in *Culture and Value* (Oxford: Blackwell, 1980), 30.

32. Tim Murphy rightly warns us against putting too much weight on what Nietzsche says about Paul at the expense of what he makes of the early Christian community more generally: *Nietzsche, Metaphor, Religion* (Albany: State University of New York Press, 2001), chap. 8. In his essay "Nietzsche's Understanding of the Apostle Paul," in *Studies in Nietzsche and the Judaeo-Christian Tradition,* ed. James C. O'Flaherty, Timothy F. Sellner, and Robert M. Helm (Chapel Hill: University of North Carolina Press, 1985), Jörg Salaquarda argues that Nietzsche moved from seeing Paul as one of the principal figures to seeing him as the decisive figure in the origins of Christianity.

33. *EH,* "Why I Am So Clever," 3. The contrast with Montaigne would be helpfully illuminated by looking at Montaigne, but it would take us too far afield. I was guilty of turning this question into an affirmation in Stephen N. Williams, *Revelation and Reconciliation: A Window on Modernity* (Cambridge: Cambridge University Press, 1995), 20.

Pascal, like Montaigne, was one of Nietzsche's eight shades. In *AOM*, Nietzsche numbered four pairs of figures in the underworld with whom he could converse, from whom he would "accept judgement," to whom he would "listen when in so doing they judge one another" (408). They are Epicurus and Montaigne, Goethe and Spinoza, Plato and Rousseau, Pascal and Schopenhauer. In light of Nietzsche's hostility to Christianity, Pascal is an outstanding presence in this company.[34] Nietzsche's respect for Pascal is noble respect for a worthy enemy. He could "almost love" Pascal, he said, "because he has taught me such an infinite amount—the only *logical* Christian."[35] Yet Nietzsche offers his observations about Christianity having "taken the side of everything weak, base, ill-constituted" and "made an ideal out of *opposition* to the preservative instincts of strong life." Then he avers that "it has depraved the reason even of the intellectually strongest natures by teaching men to feel the supreme values of intellectuality as sinful, as misleading, as *temptations*" (*A* 5). The supreme example, meaning the "most deplorable example," is that of Pascal. Pascal's faith "has the gruesome appearance of a protracted suicide of reason" (*BGE* 46). Christianity has corrupted both Pascal's reason and what Pascal thinks of reason. Further, Pascal exemplifies the Christian view of humanity beyond the call of epistemological duty. For he has a characteristically Christian self-hatred probably extended "towards mankind as a whole" (*D* 63).

> Christianity possesses the hunter's instinct for all those who can by one means or another be brought to despair—of which only a portion of mankind is capable. It is constantly on their track, it lies in wait for them. Pascal attempted the experiment of seeing whether, with the aid of the most incisive knowledge, everyone could not be brought to despair: the experiment miscarried, to his twofold despair. (*D* 64)

Voltaire memorably dubbed Pascal "the sublime misanthropist."[36] Pascal is unusually interesting for anyone who wants to penetrate Nietzsche's critique of Christianity, quite apart from possessing the intrinsic interest of a seventeenth-century believer whose writings can be read with such extreme profit in modern and postmodern times. A perusal of Pascal

---

Nietzsche is presumably making the affirmation, but it is well to leave it as a grammatical interrogative.

34. This is not to pronounce on the religion of Montaigne or Rousseau, but the religion of Pascal is cut from an entirely different cloth.

35. *SL*, November 20, 1888.

36. Voltaire, *Letters on England* (Harmondsworth, UK: Penguin, 1980), 25, 120. Voltaire's response to Pascal is altogether more challenging than Nietzsche's. In light of Nietzsche's reference to Pascal inducing despair, observe Rousseau's accusation that Voltaire tries to bring us to despair: see Bertrand Russell, *History of Western Philosophy* (London: Allen & Unwin, 1961), 664.

enables us to see how terribly one-sided, at best, Nietzsche was in his account of practically the only Christian enemy worth having. Nietzsche ignores the elements of Pascal's work that directly impinge on his own criticisms. We need to pause with Pascal, who without God, it has been said, was "the most accomplished of nihilists," and without God was reincarnated in the Marquis de Sade.[37]

Pascal prioritizes the question of truth as ardently as does Nietzsche himself. "The sincere quest for truth alone brings peace," though there is a difference "between peace and the certainty of conscience. Truth alone brings certainty."[38] As Nietzsche speaks in *HH* of "Man on His Own" and wearies of the rabble, so Pascal says:

> It is absurd of us to rely on the company of our fellows, as wretched and helpless as we are; they will not help us; we shall die alone. We must act then as if we were alone. If that were so, would we build superb houses etc? We should unhesitatingly look for the truth. And, if we refuse, it shows that we have a higher regard for men's esteem than for pursuing the truth. (211)

This entails placing a premium on thinking, and Pascal is again at one with Nietzsche in the importance he attaches to it. "Man is obviously made for thinking. There lies all his dignity and his merit, and his whole duty is to think as he ought."[39] Faith does not contradict the imperative either to seek truth or to think. "There are few true Christians. I mean even as regards faith. There are plenty who believe, but out of superstition. There are plenty who do not believe, but because they are libertines; there are few in between" (179). Here we might recall Nietzsche's tribute:

> One cannot deny that the French have been *the most Christian* nation on earth: not because the faith of the masses has been greater in France than elsewhere, but because the most difficult Christian ideals have been transformed into men and not remained merely ideas, beginnings, falter-

37. These descriptions by Suárez and by Crocker—quoted in Thomas V. Morris, *Making Sense of It All: Pascal and the Meaning of Life* (Grand Rapids: Eerdmans, 1992), 11—are dangerous and misleading but nonetheless significant. Nothing that follows is affected by the story of the successive editorial arrangements of Pascal's *Pensées* between Pascal's time and Nietzsche's or between Nietzsche's time and ours.

38. Blaise Pascal, *Pensées*, trans. A. J. Krailsheimer (London: Penguin, 1966), 599. References from now on are usually in the text and are to the sections and not the pages in Krailsheimer's edition.

39. Ibid., 620. However, he continues: "Now the order of thought is to begin with ourselves, and with our author and our end." The salient point of positive comparison with Nietzsche, though, is picked up again at the end of the section, in Pascal's remark about the world's failure to think about "what it means to be a king or to be a man."

ings. There stands Pascal, in unity of fervour, spirit and honesty the first of all Christians. (*D* 192)

In the passage above, where he distinguishes between faith and superstition, Pascal concludes: "I do not include those who lead a really devout life, nor all those who believe by intuition of the heart." Is true faith, then, on the one hand bound to the search for truth, committed to the supreme dignity of thought, distanced from superstition, and on the other hand just an "intuition of the heart"? Quite early in life Nietzsche concluded that something like this is the case with faith, and in contradistinction he aimed to bestow its rightful place on reason. Is Nietzsche right, then, that, for all his pretensions, Pascal practically sacrificed reason? It is dreadfully hard—indeed, impossible—to buy that interpretation. In any comprehensive negotiating of our way around Pascal's various statements, we must certainly be prepared to find contrasting emphases, if not inconsistencies. But we also find certain quite clear and prominent trajectories of thought, and it is difficult to expose oneself seriously to Pascal and emerge with the judgment that is often offered, that he was a fideist. Keeping within lines that relate to Nietzsche's own position on Christianity, it is profitable to ask about Pascalian reason.

Divine wisdom declares as follows: "I do not demand of you blind faith" (149). Near the beginning of Pascal's papers, as classified in the edition we are following, we read:

> *Order*. Men despise religion. They hate it and are afraid it may be true. The cure for this is first to show that religion is not contrary to reason, but worthy of reverence and respect. Next make it attractive, make good men wish it were true, and then show that it is. Worthy of reverence because it really understands human nature. Attractive because it promises true good. (12)

Things become rationally stronger, however, than the claim that faith is not contrary to reason. Pascal is eager for us to get things straight here. In the first section of the chapter "Submission and Use of Reason," we read: "Submission and use of reason; that is what makes true Christianity" (167). "The way of God, who disposes all things with gentleness, is to instil religion into our minds with reasoned arguments and into our hearts with grace, but attempting to instil it into our hearts and minds with force and threats is to instil not religion but terror. *Terror rather than religion*" (172). Nietzsche might scoff at divine gentleness and point out that on this point we are to read pacific Pascalian protestations of antiterrorism in the light of later threats.[40] But Pascal, convincingly

40. "One of the ways in which the damned will be confounded is that they will see themselves condemned by their own reason, by which they claimed to condemn the

or not, adduces evidences for Christian belief, demonstrating that his
point about reasoned argument is not only theoretically important but
also followed through in practice. Whatever else it is doing, the contrast
between mind and heart is not undermining reasoned argument. It is
rather a question of putting everything in its proper place, as it is in the
Augustinian tradition to which Pascal belongs. Nietzsche gives him no
credit whatsoever for this.

"One must know when it is right to doubt, to affirm, to submit. Anyone who does otherwise does not understand the force of reason" (170).
Pascal is just endorsing Augustine: "Reason would never submit unless
it judged that there are occasions when it ought to submit" (174). Self-
limitation is a form of self-regulation. "There is nothing so consistent
with reason as this denial of reason" (182). The "denial" of reason is
not a priori, not the product of faith's wicked fiat. It is the terminus of
rational processes. "Reason's last step is the recognition that there are
an infinite number of things which are beyond it. It is merely feeble if
it does not go so far as to realize that" (188). So, pithily, there are "two
excesses: to exclude reason, to admit nothing but reason" (183).

Where do we draw the line? Superficially, it may appear that reason
is capacitated for the natural while faith is geared to the sphere of the
supernatural. If so, Pascal may appear deliberately to be courting rational
mystery in order to set up another (supernatural) realm where faith can
frolic. This is how Nietzsche likely understands him. Those who concur
in Pascal's claim that if "we offend the principles of reason our religion
will be absurd and ridiculous" might understandably be suspicious on
learning at the same time that if "we submit everything to reason our
religion will be left with nothing mysterious or supernatural" (173).
However, the natural/supernatural distinction does not structurally cor-
respond to the reason/faith distinction in Pascal. The discussion on the
"Submission and Use of Reason," as we presently have it, concludes with
a question: "If natural things are beyond it, what are we to say about
supernatural things?" (188). Reason discovers its limitations within the
natural, not at the boundary of natural and supernatural.

With all his distinctiveness, Pascal's thought has affinities at this point
with the empirical tradition in seventeenth- and eighteenth-century English-speaking philosophy of religion, a tradition whose deployment of
reason Nietzsche ignores just as he effectively does in the case of Pascal.[41]

Christian religion" (175). Pascal is averring that this terrorism is partly instigated by our
own reason.

41. I am not defending the tradition, just observing how Nietzsche's averments on
Christianity and reason ignore it. See Joseph Butler's discussion in *The Analogy of Religion:
Natural and Revealed* (London: Dent, 1906), where he argues that putative obscurity in the
sphere of revelation does not warrant dismissal of revelation, because obscurity attends

But there are differences, and if we track them down from Pascal's end, we shall encounter the connection between epistemological skepticism and putative misanthropy, which Nietzsche abjures. Arguments for skepticism, according to Pascal, can be generated by the reflexive operations of reason. "It may be that there are such things as true proofs, but it is not certain" (521). In true Pyrrhonic form, Pascal adds: "But that only proves that it is not certain that everything is uncertain. To the greater glory of scepticism."[42] Because reason cannot unravel the skeptical tangle, it ought to acknowledge its own limits. Skepticism, moreover, forms a lacuna within a person, for it leaves us in a double bind: we are ignorant and we are unhappy in our ignorance. Ignorance may be wise:

> The world is a good judge of things, because it is in the state of natural ignorance where man really belongs. Knowledge has two extremes which meet; one is the pure natural ignorance of every man at birth, the other is the extreme reached by great minds who run through the whole range of human knowledge, only to find that they know nothing and come back to the same ignorance from which they set out, but it is a wise ignorance which knows itself. (83)[43]

But wise ignorance is also unhappiness:

> Ecclesiastes shows that man without God is totally ignorant and inescapably unhappy, for anyone is unhappy who wills but cannot do. Now he wants to be happy and assured of some truth, and yet he is equally incapable of knowing and of not desiring to know. He cannot even doubt. (75)

The move from epistemological skepticism to anthropological infelicity is mediated, and quite importantly so, by reflection on the humility proper

---

the realm of nature as well. More striking is a comparison between Pascal's and Locke's analyses of what is according to, contrary to, and above reason in John Locke, *An Essay on Human Understanding* (Oxford: Clarendon, 1975). Locke's argument should be picked up from around 4.14.

42. For Pyrrho and the interest in him, see Richard H. Popkin, *The History of Scepticism from Erasmus to Spinoza* (Berkeley: University of California Press, 1979). Pascal's reasoning is questionable. If "proof" is the eminent form of certainty, from the fact that we cannot be certain that there are true proofs, we might conclude that everything is uncertain. But if we bracket this claim about proof, what seems to follow from Pascal's premise is that it is certain that everything is uncertain, not that we cannot be certain that everything is uncertain. This latter claim may be true, but it does not follow from what Pascal has premised. His deduction seems to work only if the initial claim is self-referential—if the claim that "it may be that there is such a thing as true proofs, but it is not certain" itself possesses a "true proof."

43. The rest of the section must be omitted here for reasons of space, but it is rewarding to read on.

to our disposition. Pascal insists that this is the only proper attitude as we contemplate self and the universe. This comes out with special force in a long section titled "Disproportion of man" in the chapter "Transition from Knowledge of Man to Knowledge of God" (199). "Man is to himself the greatest prodigy in nature, for he cannot conceive what body is, and still less what mind is, and least of all how a body can be joined to a mind. This is his supreme difficulty, and yet it is his very being." But what does this do to us? It may make us unhappy; it should make us humble; but it contextualizes without denying the claim that humans possess greatness. "Man's greatness and wretchedness are so evident that the true religion must necessarily teach us that there is in man some great principle of greatness and some great principle of wretchedness" (149). More: "Man's greatness comes from knowing he is wretched. . . . Thus it is wretched to know that one is wretched, but there is greatness in knowing one is wretched" (114). In fact, it is dangerous and erroneous to tell people that they are wretched without telling them that they are great as well; it is as dangerous to speak of human wretchedness without human greatness as it is of human greatness without human wretchedness (e.g., 121). Nietzsche may dislike this, but one would never guess, from his remarks, that Pascal has said anything like it. Taking into account what we have just heard from Pascal, we must say that Nietzsche simply distorts the thought of his worthy Christian opponent. In the same breath, he distorts Christianity.

This is not to deny that there are important strands in Pascal to which Nietzsche can justifiably point and from which many in the Christian tradition might want to demur.[44] But Pascal everywhere tries to orient the mind to the doctrine of creation and not just the fall. He is bent on getting us to listen, not just to believe; to get a grip on our greatness, not just on our wretchedness. Nietzsche is scornful of Pascal's defense of the belief that there is something or someone to be listened to.

> A god who is all-knowing and all-powerful and who does not even make sure that his creatures understand his intentions—could that be a god of goodness? Who allows countless doubts and dubieties to persist, for thousands of years, as though the salvation of mankind were unaffected by them, and who on the other hand holds out the prospect of frightful consequences if any mistake is made as to the nature of the truth? . . . But perhaps he is a god of goodness notwithstanding—and merely *could* not express himself more clearly! . . . On the "hidden god," and on the

44. A sympathetic exponent such as Morris, *Making Sense of It All*, 202, remarks that there is "nothing in Pascal's notes so shocking to first-time readers as his strident denunciation of self-love and a completely unexpected recommendation of self-hatred."

reasons for keeping himself thus hidden and never emerging more than half-way into the light of speech, no one has been more eloquent than Pascal—a sign that he was never able to calm his mind on this matter: but his voice rings as confidently as if he had at one time sat behind the curtain with this hidden god. He sensed a piece of immorality in the *"deus absconditus"* and was very fearful and ashamed of admitting it to himself: and thus, like one who is afraid, he talked as loudly as he could. (*D* 91)

The logical problem of evil is typically couched in terms of whether God is limited in his desire or in his power to prevent evil. Nietzsche tries to impale the theistic believer in revelation on the horns of a similar dilemma.[45] He not only rejects what he takes to be the most eloquent available defense of the "hidden god," that of Pascal; he also affirms that Pascal is himself dissatisfied with it. This latter affirmation seems to be gratuitous.[46] But how does Pascal argue his point? In the chapter "At Port Royal" (149), Pascal reasons that humans want both to be self-centered and to get what they want. If revelation and redemption occur in such a context, it is an act of mercy. "God's will has been to redeem men and open the way of salvation to those who seek it, but men have shown themselves so unworthy that it is right for God to refuse to some, for their hardness of heart, what he grants to others by a mercy they have not earned." God is certainly capable of revealing himself unmistakably. But that is an eschatological prospect. If humans here and now do not actually want to know and serve God, why should he reveal himself clearly in the present?

It was therefore not right that he should appear in a manner manifestly divine and absolutely capable of convincing all men, but neither was it right that his coming should be so hidden that he could not be recognized by those who sincerely sought him. He wished to make himself perfectly recognizable to them. Thus wishing to appear openly to those who seek him with all their heart, he has qualified our knowledge of him by giving signs which can be seen by those who seek him and not by those who do not.

45. However, the same basic objection can be made without the conundrum. "The worst part of it is: he [God] seems unable to communicate in an intelligible manner: is he unclear?" (*BGE* 53).

46. "Nietzsche's post-theistic autopsy of Pascal's argument is only instructive if the idea of the hidden God is as incoherent as Nietzsche makes it. If not, his impugning of Pascal's motives is *ad hominem* and begs the question," writes Douglas Groothuis, *On Pascal* (Victoria, Australia, and Belmont, CA: Thomson/Wadsworth, 2003), 55. Of course, from a logical point of view, the argument might be coherent and Pascal yet be uneasy about it, but Groothuis is broadly correct. See his whole chapter in exposition and defense of Pascal on this point.

There is enough light for those who desire only to see and enough darkness for those of a contrary disposition.[47]

In terms of Nietzsche's conundrum, Pascal's resolution is that God
can, but does not want to, reveal himself completely and transparently
unmistakably. This would probably be perverse to the point of making
the idea of divine goodness incoherent, if humans were naturally sincere and honest seekers. They are not—something that Nietzsche, in his
way, hammers home on behalf of himself and a handful of other sincere
philosophers. So why should God be obligated to reveal himself in the
only way that Nietzsche deems consistent with God?[48] What Pascal says
about the hidden God can, in any case, not be detached from what he
says about evidences, and this occupies quite considerable stretches of
the *Pensées*. These may not be of the kind popularly touted these days,
with miracles and prophecies taking pride of place. But they indicate
the scope that Pascal gives to reason and the presence of an evidentialist
streak along with an experientialist one in his apologetic. Pascal's own
fiery certainty was not the product of a rational calculation. There are,
nevertheless, evidences of the kind that should allow no one to judge
Christianity irrational in any pejorative sense.

"A man should always wear a garment with two pockets. In one pocket,
there should be a note which reads, 'I am but dust and ashes.' In the
other pocket, there should be a paper which says, 'For me, the world was
created.'"[49] What Pascal famously carried about in a space even more
occluded than a pocket was something different, a testimony to his fiery
certainty.[50] But the Hasidic sentiment chimes in adequately well with
something that Pascal emphasizes. Nietzsche examines just one pocket
of both the specifically Pascalian and the generically Christian garment
and certainly does not run through his hands its seamless fabric. At

47. Cf. Richard Swinburne, approaching the question a priori, on the point "that
the revelation should not be too open, but something to be looked for and found," in his
Revelation: From Metaphor to Analogy (Oxford: Clarendon, 1992), 74.

48. Here I must demur at the way Morris puts things in *Making Sense of It All*. After
giving an example from human life of how easily puffed up we become when we know
someone famous, he states that "Pascal wants us to imagine what would happen if any of
us came to know God in a close encounter without being properly prepared. His suggestion is that we would quickly hit the zenith of pridefulness, as many people do who falsely
take themselves to be in special, intimate communion with God" (100–101). But that is not
Pascal's point. He is concerned about the pride that is innately ours and that contributes
decisively to the fact that divine revelation does not take a completely perspicuous form,
not the pride that would be ours if we claimed of God a knowledge by acquaintance.

49. A piece of Hasidic wisdom quoted in Thomas V. Morris, *If Aristotle Ran General
Motors: The New Soul of Business* (New York: Holt, 1997), 214.

50. For this famous "Memorial," see *Pensées*, 913.

least, that is how it appears from his published criticisms of revelation, reason, humanity, and redemption in Christianity.

Nietzsche admitted that he risked being unfair toward Christianity, adding to his admission: "The conviction that life is valueless and that all goals are illusory impresses itself on me so strongly, especially when I am sick in bed, that I need to hear more about it [Buddhism], but not mixed with Judaeo-Christian phraseology, a surfeit of which, at some time or another, has so disgusted me with it."[51] One reason for Nietzsche's frequent inability to read or hear with the objectivity or the care that he trumpets as endemic to a good philologist appears to be an overestimation of his own prowess as a psychologist. On reading Augustine's *Confessions*, for example, he commented that "one sees into the guts of Christianity in this book."[52] When he analyzes his petty youthful theft, Augustine's psychology is risibly false. When he speaks of sharing one soul with his friend and of going on living so that his friend might also go on living in soul, if not in body, Augustine's dishonesty is "revolting." The philosophical value of *Confessions* is "zero," representing, as it does, "*vulgarised* Platonism—that is to say, a way of thinking which was invented for the highest aristocracy of soul, and which he adjusted to suit slave natures."

Obviously, Augustine's psychological and philosophical analyses are open to challenge. But the terms of Nietzsche's dismissal suggest that he is possessed of an excessive pyschoanalytic self-confidence born of what we might term an "antithetical" attitude.[53] This attitude seems to lie behind the apparently groundless assertion that Pascal was himself unconvinced by his argument for the hidden God. However, perhaps it is unfair to press this point without sketching out a prima facie defense of Augustine on the matters Nietzsche picks out, certainly not a task for this place and time.[54] We conclude this phase of the discussion by referring to the end of *GS* book 3, where Nietzsche fires a series of eight questions and provides

51. *SL*, December 13, 1875, 139. These words may be quoted without recognizing that Nietzsche at the same time speaks of the risk of misunderstanding Christianity: see, e.g., Robert G. Morrison, "Nietzsche and Nirvana," in *Nietzsche and the Gods*, ed. Weaver Santaniello (Albany: State University of New York Press, 2001), 89.

52. To Overbeck, *SL*, March 31. Overbeck was an expert in and hostile to Augustine; see Laurence Lampert, *Nietzsche and Modern Times: A Study of Bacon, Descartes, and Nietzsche* (New Haven: Yale University Press, 1993), 364.

53. "His stance towards himself is the antithesis of, say, St. Augustine's; instead of judging, condemning, and paring away at his impulses, Nietzsche says he has simply tried to arrange them so that they might co-exist," writes Henry Staten, *Nietzsche's Voice* (Ithaca, NY: Cornell University Press, 1990), 22.

54. Philippa Foot is surely right to curb praise for Nietzsche as a wonderful psychologist; see "Nietzsche's Immoralism," in *Nietzsche, Genealogy, Morality: Essays on Nietzsche's "Genealogy of Morals,"* ed. Richard Schacht (Berkeley: University of California Press, 1994), 13.

eight answers. In between the questions and the answers, I provide in my own parentheses what Nietzsche implies is the Christian answer.

> *"What makes one heroic?"* ("Heroism is wrong; you are a worm before God.")
> "To approach at the same time one's highest suffering and one's highest hope."

> *"What do you believe in?"* ("Things with no foundation in reason.")
> "In this, that the weights of all things must be determined anew."

> *"What does your conscience say?"* ("You are a miserable little sinner.")
> "'You should become who you are.'"

> *"Where lie your greatest dangers?"* ("In self-assertion.")
> "In compassion."

> *"What do you love in others?"* ("Their sheer humanity.")
> "My hopes."

> *"Whom do you call bad?"* ("Everyone, by nature.")
> "He who always wants to put people to shame."

> *"What is most human to you?"* ("Pity, I suppose.")
> "To spare someone shame."

> *"What is the seal of having become free?"* ("Feeling forgiven.")
> "No longer to be ashamed before oneself."

Nietzsche is quite transparent here. As the exchange proceeds, we see that the question of shame looms large in his quarrel with Christianity. Pascal said: "How little pride the Christian feels in believing himself united to God! How little he grovels when he likens himself to the earthworm!" (358). Elsewhere: "Jesus is a God whom we can approach without pride and before whom we can humble ourselves without despair" (212). Nietzsche, however, reckoned that there was nothing he could derive from Christ that would rout the shame and the attendant wretchednesses of Christian anthropology. But before we learn how Nietzsche regarded Jesus Christ, we have to reckon with someone he regarded as greater than either Jesus or himself. The scene is now set for the appearance of the one who will expunge what is rotten in Christian anthropology and vanquish Christianity. *Incipit tragoedia*: the tragedy begins.

The Birth of Zarathustra

WS was published in 1880, *D* in 1881, *GS* in 1882. In its initial form of four books, *GS* ended with "*Incipit tragoedia*.—When Zarathustra was thirty years old, he left his homeland and Lake Urmi and went into the mountains" (342). So Nietzsche had given birth to Zarathustra in the work immediately preceding *Z*. The year 1881 was momentous. During that summer, he was informed by a Swiss native about the beauties of Sils-Maria in the mountains, and his association with Sils-Maria turned out to be dramatically eventful. First, he discovered Spinoza, or at least his kinship with Spinoza.[55] Then, in August, up at high altitude, he had some revelation of the truth of "eternal recurrence." In *Z*, he transmitted the revelation to those with ears to hear. It is as hard to know what to make of the revelatory occurrence as it is to construe the revealed content, if we insist on pressing beyond the fact that it was some kind of intellectual-cum-spiritual illumination. Momentous as this was, it was not the only thing that renewed Nietzsche in 1881. On November 27 he heard Bizet's *Carmen* and again aspired to be a musician.[56] It improved his health.[57] But then in 1882, Lou Salomé turned up.

> The hills look over on the South
> And southward dreams the sea;
> And with the sea-breeze hand in hand
> Came innocence and she.[58]

Though I have not resisted taking topographical liberties here, a biographical account certainly must be resisted. Reluctantly! Salomé was a twenty-one-year-old Russian with Danish and German blood coursing through her veins. Very intelligent, attractive, possessed of an intellectual eagerness that matched her precocity, her meeting with Nietzsche had a

55. See Nietzsche's letter to Overbeck on July 30 of that year (1881) in *SL*, which specifies five points of kinship. But Spinoza already featured as one of the eight shades of *AOM* 408, to which I have alluded.

56. Gianni Vattimo's "Chronology of Nietzsche's Life and Work," in *Nietzsche: An Introduction* (London: Athlone, 2002), part 4, pays instructive attention to the musical dimension in Nietzsche's life.

57. To Peter Gast, *SL*, December 5, 1881.

58. Francis Thompson, "Daisy," in *Poems of Francis Thompson*, rev. ed. (New York: Apple-Century, 1941).

deep impact on him. Together with another male friend (Paul Rée), he thought at one stage that he would set up a domicile with Salomé. At a time when he was brimming over with the ideas of Z, Salomé came into his life. Things soon went wrong in the relationship, with Nietzsche's sister, Elisabeth, in the middle of the fray. Nietzsche met Salomé as spring turned to summer. By autumn she was gone.

> She went her unremembering way,
> She went and left in me
> The pang of all the partings gone,
> And partings yet to be.

And with her went joy.[59]

Salomé's account of Nietzsche, the man and his thought, honed through the months that she spent with him, is highly instructive, even if we must read her account critically.[60] Published in 1894, it covers the "essence," "transitions," and "system" of Nietzsche.[61] Salomé takes us through his solitude, self-laceration, and inner multiplicity as we "hear ideas clash, see worlds sink, and new worlds emerge" in his thought.[62] She identifies the "four ideas rife during Nietzsche's first philosophical phase, which continued to engage him in constantly changing guise and view until the end: the Dionysian, decadence, the untimely, and the cult of genius."[63] It is Salomé's central contention that we must interpret Nietzsche as a religious thinker. Nietzsche is "a genius of religious speculation." His whole development is explicable from the loss of religious belief, but he remains chained to a natural affinity for the form of religious life with which he was familiar from home and childhood.[64] What comes to such dramatic expression in Nietzsche's work is a religious soul.

As Salomé interpreted matters, the time in which she and Nietzsche lived was a time when a basically religious drive and disposition were

59. The poem's last stanza reads: "Nothing begins, and nothing ends, / That is not paid with moan; / For we are born in others' pain, / And perish in our own." Nietzsche might have added that moan and pain also mark our course between the beginning and the end.

60. For what follows, see Siegfried Mandel's translation of Lou Salomé, *Nietzsche* (Urbana: University of Illinois Press, 2001).

61. "The notion of a 'system' in Nietzsche's works relies more upon an over-all mood than a clear-cut unity of defined deduction" (ibid., 91). By contrast, though not necessarily in opposition, see Karl Lowith, *From Hegel to Nietzsche: The Revolution in Nineteenth Century Thought* (London: Constable, 1965), 193: "Nietzsche's actual thought is a thought system, at the beginning of which stands the death of God, in its midst the ensuing nihilism, and at its end the self-surmounting nihilism in eternal recurrence."

62. Salomé, *Nietzsche*, 29.

63. Ibid., 48. Much is illuminating in her work, including important remarks on how master morality and slave morality are embodied in Nietzsche himself (113).

64. Ibid., e.g., 17, 26, 32.

culturally most naturally convertible into a drive toward the acquisition of knowledge. Intellectual force draws upon spiritual energy. The standard direction in which such a drive is expressed is external. Nietzsche's drive was inwardly directed. The result is that the fundamentally unifying impulse that aspires to reconcile knowledge and being becomes a fragmenting impulse as redirected spiritual force centrifugally scatters the drives.[65] The result is destructive, but Nietzsche paradoxically triumphed in the midst of self-division. Destruction swivels around in the direction of deification; life's sacrifice becomes apotheosis.

In the discussion that climaxes her treatment of Nietzsche's "Transitions," Salomé is adamant about Nietzsche's religion. "His various philosophies are for him just so many surrogates for God," and the closer Nietzsche gets to the realization that something like this is the case, the more intense the internal conflict between subliminal religious affirmation and professed religious repudiation. This is the road to Zarathustra. It is also the road to mysticism. Z is a mystical work, and Zarathustra a mystical being.[66] But it is a mysticism rooted in an extreme union of self-deification and self-sacrifice. With some force Salomé writes about Nietzsche's relationship to Zarathustra, of Zarathustra as the "superior Nietzsche," Nietzsche's double.[67] But was she right on Nietzsche's religious instinct and philosophy?

Despite quite a lot of attention that has been paid to this question, I am not persuaded that anything much hangs on an answer, from a theological point of view. "Religion" as a generic term may not be entirely unmanageable, and reflection on the distinction between the "religious" and the "secular" is of some importance in the contemporary global context. Furthermore, it may be claimed that all human thought is fundamentally religious.[68] That said, the question of whether a philosophy counts as more specifically religious is partly a definitional question, and the question of whether Nietzsche was religious is partly a definitional and partly a psychological question.[69] Similarly, I am not convinced that a theological response to Nietzsche needs to adjudicate the question of his mysticism.[70] But in general, Salomé seems to me to be persuasive

65. In interpreting Salomé here in terms of knowledge and being, I may, however, be missing the mark.

66. Salomé, *Nietzsche*, 91, 138.

67. Ibid., 123–24.

68. E.g., Herman Dooyweerd, *In the Twilight of Western Thought* (Nutley, NJ: Craig, 1972).

69. I think that Salomé was fundamentally right to say that "a genuine Nietzsche study would require the psychology of religion that would spotlight the meaning of his being, his suffering and his self-induced bliss" (*Nietzsche*, 26).

70. See Tyler T. Roberts's helpful essay "Ecstatic Philosophy," in *Nietzsche and the Divine*, ed. John Lippitt and Jim Urpeth (Manchester, UK: Clinamen, 2000), 200–225.

on Nietzsche and religion, though we have to watch for distortions in her perspective.[71]

More striking, I think, and ultimately more rewarding in a consideration of Nietzsche on Christianity is a related question that arises from both Salomé's work and that whole period of Nietzsche's life. Nietzsche is desperate to love and to be loved and is very lonely. Thomas Mann spoke of Nietzsche's "painful longing for the dew of love."[72] Nietzsche is surely being straight, with little or no irony, when he says: "It moves the observer to tears to see the admiring look of happiness with which a pretty young wife gazes up at her husband. One is filled with autumnal melancholy to think of the greatness as well as the transitoriness of human happiness" (*WS* 271). On a Christian account of things, there is nothing amiss in Nietzschean desperation. For Nietzsche, the "demand to be loved is the greatest of all pieces of presumption" (*HH* 523); for the Christian, the desire for it is not. Nietzsche's desire was wide-ranging. It included the need for mother love.[73] To Lou herself, Nietzsche said: "I want to be lonely no longer, but to learn again to be a human being."[74] His desire was unfulfilled. Over five years later, he would tell Rohde: "I have forty-three years behind me, and am just as alone as when I was a child."[75]

In the midst of all this, Zarathustra appeared.

71. See Carol Diethe, "Lou Salomé's Interpretation of Nietzsche's Religiosity," *Journal of Nietzsche Studies* 15 (1998).

72. Thomas Mann, "Nietzsche's Philosophy in the Light of Recent History," in *Last Essays* (London: Secker & Warburg, 1959), 167. Mann, winner of the first Nietzsche Prize, is a most illuminating exponent of Nietzsche.

73. See the communication to Malwida von Meysenburg in *SL*, April 14, 1876, although this is earlier than the period immediately surrounding *Z*.

74. *SL*, July 2, 1882.

75. *SL*, November 11, 1887.

5

Azure Existence

From my youth upwards
My spirit walk'd not with the souls of men,
Nor look'd upon the earth with human eyes;
The thirst of their ambition was not mine,
The aim of their existence was not mine;
My joys, my griefs, my passions, and my powers,
Made me a stranger.

Byron, *Manfred*, act 2, scene 2

THOSE EIGHTEEN MONTHS between Lou Salomé's departure and the publication of what was initially meant to be the third and final part of *Z* were emotionally charged. Not only did Salomé depart and Zarathustra appear, but also Richard Wagner died, on February 13, 1883. News of his death affected Nietzsche both physically and emotionally. He knew how close they had been and how great the angst of separation. *Z* was the child of suffering as well as exhilaration. Some of it was conceived before the meeting with Salomé and the death of Wagner. According to Nietzsche, "This work stands altogether alone. Let us leave the poets aside: perhaps nothing at all has ever been done out of a like superfluity of strength" (*EH*, "Thus Spoke Zarathustra," 6). *EH*, where he said this, recounts both Nietzsche's qualities and his works. *Z* dominates. By the time he comes to give it detailed treatment, we are already in a state of anticipation, and in the course of his treatment he furnishes us with some hermeneutical aid for its interpretation. Nietzsche hoped that, one day, university chairs would be established for the interpretation of this text. In *EH* he comments about different sections of it, but it is especially significant that he tells us how in this work his "concept 'Dionysian' has here become the *supreme deed*." Regarded from the standpoint of the "deed," Nietzsche achieves supreme affirmation contingent on exuberant destruction. Regarded in terms of attitude, supreme melancholy is allied with supreme affirmation. Prosaically described, *Z* prescribes the overcoming of morality and the moral self in the cause of unsparing truthfulness.

But *Z* is not prosaic. It is a kind of scripture, subject to commentary of a type not unlike some biblical commentaries.[1] Should we consider it as the scripture of the Antichrist, especially since the author from the beginning invites us to pit Zarathustra in opposition to Jesus? Perhaps Nietzsche would say so. Yet Nietzsche's treatment of Jesus, which we shall consider in the next chapter, makes such a description ring somewhat strange on the ear. In "The Intuitive Mode of Reason in *Zarathustra*," James O'Flaherty concluded that "ironically, Nietzsche has done his great adversary, Christianity, a notable service by vindicating its conception of the proper role of reason as exemplified in its Scriptures."[2] The role in question was imputed to Hamann by Kant and derived by Hamann from the Bible. It goes under the heading "Intuitive Reason." O'Flaherty even thinks that *Z* is not simply a parody of the Gospels but an "unsurpassed vindication of the mode of thought that informs them."[3] However, this overlooks the empirical component in Scripture, an element often pedestrian in the extreme for connoisseurs of purely literary delight, yet testifying to one who actually lived, suffered, and died, unlike Nietzsche's Zarathustra.[4] Nevertheless, O'Flaherty's is an important reminder of how this work should be read. He is further right to insist that because "the form of the work is quasi-biblical, one can expect it to be informed by considerable multivalence," although we might want to subject "multivalence" to the same kind of theological-hermeneutical check as "intuition."[5]

1. Laurence Lampert, *Nietzsche's Teaching: An Interpretation of "Thus Spoke Zarathustra"* (New Haven: Yale University Press, 1986), set the standard here. See too Stanley Rosen, *The Mask of Enlightenment: Nietzsche's Zarathustra* (Cambridge: Cambridge University Press, 1995), which is more selective. Robert Gooding-Williams, *Zarathustra's Dionysian Modernism* (Stanford, CA: Stanford University Press, 2002), a thorough piece of work, is also commentary.

2. James C. O'Flaherty, "The Intuitive Mode of Reason in *Zarathustra*," in *Studies in Nietzsche and the Judaeo-Christian Tradition*, ed. James C. O'Flaherty, Timothy F. Sellner, and Robert M. Helm (Chapel Hill: University of North Carolina Press, 1985), 293.

3. Ibid., 294.

4. I have already mentioned that there was a historical Zarathustra (Zoroaster), whom Nietzsche is not trying to portray.

5. O'Flaherty, "Intuitive Mode of Reason," 285.

It is doubtless as true now as it was when it was said of Z in 1988 that not only is there "nothing close to a standard reading of the work's intention, form, development, resolution" but also "there are not even standard disagreements."[6] While Z declares the heart of Nietzsche's philosophy, especially in its revelation of the teaching of eternal recurrence, a history of the interpretation of this teaching alone would require a quite hefty volume, at the end of which we could still leave the reader to pick his or her own option. Eternal recurrence is just one thing that comes up in my following account, a fact indicating that my treatment is bound to be superficial at best—but certainly not misleading, I hope. Zarathustra's teaching is set in the framework of a narrative, and the narrative and teaching together introduce Zarathustra in person as well as in word. We might draw a comparison with Kahlil Gibran's classic, *The Prophet*. He apparently took the idea for its form from Z.[7] Gibran's is a work of teaching, but to convey the teaching is not to convey the book. Our minds are drawn to the teacher along with the teaching, and the narrative gives far more than just a contingent framework for the teaching; it generates a distinctive ethos. Suffused as it is with mystical teaching, the atmosphere of Gibran's classic is largely created by the coming and going of the prophet from place to place over land and sea, the stranger who arrives and instructs, leaves and leaves the hearers nostalgically fulfilled. Yet this figure is shrouded in self-effacement far more than is the figure of Zarathustra in Nietzsche's much longer work.

In what follows, I try to give a flavor of the work by a summary rendering of its matter, mood, and movement. I hope the résumé is more expository than impressionistic and that expository comment is more illuminating than intrusive. The exercise is rather like constructing a large signpost. The contours of the teaching of Z will be limned rather too vaguely for my liking, but then Z is in some respects a mysterious book, and it would be impossible to sketch out its teaching in short compass with bold confidence.[8] Much is missed in Z by failing to attend not just to the detail of the text and its philosophical interpretation but also to

6. Robert B. Pippin, "Irony and Affirmation in Nietzsche's *Thus Spoke Zarathustra*," in *Nietzsche's New Seas: Explorations in Philosophy, Aesthetics, and Politics*, ed. Michael Allen Gillespie and Tracy B. Strong (Chicago: University of Chicago Press, 1988), 45.

7. See Kahlil Gibran, *The Prophet* (London: Penguin, 2002), x.

8. The limits of my account force on it a unidimensionality that may mislead. This is especially the case if Gooding-Williams is right: "The essence of Nietzsche's rigor is his relentless, if often stressful, practice of thinking against himself" (*Zarathustra's Dionysian Modernism*, 83). Associated with this is the problem of deciding whether Zarathustra unequivocally speaks for Nietzsche. To the extent that he is Nietzsche's ideal self, he presumably does.

Plato and the Greeks, Hegel and the Bible, Schopenhauer and Wagner.[9]
Nevertheless, we must have a go at it.

Prologue

"When Zarathustra was thirty years old, he left his home and the
lake of his home and went into the mountains."[10] Ten years' enjoyable
solitude followed. But then he thought about the sun. How could it be
happy unless it had those on whom it could shine? A lesson; indeed, a
parable. Zarathustra must shine on others too. "Go down, Zarathustra,
and give." So he does. He wastes no evangelistic time. God is dead, so
his first word to the first crowd that he encounters in a market square is
this: *"I teach you the Superman."* With this declaration, we are propelled
into the heart of things from the beginning, much as in the case of the
announcement of the kingdom of God in the Gospel of Mark, chapter
1. Who or what is the Superman?

Almost ninety years ago, Figgis said: "Probably no two people to the
end of time will be in precise agreement as to the significance of the
Übermensch."[11] "Significance" here encompasses "meaning." The very
word "Superman" as a translation of *Übermensch* is problematic, and
there is a case either for alternatively translating it or, as I shall sometimes
be doing, for leaving it untranslated.[12] Other words compounded with
the affix *"über"* are sprinkled throughout Z. The *Übermensch* surely has
a rangy connotation: the man who overcomes, the overcoming man, the
overman, the one who as man overcomes, and who overcomes himself
as man. It is also the man of the future, the man of the "beyond," who
does and will transcend good and evil. But we are aptly warned not to
overdetermine the idea.[13] The best way to interpret it is to give an inductive account of what Zarathustra teaches. Zarathustra, who starts life as

9. Studies such as those mentioned frequently bring out these things. I venture to
think, however, that Heraclitus might sometimes have a higher profile than he does in
these accounts.

10. In Z, "Prologue," 1. In what follows, I shall be keeping references to a minimum
since I am usually following the plotline of Z.

11. John Neville Figgis, *The Will to Freedom, or The Gospel of Nietzsche and the Gospel
of Christ* (London: Longmans, Green, 1917), 6.

12. Where I retain it, it is principally because I am using Hollingdale's translation.

13. See Bernd Magnus, "Jesus, Christianity, and Superhumanity," in *Studies in Nietzsche*, ed. O'Flaherty, Sellner, and Helm. Rosen in *Mask of Enlightenment*, 20, interprets
Zarathustra "as an indeterminate human being, somewhere between a man and a superman." "Indetermination" is not the same as lack of "overdetermination." Certainly, the
Übermensch identified "a stronger species, a higher type that arises and preserves itself
under different conditions from those of the average man" (*WP* 866).

Superman's prophet, comes to look a bit more like the preincarnation of the *Übermensch* by the end, having broken through to the attainment of true doctrine.[14] We read a story of Zarathustra's own becoming, which includes becoming a properly refined philosopher.

Man and earth are intimately associated in the view of things that Nietzsche advocates via the *Übermensch*. "I entreat you, my brothers, *remain true to the earth*, and do not believe those who speak to you of superterrestrial hopes! They are poisoners." There is God and there is the earth; God is dead; therefore, there remains the earth. God was correlative to one sort of humanity; now a new sort of humanity must be correlative to the earth. Earth means body, and with the death of God, the soul that despised the body also dies. So now we just have the body. With God and soul you have reason, virtue, justice, and pity. Jettison them. Is that sin? Sin is not your problem. Your problem is your base mediocrity. You're not even capable of a little *pecca fortiter*.[15] The Superman is the sea into which you must flow, the lightning that will shock your life.

Much of Nietzsche's teaching is packed into these opening salvos in the "Prologue." There is much more to come, but no time is wasted in getting down to first principles in proclamation. The action continues in the market square, where a crowd has gathered to see a tightrope walker. The walker apparently thinks that Zarathustra's declarations are a sign for him to begin his antics, which the crowd is eager to observe. "Man," Zarathustra assures the listeners, "is a rope, fastened between animal and Superman—a rope over an abyss, . . . a bridge, and not a goal." Dangerous business—and Zarathustra loves those who engage in it, engage even unto their downfall, in our flaccid age. Zarathustra is the prophet of the Superman. But what an age in which to prophesy! "No herdsman and one herd. Everyone wants the same things, everyone is the same: whoever thinks otherwise goes voluntarily into the madhouse." Thus spoke Zarathustra, but the ears of the listeners are worse than those of the deaf. They're happy to leave Supermen to Zarathustra and revel in the image of "man" that is small and perishing.[16]

14. Questions have also been asked about the centrality of the notion of the *Übermensch*. As *Z* progresses, the term fades away, though it reappears in part 4. Lampert, who treats part 4 as an appendix to his commentary, remarks in *Nietzsche's Teaching*, 258: "It seems to me that one of the greatest single causes of the misinterpretation of Nietzsche's teaching is the failure to see that the clearly provisional teaching on the superman is rendered obsolete by the clearly definitive teaching on eternal return."

15. Luther's "sin boldly." This is my own gloss on *Z*.

16. Again, whether we should retain the gender-specific word "man" in describing Nietzsche's ideas is sometimes hard to decide. The "masculine" orientation of his positive philosophy, if that is not too crudely put, encourages the frequent retention of "man" to advertise its gendered connotation in Nietzsche. But the decision can sometimes be a rather narrow one.

Drama sets in on the high rope. Another character appears on it, taunts the rope walker, and leaps over him. The effect is that the disconsolate walker despairingly precipitates his own fall and crashes down onto the market square. Regaining consciousness, he assures Zarathustra, who is now kneeling beside him, that he knew the devil would trip him up. But there is no devil, says Zarathustra. The man decides that he has nothing to live for because soul, God, and hell have all vanished. He dies. It is night, and Zarathustra, taking the corpse on his back, trudges out of town. Sleep follows in the forest. On waking, Zarathustra realizes anew that he needs living companions. What he does not need is the rabble, the herd. He must have the few. The "good and the just"—they will hate the teaching that he will mete out to his disciples. "Whom do they hate the most? Him who smashes their tables of values, the breaker, the law-breaker." Nevertheless, Zarathustra adds, "He is the creator." Nothing becomes more important in Z than the elaboration of this point. Meanwhile, the moment has come. From the sky comes an eagle, a serpent coiled around it, companion rather than foe or prey. Zarathustra rejoices to see his animals, the eagle being the proudest of animals, the serpent the wisest. Together the three venture forth, though it is some time before the animals feature again in Z. "Thus began Zarathustra's down-going."

What is going on in the "Prologue"? Poetically, it is stacked with metaphor. The rubric under which it sets out the following books of Z is clear: it is the thought of the *Übermensch* instead of God. The market square and listeners remind us of the passage on the death of God in GS. Zarathustra and his teaching are reverse images of Jesus and his teaching (and at this point perhaps of Plato). So, for example, Zarathustra is thirty years old when he leaves home. There is a scene where a hermit offers bread and wine to him and his accompanying corpse. Zarathustra will seek choice disciples and not the herd, for he is against pity: "Is not pity the cross upon which he who loves man is nailed? But my pity is no crucifixion!" If Jesus's teaching is epitomized in the Sermon on the Mount, where he speaks to his disciples of the higher righteousness, the reference in Z to smashing tables of the law and creating new ones takes us to the heart of Zarathustra's reversal of Moses and of Jesus, reaching its pivotal expression in the third part in the chapter "Of Old and New Law-Tables" (Z 3.56). This action at least is the passage to, if not an expression of, the *Übermensch*. We must keep this action in mind as we pass on to the rest of the book, compelled to be rather niggardly prosaic, at certain points, in reproducing the doctrinal tenets of Zarathustra's discourses.

Part 1

The discourses that constitute part 1 take place in a town called the "Pied Cow," to which, we are told, Zarathustra's heart was attached.[17] When he eventually makes his exit from it, many would-be disciples follow him. The teaching at the beginning of this part is a good early example of an indubitably important discourse, whose interpretation nevertheless is controversial. We are introduced to the "three metamorphoses": camel, lion, and child. The camel is a beast of burden: "It renounces and is reverent." The lion will have nothing of the "thou shalt": it says, "I will." But metamorphosis from camel to lion does not produce the being that creates new values. Rather, it produces the creature of freedom, and this establishes the condition for the creation of new values. Another metamorphosis is required to become the author of value creation. To enter that kingdom, we must become as children, innocent and forgetful. The child can always start again. But is the camel the old self that never dreams of creation and thus must be renounced? Or is it the self that actually takes on the burden of the task of creation, for which, however, it is precisely a burden, so that nothing issues forth in creation before subsequent metamorphosis? And notwithstanding rival readings of it, should we find in the chapter a clue to the conceptual structure of *Zarathustra*?[18]

This is just one, albeit important, example of controverted readings of Z, hitting us right from the start of the discourses. However we read this particular section, the business of "overcoming" is at the heart of it all as the subsequent speech illustrates, though it is not a speech given by Zarathustra himself, and Zarathustra is its critic. We are apparently given a clue to Zarathustra's own self-overcoming when we learn that he made for himself "a brighter flame," and in its light and heat the old "phantom" of God and of man *"fled* from me." Zarathustra's words here are a vehicle for Nietzsche's suggestion that it is the higher possibility that expels Christianity. The prophet of the Superman has attained a measure of the self-overcoming that he presages and prophesies. Certainly, once you've gone as far as Zarathustra has, you can't go back to that weary sense of suffering and impotence that created gods and beyonds. We must convalesce from this, and a highly significant chapter on convalescence comes later, in part 3, straight after the chapter "Of Old and New Law-Tables." Nietzsche has thrown down the gauntlet early. On the one hand are those who "are always looking back to dark ages," days of faith and not of reason, when "doubt was sin." For them, the

17. We are told this at the end of part 1, "Of the Bestowing Virtue," Z 22.1.
18. See Gooding-Williams, *Zarathustra's Dionysian Modernism,* 31–44.

afterworld and the soul's redemption. On the other hand is the teaching of Zarathustra, which is focused on this world and the body. The body is "the meaning of the earth," and after sharing this discovery, Zarathustra discourses on the "despisers of the body." What is it about the body that Zarathustra wants to liberate and celebrate?

We recall that "Zarathustra's secret" has been regarded as homosexuality. Just possibly it is a secret, even *the* secret, but talk of corporal nakedness, which peppers the discourses, functions to advertise body and embodiment in a wider sense. Here we pay the price of a refusal to delve much below the surface of the text, where "body" appears to be frequently literal, but "nakedness" metaphorical. However, generalization in interpretation at least points us in a general direction. We can at least say that Zarathustra's statement of his philosophy is broadly materialist, and the emphasis seems to lie on persuading people to rid themselves of the idea of the soul and to make the body, in its innocent givenness, the fount of creativity. Sure, it is the seat of conflicting drives. When one tries to come to terms with it, one's self can seem like "a knot of savage serpents that are seldom at peace among themselves."[19] The enterprise of revaluation will be demanding. The crucial thing is, surely, that Zarathustra does not prescribe *what* revaluing will amount to, once one begins with the body, but rather that the body must be the site of revaluation. What other site is there if God is dead and there is no immaterial soul? Valuing is to be centered on the senses, whatever that entails in the valuing process.

None of this will come easy. We may judge ourselves to be enlightened folks, but the fact is that "once spirit was God, then it became man, and now it is even becoming mob." Zarathustra oscillates between self-disclosure and instructing the other.[20] He reveals to us his serious, deadly serious, heart. But the Spirit of Gravity can kill you, so you need to laugh. Again, we must refer to part 3, where, at what is perhaps the dramatic high point of the whole work, the Spirit of Gravity strikes hardest.[21] In this last passage, Zarathustra ends up laughing, but first he has had to fight off the Spirit of Gravity. Dionysus must suffer, but suffering and laughter are intertwined. And Zarathustra is the ideal, or idealized, embodiment of Dionysus.

As the Gospels take an interest in Jesus's various disciples and not just in Jesus himself, so *Z* with regard to disciples, though there are sig-

19. These words come from the chapter "Of the Pale Criminal," *Z* 1.6; Rosen in *Mask of Enlightenment*, 87, thinks it "contains the most difficult of all the parts of *Zarathustra*." It seems to deal largely with the question of justice, so I am displacing these words from their context.

20. I refer to the explicit presentation: "oscillate" is not meant to suggest something loose or casual in the literary structure of *Z* at this point.

21. "Of the Vision and the Riddle," *Z* 3.46.

nificant differences, not least in the general anonymity of Zarathustra's addressees. Zarathustra tells them that the path is hard and narrow. At one stage in part 1, the literary flow of Zarathustran speech is calculatedly interrupted by the sight of a young man who is avoiding him (Z 1.8). The youth is leaning wearily against a tree. He has accepted what Zarathustra teaches: we are as trees in that the more we want to grow upward, the more we sink our roots into the earth. And the earth is dark, deep—evil. But what has happened as a result of his accepting all this? He no longer trusts himself and is trusted by no one. There is no constancy to the days of his life. He is alone. Contempt grows with desire. He climbs, but stumbles and envies those who can fly, including Zarathustra. Articulating this confession is too much for the man, and he breaks down, weeping. With all the appearance of gentle compassion, Zarathustra puts an arm around him. They start walking, and eventually Zarathustra starts talking, to this effect:

Friend, you're searching for freedom, but you're not free yet. Don't lose heart. There are plenty of preachers of death around, life-denying devotees of eternal life, who see only suffering existence about them. Fight. The golden rule is, "Man is something that should be overcome." And much is arrayed against you here, for the political order of the state achieves anything but the elevation of humanity. State and market square, public space, are sites of inflexibility. "Flee into your solitude!" "I see you," Zarathustra tells the young man, "wearied by poisonous flies"—small drops, small wounds, from small men—this can get to you and hollow you out. Greatness offends the little. Flee into solitude.

Zarathustra is thus preaching a form of life (solitude) in order to attain its fullness (creation). As he follows this with discourses on relationships, chastity, friendship, neighbor, and woman, the logic seems to be that the summons to solitude, while intelligible in contrast to the company of the rabble in the civic and political order, apparently requires something to be said about the whole span of relationships. Zarathustra's objective is broadly similar in all these cases. He summons us to evaluate the realities involved here, to unmask and to probe actualities. Actualities include cultural variables. In all these variables, one is dealing with evaluations, for that is life. And as "a table of values hangs over every people," and "it is the table of its overcomings," so it is all "the voice of its will to power." This last is a phrase that receives its important elaboration in the next part.

What of the variables? There are a "Thousand and One Goals," but "men have given themselves all their good and evil. . . . Man first implanted values into things to maintain himself. . . ." As it has actually been for mankind, so it must now be consciously and anew. To evaluate is to create; value is simply the product of evaluation. And the Zarathustran program is more or less contained in this: "He who has to be a creator always has to destroy." People have always created, but they have done so *as a people*. Now the individual must create. Individual is rightly pitted against neighbor in this perspective, for "you flee to your neighbour away from yourselves and would like to make a virtue of it. . . ." Think afresh. "Higher than love of your neighbour stands love of the most distant men and of the men of the future. . . ." A *friend*—now that may be different if you order friendship to the correct priorities that do not impede self-development. But that does not obviate the fact that the creator is hard and lonely.

> It is terrible to be alone with the judge and avenger of one's own law. It is to be like a star thrown forth into empty space and into the icy breath of solitude. . . . But one day solitude will make you weary, one day your pride will bend and your courage break. One day you will cry: "I am alone." ("Of the Way of the Creator," Z 1.17)[22]

Zarathustra's speeches wend their way back from the despairing youth to the audience of disciples, and as this part draws to its close, he is found in their company again. Of the eagle and the serpent we have heard nothing since their appearance, but the serpentine theme is taken up when an adder bites Zarathustra, prompting a prophetic proclamation that revalues what Jesus preached about requiting good for evil, blessing and not cursing your enemies. This dominical pseudo-wisdom from Jesus just brings shame on people. It is very unworthy. So we should move on from it and move up a notch in what we make of man. It is better to breed creators through marital procreation than to breed shame in the enemy. A challenge is issued: "A creator's thirst, arrow, and longing for the Superman: speak, my brother, is this your will to marriage?" It should be so.

By now, Zarathustra is musing on Jesus. We have touched on the birth of creators; should we not, then, touch on death? It must not be conceived of as do the preachers of death. Rather, make it (death) good and make it timely. Jesus didn't. Zarathustra is about forty, regarded by the Greeks as the perfect age. However much Zarathustra may want to die, he lives on to instruct his friends. It was different with the other, his opposite number.

> Truly, too early died that Hebrew whom the preachers of slow death honour: and that he died too early has since been a fatality for many. As yet he knew only tears and the melancholy of the Hebrews, . . . He died too early;

---

22. I leave aside what Zarathustra says about woman, a riddle apparently destined for submissiveness. I regret this gap in my treatment of Nietzsche in this volume.

he himself would have recanted his teaching had he lived to my age! He was noble enough to recant! But he was still immature. (Z 1.21)

Moreover, he mixed more than was good for him with "the good and the just"—yesterday's Pharisees, today's conventionally religious.

So Nietzsche presents us with the alternative: Zarathustra or Jesus? Beyond the order of good and evil, or enslaved to the order of good and evil? Creator, or Creator's subject and instrument? As Zarathustra also prepares to leave, we are left with such questions. A farewell speech commends the serpent of knowledge as the symbol of new power, whereas new virtue is symbolized by the sun. No less than Jesus does Zarathustra love his disciples, but he does so more wisely. His parting entreaty is to "stay loyal to the earth." "May your spirit and your virtue serve the meaning of the earth, my brothers; and may the value of all things be fixed anew by you. To that end you should be fighters! To that end you should be creators!" A thousand paths lie before. And their end? From you will come a chosen people; from the chosen people, a Superman.

Zarathustra must go away and be alone; the disciples must remain bereft. If they believe in Zarathustra, they reinvent the wheel, because the point of finding Zarathustra is to seek yourself. Zarathustra knows that his disciples will deny him, but he will come back. After that, there will be further departure and return. And after that? Banquet and celebration. Above the celebrations flies the banner: "*All gods are dead: now we want the Superman to live*' . . . Thus spoke Zarathustra" (Z 1.22).

Part 2

As there are various interpretations of Z, so there are various views on its intellectual and literary merits. Is it an effective vehicle for something like a philosophical communication? Is it good philosophy? However we answer those questions, sustained exposure to Z impresses us with a sense either of its basic substantive monotony or of its particular detailed variety. It is possible to combine these responses, especially if the variety in question pertains to figure and trope. The surface of Z is strewn with image after image poured out onto the page, resplendent and evocative, shaded in hue, multicolored in mood. We might detect variety in substance, too, if we become engrossed in meticulous commentary on Z, interpreting word and image, background and concept, textually, philologically, historically, and philosophically. Despite this, an impression of substantive monotony remains (I do not mean it pejoratively); considerable thematic reiteration spans parts 1 and 2. Yet there is novelty, so we press on with sequential exposition.

"A sower," said Jesus, "went forth to sow." Jesus was the greatest of sowers, and his seed was the word of God.[23] No less is Zarathustra a sower, and he is a finer pedagogue. He has returned to his solitary mountain cave but longs to give again to his disciples. Years go by, and Zarathustra increases in wisdom and in pain. He cannot remain. Weeds are surely growing on the soil where he sowed his doctrine. What has become of his friends? Although the scenes that follow initially appear to shift between his traditional haunt (the forest) and the blissful islands, where we learn that Zarathustra is dwelling, this is probably appearance only; the forest of part 2 is presumably an island forest, not the main-land forest where Zarathustra was before, so the action is taking place on the Blissful, and maybe other, Isles. It is certainly important that the Blissful Isles are the scene of at least some of Zarathustra's doings, for in antiquity, these are the islands where dwell the virtuous heroes, the cream of the human race.

Although we are amply warned in the opening chapter to expect new teaching, it starts off in continuity with the old. "Once you said 'God' when you gazed upon distant seas; but now I have taught you to say 'Superman.'" If it is too much for this generation to create the Super-man, "you could transform yourselves into forefathers and ancestors of the Superman." To create a person is to create an outlook, a worldview based on the senses. God, in contrast,

> is a thought that makes all that is straight crooked. . . . I call it evil and misanthropic, all this teaching about the one and the perfect and the un-moved and the sufficient and the intransitory. . . . The best parables and images should speak of time and becoming: they should be a eulogy and a justification of all transitoriness.

Zarathustra is not about to concur with Hegelian revisionism in the concept of God, substituted for a more nearly Platonic understanding. Human creating is the antidote, but you have to suffer before being creator. The act of willing allies joy to suffering sensibility. Zarathus-tra heavily accents creative "will." "What would there be to create if gods—existed?" Zarathustra must work on humanity, "an image sleeping in stone." What emerges will be a thing of beauty. And then, how could the divinity presently familiar to us hold a candle to the excellence of the Superman? We are not surprised at what kind of man will emerge. It is someone rooted in the vocation to revalue values. Hitherto, "shame, shame, shame—that is the history of man." The virtues of compassion and pity establish shame. So disestablish compassion and pity. Or be

23. Again, my gloss: Nietzsche does not explicitly refer to this.

compassionate according to your sovereign and occasional will, but do not kowtow to it as a virtue. You want to love as well? Fine; just stop pitying. Steel yourself. The whole business of Christian virtue and value is painful. Look at the priests, if you can bear it. See them cast "into the bondage of false values and false scriptures. Ah, that someone would redeem them from their Redeemer!" Zarathustra's targets are advertised in the chapter titles (Z 2.25–29): "Of the Compassionate"; "Of the Priests"; "Of the Virtues"; "Of the Rabble"—the "power," "scribbling," and "pleasure" kinds of rabble. He goes on to talk "Of Tarantulas," and at this point we must introduce the possibility of a "political" interpretation of Z.

The question of political interpretation goes quite deep. Nietzsche and Z were put to political use by the Nazis, but both then and since, it was frequently assumed that the political dimension of Nietzsche's literature, considered in its own right, is not very marked. An individualistic and existentialist Nietzsche appeared truer to the literature. In the scholarship of recent years, the political dimension has again come to light.[24] Discussion of the question of whether and to what extent Z should be treated as a political document is outside my remit. However, it undoubtedly has a significant political dimension, and the discussion of tarantulas, for instance, exemplifies a hostile interest in socialism. Tarantulas are poisonous, harboring the poison of revenge. Earlier, the "preachers of death" have been attacked. Now it is the turn of the "preachers of equality," searching after *justice*; operating in the name of *virtue*; opposing *power*. "Mistrust all those who talk much about justice." They are a deceitful bunch; they *seem* to be life-affirming, and life-affirmers *seem* to be allies of Zarathustra, but in reality they belong to the preachers of death, who include priests. "Men are not equal." Sad to say, philosophers are not necessarily better than priests and egalitarians. They are usually servants of the people, not of the truth. Of spirit, solitude, and strength, they know nothing. The malaise of culture is not merely religious.

Though Zarathustra constantly returns to the question of destroying before creating, there are many tensions in his soul. The spirit of joy and celebration, of creation and affirmation, is joined with discourses that are critical and destructive, no-saying and prohibitive. When Zarathustra bursts into song, in three chapters of part 2, he bares a divided soul (Z 2.31–33). Thus, in "The Night Song" we find that in solitude he longs for speech, and in love he longs for giving. Then, in "The Dance Song," brought on by the sight of girls dancing in the forest, he provides a counterpoint to the song of Cupid and the dancing girls. But his dialogue with Life and Wisdom make him sad. When the dance ceases,

24. See, e.g., Keith Ansell-Pearson, *An Introduction to Nietzsche as Political Thinker* (Cambridge: Cambridge University Press, 1994).

Zarathustra strikes up a "Funeral Song." Surely we draw very close to Nietzsche's own experience here as Zarathustra sings of vanished youth and clings to his savior: "Will." It is not surprising that when he breaks off singing to resume speech, his subject is "Self-Overcoming" (2.34). And here we come to a philosophical move that, if not entirely new in *Z* and Nietzsche's work, is at least distinctly emphasized.

In reflection ultimately designed as an address to the wisest, Zarathustra avers: "Life itself told me this secret: 'Behold,'" it said, "'I am that *which must overcome itself again and again.*'" The secret is more than just that; it is that the will at the heart of self-overcoming is the will-to-power. On one interpretation of things, will-to-power takes over from the *Übermensch*, not as its contradiction, but as its clearer conceptual, philosophical, even metaphysical substitute. The history of the interpretation of Nietzsche via this concept is rich, taking us into the labyrinths of the early compilation of Nietzsche's unpublished later notebooks and into the celebrated expositions by Martin Heidegger. In the previous chapter, I observed that here a critique of and advance on Darwin is involved and that the question of perspectivism arises. A point *Z* certainly wants to make is that life is optimally lived—unless we perish of dire mediocrity and religion—under the rubric of a biology and philosophy expressed as will-to-power.[25] Sticking just with what Zarathustra says:

> You too, enlightened man, are only a path and footstep of my will: truly, my will to power walks with the feet of your will to truth! He who shot the doctrine of "will to existence" at truth certainly did not hit the truth: this will—does not exist! For what does not exist cannot will; but that which is in existence, how could it still want to come into existence? Only where life is, there is also will: not will to life, but—so I teach you—will to power!

At the heart of existence is will, and underlying the putative will-to-truth is will-to-power. Arguably, this succinctly defines Nietzsche's relation to Schopenhauer. With Schopenhauer, will is at the heart of things; against Schopenhauer, it must exercise and not renounce its strength. This connection and contrast must not conceal the fact that Schopenhauer has in mind something like a unitary metaphysical entity, whereas Nietzsche is reckoning in terms of an aggregate of physiological drives.

Discoursing on will-to-power conveys insight, but it also puts clear water between Zarathustra and the men of the present. These men are memorably portrayed. "And if one tests your virility, one finds only steril-

---

25. Perhaps the cowardly, perhaps the correct, way of describing this is in terms of a quasi-constructivist biology. Cowardice would soon have to break cover, however, in any detailed exposition, for the devil would still lie in the interpretation of "quasi."

ity! You seem to be baked from colours and scraps of paper glued together."
So it is not to the present and the men of the present that Zarathustra
must turn his gaze. Rather, it is to *"my children's land."* His enemies in the
present cause him to be angry, compounding their vaunted contempt of
the earth with hypocrisy. "Your spirit has been persuaded to contempt of
the earthly, but your entrails have not; these, however, are the strongest
part of you!" "Oh, you sentimental hypocrites, you lustful men! You lack
innocence in desire: and therefore you now slander desiring!" Denial of the
senses and the body is both theoretical rubbish and practical impossibility.
Zarathustra gets as bitter on this point as we have found him hitherto.
"Distance concealed from me the serpent-filth, and the evil odour, and
that a lizard's cunning was prowling lustfully around."[26]

We are reminded, if we need to be, of the hermeneutical agonies of
interpreting *Z* by a caveat about poets that ushers in the final sequence
of this part. Irony hovers when the question is raised whether Zarathustra, as poet, lies, as poets lie; it is a question not answered with a plain
negative.[27] Yet irony as a literary trope or a pervasive mood does not
seem to cling particularly to this section. There appears to be a strict
sobriety of soul that qualifies or modulates any exhibition of irony.[28] But
the caveat ushers in the chapter "Of Great Events" (*Z* 2.40). The time
is nigh for something. Zarathustra has briefly disappeared, and rumor
has it that he has made his way to the heart of the earth. Down at the
depths of things, he is impressed by the fact that the danger of nihilism
is very real. Nihilism is a negative, fatalistic post-Christian lassitude.[29]
We are at the twilight juncture of the old and the new. Zarathustra is,
candidly, terrified.[30] Do we not hear the sepulchral tones of Edgar Allan
Poe: "Terror is not of Germany, but of the soul"?[31] A beloved disciple

26. On lizard imagery, see Joachim Köhler, *Zarathustra's Secret: The Interior Life of
Friedrich Nietzsche* (New Haven: Yale University Press, 2002), 166–69.

27. The ghost of Thomas Gray informed Coleridge that "all poets go to hell, we are
so intolerably addicted to lying"; see Heathcote W. Garrod, *Coleridge: Poetry and Prose*
(Oxford: Clarendon, 1925), ix.

28. See *HH* 372 for Nietzsche on irony. For a critique of Paul de Man's reading of *Z* as
ironic allegory, see Gooding-Williams, *Zarathustra's Dionysian Modernism*, esp. 80ff. See
also Pippin's essay "Irony and Affirmation." Staten makes the characteristically interesting
observation that "Nietzsche, despite what is constantly said about him, is in some very
deep sense incapable of irony"; see Henry Staten, *Nietzsche's Voice* (Ithaca, NY: Cornell
University Press, 1990), 45.

29. See Michael Allen Gillespie's important study *Nihilism before Nietzsche* (Chicago:
University of Chicago Press, 1996).

30. See "The Prophet," or "Soothsayer" (*Z* 2.41). I am skipping over political interpretation again, assuming that a fire-hound (2.40) that turns up in the narrative is a political
revolutionary.

31. Quoted in Graham Clarke's introduction to Edgar Allan Poe's *Tales of Mystery and
Imagination* (London: Dent, 1993), xxvii.

tries to prop up Zarathustra's soul. Surely, Zarathustra is the terror of the life-denying and the weary. He has taught innocence and laughter. Surely, he need not be terrified. Zarathustra speechlessly seems not to see things this way, but he summons up strength to offer teaching on a theme as important as any in the book. This is in the chapter "Of Redemption" (2.42), and Lampert is surely close to the mark when he calls this "the most astonishing of all the chapters of *Thus Spoke Zarathustra*."[32]

The narrative setting is striking. Cripples and beggars come to Zarathustra for doctrinal healing. Zarathustra will not give it; instead, in rather ill-humored vein, he discourses as follows. At his first exodus from solitude, he saw worse things than cripples, beggars, and hunchbacks.

> Truly, my friends, I walk among men as among the fragments and limbs of men! The terrible thing to my eye is to find men shattered in pieces and scattered as if over a battle-field of slaughter. And when my eye flees from the present to the past, it always discovers the same thing: fragments and limbs and dreadful changes—but no men! The present and the past upon the earth—alas! my friends—that is my most intolerable burden; and I should not know how to live, if I were not a seer of that which must come. (Z 2.42)

Past and present must be redeemed. How? The answer to that question constitutes the essence of Nietzsche's contra-Christian teaching. It is this: "To redeem the past and to transform every 'It was' into an 'I wanted it thus'—that alone do I call redemption." This is reiterated later in the chapter "Old and New Law-Tables" (Z 3.56), and it is emphasized in the exposition of Z in *EH*. To own and to embrace necessity by understanding it as the will that finds its personal expression in me—that is victory. We are redeemed not from sin but from guilt, for there is no sin, and so there must be no guilt. Nor remorse. "The highest state a philosopher can attain: to stand in a Dionysian relationship to existence—my formula for this is *amor fati*" (WP 1041).[33] We are beyond the Spinozistic *amor fati* here, the serenely passionate embrace of that which is. We have become the *creator fati*. However we are supposed to do it, necessity must apparently be subjected to creative will.

But surely Old Father Time thwarts thought's movement in this direction. "The will cannot will backwards; that it cannot break time and time's desire—that is the will's most lonely affliction." Yet, says Zarathustra,

---

32. Lampert, *Nietzsche's Teaching*, 140.
33. Cf. Arthur Schopenhauer, *The World as Will and Representation*, 2 vols. (New York: Dover, 1966), 1:306: "There is no more effective consolation for us than the complete certainty of unalterable necessity."

"it is all my art and aim, to compose into one and bring together what is fragment and riddle and dreadful chance." Now:

> All "It was" is a fragment, a riddle, a dreadful chance—until the creative will says to it: "But I willed it thus!" . . . But has it ever spoken thus? And when will this take place? . . . The will that is the will to power must will something higher than any reconciliation—but how shall that happen? Who has taught it to will backwards, too?

This riddle is a matter of life and death. God, if we may interrupt Zarathustra for a second, had tremendous power. He held not just the present and future in his hands; he had the past there too. That is unparalleled power. Now the creative will must break free of him; yet surely humans cannot rise as high as the God (or the gods), once we have conceived them. Assign to humanity the greatest power. Put present and future potentially in the hands of the human who has the courage to dare and to create. But the past? Surely there is no way of willing backward. Or . . . unless—"At this point of his discourse, Zarathustra suddenly broke off and looked exactly like a man seized by extremest terror." Cut. But an inquiring hunchback slowly pursues a discerning line of questioning. Zarathustra, he observes, speaks differently to cripples than he does to disciples. The point cannot be shrugged off. Indeed, it can be pushed a stage further: "Why does Zarathustra speak to his pupils differently—than to himself?" Zarathustra does not answer directly. "My will clings to mankind, I bind myself to mankind with fetters, because I am drawn up to the Superman: for my other will wants to draw me up to the Superman." So Zarathustra confesses his heart's twofold will. Now the time has come for Zarathustra to go away again.

A heavy weight lies on the final scene of part 2. The increased wisdom and pain that Zarathustra experienced in his sojourn in the cave, between the first and second downgoings, has been reflected in the story and teaching of this part. If a distinctive feature of the increased wisdom be picked out, it apparently lies in the teaching of the will-to-power. Increased pain is caused not by rejection and sorrow but by terror and inward perturbation. There is something as yet undisclosed, perhaps suspected or inchoately known. What? That he must command? That prophet must metamorphose into lawgiver? "Do you know," said something voicelessly to Zarathustra in a dream, "what it is all men most need? Him who commands great things." That is a harder business than doing. And the voiceless voice chides or chastises: "This is the most unpardonable thing about you: You have the power and you will not rule." Zarathustra's fruits are ripe, but Zarathustra is not ripe for his fruits. So back to solitude. Zarathustra weeps at departure; nevertheless, he goes. Once more, he will return, whether or not as commander, certainly as bearer of the essential Nietzschean philosophy: the doctrine of the eternal recurrence of the same.[34]

Part 3

The departure at the end of the second part is different from that at the end of the first, since it is viewed as a kind of forsaking. The narrative line of part 3 is Zarathustra's return to the cave. Leaving his disciples, Zarathustra traverses the island and boards a ship. The voyage lasts four days. On gaining terra firma, he indirectly heads for his famous mountain retreat, wandering about, seeing what has become of humankind. So he comes back to the Pied Cow, two days away from his cave, where his animals await him and which he is eager to reach. The tale ends with his arrival at the cave, whence issues forth the song of revelation and of Revelation, climaxing what was originally the last book of Z.

It is specifically stated that Zarathustra's objective in adopting an indirect route back is the discovery of whether men have "become bigger or smaller."[35] He appears to obtain an answer quickly, and the title of the discourse "Of the Virtue That Makes Small" tells us what that answer is (Z 3.49). Zarathustra has both his overtly philosophical and his emotionally distant moments in reacting to people's reaction to him and to his teaching. They are in a different world, but he nonetheless determines to stay civil toward them. People are definitely diminishing, however, *"and their doctrine of happiness and virtue is the cause."* They don't see that what they account "good" is really "weak." "They are frank, honest, and kind to one another, as grains of sand are frank, honest, and kind to grains of sand," Zarathustra memorably judges. Yet, phlegmatic as he can be, passion also breaks the surface of relative composure. How can it be otherwise when you are facing falsehood and apostasy? Zarathustra rails at the "teachers of submission! Wherever there is anything small and sick and scabby, there they crawl like lice; and only my disgust stops me from cracking them." One cannot become much bitterer than that, and in contemptuous defiance Zarathustra trumpets that he is "Zarathustra the Godless." These people can't even will. They diminish; Zarathustra grows.

Danger lurks. Zarathustra began his ministry by loving, cultivating a strong and proper self-determining and nonpitying sort of love; if he

34. Just "once more," if we assume that the work ends with part 3.
35. I am picking up the story from the start of the section "Of the Virtue That Makes Small," Z 3.49.

does not sustain such love appropriately, he will capitulate to the smallness of those who appear outwardly to indict exactly what Zarathustra indicts. A case of this appears when a fool called "Zarathustra's ape" eloquently castigates the shriveled soul of the religious, state-worshipping, newspaper-reading, festering masses (Z 3.51). "Well said," we may mutter on Zarathustra's behalf, but Zarathustra repudiates the fool. If one cannot love, one should pass by. Here Nietzsche keeps in his hand a number of threads: questions about society, state, politics, and religion are interwoven, though Z persistently returns to the central religious question. This latter point is illustrated in the chapter on apostates who have tragically returned to religion and so denied Zarathustra (3.52). God and the cross: what can be worse? In the end, solitude it must be. Among the people Zarathustra is lonely, but in solitude he finds contentment. So he comes home, where he can muse on pleasure, power, selfishness, and the "Spirit of Gravity," which makes life hard to bear and stops one from being oneself. "Man is difficult to discover, most of all to himself; the spirit often tells lies about the soul. The Spirit of Gravity is the cause of that." The great stumbling block is that "almost in the cradle are we presented with heavy words and values: this dowry calls itself 'Good' and 'Evil.'" This absolutely has to go. So Nietzsche arrives at "the decisive chapter," "Of Old and New Law-Tables" (3.56), and his next book after Z is titled *Beyond Good and Evil*, a more prosaic rendering, Nietzsche insisted, of what Z had to say.

"Of Old and New Law-Tables" is both retrospective and prospective reflection. "When I visited men, I found them sitting upon an old self-conceit. Each one thought he had long since known what was good and evil for man." Zarathustra has taught them differently, proposing to them that they become creators. So, for the first time in part 3, we are reminded of the "Superman." Creation presupposes redemption, for we shall not create until the past is owned as the product of my will, which puts us en route to redeeming it. But self-redemption is not complete before creation because it is also part of the creative endeavor. Creativity arches over past and future in its scope. In creative redemption, we must shatter the old law-tables, upon which are inscribed life-denying injunctions. The Ten Commandments must vanish, and the "worst of all trees, the Cross," must vanish with them. The imperative is *Will*! "Willing liberates: for willing is creating: thus I teach." You will be called lawbreaker, and they'll crucify you for that. Do it anyway. "Creators are hard. And it must seem bliss to you to press your hand upon millennia as upon wax, bliss to write upon the will of millennia as upon metal—harder than metal, nobler than metal." Heaviness and frustration brood over a chapter in which Zarathustra touches on a range of "moral" questions and shows how he is constantly inhibited in his enterprise by the people around him (3.57). There is a further problem. The earlier chapter, "Redemption," (2.42) put to us a riddle: how do you will backward? "Eternal recurrence" seems to be the answer to this, and on the face of it, it receives its clearest expression in the chapter (3.57) that follows the one on law-tables. Eternal recurrence unites redemption and creation. But how?

Early in part 3 Zarathustra has shared "a vision and a riddle." Mounting higher and higher, accompanied by the Spirit of Gravity, "half dwarf, half mole" squatting upon him, menacing and thwarting, Zarathustra reaches a gateway. Two unending paths meet there. One runs forward; one runs back. Zarathustra speculates:

> Must not all things that *can* run have already run along this lane? Must not all things that *can* happen *have* already happened, been done, run past? . . . Are not all things bound fast together in such a way that this moment draws after it all future things? . . . For all things that *can* run *must* also run once again forward along this long lane, . . . and I and you at this gateway whispering together, whispering of eternal things—must we not all have been here before?—and must we not return and run down that other lane out before us, down that long, terrible lane—must we not return eternally? (Z 3.46)

On the face of it, any obscurity in the meaning of this is cleared up by Zarathustra's animals when they show that they understand what no one else seems to understand. This happens in the later chapter, "The Convalescent."

> For your animals well know, O Zarathustra, who you are and must become: behold, *you are the teacher of the eternal recurrence*; . . . you have to be the first to teach this doctrine . . . that all things recur eternally and we ourselves with them, and that we have already existed an infinite number of times before and all things with us. . . . "Now I die and decay," you would say, "and in an instant I shall be nothingness. . . . But the complex of causes in which I am entangled will recur—it will create me again! I myself am part of these causes of the eternal recurrence. . . . I shall return eternally to this identical and self-same life." (Z 3.57)

From Nietzsche's notebooks of 1881 onward, we know that he chewed on the notion that there is only a finite number of states of affairs but that time is infinite and that in infinite time, the combinations of events that have occurred will recur.[36] In the literature on Nietzsche, we find discussions not just of the philosophy but also of the mathematics and

---

36. This is quite generally put. We could describe the issue in relation to energy or force (e.g., *WP* 1066).

the physics of eternal recurrence.[37] Nietzsche's unfulfilled ambition to spend a number of years studying science, apparently to clear up his thinking on this, also seems to testify to the fact that we are dealing here with a cosmological theory.

But this is contestable. Gilles Deleuze regarded a literal-scientific reading of Nietzsche's eternal recurrence as plain "childish," though he offered no exegesis of the passages in Nietzsche's notebooks or anywhere else that appear to command such a reading.[38] More forceful is the proposal that Nietzsche is treating eternal recurrence as the ground of an "existential imperative": what if your life were to recur eternally? Live *as though* it were to recur eternally. Lou Salomé was not alone in regarding a passage in *GS* as key here:

> What if some day or night a demon were to steal into your loneliest loneliness and say to you: "This life as you now live it and have lived it you will have to live once again and innumerable times again; and there will be nothing new in it, but every pain and every joy and every thought and sigh and everything unspeakably small or great in your life must return to you, all in the same succession and sequence. . . . Would you not throw yourself down and gnash your teeth and curse the demon who spoke thus? Or have you once experienced a tremendous moment when you have answered him: "You are a god, and never have I heard anything more divine"?[39]

Perhaps Nietzsche was less committed to a cosmological doctrine of eternal recurrence than committed, at least at one stage, to probing its possibility. Meanwhile, it yields its requisite existential, metaphorical sense. Requisite for what? The creative and redemptive mandate.

The merits of these alternative readings, crudely generalized and reported above, cannot be adjudicated here.[40] We must bear in mind that

37. See, e.g., Robin Small, *Nietzsche in Context* (Burlington, VT: Ashgate, 2001).

38. Gilles Deleuze, *Nietzsche and Philosophy* (New York: Columbia University Press, 1983), xi.

39. *GS* 341. This is the penultimate section in what at the time of writing was the last book of *GS*, followed only by an introduction to Zarathustra that Nietzsche proceeded to take up in *Z* itself. As in "The Vision and the Riddle" (*Z* 3.46), Nietzsche here refers to the recurrence of spider and moonlight.

40. Even if we go no further than the introduction to eternal recurrence in *Z*, in the chapter "The Vision and the Riddle" (*Z* 3.46) what is pictured and what is proposed are not unambiguously clear. What do we have? Picture? Concept? What Rudolf Otto called an "ideogram" in *The Idea of the Holy* (New York and London: Oxford University Press, 1926), 19–24, 35? All of them? When the arch-inimical dwarf affirms that time is a circle, does Zarathustra repudiate the notion or just its dwarfish appropriation? For everything to recur, does not time need to be cyclical, and are the lanes pictured in this chapter curved in order to give a circular possibility? And does the cyclical need to be circular? Is it helpful to conceive of a wheel, which describes an eternally identical cyclical motion while

Nietzsche knew something along these lines had been debated in ancient philosophy as a cosmological theory.[41] It might still be a novelty either as something demonstrably scientifically viable or as a mystical revelation that hit Nietzsche himself. What is apparently novel in Nietzsche over against the ancients, however we are reading him on eternal recurrence, is the redemptive reading of life entwined with the teaching. The crown of Christianity, its teaching on redemption, is now placed on the head of the teaching on eternal recurrence. The question: How can the will will backward? is not the question: How can I *change* the past?[42] The question is about affirming the past in the sense of apprehending it gladly and decisively as my own by willing it to be what it is and was. How can we will what is past? One promising line seems to be the following: Suppose I entirely embrace what I am today and will be tomorrow. On this view of things, I have a liberty of spontaneity; I express the most perfect *amor fati*.[43] I want things to be thus and want them to be nothing but thus: I shall will them in any existential (or metaphysical) way that I can. But I am what I am and will be what I will be by virtue of what is past. Without my past, I cannot be what I am to be—and now resolve to will to be—tomorrow. Therefore, in willing the future, I must will the past as well.

While all this is, I think, implicit in Nietzsche, it still does not explain eternal recurrence. It requires only the affirmation of my past and future. True, that is the affirmation of the whole cosmic past and future, since I am what I am because of the intertwining of all things, past, present, and future.[44] Yet it does not require eternal recurrence. However, if I do affirm eternal recurrence and will my own redemption, I have secured

---

traversing perpetually and linearly? Should we be asking these questions? And so on. In the spirit of his interpretation at this point, with its balanced combination of exposition and tentative refusal to be dogmatic, Alexander Nehamas in *Nietzsche: Life as Literature* (Cambridge: Harvard University Press, 1985) is admirable. Yet his conclusion is surely not persuasive. He takes the fundamental proposition about eternal recurrence to be of the form "If my life were to recur, then it could recur only in identical fashion" (153). A logical claim mounted on a conditional proposition seems to me too existentially remote from Nietzsche's thinking.

41. See, e.g., the generally informative study by Patrick Moroney, *Nietzsche's Dionysian Aristocratic Culture* (Maynooth, UK: Kairos, 1986).

42. So, mistakenly, Giles Fraser, *Redeeming Nietzsche: On the Piety of Unbelief* (New York: Routledge, 2002), 109.

43. Liberty of spontaneity denies a libertarian view of freedom but affirms a compatibility between freedom and determination. Admittedly, it may be altogether too dangerous to try to plot Nietzsche's position in relation to this terminology, and if we do, how exactly should we do it?

44. "To desire that something should be different from what it is means to desire that everything should be different—it involves a condemnatory critique of the whole. But life itself is such a desire!" (*WP* 333). Cf. *WP* 1032.

the grandest imaginable scheme. Nietzsche was in pursuit of that. The passage in *GS* on the death of God requires that we be worthy of the deed. Christianity, or Judeo-Christianity in alliance with Platonism, devised the greatest idea going: a God who is eternal, who creates and redeems. Here Nietzsche has more than matched that. What is eternal will recur.[45]

However much sleep we might lose over the interpretation of the doctrine of eternal recurrence, Zarathustra certainly lost sleep over it, for it has nasty entailments. It is one thing if Zarathustra (or Nietzsche) returns or recurs—that gives world history its highest value.[46] But a recurrent Zarathustra (or Nietzsche) must be locked in perpetual Heraclitean strife with the little people, who will also recur. "'Alas, man recurs eternally! The little man recurs eternally!' . . . eternal recurrence even for the smallest! that was my disgust at all existence! Ah, disgust! Disgust! Disgust!" ("The Convalescent," *Z* 3.57.2). At this point the animals cut him off, which is surely one reason for being cautious about taking their description of Zarathustra's teaching as the hermeneutical key to it.[47] Zarathustra's triumph consists of his biting this bullet.[48] Part 3 ends with "The Seven Seals (or: The Song of Yes and Amen)" (3.60), echoing the triumph of the book of Revelation. Zarathustra proclaims aloud his love of eternity. According to Tyler Roberts, "Nietzsche figures two modalities of desire: suffering desires life, though not its own, and joy desires eternity."[49] I am not sure if it is the case that suffering does not desire its own life, but if Roberts is right, it would be worth asking how to counterpose to this the twin modalities of suffering and joy in Christianity. Still, what we certainly find at the end of Revelation, we also find here in Nietzsche: a shadow.[50] The shadow is shaped more by mood than by word, at least in these closing songs. It is more than the

45. We must highlight the qualitative magnitude of Nietzsche's conception. Even if we should not strictly cavil at Ian Markham's way of putting it—"Live every moment as if you will live it a million times"—the numerical specification seems to me somehow to risk weakening the strength of Nietzsche's affirmation about infinite reality; see Ian Markham, *Truth and the Reality of God: An Essay in Natural Theology* (Edinburgh: T&T Clark, 1998), 111.

46. Although some will want to draw a distinction between "returning" and "recurring," I am using both words to say the same thing at this point.

47. Another reason, perhaps, is that Zarathustra does not respond to them. But we are exercising caution, not denying that the key may be here.

48. Or biting off the head of the snake, if that is what is in mind in "Of the Vision and the Riddle," *Z* 3.46.2.

49. Tyler T. Roberts, *Contesting Spirit: Nietzsche, Affirmation, Religion* (Princeton, NJ: Princeton University Press, 1998), 135.

50. See Rev. 22:15. For the book of Revelation and the structure of *Z*, see Laurence Lampert, *Nietzsche and Modern Times: A Study of Bacon, Descartes, and Nietzsche* (New Haven: Yale University Press, 1993), 368.

pathos of desire. It invites application to Z of a remark by Julia Kristeva: "If there exists no writing that is not amorous, then neither does there exist imagination that is not, manifestly or secretly, melancholic."[51] And that is eternally that, as far as Z goes. Or so it seemed. But as a matter of fact, it was not the end. Zarathustra returned.

Part 4

Z was on its way into print early in 1884, but later in that year Nietzsche took up the tale again, and this fourth and—as it transpired, final—book was privately circulated for some time before it joined the other three. The circumstances surrounding its addition have led Rosen, for example, to conclude that "it is obviously impossible to arrive at a final interpretation of the work as a whole."[52] Even after learning how Nietzsche crafted this part in relation to the first three, we cannot interpret it definitively.[53] Judgments will still differ on the significance, value, and literary quality of part 4.[54] It supplements, if not completes, the earlier parts in at least two major ways. First, without necessarily advancing their conceptual connections very far, it reintroduces the vocabulary of *Übermensch* and links it with eternal recurrence. Second, at the end of part 3 we may well ask: What of Zarathustra's disciples? Part 4 at least gives some answer.

In atmosphere, it differs from the others. There is a cloying and brooding feel to it. More than in the other parts, it conveys something of the sense and ethos of the barren godlessness spreading over late-nineteenth-century German culture and society. The story line itself is tighter than in the other parts and thrown into bold relief. After the renewed isolation that concludes part 3, "months and years passed over Zarathustra's soul, and he did not heed it; his hair, however, grew white." At his animals' suggestion, he climbs a mountain. There, solitary and laughing, he muses. Whatever wisdom he has gained, the issue of disciples, or at least pupils, remains unresolved. So the encounters begin again, sparked off by a challenge offered by a soothsaying figure. Zarathustra's test will have to do with pity and with a search for, or reckoning with, "higher men."

51. "On the Melancholic Imagery," in *Discourse in Psychoanalysis and Literature*, ed. Shlomith Rimmon-Kenan (London: Methuen, 1987), 105.

52. Rosen, *Mask of Enlightenment*, 207.

53. Details of the crafting are in Lampert, *Nietzsche's Teaching*, 287ff.

54. Deleuze, ever independent and a trifle gnomic, says: "This book is the essence of the published Zarathustra" (*Nietzsche and Philosophy*, 164). See too Philip Pothen, *Nietzsche and the Fate of Art* (Burlington, VT: Ashgate, 2002), 90–97.

"Pity," or "compassion," is one of the most important themes in Nietzsche's literature. It is also deep. Both English words are used to translate the German *Mitleid*. This may not be an optimal state of affairs, and yet it may be hard to avoid. In English, "pity" is probably liable to contain a note of condescension not present in "compassion."[55] One criticism of Nietzsche is that he reduces all forms of compassion to a form of pity.[56] *"Where lie your greatest dangers?"* we recall Nietzsche asking and then answering: "In compassion" (*GS* 271).[57] This is where Schopenhauer went so badly wrong, from Nietzsche's point of view. The pity mentioned at the present juncture of *Z* is presumably pity at the plight of "higher men" whom Zarathustra will encounter. At all events, a cry of distress rings out, and Zarathustra sallies forth. Conversations begin. First, he meets two kings leading an ass, presumably breaking from the rabble and purporting to be in search of the Highest Man (*Z* 4.63). Then he stumbles across a self-styled *"conscientious man of the spirit,"* apparently a man of science, his blood flowing after a leech has laid into him (4.64). Then we have a character who part-simulates and part-exhibits penitence of spirit; apparently it is Wagner, or a Wagnerian type (4.65). He is a sorcerer. But then comes an encounter with an old pope, and this encounter is different (4.66).

In the course of these previous meetings, *Z* emphasizes that the forests and mountains Zarathustra traverses are now the terrain and kingdom of Zarathustra, wherein he offers refuge for the afflicted in his own cave. The kings and the victim of the leech need Zarathustra, and in their conversational exchanges with him, the question of God has scarcely arisen.[58] With the sorcerer, things changed. He was one with the others in his need for Zarathustra and in his eventual receipt of an invitation to the cave. But he roused in Zarathustra different emotions. Zarathustra actually started beating him with a stick, for the sorcerer was wailing away to the unknown god (God?), who is a malicious and tormenting huntsman, a jealous hangman, hidden and

---

55. When Alasdair MacIntyre, to whose work we refer in a subsequent chapter, is discussing Aquinas, he retains *misericordia* to avoid the connotations of "pity" in English; see *Dependent Rational Animals: Why Human Beings Need the Virtues* (London: Duckworth, 1999), 123. Also see Oliver O'Donovan's comment on the further distinction between compassion and sympathy, in *The Desire of the Nations: The Roots of Political Theology* (Cambridge: Cambridge University Press, 1996), 276.

56. Martha C. Nussbaum, "Pity and Mercy: Nietzsche's Stoicism," in *Nietzsche, Genealogy, Morality: Essays on Nietzsche's "Genealogy of Morals,"* ed. Richard Schacht (Berkeley: University of California Press, 1994), helps us get a grip on some important distinctions here.

57. Walter Kaufmann's translation of *The Gay Science* (Vintage: New York, 1974) uses the word "pity" here (ad loc.).

58. Though see the poem at the end of "Conversation with the Kings," *Z* 4.63.1.

cruel—but finally, what else is there? Was this, strange as it may seem, directed at the Dionysiac substitute for the old God?[59] Whatever the answer to this, the character before us clearly exhibits a postreligious attitude decidedly not inculcated by Zarathustra. We certainly observe that the issue of God/god in some form remains at the heart of Zarathustra's concerns.

Now the thoughtful and relatively solemn exchange with the pope, "retired from service," centers on the question of God in a more dispassionate and sober way. This pope is the last pope and has learned that God is dead. Such news brings him no cheer, and there is no consoling alternative. Zarathustra asks him straight: "Do you know *how* he died? Is it true what they say, that pity choked him, that he saw how *man* hung on the Cross and could not endure it, that love for man became his Hell and at last his death?" Nietzsche connects the death of God with the biblical ascription of death to God the Son, as did Hegel, albeit in a different way. God's ultimate act, the climax of the drama of redemption, is the supreme expression of pity. Nietzsche is determined to effect as radical a reversal as possible of the Christian view of things, which he achieves by storming and subverting its vocabulary, tenets, and worldview and by substituting Zarathustra for Christ. This must involve the absolute rejection of pity, and Zarathustra has a persistent, though sometimes elusive, temptation in this respect.

The pope does not answer the question, but he confides in Zarathustra his feelings about God and the concept of God. As for the evolution of the concept of God, the primitive notion of the oriental potentate had yielded to the thought of a compassionate old duffer who, if not papally described as choking with pity on a cross, is described as suffocating through it in his dotage. Zarathustra's sanctioning of this line of thought is perhaps more apparent than real.[60] But he indulges in a supplementary comment: God was unclear in self-revelation and angry when victims of his unclarity did not understand. He failed in many of his acts. Whether coming as a recommendation or as a command from Zarathustra, the pope is told that he must *entirely* let God go. He, too, is welcome in the cave.

The next meeting reeks of the somber. Here the book to best effect exudes its distinctively bleak atmosphere, the pathos encompassing a nihilistic world that is posttheistic but without an alternative. Now Zarathustra encounters "the ugliest man." The scene is worth describing in Nietzsche's words:

59. See "Ariadne's Complaint" in *DD* and Hollingdale's attached comments on this (pp. 91–93).

60. Peter Berkowitz, *Nietzsche: The Ethics of an Immoralist* (Cambridge: Harvard University Press, 1995), 217.

> But when the path again rounded a rock, all at once the scenery changed, and Zarathustra stepped into a kingdom of death. Here black and red cliffs projected up: no grass, no tree, no cry of birds. For it was a valley which all beasts avoided, even the beasts of prey; except that a kind of ugly, thick, green serpent, when it grew old, came here to die. Therefore the shepherds called this valley "Serpent's Death." (Z 4.67)

A weight of recollection and reflection descends on Zarathustra's mind. He slows and stops. An ugly humanoid form appears on his path. The sight is unbearably shameful. It comes as close to vanquishing Zarathustra spiritually as anything has. In fact, for a moment it does conquer: Zarathustra sinks down in pity. Rosen opines: "He pities the human generation that must undergo a lingering death, and, in so pitying, he is pulled down to the level of the suffering of what must be overcome."[61] That may be so; we may wonder whether this sits easily with the experience of Nietzsche the man, but if we start asking that about everything, we should be spending a long time away from our text. Zarathustra is not the historical Nietzsche any more than he is the historical Zoroaster. Anyway, Zarathustra now recovers and steels himself. He identifies the man before him and it is, prima facie, a surprising identification. "'I know you well,' he said in a brazen voice: *You are the murderer of God*! Let me go.'" The ugliest man nevertheless pleads with Zarathustra. Zarathustra is his one hope, because Zarathustra will not yield to pity, having surrendered such a virtue. This constitutes the most radical contrast with God. God

> *had* to die: he looked with eyes that saw *everything*—he saw the depths and abysses of man, all man's hidden disgrace and ugliness. His pity knew no shame: he crept into my dirtiest corners. This most curious, most over-importunate, over-compassionate god had to die. He always saw *me*: I desired to take revenge on such a witness—or cease to live myself. The god who saw everything, *even man*: this god had to die! Man could not *endure* that such a witness should live. (Z 4.67)

Pity shames. Zarathustra is chilled.[62] But although Zarathustra is now in the kingdom of death and not in his own kingdom, still, this man is also invited to the cave. Never has Zarathustra more strenuously reflected on the truth that "man, however, is something that must be overcome."

This passage suggests how Nietzsche's own philosophy stands in different relation to the respective concepts of divine omnipotence and divine

---

61. Rosen, *Mask of Enlightenment*, 219.

62. The word "chilled" appears twice on 279 in Hollingdale's translation, once at the beginning of the following section, "The Voluntary Beggar." They are not exactly the same German words but are derived from the same root.

omniscience.[63] Divine power and divine knowledge surely evoke different reactions in Nietzsche. Divine power is something one can ultimately admire. Mighty "Jehovah" (Yahweh), found in the earliest strata of the Hebrew Bible, is a character one can admire for his carefree power.[64] But as for the state or activity of *knowing* everything about everyone, that is different. Power of itself is sublimely indifferent to others; knowledge that is interested in others ravages them. Even debased power is not the same as knowledge. It is bad enough for such a character to know all about us and blast everyone except groveling devotees to everlasting perdition. It is positively obscene for him to peer into what goes on in one's conscious or subconscious psyche in the long hours of the day and the small hours of the night and then to act in respect of it in a *pitying* way. Power might evoke fear. Knowledge evokes shame. There is nothing worse. It has been maintained that "since his [Nietzsche's] attack on Christianity develops out of his critique of the monotheistic vision of absolute divine power and human abjection, a Christian vision concentrating on God's vulnerability avoids the blows of Nietzsche's idol-smashing hammer."[65] Surely not. Nietzsche may dislike the concept of power in developed monotheism. But the hammer comes down with most force on anything in God that includes pity or, its companion concept, vulnerability. As for the possibility that the vulnerability of the cross arises from pity for humans and that God *knows* things about us that make him feel that way—this makes Nietzsche want to vomit.[66]

We return to the narrative. After the dire gravity of the encounter with the ugliest man, there follows an artistically elegant counterpoise, a meeting with a "voluntary beggar," which bubbles up, though not to overflow, with light and laughter (Z 4.68). This is probably Jesus, so represented on the basis of some contemporary interpretations. Finally, there is one more figure or one more voice to contend with before Zarathustra returns to his cave: his own shadow (4.69). The shadow has been a seeking wanderer; its nomadic search was its affliction. Yes—the shadow, too, may enter Zarathustra's cave. "Take care," Zarathustra

63. Weaver Santaniello, ed., *Nietzsche and the Gods* (Albany: State University of New York Press, 2001), 73–83, who argues the case for "Socrates as the Ugliest Murderer of God," speaks of divine omnipresence rather than omniscience. See Paul Tillich, "The Escape from God," in this same volume, 173–79.

64. Cf. *WP* 1037.

65. Roberts, *Contesting Spirit*, 183. Cf. Paul Tillich: "This is the God Nietzsche said had to be killed because nobody can tolerate being made into a mere object of absolute knowledge and absolute control. This is the deepest root of atheism" (*The Courage to Be* [London: Fount, 1962], 179).

66. Eberhard Jüngel makes a similar mistake in *God as the Mystery of the World* (Edinburgh: T&T Clark, 1983), esp. 109–12. Roberts (*Contesting Spirit*) and Jüngel both emphasize vulnerability rather than omniscience.

bids the shadow, "that you are not at last captured by a narrow belief, a hard, stern illusion! For henceforth everything that is narrow and firm will entice and tempt you." Though the figure of Zarathustra's shadow is fraught with interest, we must leave it shadowy.

Zarathustra is now able to appreciate afresh his love of solitude, but he is in no position to relish it immediately because, on returning to the cave, he finds his day's companions waiting, from kings to shadow (4.71). Since they are there by his invitation, their presence as such is no cause for surprise. The surprise is the cry of distress that Zarathustra hears issuing from the cave, a cry uttered by the many but heard as single, the cry that earlier in the same day first sent Zarathustra in search of the Higher Man. But he soon sums up the situation. All these may be relatively higher men, but they are not high enough. They are, at best, bridges and steps for the really higher men. Prosaically put, the break with God needs to be more radical than it is with this lot. It needs to be absolute. If it is not absolute, it is little.

Now is the time for a meal together, a Last Supper, with bread and wine, and a homily. While God lived, men were equals. Now he has died, let us set that aside so "that the Superman shall live." The question of the day is, "How shall man be *overcome*?" "The Superman lies close to my heart, *he* is my paramount and sole concern—and *not* man: not the nearest, not the poorest, not the most suffering, not the best." Courage! Resist petty egalitarianism. It will be hard, and take hardness. It will mean suffering. Calculate and strive. Don't be diverted from your task by false values. "Your work, your will is *your* 'neighbour': let no false values persuade you otherwise!" Laugh. (Remember One who didn't?) Zarathustra is "the laughing prophet."[67] And dance. "You Higher Men, the worst about you is: none of you has learned to dance as a man ought to dance—to dance beyond yourselves! What does it matter that you are failures!" But, especially, laugh.

After the speech, there is some movement to and fro, with Zarathustra stepping out of the cave and back in again, the "Higher Men" discussing, discoursing, even deliberating among themselves (Z 4.74). Overhearing them, we learn that the great threat to Zarathustra's teaching is Melancholy. His shadow puts it well: "Here there is much hidden misery that wants to speak out, much evening, much cloud, much damp air!" The "old arch-enemy," the Spirit of Gravity, is at the bottom of it, fomenting potential recalcitrance. The combat is subtle and easily turned one way or another. At one stage, Zarathustra seems to have made a breakthrough, and the sign of this is the confession of the ugliest man:

67. I am adapting the description of Democritus, the "laughing philosopher." Heraclitus was the "weeping philosopher." Nietzsche aspires to join laughter and weeping, which Dionysus will not allow to be torn asunder.

For the sake of this day—I *am* content for the first time to have lived my whole life. And it is not enough that I testify only this much. It is worth while to live on earth: one day, one festival with Zarathustra has taught me to love the earth. "'Was *that*—life?' I will say to death. 'Very well! Once more!'" (Z 4.79)

In the aftermath of this speech, victory seems complete: all seem to be converted to Zarathustra's teaching. But not quite and not really, given the way of humans. Zarathustra is solemn. Still, he sings. Back comes the theme of eternal recurrence, back the twelve chimes of the clock at midnight.[68] The teaching about the Superman that opened part 1 and that has reappeared in part 4 culminates in the celebration of eternal recurrence announced in part 3, now sung as a song of joyous affirmation in the presence of the guests. "Did you ever say Yes to one joy? O my friends, then you said Yes to *all* woe as well. All things are chained and entwined together, all things are in love."

So, Nietzsche teaches us, we must love or hate. The world must be taken as a whole, either denied, rejected, hated as a whole or accepted, affirmed, loved as a whole. Christians, like Platonists, divided the world. One (ideal) world they loved, the other (real) one they hated. You can't do that. Schopenhauer denied God but proceeded to deny the reality that was left: the world. Christianity needs to be totally inverted. Deny God and love the world. If that sounds like Christian or Platonic dualism in reverse, remember that the realm the Platonists and Christians laud is nonexistent. So love and affirm all that you are left with, and the world is all that is the case. Take the whole.

Z draws to its close. As he did at the beginning, so now Zarathustra emerges alone from his cave (4.80). The higher men sleep on. Zarathustra knows that, despite all that he has done with and for them, they are not his true companions. They are as fickle, we may assume, as any of Jesus's disciples at his Last Supper. Who are his true companions? His animals, and they multiply as doves, birds, and a magnificent lion appear. A sign. His true children are near. But Zarathustra has accomplished something. He has vanquished his highest temptation, which is to pity. His day will come; his time is near. For now, Zarathustra has put clear water between himself and others. He is solitary.

Conclusion?

What is Z? A vision? A dream? A mask? Overbeck had a letter from Nietzsche in August 1883, which said that Zarathustra was "the long-

---

68. See "The Second Dance Song," Z 3.59.3.

promised Antichrist. There has not been since Voltaire such an outrageous attack on Christianity—and, to tell the truth, even Voltaire had no idea that one could attack it in *this* way."[69] That was just over six months after Overbeck received the following communication: "All my human relations have to do with a mask of me, and I must perpetually be the victim of living a completely hidden life."[70] *Z* is subtitled "A book for Everyone and No One." In a piece called "Everything and Nothing," Borges wrote: "There was no one inside him; behind his face (which even in the bad paintings of the time resembles no other) and his words (which were multitudinous, and of a fantastical and agitated turn) there was no more than a slight chill, a dream someone had failed to dream."[71] Is that Zarathustra and *Thus Spoke Zarathustra*? Or is the truth more prosaic? "Zarathustra," Nietzsche once scribbled to himself, "is merely an old atheist" (*WP* 1038).

There is a revealing letter written by Nietzsche at the beginning of December 1882:

> One gets to love something, and one has hardly begun to love it profoundly when the tyrant in us (which we are all too ready to call our "higher self") says, "Sacrifice *that* to me." . . . I tell you frankly that I have in myself too much of this "tragic" complexion to be able not to curse it; my experiences, great and small, always take the same course. What I desire most, then, is a high point from which I can see the tragic problem lying *beneath* me. I would like to *take away* from human existence some of its heartbreaking and cruel character.[72]

Here I agree with Michael Tanner: "The most genuine tone of *Thus Spoke Zarathustra*, which surfaces in surprising places, is one of regret. The least convincing is one of exaltation and affirmation, the qualities that Zarathustra is at such pains to inculcate."[73] Given the plenitude of what Zarathustra is trying to inculcate, this is a telling truth. After all, "I teach: that there are higher and lower men, and that a single individual can under certain circumstances justify the existence of whole millennia—that is, a full, rich, great, whole human being in relation to countless

69. *SL*, August 28, 1883.

70. *SL*, received February 11, 1883.

71. Jorge Luis Borges, *Collected Fictions* (New York and London: Penguin, 1998), 319.

72. *SL*, 196–97. This is consistent with Lou Salomé's diagnosis. For suffering as the paternity of *Z*, see Nietzsche's letter of April 6, 1883, to Peter Gast. *Z* should be read alongside *DD*, perhaps especially (in *DD*) "Amid Birds of Prey," "Fame and Eternity," and "Of the Poverty of the Richest Man."

73. Michael Tanner, *Nietzsche* (Oxford: Oxford University Press, 1994), 46.

incomplete fragmentary men" (*WP* 997).[74] In relation to Zarathustra, might we not reverse Nietzsche's judgment about Hamlet, who "speaks more superficially than he acts" (*BT* 17)?

Emily Dickinson's stanza is a good candidate for summing up matters: "Adventure most unto itself / The soul condemned to be— / Attended by a single Hound / Its own identity."[75] But we must revert to Jorge Luis Borges for the wider perspective. "It also occurred to him that throughout history, humankind has told two stories: the story of a lost ship sailing the Mediterranean seas in quest of a beloved isle, and the story of a god who allows himself to be crucified on Golgotha."[76] Z emerged because the wood of the cross was dismantled and recycled to fashion an entirely new craft.

74. The "I" here is Nietzsche himself; the note contains no reference to Zarathustra.

75. Thomas H. Johnson, ed., *The Complete Poems of Emily Dickinson* (London: Faber & Faber, 1970), no. 822.

76. In Borges's haunting story "The Gospel according to Mark," in *Collected Fictions*, 400.

6

ALTERNATIVE

Yet, see, he mastereth himself, and makes
His torture tributary to his will.

Byron, *Manfred*, act 2, scene 4

Barth and Others

In the previous chapter, I have tried to convey something of the drift
of Z. How should we react? When Nietzsche went to teach classical
philology in Basel, his ex officio responsibilities included teaching at
the local high school. Among his pupils was one Fritz Barth, on whom
he made a decidedly favorable impression.[1] His son, Karl, later offered
a characteristically robust account of and response to what Nietzsche
was up to in Z.[2] A survey of the third volume of the *Church Dogmatics*
(on creation) and the fourth (on reconciliation) would yield a massive
theological counterthesis to Nietzsche's philosophical anthropology. We

1. Eberhard Busch, *Karl Barth: His Life from Letters and Autobiographical Texts*
(London: SCM, 1976), 3.
2. Karl Barth, *Church Dogmatics*, vol. III/2 (Edinburgh: T&T Clark, 1960). Page references to this volume are inserted into the text. John Macken, in his economical study
The Autonomy Theme in the "Church Dogmatics" (Cambridge: Cambridge University Press,
1990), alludes to but does not develop Christof Gestrich's observation that Nietzschean
nihilism was the background to Barth's doctrine of God (203n98).

shall merely look in at one of the sideshows, the one that specifically
features Nietzsche.

Nietzsche is discussed in the course of Barth's treatment of the christological ground of theological anthropology and a discussion of Jesus
as the "Man for Other Men." Barth's objective is to insist that "when we
think of the humanity of Jesus, humanity is to be described unequivocally as fellow-humanity" (III/2:208). "In no sense is He there for Himself
first and then for men, nor for a cause first. . . . What interests Him,
and does so exclusively, is man, other men as such, who need Him and
are referred to Him for help and deliverance" (215). The very being of
Jesus Christ

> is wholly with a view to this alien being [man]. . . . Disposed by it, He
> disposes Himself wholly and utterly towards it, in utter disregard of the
> possibility that another task and activity might better correspond to His
> divine determination and be more worthy of it. . . . "Selfless" is hardly
> the word to describe this humanity. Jesus is not "selfless." . . . For in this
> way He is supremely Himself, . . . a supreme I wholly determined by and
> to the Thou. (215–16)

This grounds our theological convictions about the "Basic Form of
Humanity," and here Nietzsche enters the frame.[3] Theologically, "we
have to rule out the possibility of a humanity without the fellow-man,"
but of this rejected possibility

> it may be argued that it is not only infinitely more appealing but even
> self-evident on a non-theological view. . . . According to this constantly
> victorious conception, humanity consists in the fact that I am, that I am
> for myself, and neither from nor to others. . . . And if, for a moment, we
> suspend our Christian judgment, we at once recognise that it is the most
> obvious thing in the world to answer the question of humanity with per-
> haps a more profound and purified and convincing modification of this
> view. (229–31)

The best and theologically most illuminating exemplar of this egoistic view is Nietzsche. Barth's exposition of Nietzsche is ordered to the
demonstration of two points. The first is that Zarathustra, who is representative of Nietzsche and what Nietzsche wrote elsewhere, is concerned with himself and himself alone. "Nietzsche was basically and

---

3. If we want to get into Barth's theological anthropology rapidly—never a particularly
good idea with anything in Barth—Stuart D. McLean gives a helpful general account in
"Creation and Anthropology," in *Theology beyond Christendom*, ed. John Thompson (Al-
lison Park, PA: Pickwick, 1986), esp. 123–33. This is a fine volume that has not received
the publicity it deserves.

properly self-consciousness and nothing more. . . . When he was not engaged in polemics but spoke positively, Nietzsche never spoke except about himself."[4] Nietzsche's description of Zarathustra in *EH* and texts from *Z* itself are cited to show how this is so. The second point is that self-asserting, self-absorbed solitariness is designed by Nietzsche as the antithesis of Christian morality and its theanthropological ascription of spiritual worth to all that is opposed to Zarathustran humanity: "the lonely, strong, proud, natural, healthy, wise, outstanding, splendid man, the superman." Earlier, Barth has broached the question of whether the self-deception entailed in this self-absorption just brings to light "the spirit of all European humanity as fashioned and developed since the sixteenth century" through Leibniz and Goethe to Nietzsche's day.[5] Now he says:

> The new thing in Nietzsche was the man of "azure isolation," six thousand feet above time and man; the man to whom a fellow-creature drinking at the same well is quite dreadful and insufferable; the man who is utterly inaccessible to others, having no friends and despising women; the man who is at home only with the eagles and strong winds; the man whose only possible environment is desert and wintry landscape; the man beyond good and evil, who can exist only as a consuming fire. And so the new thing in Nietzsche's relationship to Christianity necessarily consisted in the fact that this pressed and embarrassed him in a way which the others had not seen, or at most had only sensed.[6]

In theological opposition to this, Barth naturally says that "Christianity places before the superman the Crucified, Jesus, as the Neighbour, and in the person of Jesus a whole host of others who are wholly and utterly ignoble and despised in the eyes of the world (of the world of Zarathustra, the true world of men). . . ." Credit to Nietzsche, however; he had seen the point. Did Strauss and Feuerbach, before him, have a tacit presentiment of that point when they kept "hammering away at what they declared to be so bankrupt a thing as Christianity, especially in a century when it no longer cut a very imposing figure outwardly, and

4. The following is drawn from *Church Dogmatics*, III/2:232–42.

5. This way of tracing the lineage back to Leibniz runs parallel to the important analysis of the way in which Protestant theology went off track in the eighteenth and early nineteenth centuries. See Karl Barth, *Protestant Theology in the Nineteenth Century* (London: SCM, 1972), esp. chaps. 2–3. The historical significance of Emil Brunner's espousal of natural theology, says Barth, lies in its return to the hopeless old paths of those centuries; see *Natural Theology*, ed. John Baillie, trans. Peter Fraenkel (London: Bles, 1946), 94ff.

6. When Barth says "new," we must read it in the light of his earlier accounts of other figures, especially his treatment of Fichtean isolation (*Church Dogmatics*, III/2:103–4).

the battle against it had long ceased to be a heroic war of liberation"? Whether or not we answer this in the affirmative,

> we have certainly to ask why Nietzsche was guilty of the Donquixotry of acting in the age of Bismarck as if the Christian morality of 1 Cor. 1 constituted the great danger by which humanity necessarily found itself most severely imperilled at every turn. Yet the fact remains that Nietzsche did take up arms against Christianity, and especially the Christianity of 1 Cor. 1, as if it were a serious threat and no mere folly.

Why? Because he saw and understood the real thing when he was reckoning with Christianity. He "rejected . . . not a caricature of the Christian conception of humanity, but in the form of a caricature the conception itself."

> With his discovery of the Crucified and His host he discovered the Gospel itself in a form which was missed even by the majority of its champions, let alone its opponents, in the 19th century. And by having to attack it in this form, he has done us the good office of bringing before us the fact that we have to keep to this form as unconditionally as he rejected it, in self-evident antithesis not only to him, but to the whole tradition on behalf of which he made this final hopeless sally.

This is Barth's reaction, in brief. From a theological point of view, can we gainsay it? I have quoted him at relative length because it may appear that he adequately states on our behalf a Christian reaction to Nietzsche. Certainly, there is a lot of truth in what he says. Barth is clearly justified in positing cohumanity, being for others, as the antithesis of Nietzsche's conception and in deriving the notion of true humanity from the humanity of Jesus. Yet something is missing from his account. Recall Barth's characterization of "Zarathustra or Dionysius, the lonely, noble, strong, proud, natural, healthy, wise, outstanding, splendid man, the superman." That "lonely" should be the first word is appropriate: loneliness or solitude—words interchangeable in this context, where we are not analyzing soul emotion—is much in evidence in the *Dithyrambs of Dionysus*.[7] The reality of Nietzsche's experience and that of the ideal

---

7. In *DD* see, e.g., "The Fire-Signal": "*Six* solitudes he [Zarathustra] knew already; . . . it is a *seventh* solitude he seeks to catch," a solitude of Sabbath rest. In "The Sun Sinks" Nietzsche returns to the seventh solitude, and in "Of the Poverty of the Richest Man" he refers to the "creator on his seventh day" (both in *DD*). Cf. *GS* 285, 309, and *EH*: "Solitude has seven skins" ("Thus Spoke Zarathustra," 5). We philosophers of the future, said Nietzsche, "shall live alone and probably suffer the torments of all seven solitudes" (*WP* 988).

Zarathustra somewhat overlap here.[8] What is glaringly absent from Barth's description is any reference to tragedy and pain, suffering and sorrow. Does that not mean that he has depicted only half a Zarathustra?[9] If so, what does this mean for our assessment of his insertion of Nietzsche into the lineage of Leibniz and of Goethe, for example, and the consequent claim that Nietzsche's anthropology completes and brings to light a momentous historical development in which these thinkers feature?[10] I do not doubt that the Barthian diagnosis and remedy are right in a measure, but if something is missing in Barth's diagnosis, is there something missing in the remedy?[11] Do we require more than a supplement to it? Do we need a corrective to it?

Not necessarily. Arguably, my challenge to Barth is altogether too credulous in taking at his word Nietzsche's description of his own tragic sense and suffering sensibility. Is Nietzsche not guilty of melodramatic "kitsch," to pick up Giles Fraser's terminology?[12] Fraser makes his point quite effectively. His main criticism of Nietzsche is that he "fails to appreciate the full horror of human suffering"; Nietzsche's "sense that suffering has the capacity to edify the noble spirit, is only possible from the perspective of one who knows not the destructive power of excremental assault."[13] Unconcerned about everyday politics, Nietzsche views suffering from a privileged aristocratic perspective. He is a world away from what is truly real and abominable in suffering. At this point, at least, he is bourgeois to his boots.[14]

8. Jaspers wondered whether anyone had experienced loneliness as intensely as had Nietzsche; see Karl Jaspers, *Nietzsche: An Introduction to the Understanding of His Philosophical Activity* (Tucson: University of Arizona Press, 1965), 116. Hollingdale found it "hard to think of anyone in the middle of modern Europe who succeeded in segregating himself from almost every kind of attachment so completely as Nietzsche did" (*DD* 88).

9. A rather Kantian half? See Iris Murdoch's description of Kantian man, whom she judged to be not far from Nietzsche, in *The Sovereignty of the Good* (London: Routledge & Kegan Paul, 1970), 80. Here we might bear in mind our discussion of Barth and tragedy in chap. 2 (above).

10. I am drawing on Terence J. Reed, *Goethe* (Oxford: Oxford University Press, 1984) in making my assumption about the absence of tragic sensibility in Goethe of the kind that we find in Nietzsche. It is certainly absent in Leibniz.

11. Though see John Webster's reference to "the distress and inhumanity which faced Barth everywhere he looked as he doggedly put together his text," in *Karl Barth* (London: Continuum, 2000), 77.

12. Giles Fraser, *Redeeming Nietzsche: On the Piety of Unbelief* (New York: Routledge, 2002), chap. 6.

13. Ibid., 2, 139.

14. Fraser echoes observations made by Thomas Mann a half a century after Nietzsche died: see Philippa Foot, "Nietzsche's Immoralism," in *Nietzsche, Genealogy, Morality: Essays on Nietzsche's "Genealogy of Morals,"* ed. Richard Schacht (Berkeley: University of California Press, 1994), 7, and Thomas Mann, "Nietzsche's Philosophy in the Light of Recent History," in *Last Essays* (London: Secker & Warburg, 1959).

Now that we have opened this particular door, other challengers clamor to get in, and we should hear them in their own voice. Is Nietzsche indulgent? German philosophers, Santayana thought, "suffer and wrestle continually, and by a curious and deeply animal instinct they hug and sanctify their endless struggle all the more when it rends and bewilders them, bravely declaring it to be absolute, infinite and divine."[15] Is he adolescent? "The effect" of Z's style "is that of a person who screams for fear that people are not seriously listening; it is also extremely adolescent."[16] C. S. Lewis writes:

> "Milton was right," said my Teacher. "The choice of every lost soul can be expressed in the words 'Better to reign in Hell than serve in Heaven.' There is always something they insist on keeping, even at the price of misery. There is always something they prefer to joy—that is, to reality. Ye see it easily enough in a spoiled child that would sooner miss its play and its supper than say it was sorry and be friends. Ye call it the Sulks. But in adult life it has a hundred fine names—Achilles' wrath and Coriolanus' grandeur, Revenge and Injured Merit and Self-Respect and Tragic Greatness and Proper Pride."[17]

"Tragic Greatness" is an especially pertinent phrase here.[18] Finally, it is worth mentioning that Hesse speaks of "plaintive grievances in the manner of romantic youths who have read Heine and become enraptured with a somewhat childish sorrow."[19]

I have lumped together a number of things that are distinguishable, but they constitute a chorus of appeals that we think twice before

15. George Santayana, *Egotism in German Philosophy* (London: Dent, 1939), 6.

16. Henry Hatfield, *Clashing Myths in German Literature from Heine to Rilke* (Cambridge: Harvard University Press, 1974), 84. Cf. Brian Hebblethwaite, *The Ocean of Truth* (Cambridge: Cambridge University Press, 1988), 34, on a different component of Nietzschean adolescence.

17. C. S. Lewis, *The Great Divorce* (London: Fount, 1977), 64. The "Teacher" is George MacDonald.

18. I have quoted the whole passage from *The Great Divorce*, and not just the reference to "Tragic Greatness," because it picks up the question of rejecting remorse, which is implicated in redemption by willing backward and the doctrine of eternal recurrence.

19. Hermann Hesse, *Beneath the Wheel* (New York: Bantam, 1968), 94. I am thinking of Heine as background to Nietzsche in general, not Z in particular. That Hesse is a generation later than Nietzsche does not affect the basic point being made, nor is it affected if he is not speaking in his own voice at this point in the novel. Cf. the comment in Hermann Kurzke, *Thomas Mann: Life as a Work of Art; A Biography* (Princeton, NJ: Princeton University Press, 2002), 27. (It simply defies belief that a translation of this deficient quality would be published by Princeton University Press. Cf. "Mann in English," in *The Cambridge Companion to Thomas Mann*, ed. Ritchie Robertson [Cambridge: Cambridge University Press, 2002] for an earlier set of problems.)

taking Zarathustra's suffering with the kind of profound seriousness that seems implied in the question I have put to Barth. I do not wish either to uphold or to reject these appeals. What Santayana and Hatfield say, for example, may be correct, but it is not my prerogative to make judgments on the passional character of German philosophy or the emotional maturity that informs the Nietzschean viewpoint. It is true that many of us are pathetically self-deluded in this broad respect; our hidden depths are well hidden because there are none.[20] This applies across the board, to both the religious and the irreligious. What we regard in ourselves as deep intensity is usually a shallow film on the crest of waves of self-absorption. We are like people who cannot tell the difference between the brazen glare of an artificial and tacky electric light and the rich pallor of a natural evening sky. Giles Fraser seems to me importantly correct on the particular point that he is making, and he well draws out its implications when juxtaposing the philosophy of Nietzsche to the reality of the Holocaust. Thomas Mann spoke of the "guilt of the intellect, its unpolitical disregard of the actual world, surrender to the aesthetic enjoyment of its own audacities. . . . In these secure bourgeois times, nobody realized how easily a people can be made to believe that there are no longer any iniquities which cry out to heaven."[21] Such iniquities have generated real and horrendous suffering.

Having said all this, the possibility of a telling riposte to Nietzsche along the various but potentially convergent lines traced out in these comments should not force us to accept Barth's omission as it stands. Having heard Hesse on Heine, we should heed him again:

> A man of the Middle Ages would detest the whole mode of our present life as something far more than horrible and cruel, far more than barbarous. . . . Human life is reduced to real suffering, to hell, only when two ages, two cultures and religions overlap. . . . There are times when a whole generation is caught in this way between two ages, between two modes of life and thus loses feeling for itself, for the self-evident, for all morals, for being safe and innocent. Naturally, everyone does not feel this equally strongly. A nature such as Nietzsche's had to suffer our present ills more than a generation in advance. What he had to go through alone and misunderstood, thousands suffer today.[22]

20. To paraphrase a characteristic remark of Paul Holmer's.

21. *SL* xi. Again, the point is unaffected by the fact that Mann was of a later generation.

22. Hermann Hesse, *Steppenwolf* (New York: Bantam, 1969), 28. There is a brilliant description of how "Steppenwolf's look pierced our whole epoch" (10). The novel was first published in 1927, in German.

We could take this as kitsch as well, and Hesse does appear capable of indulgent exaggeration on the question of suffering.[23] Barth had little sympathy for Hesse.[24] But as the Second World War drew to its close, Elton Trueblood made the simple observation, applicable to Nietzsche's day, that "a great part of the suffering of our time is of the mind," and Trueblood was certainly not one disposed to think or romanticize away the stark realities of earthly, communal, civic, practical, neighborly life.[25] Surely we need to attend with theological seriousness to the fact that Nietzsche ascribes suffering to Zarathustra, even if we do so by way of a metallic concession that we should give him the benefit of the doubt that something worth analyzing remains after we have indicted him on the charge of melodramatic kitsch. "We must learn," said Dietrich Bonhoeffer, "to regard people less in the light of what they do or omit to do, and more in the light of what they suffer"; Nietzsche, for all his idiosyncrasies, was not alone in his suffering.[26] Hesse was acutely aware of that, and his awareness emerges in the connection he makes between Novalis and Nietzsche on the question of suffering.[27] Nietzsche profoundly influenced Hesse: "I lived with him," says one of his characters—at this point echoing Hesse's own experience—"felt the loneliness of his soul, shared his prescience of the fate that drove him unceasingly on, suffered with him and rejoiced that there had been one man who had relentlessly followed his destiny."[28]

Hesse knew that "all extreme individuation turns against itself, intent upon its own destruction."[29] And he clearly signals the possibility that self-contempt was a root of Nietzsche's condition.[30] I do not say that Hesse always understood Nietzsche properly; further, his main characters differ from Nietzsche in important ways.[31] But he can pick up Nietzsche quite well:

23. See Hesse's description of Hermine in *Steppenwolf*, 125, even if we allow that Hesse is not directly owning the claim that Hermine has experienced such suffering.

24. Busch, *Karl Barth*, 125.

25. D. Elton Trueblood, *The Predicament of Modern Man* (New York: Harper & Row, 1944), 12.

26. Dietrich Bonhoeffer, *Letters and Papers from Prison* (London: SCM, 1971), 10.

27. Hesse, *Steppenwolf*, 17. See Novalis and Nietzsche in Hermann Hesse's *Demian* (London: Peter Owen, 2001), 92, and Mann, "Nietzsche's Philosophy," 165–66.

28. Hesse, *Demian*, 147.

29. Hesse, *Steppenwolf*, 61.

30. Ibid., 11.

31. In *Demian*, 92, Hesse makes a faulty connection between Nietzsche and Jesus. Hesse's main characters differ from Nietzsche in other works, too, such as *Narcissus and Goldmund* (New York: Farrar, Straus & Giroux, 1968). Hesse himself was quite unlike Nietzsche. For why Hesse was not, on his own account, one of Nietzsche's followers, see Joseph Mileck, *Hermann Hesse: Life and Art* (Berkeley: University of California Press, 1978), 92n59. Mileck goes on to say that Hesse responded differently to Nietzsche at different times.

That man is not yet a finished creation but rather a challenge of the spirit;
a distant possibility dreaded as much as it is desired; that the way towards
it has only been covered for a very short distance and with terrible agonies
and ecstasies even by those few for whom it is the scaffold today and the
monument tomorrow—all this the Steppenwolf too, suspected.[32]

Without saying as much at this juncture, Barth implies that Nietzsche's
"tragic suffering" is epiphenomenal on a Promethean philosophy of
humanity and that the important thing is the underlying Promethean
substance, not the epiphenomenal presentation of suffering. Perhaps,
indeed, if philosophies inspired by Nietzsche capitalize on his solitariness and immoralism without sharing much of the tragic dimension,
they are credibly taking up some basic elements in Nietzsche's thought.
Nietzsche is no stranger to melodrama, and there is a difference between
raw, externally imposed, eventful tragedy and indulgent aristocratic
self-immolation. Yet we can never forget the grief that set in so early in
Nietzsche's life and the history and ramifications of its emotional consequences. Nor can we forget the physical suffering. Further, when we go
back to Schopenhauer, so influential on later artists, and to Wagner as
well, we find that the tragic is becoming deeply implicated in the nineteenth-century perception of life among culturally dominating figures. If
the tragic and suffering in Nietzsche turns out to be just epiphenomenal
or just kitsch—and I am deliberately going beyond Barth, Fraser, and
others in putting it so flat-footedly—at least it is profitable to consider
a response to him that takes these things into account on more or less
the terms that Nietzsche invites. But the proof of this pudding will be in
the eating. Barth postulates the social lovingness of Jesus in opposition
to the solitary lovelessness of Zarathustra and speaks of Christ's suffering in his love. Nietzsche also speaks of the love of Jesus. If critics find
adolescence in Zarathustra, Nietzsche finds something superficially more
dramatic in Jesus: immature idiocy. We turn to Nietzsche on Jesus as we
seek a way into an alternative or supplementary response to Nietzsche
but not one contradictory to what we have discovered in Barth.

Idiot?

Opinions differ on the question of how exactly Nietzsche regarded
Jesus. It is certainly true that he placed Jesus in a certain antithesis to
Christianity and that he did not feel toward him the hostility provoked
by the religion that bears his name. Surely the intrusion of irony does not

32. Hesse, *Steppenwolf*, 71.

cloud the transparency of Nietzsche's description of Christ as the "noblest human being," a phrase he uses in one of his earlier works.[33] Yet, what Nietzsche has to say about Jesus is predominantly and strongly negative. That he was the Son of God is palpable nonsense, yet he certainly "regarded himself as the innate son of God and as a consequence felt himself to be sinless" in a world where "the whole of antiquity swarmed with gods" (*HH* 113, 144).[34] The trouble is that Jesus "regarded everyone as being in the greatest measure and in almost every respect a sinner," even if he himself was not (*WS* 81). His self-consciousness led him to think that "there was nothing of which men suffered more than their sins," and this was his great error (*GS* 138). The religious topography certainly did not help him much: "A Jesus Christ was possible only in a Jewish landscape—I mean one over which the gloomy and sublime thunder clouds of the wrathful Jehovah hovered continually" (*GS* 137).

Jesus's teaching is full of foolish errors. You can't forgive people "if they know not what they do! One has nothing whatever *to* forgive."[35] Luke 18:14 would read better if amended: "He that humbleth himself wants to be exalted" (*HH* 87). There is at least a streak of dishonesty in the injunction to seek first the kingdom of God "and all these things shall be added unto you" (*D* 456; Matt. 6:33 KJV).

> The founder of Christianity was, as goes without saying, not without the gravest shortcomings and prejudices in his knowledge of the human soul, and as a physician of the soul devoted to that infamous and untutored faith in a universal medicine. At times his methods seem like those of a dentist whose sole cure for pain is to pull out the teeth; as, for example, when he combats sensuality with the advice: "If thy eye offend thee, pluck it out." (*WS* 83; Matt. 5:28–29)[36]

Jesus was neither as wise nor as intelligent as Socrates (*WS* 86). Noble as he was, he doubtless had the warmest of hearts, but he "promoted the stupidifying of man, placed himself on the side of the poor in spirit and retarded the production of the supreme intellect: and in this he was consistent" (*HH* 235). He came to an unhappy end. To "set

33. *HH* 475. "Noblest," not "the most loving of men" as in Eugen Biser, "Nietzsche's Relation to Jesus," in *Nietzsche and Christianity*, ed. Claude Geffré and Jean-Pierre Jossua (Edinburgh: T&T Clark, 1981), 61. The context of Nietzsche's comment, incidentally, illuminates the question of Nietzsche's attitude toward the Jews.

34. Nietzsche allows that the church early came to make christological claims that are unfounded in Jesus's self-understanding. Yet it remains that Jesus understood himself as Son of God in some silly and unacceptable sense.

35. *WS* 68. I call Jesus's cry a "teaching" in light of Nietzsche's treatment of it.

36. This passage is followed by a striking one suggesting Jesus's redundancy in the age of the death of God.

such store on being believed in that he offers Heaven in exchange for this belief, and offers it to everyone, even to a thief on the cross," he "must have suffered from fearful self-doubt" (*D* 67). Perhaps he was delivered from fantasy at the end, but at what a cost! "It is possible that . . . the bitterest of all exclamations 'my God, why hast thou forsaken me!' contains, in its ultimate significance, evidence of a general disappointment and enlightenment over the delusion of his life; at the moment of supreme agony he acquired an insight into himself of the kind told by the poet of the poor dying Don Quixote."[37] Poor man indeed, riding into Jerusalem on a steed called Rocinante, if Nietzsche is right.[38]

In *Z* the relationship between Zarathustra and Jesus is perhaps best described in terms of condescension. We observed both the reference to Jesus dying young—thus being spiritually immature—and the passage about his preaching to cows, in which Jesus is treated, as Berkowitz says, with "tender affection and gentle derision."[39] But no statement before *A* leads us into the description and denouement that we find there better than the following, from *BGE*:

> It is possible that within the holy disguise and fable of Jesus' life there lies concealed one of the most painful cases of the martyrdom of *knowledge about love*: the martyrdom of the most innocent and longing heart which never had sufficient of human love, which *demanded* love, to be loved and nothing else, demanded it with hardness, with madness, with fearful outbursts against those who denied it love; the story of a poor soul unsated and insatiable in love who had to invent hell so as to send there those who did not *want* to love him. (269)[40]

Commenting on this passage and on the lines that follow, Staten asked: "Does Nietzsche not know about this love? Manifestly, he does. So he is not entirely unlike Jesus; he has the same knowledge, but perhaps not the same desire?"[41] "Manifestly" is perhaps too strong, though Nietzsche, like so many of us, often seems to reject vehemently what tempts him most strongly. Nietzsche's final published reckoning with Christ comes in *A*. Here Nietzsche bitterly records how the early church distorted Jesus's teaching. Jesus rejected the contemporary Jewish "higher men,"

37. *D* 114. Cf. *WS* 80.
38. Rocinante (Supernag) was Don Quixote's hapless mount.
39. Peter Berkowitz, *Nietzsche: The Ethics of an Immoralist* (Cambridge: Harvard University Press, 1995), 219.
40. I am using R. J. Hollingdale's translation here of Friedrich W. Nietzsche, *Beyond Good and Evil* (London: Penguin, 1990).
41. Henry Staten, *Nietzsche's Voice* (Ithaca, NY: Cornell University Press, 1990), 161.

the social hierarchy besmirched by the priestly caste. That struck at the very existence of the Jewish nation, "an attack on the profoundest national instinct, on the toughest national will to life which has ever existed on earth" (*A* 27). As a political criminal, Jesus died for his own guilt, not that of others. "The word 'Christianity' is already a misunderstanding—in reality there has been only one Christian, and he died on the Cross" (39). History bears this out. "What did Christ *deny*?" Nietzsche asks in an unpublished note. "Everything that is today called Christian" is the answer (*WP* 158).

So how should we regard the only true Christian? Nietzsche attempted to identify the psychological type of which Jesus is a token, if unsurpassed, example. He believed that historical criticism would not get us far and, in the absence of nonscriptural records, that a scientific study of legends of the saints, including Jesus, was impossible. But a psychological profile of the Redeemer, limned by identifying his type, conceivably emerges. We first need to keep clear that "Christianity is a *way of life*, not a system of belief. It tells us how to act, not what we ought to believe" (*WP* 211). Examples are given in this note in *WP*, but going by Nietzsche's account in *A*, we appear to be at the heart of things with the saying "Resist not evil."[42] This is a big clue to understanding Jesus. According to Nietzsche, it is ridiculous to plump for either of two options canvassed in recent scholarship if we are trying to grasp aright the psychological type of Christ. These options are Jesus as genius and Jesus as hero.[43] He is neither. Then what is the appropriate classification? If we "speak with the precision of the physiologist a quite different word would rather be in place here: the word 'idiot'" (*A* 29).

> We recognise here a condition of morbid susceptibility of the *sense of touch* which makes it shrink back in horror from every contact, . . . a merely "inner" world. . . . "The kingdom of God *is within you*." . . . The fear of pain, even of the infinitely small in pain—*cannot* end otherwise than in a *religion of love*. (30)

Yet "one could, with some freedom of expression, call Jesus a 'free spirit'—he cares nothing for what is fixed: the word killeth, everything fixed killeth" (32).

42. Nietzsche's reading of Tolstoy probably influenced him on this point.

43. Here the celebrated biblical historian Ernest Renan was Nietzsche's target. Cf. *BGE* 48 and *TI* 9.2. See Gary Shapiro, "Nietzsche contra Renan," *History and Theory* 21, no. 2 (1982): 193–222, with 218ff. also touching on Wellhausen. If van Gogh's testimony is anything to go by, Renan was nevertheless capable of inspiring people in a way not too far removed from Nietzsche himself: see Pascal Bonafoux, *Van Gogh: The Passionate Eye* (New York: Abrams; London: Thames & Hudson, 1992), 21.

"Idiot" has a range of connotations.[44] It includes the "private citizen," the apolitical entity, and is a term that Nietzsche apparently picked up from Dostoyevsky. The apolitical element doubtless counts in both Dostoyevsky's and Nietzsche's works, but there is a deeper layer of meaning to be considered.[45] In *TI*, written just before *A*, Nietzsche has the section "The Criminal and What Is Related to Him," in which he refers to "Dostoyevsky, the only psychologist, incidentally, from whom I had anything to learn: he was one of the most splendid strokes of luck in my life" (9.45).[46] In connection with the criminal, he is apparently thinking especially of Dostoyevsky's *The Insulted and Injured*, as the title is sometimes translated. In *A*, following the foregoing physiological analysis of pain and love, Nietzsche writes of "that strange and sick world to which the Gospels introduce us—a world like that of a Russian novel, in which the refuse of society, neurosis, and 'childlike' idiocy seem to make a rendezvous. . . . One has to regret that no Dostoyevsky lived in the neighborhood of this most interesting *décadent* [Jesus]" (31).[47] "I am grateful to him in a remarkable way," said Nietzsche in a private letter, "however much he goes against my deepest instincts."[48]

Late in his intellectually active life Nietzsche encountered Dostoyevsky via the latter's desperately bleak and haunting story of the "human rag soaked in shame and servitude," whom we meet on the first page of *Notes from the Underground*.[49] The story deserves to be pondered both in its own right and for its rich suggestion of affinities with Nietzsche's frame of mind.[50] It is now widely known that Nietzsche

44. See Tim Murphy, *Nietzsche, Metaphor, Religion* (Albany: State University of New York Press, 2001), 114–18. In contrast to some other interpreters, Murphy rightly emphasizes how negative Nietzsche is about Jesus.

45. Cf. *WP* 204, 211. The range of application is perhaps indicated by the fact that Virginia Woolf's husband, Leonard, could speak of G. E. Moore as a divine "silly" in the "Idiot" mold: see S. P. Rosenbaum, ed., *The Bloomsbury Group* (London: Croom Helm, 1975), 101. Moore led the group away from Jesus (104).

46. Nietzsche adds that he has gained from Dostoyevsky even more than from the novelist Stendhal, "who has perhaps had the most thoughtful eyes and ears of all Frenchmen of *this* century" (*GS* 95). Stendhal's powerful study, *The Red and the Black* (French original, 1830; Oxford: Oxford University Press, 1991), impressed Nietzsche. We must reluctantly leave it out of this account. Gregory Moore, with special reference to another work by Stendhal, observes that "the extent of his [Nietzsche's] debt to the French novelist does not seem to be generally recognized"; see *Nietzsche, Biology, and Metaphor* (Cambridge: Cambridge University Press, 2002), 107.

47. Cf. *WP* 180: "The extraordinary company that here gathered around this masterseducer really belongs wholly in a Russian novel."

48. To Brandes, *SL*, November 20, 1888.

49. The characterization is that of René Girard in his first main work, *Deceit, Desire, and the Novel* (Baltimore: Johns Hopkins University Press, 1965), 94.

50. Fyodor Dostoyevsky, *Notes from the Underground/The Double* (London: Penguin, 1972). The underground man is forty years old, and his self-laceration is portrayed with

both devoured Dostoyevsky's major novels (with the exception of *The Brothers Karamazov*) and read some shorter works.[51] The character who is the "idiot" in the novel of that title is Prince Myshkin, memorably portrayed by the author. Intellectual stupidity is not the point, but the character possesses a kind of naïveté. Myshkin displays an innocent, ingenuous, pure moral transparency. Dostoyevsky's *Notebooks for the Idiot* show the author identifying Myshkin with Christ, the "perfectly good man." In their recent study, bringing Nietzsche into dialogue with Dostoyevsky, P. Travis Kroeker and Bruce K. Ward argue that Dostoyevsky is not trying to portray Christ in his portrayal of Myshkin but drawing on Christ's humanity to portray the pure humanity of Myshkin.[52] They judge that Nietzsche misses the point of Prince Myshkin by overlooking the prophetic element in the idiot's makeup and role and the holy folly that, in line with the Byzantine tradition, characterizes him. So where Nietzsche pits the idiot against Renan's hero or genius, Dostoyevsky, who also reckoned with Renan, crafts an idiot who combines idiocy and heroism in his peculiar fashion.[53] Mindful of some scholars' claims that Dostoyevsky had already said and seen all that Nietzsche had said and seen, and more besides, Kroeker and Ward think that Dostoyevsky challenges more than supports Nietzsche. We are not becoming sidetracked in recording their observations: "If ever two contemporaneous writers were meant for dialogue with each other, it is these two. Their dialogue . . . is a sine qua non for those concerned with the relationship between Christian faith and the modern consciousness."[54] It is obviously worth pausing with this.

Kroeker and Ward actually concentrate their analysis of Dostoyevsky and Nietzsche, where he comes into the frame, not on a different reading of *The Idiot* but on the classic sequence of "The Grand Inquisitor" in *The Brothers Karamazov*. Nietzsche particularly features in their discussion in the chapter whose title takes up words from Dostoyevsky's correspondence in the summer of 1879: "Do you despise or love humanity, you, its coming saviours?" Nietzsche despises humanity. The higher man must live for himself. Dostoyevsky, on the other hand, points to Christ. We must live for others. This may sound like what we have just heard

---

grim brilliance. For particularly rich possibilities for comparison with Nietzsche, see the remarks on morality and action (16) and the whole passage in 39–43. Just before the end, the underground man says: "I posed an empty question: which is better, a cheap happiness or lofty suffering?" (122). It certainly is empty: there is nothing lofty about the suffering of which we read, and Dostoyevsky would not have us think otherwise.

51. P. Travis Kroeker and Bruce K. Ward, *Remembering the End: Dostoevsky as Prophet to Modernity* (Boulder, CO: Westview, 2001), 144.

52. Ibid., chap. 7.

53. Ibid., 244.

54. Ibid., 142.

from Barth, but the intense sense of tragedy and pain that runs through Dostoyevsky's work and the probing identification of our cohumanity in the midst of that puts him in a rather different world from Barth, even if we are not setting foot in the kingdom of Zarathustra.[55] Kroeker and Ward's advocacy of Dostoyevsky contra Nietzsche goes like this. Nietzsche and Dostoyevsky both preach love for the earth. But Dostoyevsky's is a stronger love, rooted in the love for God, whereas Nietzsche grounds everything in self-will. On Nietzsche's own criterion of truth as that which affirms life, Dostoyevsky succeeds better. He exposes the blatant tenuosity of Nietzschean life-affirmation. By grounding a hope for the self and the world in a love that, according to faith, will triumph, Dostoyevsky places before modernity the mirror of apocalypse and at the same time rivets humanity to love for the earth more firmly than does Nietzsche or Zarathustra.[56]

The conclusion about Nietzsche and Dostoyevsky's respective loves of the earth may be sound enough, but I doubt that we should accept this argument as it stands. The two men differ considerably in both what they affirm about life and how they affirm it. In Dostoyevsky's case, love is holistic, integrating earth and neighbor; in Nietzsche's, it is apparently exclusive of neighbor or, at best, only contingently inclusive of neighbor. This surely means that Dostoyevsky is not demonstrably more successful than Nietzsche on Nietzsche's terms, because he injects into those very terms a radically different meaning from that which Nietzsche gives them. Even so, the comparison between the two, adjudged so important if we want to place Christian faith in relation to modern consciousness, is certainly fruitful, and it is possible to attempt it in particular connection with Nietzsche by taking a different trajectory out of Dostoyevsky's work. A satisfying response to Z demands attention to Nietzsche's remarks on Jesus; the remarks on Jesus demand attention to Dostoyevsky. One thing we can safely say: there is nothing kitsch about Dostoyevsky.[57]

55. Barth indicates his own positive indebtedness to Dostoyevsky in the preface to the second edition of his commentary on Romans, and Dostoyevsky certainly crops up at unexpected junctures throughout it; see Karl Barth, *The Epistle to the Romans* (London: Oxford University Press, 1968), 4.

56. Kroeker and Ward (*Remembering the End*) do not mention Z here, but in part 1 of Z, love for the earth is a major consideration. Cf. Hölderlin: "Who has thought about the deepest, loves what is most alive," quoted in Karl Jaspers, *Reason and Existence* (London: Routledge & Kegan Paul, 1956), 76.

57. Eberhard Jüngel's remark, though not directed to it, captures at least an element in Dostoyevsky's literature: "Between love and nonlove there is a yawning chasm, in comparison with which the contrast between heaven and earth threatens to lose its significance"; *God as the Mystery of the World*, trans. Darrell L. Guder (Edinburgh: T&T Clark, 1983), 325.

True Love

When Nietzsche read Dostoyevsky, he knew he had a challenge on his hands. Dostoyevsky throws down the gauntlet. There are some quite striking echoes of Dostoyevsky in Nietzsche. In the last section of *EH* we read: "The *unmasking* of Christian morality is an event without equal, a real catastrophe. He who exposes it is a *force majeure*, a destiny—he breaks the history of mankind into two parts. One lives *before* him, one lives *after* him" (*EH*, "Why I Am a Destiny," 8). Compare these words with those of Kirillov in Dostoyevsky's novel *Devils*:

> He who conquers pain and fear will become God. Then a new life will dawn; there'll be a new man; everything will be new. . . . History will be divided into two parts: from the gorilla to the destruction of God, and from the destruction of God to . . . the physical transformation of the earth and of man.[58]

If *Notes from the Underground* portrays a sick man and ends with no hope of redemption, *Devils* portrays a sick nation whose hope of redemption appears like a star over the blighted lives of the Russian people, right at the end of the novel, in the memory that Jesus expelled the demons from the unfortunate victim in the story of the Gadarene swine (Mark 5). Collision between Nietzsche and Dostoyevsky is most obviously staged in connection with the prospect of redemption through love. Dostoyevsky's earlier novel *Crime and Punishment* illustrates this, and if Kirillov's words invite positive comparison with Nietzsche, the climax of *Crime and Punishment* illustrates the critical contrast. In the novel, Raskolnikov brutally murders an elderly lady, virtually without reason and "without cause," as we normally understand these words, though he does have some reason and cause to resent her. Author of a treatise on criminology, he is clinically interested in the "extraordinary man." Such a man is not bound to flout morality, but neither is he bound to abide by it. There is a panegyric upon the "man of the future": where

58. Fyodor Dostoyevsky, *Devils* (Oxford: Oxford University Press, 1992), 121. On the contrast between the "God-man" and "man-god," see the discussion in "Night," 219–71. Also see the contrast later between the old (the God-man) and the new (the man-god), 215. Despite Girard's well-taken words, that "this inexhaustible work contains the real dialogue between Nietzsche and Dostoevsky" (*Deceit, Desire, and the Novel*, 274), the context in which I have introduced Dostoyevsky into the present volume means that we cannot follow this up. Charles Taylor, who regards this work as "one of the great documents of modern times," observes that the "character Kirillov in *The Devils* sounds in some respects like a fictional anticipation of Nietzsche"; see *Sources of the Self: The Making of Modern Identity* (Cambridge: Cambridge University Press, 1989), 517, 452. Adjudicating that point is a complex affair.

the man of the present preserves the world, men of the second type move the world and guide it to its goal.[59] Then there is the genius, a man in at least a million, and the great genius, a man in many thousand millions. Time and again, Raskolnikov reverts to Napoleon, who if not necessarily a genius is a man of consummate self-command, a man who could flout any kind of law without premeditation or remorse if he wanted and was able to do so. Nietzsche, who so admired Napoleon, mentions him in *TI* in connection with Dostoyevsky: he is the man who "shows himself to be stronger than society."[60] (We shall touch later on Napoleon's significance for Nietzsche.)

Raskolnikov is caught, tried, convicted, sentenced, and imprisoned. But as the story unfolds, so docs love, in the form of his relationship with the prostitute Sonya. Raskolnikov is renewed in her love. As the book closes, the possibility hovers over its pages that he will open her New Testament, now in his possession, from which she once read to him the story of Lazarus and the resurrection to life (John 11). Dostoyevsky tells us that Raskolnikov's life was indeed renewed, but he tells us no more before ending his story. In the climax to Dostoyevsky's novel, the shadow of the Nazarene is taking pale form around the edges of the pale criminal's life.[61] To love and be loved, to survey the possibility of redemption and the new life—these are better than being an immoralist and better than being Napoleon. Crudely put, that is what is at issue between Dostoyevsky and Nietzsche. So our question is: How is this problematic illuminated by their respective accounts of Jesus Christ? In *The Brothers Karamazov* we find the most forceful statement by Dostoyevsky on this point, although *The Idiot* was published before it. The *Brothers Karamazov* contains the scene that surely features the most telling confrontation between Dostoyevsky and Nietzsche on Christ, humanity, love, and redemption—in short, on Christianity. Although the dialogue between the two authors, even on Christology, can be set up in various ways, the point of entry we take here is one of the most famous and, surely, greatest passages in all literature: the encounter of

59. Fyodor Dostoyevsky, *Crime and Punishment* (Oxford: Oxford University Press, 1998), 238–57.

60. *TI* 9.45. Would Nietzsche have agreed with Borges that "Raskolnikov's undertaking was more difficult than Napoleon's"? See Jorge Luis Borges, *Collected Fictions* (New York: Penguin, 1998), "*Deutsches Requiem*," 231.

61. The section "Of the Pale Criminal" in *Z* 1.6 was written before Nietzsche read Dostoyevsky. On the contrast between Raskolnikov and Nietzsche, see Anton Uhl, who discusses Raskolnikov as the Pale Criminal, in "Suffering from God and Man: Nietzsche and Dostoevsky," in *Nietzsche and Christianity*, ed. Geffré and Jossua, 32. Uhl appears to collapse the various Christ-figures in Dostoyevsky. The "Pale Criminal" connection is also made by Berkowitz, *Nietzsche*, 166.

Christ with the Grand Inquisitor. I shall be brutally restrictive in the use I make of it.[62]

The confrontation between Christ and the Grand Inquisitor occurs when Christ turns up at the height of the Spanish Inquisition, when the heretics are being burned, and he begins to perform miracles of healing. Hauled up to appear before the Grand Inquisitor himself, the captive is harangued by the Inquisitor, who lays out the terms of their opposition. Jesus has failed because he refused to take up the opportunity offered by the tempter in the desert. If people are to be made happy, they are to be given bread; their conscience must be subject to the right authority; they must have peace and security. The church has provided just that. Its task is not yet complete, which is why there is a need for the Inquisition. But it has exercised the power of "miracle, mystery and authority." Through this, it has met human needs. By contrast, Christ had the perversity to refrain from taking that route and proposed instead an impossible one. Knowing and bearing the truth, he wanted people to be free. They had to be faced with the knowledge of good and evil—and choose. The burden was intolerable. Only the few can actually shoulder that burden, a few "great and strong," but for the majority Jesus's way amounted to a counsel of despair. Yet, he was adamant. The perversity of perversities is that Christ operated like this in the name of love. A love that was real and realistic would have led to the path of the church, represented by the Grand Inquisitor. As it is, Christ forfeited humanity, human happiness, and indeed forfeited truth:

> Instead of the firm ancient law, man had henceforth to decide for himself, with a free heart, what is good and what is evil, having only your image before him as a guide—but did it not occur to you that he would eventually reject and dispute even your image and your truth if he was oppressed by so terrible a burden as freedom of choice? They will finally cry out that the truth is not in you, for it was impossible to leave them in greater confusion and torment than you did, abandoning them to so many cares and insoluble problems. Thus you yourself laid the foundation for the destruction of your own kingdom, and do not blame anyone else for it.

This is all because Christ "desired the free love of man, that he should follow you freely, seduced and captivated by you." And so the solemn pronouncement is firmly made: Christ must go to the stake. Tomorrow he will die.

Let us first put a point domestically: on this presentation of the case against him, Jesus stands against some of the things that Nietzsche

---

62. Kroeker and Ward (*Remembering the End*) helpfully reproduce this portion in full, but there is no substitute for reading the whole novel.

stands against in Christianity. "You thirsted for a love that is free, and not for the servile rapture of a slave before a power that has left him permanently terrified." At the same time, on Dostoyevsky's account, in judging Christ, the Grand Inquisitor makes some of the same mistakes as Nietzsche does. The Grand Inquisitor "insinuates, on the basis of his own application of suspicion to Christ, that the great idealist's rejection of the three temptations was motivated more by the desire to be loved in a certain way than by compassionate love for human beings as they actually are."[63] Nietzsche thinks that there is a distance between Jesus and primitive Christianity and finds in Jesus's "thirst" for love a tragic pathos. Dostoyevsky crafts the speech of the Grand Inquisitor in a way that allows the sympathetic reader to distinguish between the true and the false in his portrayal of Jesus. If we are absorbed in the Nietzschean enterprise of trying to identify psychological types, one christological lesson that we can derive from the passage is this: the ministry of Jesus evidences nothing like a pathetic or misguided slaking of thirst or a fantastic idealism in putting on humanity a burden of freedom. Deep calls to deep. Just as, earlier, Ivan Karamazov has advanced an extraordinarily powerful case for the impossibility of worshipping God in a world of suffering and cruelty, now Jesus with equal tenacity refuses to act in any other way than to preserve human freedom *coram deo*. The dilemma of theodicy has its counterweight in action in freedom. Jesus jeopardizes the public acknowledgment of truth so that its personal appropriation might be authentic. Love allows its own rejection so that it might be born only in the passion for truth.

This portrayal of Jesus not only distances Dostoyevsky's Jesus from that of Nietzsche. It also reverses the relative strengths and weaknesses of Zarathustra and Jesus. Dostoyevsky's Jesus has a power to love that involves neither coercion nor sensitive morbidity. Zarathustra lacks the strength for that. He preserves his strength only by preserving himself from others. Further, for Zarathustra to yield would be to yield to the temptation to pity. In the case of Jesus, compassion does not trample on respect. Compassion may be present, yet Jesus deals with humans not according to pity but according to a respect that leaves humans in their strength. It is not a craven respect. It is the recognition—and by recognition, existential establishment or exaltation—of their humanity in and to its highest possible degree. This is what Zarathustra cannot offer. Just conceivably, he may aspire to respect others by setting an example. But he needs solitude to do it. Jesus is able to relate to the other with his whole heart and life and do so in a way that maintains the integrity of that other.

63. Ibid., 138–39.

I am not saying that Dostoyevsky is altogether right or that I have presented him altogether right. Anyway, it would be asking for trouble to try to offer a snap comment on Dostoyevsky's Christology. But the Grand Inquisitor sequence certainly indicates an important route toward christological engagement with Z. I do not think that we are wasting time here, dwelling on the idiosyncrasies of a dead thinker (Nietzsche, not Dostoyevsky) whose interpretation of Jesus may be regarded as completely absurd and his concoction of Zarathustra as completely fantastic. Both these judgments may be correct, but it is nevertheless worth drawing out an alternative perception of the nature of Jesus's love, in response to what Nietzsche thinks. If there is anything more deeply pathetic than Zarathustra's desperate affirmation of self and life, won at the cost of teaching eternal recurrence and eschewing shame, it is Nietzsche's idea of what Jesus must have been like. He rightly detects a profound connection between suffering and love. But even allowing for what he takes to be the limits of historical-critical investigation, Nietzsche seems clueless about the possible form of their coexistence in Jesus. He does not perceive the connection between divine power and divine love in Christ. Why conclude that Nietzsche has profounder christological insight than Dostoyevsky?

On the perception alternative to that of Nietzsche, Jesus did not crave love, still less have a physiological need of it, in the senses that Nietzsche tentatively detected. Jesus knew love as the only mode proper to his being, overflowing from a plenitude of strength. Nietzsche appears to get Jesus as completely upside down as he can, seeing tragically little of the biblical portrayal of Jesus's love. Nietzsche thought that vaunted love is the "subtlest artifice which Christianity has over the other religions" (*AOM* 95). There is no need to deny that Nietzsche said much on love that is worth considering or endorsing; it is worth trawling through his work to find out what.[64] But if anything is an active and not a reactive force in Jesus—the canonical Jesus, not just that of Dostoyevsky—it is love.[65] Z pits a Zarathustran style of suffering and giving against a fantasy about what its opposite in Jesus amounted to. Of course, if we know little of the historical Jesus; we are entitled only to contrast ideal types, not a historical reality (Jesus) with an ideal type (Zarathustra). But the point is that Dostoyevsky has presented us with a possible view of love,

---

64. From early works, see, e.g., *HH* 601, 603; *AOM* 75, 273, 342, 351. We should need to consider many dimensions of love and of Nietzsche's understanding of it in order to do him justice. See, e.g., Wolfhart Pannenberg, *Systematic Theology*, vol. 3 (Grand Rapids: Eerdmans; Edinburgh: T&T Clark, 1998), 184.

65. I am using this vocabulary of active and reactive with Gilles Deleuze, *Nietzsche and Philosophy* (New York: Columbia University Press, 1983), chap. 2, in mind, though employing it less technically than he does.

and its attribution to Jesus is every bit as credible as anything Nietzsche offered. Such is the case in *The Brothers Karamazov*, at least.

Regarding *The Idiot*, it seems to me that there is not too much distance between Dostoyevsky's portrayal of the idiot and Nietzsche's conception of Jesus.[66] *The Idiot* does not challenge Nietzsche's relative valuations of immoralism and vulnerability as much as do *Crime and Punishment* and *The Brothers Karamazov*—at least, not overtly. In salient respects Prince Myshkin is doubtless the opposite of a Nietzschean immoralist. More, he is the telling expression of its vulnerable opposite. But he exudes little sense of a redeeming power that is other-directed with holy concentration, untrammeled by the pain of an innocent soul. The Christ of the Gospels, on the other hand, if allowed to stand in his own evangelically portrayed right and considered apart from Nietzsche's reconstruction, does not exhibit that morbid sensibility that Nietzsche plausibly seems to detect in Prince Myshkin, the "Idiot." It is in *The Brothers Karamazov* that the real force of Dostoyevsky's christological alternative to Nietzsche comes to expression.[67]

Barth positioned the love of Jesus in opposition to the egoism of Nietzsche, supremely expressed in Z. I have suggested that Nietzsche did not grasp the nature of that love, judging it peculiarly tragic but not tragic in a Dionysian, Zarathustran way. Zarathustra's suffering gives us a key to his character, a fact that brings Jesus and Zarathustra into dialogical relationship if we bracket the allegation of kitsch. Barth did not reckon with this dimension in his discussion of Nietzsche. My preceding discussion, as far as it goes, amounts to a major supplement to, rather than decisive modification of, Barth's critique. Barth rightly posited the cohumanity of Jesus in opposition to the loneliness of Nietzsche. Yet even here, there is scope for further probing. We are usefully guided into this examination by an author of whom Hesse thought extremely highly and who had a very interesting impact on Berlin and beyond in the interwar period: the Southern writer from North Carolina Thomas Wolfe.[68]

66. On this score, some reservations I have about Kroeker and Ward's volume (*Remembering the End*) are given in my review of their work in *Studies in Christian Ethics* 16, no. 1 (2003).

67. With respect to a christological interest in *The Brothers Karamazov*, describing the terms of an encounter between Nietzsche and Father Zosima would also be relevant. Further, there is the possibility of regarding Alyosha as a Christ figure, of whom Rorty said that he did not know whether "to envy or to despise Alyosha, creature of 'incommunicable private bliss'"; see Richard Rorty, *Philosophy and Social Hope* (London: Penguin, 1999), 10.

68. Hesse reckoned Wolfe's *Look Homeward, Angel* in some respects "the most powerful piece . . . I know of": Hermann Hesse, *My Belief: Essays in Life and Art* (London: Triad/Paladin, 1989), 355. For Wolfe in Germany, see Elizabeth Nowell, *Thomas Wolfe: A Biography* (London: Heinemann, 1961), chap. 23.

God's Lonely Man

Although I have given a good deal of the time of day to other writers—Barth, Hesse, Dostoyevsky—it should be rewarding to continue in parasitic vein and now take up a short essay in which Thomas Wolfe proposes himself as an authority on loneliness.[69] "My life," he opens, "more than anyone I know, has been spent in solitude and wandering," and he undertakes to give an incomparable account of loneliness. In announcing that he is doing so, he denies that he is being arrogant. Indeed, this is our first lesson. The most utterly lonely person cannot be arrogant.

> The surest cure for vanity is loneliness. For, more than other men, we who dwell in the heart of solitude are always the victims of self-doubt. Forever and forever in our loneliness, shameful feelings of inferiority will rise up suddenly to overwhelm us in a poisonous flood of horror, disbelief, and desolation, to sicken and corrupt our health and confidence, to spread pollution at the very root of strong, exultant joy. And the eternal paradox of it is that if a man is to know the triumphant labour of creation, he must for long periods resign himself to loneliness, and suffer loneliness to rob him of the health, the confidence, the belief and joy which are essential to creative work.

Wolfe proceeds with an invocation of the intense moods that possess such a person. They include "this hideous doubt, despair, and dark confusion of the soul a lonely man must know, for he is united to no image save that which he creates himself." In the midst of this, such a person experiences hope gone, time gone, strength gone. On the other hand, there are also experiences of the apparently spontaneous resurrection of spirit in jubilant invincibility. "All his old strength is his again: he knows what he knows, he is what he is, he has found what he has found. And he will say the truth that is in him, speak it even though the whole world deny it, affirm it though a million men cry out that it is false." At the heart of his essay, Wolfe discloses: "The fact is this: the lonely man, who is also the tragic man, is invariably the man who loves life dearly—which is to say, the joyful man." He proceeds to speak of tragedy and joy; of the loneliness, rather than conflict, that lies at the heart of tragedy; of how the tragic writer learns, encompassed by the sense of death and of loneliness, that joy and sorrow, ecstasy and pain

69. Thomas Wolfe, "God's Lonely Man," in *The Hills Beyond* (Baton Rouge: Louisiana State University Press, 2000). This essay appears in the original 1941 edition (New York: Harper) but is omitted from some editions of *The Hills Beyond*. Since it is a short essay, I am not putting page references to quotations in the text above.

are woven into life at its very deepest levels; of how the lonely man is pitted against the constant threat of death, which is a certain prospect. Joy is rooted in the sorrow embedded in such knowledge.

We meet in Wolfe, as we meet in Nietzsche, a "wanderer and his shadow." I have turned to this essay for two reasons. First, what he says rings true as a description of Nietzsche. It is true that Wolfe's account has its intrinsic shortcomings, and also that his person, life, and authorship were significantly different from that of Nietzsche.[70] But Wolfe was not only capable of the most penetrating understanding of himself and his fellow humans; he is also capable of illuminating us about Nietzsche in a way that does not really come to light in Nietzsche's self-assessment.[71] Wolfe rather dramatically alerts us to the need to ponder the nexus of creativity and despair, jubilation and tragedy, solitude and death interwoven in the experience of someone like Nietzsche, assuming that, for all his individuality, Nietzsche still belongs in a larger company. Z becomes the more intelligible, if no less idiosyncratic, when read in a context much broader than provided by simply reflecting on Nietzsche himself.

However, there is a second reason for turning to Wolfe's essay if we are considering not Nietzsche in his own right but Nietzsche and Christianity. In it, Thomas Wolfe muses on the connections between his experience, slices of Old Testament Wisdom literature, and the Gospel accounts of Jesus. Wolfe's Old Testament reflections are concentrated on the book of Job, "the most tragic, sublime, and beautiful expression of human loneliness which I have ever read." Contrary to superficial impressions, "it wears at the heart of its tremendous chant of everlasting sorrow the exulting song of everlasting joy." And he quotes from Job 39:

> Hast thou given the horse strength? hast thou clothed his neck with thunder? Canst thou make him afraid as a grasshopper? the glory of his nostrils is terrible. He paweth in the valley, and rejoiceth in his strength: he goeth on to meet the armed men. He mocketh at fear, and is not affrighted; neither turneth he back from the sword. The quiver rattleth against him, the glittering spear and the shield. He swalloweth the ground with fierceness and rage; neither believeth he that it is the sound of the trumpet, He saith among the trumpets, Ha, Ha; and he smelleth the battle afar off, the thunder of the captains, and the shouting. (vv. 19–25 KJV)

70. Wolfe never clarifies the exact connection between physical loneliness and the loneliness of "the manswarm that passes us in the streets."

71. My judgment on Wolfe is made on the basis of his literature as a whole, not this one essay. Despite their differences, we might apply to Wolfe, mutatis mutandis, what Hayman says about Nietzsche: "He had formed the habit of writing about moods and emotions in superlatives: whatever he felt could never have been felt more intensely by himself or by anyone else"; Ronald Hayman, *Nietzsche: A Critical Life* (London: Phoenix, 1995), 274.

Wolfe comments:

> That is joy—joy solemn and triumphant; stern, lonely, everlasting joy,
> which has in it the full depth and humility of man's wonder, his sense
> of glory, and his feeling of awe before the mystery of the universe. An
> exultant cry is torn from our lips as we read the lines about that glori-
> ous horse, and the joy we feel is wild and strange, lonely and dark like
> death.

As Nietzsche discovered in the Hebrew Bible heroes on a scale greater
than anything he found in the Greeks, so Wolfe believes that this joy is
"grander than the delicate and lovely joy that men like Herrick and The-
ocritus described, great poets that they were."[72] After some remarks on
the Old Testament, Wolfe comes to Christ. Jesus is "God's lonely man."
According to Wolfe, "the books of the Old Testament, in their entirety,
provide the most final and profound literature of human loneliness that
the world has known," but now we discover a contrast: "Just as the Old
Testament becomes the chronicle of the life of loneliness, the Gospels
of the New Testament, with the same miraculous and unswerving unity,
become the chronicle of the life of love." Christ is the teacher of love, the
teacher of the unity of the human family through love. Following from
this objective of unity, "the central purpose of Christ's life, therefore, is
to destroy the life of loneliness and to establish here on earth the life
of love." The evidence is quickly marshaled. As biblical joy is found in
Job, so biblical love is exemplified in Jesus. Yet there is something else.
"Christ himself, who preached the life of love, was yet as lonely as any
man that ever lived."

The reasoning is not always as clear as it might be. In relation to Job,
Wolfe speaks of what is "at the heart of its tremendous chant of everlasting sorrow, the exulting song of everlasting joy." "At the heart" suggests
a kind of finality, the triumphant finality of joy. If that is intended, the
conceptual scene shifts somewhat, without warning. For we learn that
ecstasy is shot through with pain and desire, and possession is robbed
of victory by the sense of loss and death. "Joy is rooted at the heart of
sorrow," but this now reads like a description of where joy is found:
joy is here and not somewhere else, in the center, in the midst of sorrow. That is different from saying that sorrow is bound to harbor joy in
or as its root. I am not oblivious to the need to press Wolfe's essay on
these points if we want it maximally to illuminate the issues raised by
Nietzsche's response to Christianity.

72. Robert Herrick was a seventeenth-century member of Ben Jonson's "circle"; The-
ocritus was a Greek poet of the early third century BCE. Presumably, it is their accom-
plishments in lyrical form that unite them in Wolfe's commendation.

However, we do better still to think about Job in light of what Wolfe is obviously trying to make clear.[73] In the canonical story of Job, it is God who declares and describes the qualities of the horse. It is not Job who salvages joy from sorrow by equine observation. From a literary point of view, we might say that the author of the book of Job vents his sense of exuberance in a world of suffering and uses the speech of God as his conduit.[74] Wolfe plausibly introduces us to the possibility that we are encountering here what we might term, ad hoc, a Dionysian canonical moment. God revels in the equine exuberance, which is his own creation. We might almost say that he revels nakedly in his creation, but the Deus absconditus towers over the book, and this prevents us from being as categorical as "nakedly" implies. Certainly, it is proposed to humans that they share in divine "delight"—and that is not too strong a word—in the horse. The horse is a divine creature, for without God there is and can be nothing. But what God creates is glowing life, life that has its own characteristics, life that paws and snorts and charges in a way that God does not and cannot—all to the divine enjoyment. God has a powerful Dionysian strain. In the midst of life is glee, despite suffering.

Nietzsche was partial to the uncanny primitive Israelite Deity of wind and storm. Nietzsche, too, wrests joy out of the heart of creation. Joy—but not justice. As far as Nietzsche is concerned, if we speak of justice, we must speak of life as justice, speak of what there is, not of eschatological vindication by an eschatological judge. The book of Job may or may not hold out the possibility of some form of eschatological or redemptive justice; the famous verses (19:25–29) are notoriously difficult to translate and interpret. At all events, on a canonical reading of Job, the questions of the rectification of injustice or deliverance from suffering, sorrow, and sin in the Old Testament are canvassed without any embarrassing need to neglect Job's horse. The horse is mighty high, but it portends still higher things. Perhaps human and cosmic suffering intensify our exuberance at the sight of the exuberant steed. Even if we must go outside Job for eschatology, what we cannot suppose is that the possibility of redemption, as it emerges in the canonical Scriptures of the Christian church, wrecks the natural vitality of the natural order by positing another world that relativizes this one and stymies delight in the horse. Nietzsche thinks that this sort of relativization and demotion of the natural order is bound to happen as soon as the whiff of a transcendent redemption or justice clings to the biblical text, but he is not at all right. The God who

73. In Wolfe's account of Job, there is the suggestion that poetry itself can achieve the soul's victory in life, something that enables comparison with Hölderlin, if we want to tie together some threads in my overall account.

74. This can be formulated in a way that does not prejudice the belief that the book of Job gives an inspired account of God's speech.

rejoices in the horse does so as its Creator. If God occupies the office of
the world's Redeemer, this does nothing to cloud his joy in the actual.
On the contrary, God has joy. The possibility of a realm of transcendent
justice and redemption, far from banishing interest in what happens on
earth, as Nietzsche would have it, enhances it without subtracting from
earthly actuality. The Joy that created the magnificent horse, and other
magnificent creatures like it, is not weakened, shamed, or clouded by
the design of having communion with humankind. Nor does immortal
joy suffer by contriving a device for redeeming humankind.[75] Divine joy
does not have to countenance the finality either of loneliness or of an
unredeemed world in order to preserve its own exuberant superequine
strength. The transcendent exalts and does not squash the natural.[76]

If Wolfe is right and Job is illuminating, then loneliness and the natural, transcendence and redemption are patient of deep and harmonious
consistency for those who do not find difficulty in integrating Job into
the rest of the Scriptures. But what, then, of Jesus? Nietzsche's complaint
is that, with Jesus, it is a different matter. He thinks that where communion with God and redemption from sin are thrust before us in the
New Testament, it is on ground never trodden by the God of Job, ground
occupied by an altogether less attractive deity and who displaces him
in the canon. And the question is appropriately and indeed unavoidably
before us: if the God of Job establishes at least the possibility of allying
exuberant joy with hope of immortality and even the promise of some
sort of communion, is the possibility indeed realized in Jesus? Earlier
we referred to the sequence in C. S. Lewis's *Prince Caspian* that featured
revelry in the presence of Aslan. Why does Aslan himself not dance?

Of course, some say that he does, not in Lewis's tale but on the scene
of human history:

> If we look with the eyes of faith we'll catch a glimpse of ourselves as we
> were meant to be, neither impotent motes nor defiant dragon slayers, but
> a redeemed humanity dancing with joy even in the dragon's jaws. We can
> catch that glimpse because One danced before us, a dance of empowered
> suffering on a cross, which paradoxically overcame the dragon when a
> direct attack could not.[77]

75. The only explicit reference to Job in the New Testament is James 5:11, but this
is not to be taken as a sign that redemption standardly takes the earthly form described
in Job 42:10–17.

76. For a striking reflection on God's joy, controversially ascribing impassibility to God,
see Friedrich von Hügel, "God and Suffering," in *Essays and Addresses on the Philosophy
of Religion*, vol. 2 (London: Dent; New York: Dutton, 1926).

77. J. Richard Middleton and Brian J. Walsh, *Truth Is Stranger Than It Used to Be:
Biblical Faith in a Postmodern Age* (London: SPCK, 1995), 141–42. See also Nietzsche's
reference to Z in *WP* 1038. Cf. Hatfield, *Clashing Myths*, 145.

Naturally, there follows a reference to the "Lord of the Dance." Many things are well said in the volume from which I take these words, and its discussion of "The Empowered Self" is good in contraposition to Nietzsche's view of the Christian understanding of humanity. But when it comes to the dance, we should demur and allow the Nietzschean objection to stand momentarily. The cross was deepest suffering, sheer agony, and only romanticization can regard it otherwise.[78] There is no dancing here. Scripture is severely economical on the joy of the earthly Jesus. True, the face turned toward the Father in communion and prayer doubtless reflected the deep joy that possessed Jesus in the Father's presence. But we only glimpse that face so turned, and, more usually, we see the face turned toward us and toward his destiny. Concerning this destiny, the writer to the Hebrews tells his readers that it was for the joy set before him that Jesus endured the cross; it is joy deferred (Heb. 12:2). Herein lies the answer to the question about Aslan and to any skepticism on the part of Nietzsche about the possibility of joy in Jesus. On the comprehensive scriptural account of things, the Son moved from eternal joy (filled with delight day after day, rejoicing always in God's presence) to unending joy (he will drink again of the fruit of the vine in the consummated kingdom of God).[79]

Nietzsche judged the doctrine of incarnation to be contemptible hogwash and certainly did not discern the face of God in the features of Jesus. The former is a detestable lawgiver; the latter, a pathetic lover. However, from the standpoint of a broadly based biblical theology, the execution of a saving design that includes redemptive suffering means that the joy of the Creator Lord and the joy of the creature who dances in his presence are not directly or translucently mirrored in the life and time of Jesus between baptism in the Jordan and death on Calvary. That is because Jesus forfeits joy in the cause of joy. In that forfeiture, he is indeed lonely. "Christ is alone because he alone loves the other person."[80] In loneliness, Christ sacrificed himself for the sake of disciple and antagonist alike. Zarathustra cannot forgive Jesus the use that he makes of his loneliness. According to Zarathustra, if Christ had been maturer, he would have known that love should not get in the way of joy.

Surely the collision of love and joy is close to the heart of Z. Schopenhauer found the cosmic order joyless and opted for love as a kind of

---

78. For similar reasons, Willard's talk about God's joy as involving God in leading "a very interesting life" is a world removed from the canonical portrayal of God: Dallas Willard, *The Divine Conspiracy: Rediscovering Our Hidden Life in God* (London: Fount, 1998), 72. It is arguably not an apt description even of the testimony of the book of Job.

79. Prov. 8:30; Mark 14:25. I cannot here defend the propriety of a christological use of this text in Proverbs. Cf. John 17:5.

80. Dietrich Bonhoeffer, *Creation and Fall: A Theological Exposition of Genesis 1–3* (Minneapolis: Fortress, 1997), 96.

redeeming compensation. Nietzsche rather reverses things: he finds the cosmic order Dionysian and rejects the redeeming role of love. Christianity maintains that divine joy countenances temporal self-giving in order to secure its own eschatological finality. Joy is the destiny of love. Timothy Gorringe, glossing Barth, remarks: "Joy may not be constitutive of freedom in the way that love is."[81] This reverses Nietzsche's ambition, though in *Z* his love is directed to an *object*: the "ring of eternity." But Nietzsche should not force Christianity to a choice between love and joy in favor of love. There is something strangely amiss either in historical or in contemporary Christianity if Stanley Hauerwas can say: "It may seem strange to stress the significance of joy for the Christian life."[82] We need to direct attention to the positive place of joy in Christian thinking in order to engage aright with Zarathustra and with Nietzsche. Loneliness, love, and joy are, or should be, linked in the Christian scheme of things.[83]

Toward the close of his essay, Thomas Wolfe makes a hugely significant admission, quite telling in relation to both Nietzsche and Christianity. He confesses, in effect, that solitude is addictive. "And now I know that though the way and meaning of Christ's life is a far, far better way and meaning than my own, yet I can never make it mine; and I think that this is true of all the other lonely men that I have seen or known about." Why can Wolfe not make it his own? "For I have found the constant, everlasting weather of man's life to be, not love, but loneliness." Love is "the rare, the precious flower," but while it can bring life, it can also bring death, pain, and darkness. Loneliness is Wolfe's destiny and that of people like him,[84] including Nietzsche. Behind one of Nietzsche's descriptions, there is surely a similar hint. "Hundreds of profound lonelinesses together form the city of Venice—this is its magic. A picture of the future."[85] Ultimately, Nietzsche must bestow on Eternity, his Ariadne (sometime wife of Dionysus), a love that he cannot direct to a human other—just as Wolfe, for all that his experiences in this sphere of life

81. Timothy J. Gorringe, *Karl Barth against Hegemony* (Oxford: Oxford University Press, 1999), 278. He continues: "But it is a dismal freedom, and a very curious love, which knows no joy."

82. Stanley Hauerwas, *The Peaceable Kingdom: A Primer in Christian Ethics* (Notre Dame, IN: University of Notre Dame Press, 1983), 147.

83. For some brief remarks on this, see Stephen N. Williams, "Dionysus against the Crucified: Nietzsche *contra* Christianity," part 2, *Tyndale Bulletin* 49, no. 1 (1998): 143ff., though I was wrong to conflate Bonaventure's "Dionysianism" with that of Nietzsche, leaving the former "undefined" (150).

84. Given our earlier connection between solitude and nomadism in Nietzsche, observe how Ben Mijuskovic uses the language of "nomadic prison" in relation to Wolfe in Hywel D. Lewis, *Freedom and Alienation* (Edinburgh: Scottish Academic Press, 1985), 117.

85. Quoted by Karl Jaspers, *Nietzsche: An Introduction*, 283.

differed from Nietzsche, must confer on Loneliness a sort of friendship that he found difficult to sustain interpersonally.[86] Eternity and Loneliness: ersatz deities.

What Barth says about Jesus, love, and cohumanity is amply warranted. But I have suggested a different line of response to Nietzsche and Zarathustra, guided by the fact that Barth shows a resolute lack of interest in the tragic dimension of Z. Christ knew a kind of loneliness; Wolfe says it, and in fairness, Barth would not deny it. If Jesus passes Nietzsche's test for being taken seriously as a human being—and the discussion in A shows that Nietzsche certainly does take him seriously in that regard—and we must choose between cleaving to Zarathustra and to Jesus, then are we really and sanely to opt for the former? In our imagination, Zarathustra lives as Dionysus cavorts; Jesus trod our actual soil. Christians will not be alone in insisting that Nietzsche badly mistook the image of Jesus when he felt the need to create Zarathustra. That is the real tragedy of the situation.

However, a respected philosopher tells us that the "*Übermensch* and the Sartrian Existentialist-cum-Marxist belong in the pages of a philosophical bestiary, rather than in serious discussion."[87] He adds that "both by contrast are at their philosophically most powerful and cogent in the negative part of their critique." Sartre we leave aside. For purposes of expounding Nietzsche on Christianity, I have devoted more time to Z than some will consider profitable.[88] Where the rubber really hits the road, we may say, is at the point where moral philosophy is directly under consideration. Accordingly, we now train our sights in that direction.

86. Perhaps this is too hard on Wolfe. And nothing in Nietzsche parallels what amounts to an absolutely tremendous climax to Wolfe's work in "A Wind Is Rising and the Rivers Flow," book 7 of *You Can't Go Home Again* (New York: Harper Perennial, 1998; but the editorial blurb for this edition is a mass of unreliable chaos). Wolfe was sobered by the Hitlerism that, it has been alleged, Nietzsche had done so much to foster. In the next chapter I turn to this question briefly.

87. Alasdair MacIntyre, *After Virtue: A Study in Moral Theory*, 2nd ed. (London: Duckworth, 1985), 22.

88. Though, with an eye on Z, we might juxtapose to MacIntyre's judgment a remark that Reed makes: "Philosophy invites a general assent; literature compels an initially specific compassion. That is its distinctive approach to the task of civilizing society" (*Goethe*, 20).

7

THE SHADOW OF GOD

I disdained to mingle with
a herd, though to be leader.

Byron, *Manfred*,
act 3, scene 2

Morality

The excesses of Z's *Übermensch* did not deflect Alasdair MacIntyre from the judgment that Nietzsche is *the* moral philosopher of our day.[1] This plain judgment is offered in the course of a now-celebrated account of the claim that our morality is in a mess. Up till the Enlightenment moral ideas were embedded in a broadly Christian conception of human nature, which accommodated features of Aristotelian moral anthropology. The Enlightenment effectively sought to jettison the underlying conception of humanity while trying to retain key components of the moral scheme embedded in it. This turned out to be incoherent, leaving us with a moral vocabulary detached from the context in which it arose and unable to find its home in any other context, unless we espouse emotivism, which MacIntyre regards as proposing a flawed account of moral language. Nietzsche was the first to see the crisis in morality so

1. Alasdair MacIntyre, *After Virtue: A Study in Moral Theory*, 2nd ed. (London: Duckworth, 1985), 107.

209

caused. He spotted the fact that eighteenth-century morality, rationalistic and based on an understanding of human nature that it had putatively discarded, was incoherent.

MacIntyre is among the best known of those who have contributed to the English-speaking world taking Nietzsche with increasing seriousness when it comes to moral philosophy.[2] Yet as recently as 1994, many years after the publication of MacIntyre's influential volume, Philippa Foot could ask: "Why do so many contemporary moral philosophers, particularly of the Anglo-American analytic school, ignore Nietzsche's attack on morality and just go on as if this extraordinary event in the history of thought had never occurred?"[3] Whatever the right answer to this question, it contains a notably strong description of Nietzsche's significance. By the third millennium, Heidegger no longer sounds particularly "continental" when he says that everyone who thinks today does so in Nietzsche's light and shadow.[4] "Friedrich Nietzsche is certainly the most influential philosopher in the Western non-Marxist world," Rosen confidently declares, going beyond Charles Taylor's characterization of all European philosophy as "neo-Nietzschean."[5] Nietzsche's moral philosophy is at the bottom of these descriptions. Our account in this area will thus be judged by many to be an account of what is most significant in Nietzsche's thought.

Yet the limits of my account are especially severe at this juncture. A satisfactory expository and critical treatment of Nietzsche's moral thought that got into not just Nietzsche but also the big issues surrounding his contribution should properly take in the work of Robert Adams, Philippa Foot, Alasdair MacIntyre, Charles Taylor, James Mackie, Martha Nussbaum, Richard Rorty, and Bernard Williams, just to kick off the list. In addition, there are tens of scholarly treatments of Nietzsche that are devoted to or touch on his moral thought specifically. Foot's essay, from which I have quoted above, heads up a detailed volume dedicated to Nietzsche's *On the Genealogy of Morality*. If we take just one of these

2. Bernd Magnus and Kathleen M. Higgins (eds., *The Cambridge Companion to Nietzsche* [Cambridge: Cambridge University Press, 1996], 2) were glad to draw attention to this interest in 1996.

3. Philippa Foot, "Nietzsche's Immoralism," in *Nietzsche, Genealogy, Morality: Essays on Nietzsche's "Genealogy of Morals,"* ed. Richard Schacht (Berkeley: University of California Press, 1994), 3. Pannenberg thinks that Nietzsche's negative influence on traditional piety was greater than his effect on the erosion of moral norms: see Wolfhart Pannenberg, *Christian Spirituality and Sacramental Community* (London: Darton, Longman & Todd, 1984), 19.

4. Martin Heidegger, as quoted in Keith Ansell-Pearson, *An Introduction to Nietzsche as Political Thinker* (Cambridge: Cambridge University Press, 1994), 1.

5. See Robert B. Pippin, *Modernism as a Philosophical Problem: On the Dissatisfactions of European High Culture* (Oxford: Blackwell, 1999), 82.

essays—for example, Robert C. Solomon's "One Hundred Years of *Ressentiment*: Nietzsche's *Genealogy of Morals*"—there is enough to keep us occupied for a good while, not just in general relation to moral philosophy but also in particular relation to Christian thought. For example, we have an argument, positioned in contrast to Nietzsche's ideas, that concludes that "resentment . . . is the emotion of legitimacy—the emotion that more than any other prompts the 'slavish' demand of the 'herd' . . . for justice and justification."[6] "Resentment," or "*ressentiment*," as Nietzsche tended to say, is an important item in Nietzsche's thought, forcefully related to the question of Christianity. So the question of whether Solomon is right is highly pertinent to our theme.[7] However, it will receive no treatment, just as plenty that is important in Nietzsche's moral philosophy will barely be mentioned, let alone discussed.

Nietzsche has much to say about the form and substance, basis and principles, point and meaning of morality. His vocabulary consists of different words that, whether with strictest justification or quite loosely, we might translate into English as "morality." Conversely, a single German word so translated can have more than one meaning or shade of meaning. Ignoring as much as I do, what follows can but glean about the edges of Nietzsche's moral philosophy considered in its own right.[8] Yet two aspects of Nietzsche's thought that we have already encountered are so fundamental to his moral philosophy that we must highlight them again.

The first is his philosophy of mind or self. "The most radical feature of Nietzsche's psychology—generally neglected or not well understood in the secondary literature—is his conception of the psyche as a *multiplicity*, in comparison with the traditional idea of the soul as something

6. Robert C. Solomon, "One Hundred Years of *Ressentiment*: Nietzsche's *Genealogy of Morals*," in *Nietzsche, Genealogy, Morality*, ed. Schacht, 124.

7. See the contrasting theological approach to justice taken in Irving M. Zeitlin's *Nietzsche: A Re-examination* (Cambridge, UK: Polity, 1994), culminating in the "Epilogue." Alasdair MacIntyre's own line on Nietzsche is equally deserving of study as he engages Nietzsche in his *Three Rival Versions of Moral Enquiry* (London: Duckworth, 1990). For some important criticisms of MacIntyre on Nietzsche, see, e.g., Alexander Nehamas's essay "Nietzsche, Modernity, Aestheticism," in *Cambridge Companion to Nietzsche*, ed. Magnus and Higgins. Also see Stephen N. Williams, "Dionysus against the Crucified: Nietzsche *contra* Christianity," part 1, *Tyndale Bulletin* 48, no. 2 (1997): 223–25. For a change in his own general emphasis, see Alasdair MacIntyre, *Dependent Rational Animals: Why Human Beings Need the Virtues* (London: Duckworth, 1999).

8. On how to understand "morality" in Nietzsche, see, e.g., Maudemarie Clark, "Nietzsche's Immoralism and the Concept of Morality," in *Nietzsche, Genealogy, Morality*, ed. Schacht. We cannot even touch on everything pertinent to Christianity. E.g., for Nietzsche on the laws of Manu as a felicitous exemplification of what is moral in moral lawgiving, see *SL*, May 31, 1888. "One catches the *unholiness* of the Christian means *in flagranti* when one compares the *Christian* purpose with the purpose of the Manu Law-Book" (*A* 57).

unitary."[9] In an earlier chapter I stated that if we want to understand
Nietzsche's intellectual project, it is difficult to exaggerate the importance of his beliefs about the soul. "Our body is, after all, only a society
constructed out of many souls" (BGE 19), so that to identify an "ego"
as a source of moral action is mistaken. It is impossible to describe or
engage properly with Nietzsche's moral thought without a focused treatment of what he has to say about mind and self. That, in turn, would
take us into the vexed interrogations of the constitution of mind and self
that have coursed through the Western philosophical tradition, not to
mention leading us to consider his philosophical relationship to Eastern
thought. The theological significance of Nietzsche's moral philosophy
and philosophy of mind is clear:

> But if the idea of God falls away, so does the feeling of "sin" as a transgres-
> sion against divine precepts, as a blemish on a creature consecrated to God.
> . . . If a man is, finally, able to attain to the philosophical conviction of the
> unconditional necessity of all actions and their complete unaccountability
> and to make it part of his flesh and blood, then that remainder of the pang
> of conscience also disappears. (HH 133)

This is the flesh and blood of Nietzsche's declared philosophy, and it
is also his inmost sentiment.[10] With "flesh and blood" we come to the
second aspect. Nietzsche takes a strong line on the physiological basis
of morality. He thought that there was a field day for research here. For
example: "Do we know the moral effects of foods?" (GS 7). In a note
appended to the end of the first essay in OGM, Nietzsche expresses his
interest in seeing medical professionals come to the assistance of linguists
in figuring out how moral ideas evolved. Physiological investigation,
followed by medical critique, should lay bare the origins and history
of values. If one cannot, for example, derive altruism from physiology,
given the nonexistence of a "transcendent" or "ideal" realm, one had
better give an account of where it does come from (WP 52). We shall
scarcely reach closer to the foundation of Nietzsche's thinking than by
attending to the following from A, which demonstrates the unity of the
two features to which we draw attention.

9. Graham Parkes, *Composing the Soul: Reaches of Nietzsche's Psychology* (Chicago:
University of Chicago Press, 1994), 251.

10. Daniel Conway writes that Nietzsche's "attack on Western morality is specifically
directed not toward its normative character *per se* but toward its metaphysical foundation—that is, its reliance on the metaphysical apparatus of free will, responsibility, blame
and guilt"; see his "Genealogy and Critical Method," in *Nietzsche, Genealogy, Morality*, ed.
Schacht, 320. I wonder if he goes too far on the "normative character," but he is generally right, as also when he adds that Nietzsche finds our "moral mode of evaluation . . .
predicated on an egregious misinterpretation of certain physiological conditions."

As regards the animals, Descartes was the first who, with a boldness worthy of reverence, ventured to think of the animal as a *machine*: our whole science of physiology is devoted to proving this proposition. Nor, logically, do we exclude man, as even Descartes did: our knowledge of man today is real knowledge precisely to the extent that it is knowledge of him as a machine. Formerly man was presented with "free will" as a dowry from a higher order. (14)

So long as we neglect discussion of the anthropological constituents of Nietzsche's philosophy that come to light in these two related areas, we do not even reach first base in an examination of Nietzsche's moral thought, considered in its own right and on its own terms. Yet, I shall neglect to do more than indicate it, in the interests of not deviating too far into a general examination of Nietzsche's thought. By now, I have protested too much. We are obviously bound to describe some key features of Nietzsche's approach to morality, particularly as they surface in the two works that followed *Z*, which are germane to the question of his critique of Christianity. And since Nietzsche treats morality with an eye on Christianity, we shall hope to touch on a number of the principal features of his moral thought. But—one more protest—"hope" and "touch" are the keywords.

Nietzsche's form of determinism (exonerating us from responsibility) and of naturalism (the body is all that is) naturally invites theological response. But the same goes for other things involved in his moral thought, too easily regarded as relatively unimportant compared with these great planks at the foundation of his philosophy. For example, we need to take account of Nietzsche's insistence on the benefits of psychological observation, to which an earlier chapter referred. In discerning and discovering, identifying and exploring the actual play of motive and character, speech and act, as it typically expresses itself in the life of Homo sapiens, Nietzsche frequently says much that is important and telling, as we have seen, expressing it in aphorisms. "Nietzsche always attacks principles for being too general in relation to what they condition," Deleuze remarks, "for always having too broad a mesh in relation to what they claim to capture or regulate."[11] Nietzsche insisted: "All that philosophers have been handling for thousands of years is conceptual mummies; nothing real has ever left their hands alive" (*TI* 3.1). Christians should take heed. We often work with huge block ideas—God, human nature, moral law—and try to catch life in their net. They may, indeed, shape the interstices of any net that is of authentic Christian design, but

11. Gilles Deleuze, *Nietzsche and Philosophy* (New York: Columbia University Press, 1983), 50.

we often weave the holes too large to capture multiform human life in its actuality.[12]

What makes of Nietzsche's moral thought an "extraordinary event," as we heard Foot describe it earlier? Basically and generally, it is Nietzsche's uncompromising insistence that, if God is dead, morality is dead as well. This is how he spoke about George Eliot:

> They are rid of the Christian God and are now all the more convinced that they have to hold on to Christian morality: this is an *English* consequential reasoning which we will not hold against the moralizing little woman *à la* Eliot. In England, after every little emancipation from theology people have to regain their respectability in a terrifying manner, as moral fanatics. . . . The rest of us see things differently. If you abandon the Christian faith, at the same time you are pulling the *right* to Christian morality from under your feet. (*TI* 9.5)

In fact, those "who have abandoned God cling that much more firmly to the faith in morality" (*WP* 18). It is not the only time that Nietzsche turns his guns against English or British moral philosophy.[13] In Nietzsche's vocabulary, the English have failed to appreciate the significance of the death of God. God being dead, he is survived by no realm of values, no sphere stacked with moral truth that objectively confronts the world and human existence. We are not under obligation to a moral law that exists and is valid independently of what we create. Is this just a matter of denying traditional transcendence but allowing for the relocation of moral objectivity? The answer to this must be as firm as the question is fair. Nietzsche rejects the notion that there is any moral truth inhering anywhere in the world, generically pertaining to human existence. Existence has the amoral character that Schopenhauer ascribed to it. Where Schopenhauer went wrong was in missing human existence as will-to-power. He should never have invited the human will to turn against its own fundamental impulse, in an act of bleak resignation. In conjunction with his conviction that the springs of morality are rooted in the human heart, despite the purposelessness of the existence in which morality is embedded, Schopenhauer was led to reheat the main

12. We might, e.g., pause over chaps. 6 and 7 of *HH* to put flesh on the above. Robert Alter's work, *The Art of Biblical Narrative* (New York: Basic Books, 1981), furnishes moral and systematic theologians with a good agenda in this connection.

13. Nietzsche tackles their company from the beginning of the first essay in *OGM*. Herbert Spencer receives about as hard a time of it as anyone: *EH*, "Why I Am a Destiny," 4; *WP* 53, 382, 901, 944. If we were to follow through and expound Nietzsche's comments on Spencer, we would plow through a fair amount of Nietzsche's moral philosophy. For an illuminating passage on Nietzsche and Spencer, see Gregory Moore, *Nietzsche, Biology, and Metaphor* (Cambridge: Cambridge University Press, 2002), 61–72.

ingredients of Christian morality, shorn of their peculiar religious flavor. "Will-to-power" ties together life and evaluation; the power of life is the power of evaluation. That amounts to the creation of value. To repeat what was quoted earlier: there are no such things as moral phenomena, only moral interpretations of phenomena. According to Nietzsche, he was the first to formulate the insight *"that there are no moral facts at all"* (*TI* 7.1). Naturalness is immorality (*WP* 120) in the strict sense of being nonmoral or amoral.

On one definition of it, "moralism" is something that Christians have inveighed against, and many of this number will join Nietzsche in his complaint: "Christianity has thus crossed over into a gentle *moralism*: it is not so much 'God, freedom, immortality' that have remained, as benevolence and decency of disposition, and the belief that in the whole universe too benevolence and decency of disposition will prevail: it is the *euthanasia* of Christianity" (*D* 92). Nietzsche, of course, goes much further than this. He puts the choice before us: either God plus morality or no God and no morality. Since there is no God, the fate of morality is sealed. What spin in this Nietzschean proposition constitutes a novelty in intellectual history is an interesting question for intellectual historians. The proposition certainly emerges distinctively and influentially in Nietzsche.

Obviously, the importance of the matter in hand can hardly be exaggerated. Christianity and the Greeks, Christianity and culture, faith and reason, Christology and redemption—intellectual historians, philosophers, and theologians can pound away at all these, submitting their considered judgments. But the dilemma surrounding morality has long stared us all in the Western face.[14] Its staring eyes mirror an abyss. The question that arises in relation to Nietzsche's claim is frequently couched in terms of the Holocaust or other phenomena commonly designated "atrocities." Are we not to call Hitler's notorious actions morally wrong and indeed evil? Various responses are possible. Some maintain that they were evil and that there is a moral order but not one in which humans are placed by God or one that covertly trades off Platonic idealism. Alternatively, there is no moral order as such, but reason may and must be given for avoiding, rejecting, condemning what Hitler did. When cognate questions arise in academic circles, they generate the terminology of realism and relativism, objectivity and subjectivity.

In *D*, Nietzsche makes a statement that we should bear in mind, as long as we are thinking of the twentieth-century fallout of his beliefs about the abandonment or reconfiguration of moral space. After ex-

---

14. In saying this, I do not suggest that it is more important to comment on the West than on other forms of civilization. I simply do not want to complicate a sketchy account.

plaining that he denies "morality as I deny alchemy, that is, I deny their premises," Nietzsche proceeds:

> It goes without saying that I do not deny—unless I am a fool—that many actions called immoral ought to be avoided and resisted, or that many called moral ought to be done and encouraged—but I think the one should be encouraged and the other avoided *for other reasons than hitherto*. We have to *learn to think differently*—in order at last, perhaps very late on, to attain even more: *to feel differently*. (103)

This is an important declaration, but Nietzsche's authorship was cut short before he got around to a focused and constructive elaboration of the new reasons.[15] It gives us a clue to one likely element in his hypothetical reaction to Hitler.[16] But although keeping Hitler in mind can help us to focus on the issues that arise out of Nietzsche's work—unless we prefer academic games, which Nietzsche surely did not—we risk distorting his thought if we do not ask in the first instance, forgetting Hitler and bearing in mind the limits that we have announced: How does the issue of morality shape up in his own thought, in its relation to Christianity? As a text, we could take the following: "After Buddha was dead, they still showed his shadow in a cave for centuries—a tremendous, gruesome shadow. God is dead; but given the way people are, there may still for millennia be caves in which they show his shadow.—And we—we must still defeat his shadow as well!" (*GS* 108).

The Curse of Mediocrity

After completing *Z*, Nietzsche revised prefaces to his previous works and, after supplementing *Z* with the fourth part, supplemented *GS* with a fifth part. *Beyond Good and Evil* was completed early in 1886, before the last part of *GS*, and in the following year, *On the Genealogy of Mo-*

15. At one stage he had been hoping to produce a work that revalued all values, but he did not get far with it. Peter Berkowitz's account, *Nietzsche: The Ethics of an Immoralist* (Cambridge: Harvard University Press, 1995), has to be reckoned with for anyone who wants to see what we should make of *D* 103 in the context of Nietzsche's wider authorship.

16. The question of postmodernism rears its head when it comes to "new reasons." For an attempt to salvage Nietzsche from postmodernism's clutches, see Alistair Kee, *Nietzsche against the Crucified* (London: SCM, 1999), chap. 12. One approach to Nietzsche and postmodernity is via the question of the nature and objectivity of historical investigation. In his balanced work *In Defence of History* (London: Granta, 1997), Richard Evans introduces a number of pertinent considerations. He observes that "Nazi Germany seemed to postmodernism's critics to be the point at which an end to hyper-relativism was called for. . . . It trivializes mass murder to see it as a text" (124).

rality was dashed off at some speed. In a letter to Karl Kurzke, written about six months before his final breakdown, Nietzsche remarked that while *D* and *GS* were his favorite works, being his most personal, *BGE* and *OGM* were the "most far-reaching and important."[17] The latter of these has commanded special attention in the exploration of Nietzsche's moral philosophy. In prefacing it, Nietzsche drew attention to a number of his own previous discussions. They take us back as far as the second chapter of *HH*. Although Nietzsche may have selected particular passages in order to distance himself from the suggestion that he was dependent on the work of his friend Paul Rée, it is worth noticing the passages that he cites from his previous work.

The common thread running through these is a search for roughly genealogical accounts. Where do good and evil come from? Do not moralities derive from customs? How did ascetic morality come about? Where do our notions of punishment originate? Investigations into these questions begin in *HH* and are brought to a form of provisional resolution in *OGM*. The moral theme is not equally distributed throughout the intervening literature. When we study the two-volume *HH*, we find that *WS* contains rather more on morality than does *AOM*. The subsequent work, *D*, is subtitled *Thoughts on the Prejudices of Morality*, self-evidently announcing Nietzsche's concentration on the subject of those prejudices. However, if we jump from the discussions that Nietzsche cites in the preface to *OGM* to the arguments of *OGM* itself, we miss what surely ranks with the most illuminating of Nietzsche's works: *BGE*. Commentators have often been puzzled by Nietzsche's avowal that it says the same thing as *Z* but says it differently.[18] But this claim is not implausible when we attend to what Nietzsche says in *BGE* about modernity, "man," and mediocrity, the fittingly alliterative triumvirate of subjects that steer his observations on morality. If *BGE* really reproduces *Z*, to the extent that it does, it might turn out, like *Z*, to be the "portico" of Nietzsche's philosophy.[19] I shall neither be offering a systematic account of *BGE* nor speculating on the way it is related to *Z*. But it is an extremely important piece of work.

In *EH*, Nietzsche described *BGE* as "in all essentials a *critique of modernity*."[20] Its discussion of morality is lodged firmly within the framework of this critique and cannot be detached from it. Alert to Nietzsche's awareness of modern Europe, it is tempting to let our minds swivel about the poles of two dominating questions: What kind of thing is moral-

---

17. *SL*, June 21, 1888. In this connection the omission of reference to *Z* is presumably insignificant; there is surely a circumstantial explanation or an assumption being made.

18. To Burckhardt, *SL*, September 22, 1886.

19. *SL*, April 7, 1884. This is quite a provocative characterization of *Z*.

20. *EH*, "Beyond Good and Evil"; cf. *TI* 9.39.

ity? What kind of person is the modern European? However, Nietzsche would have us first of all attend to a third: What kind of person looks for and finds answers to these questions? Answer: The free spirit. It is time for us to come back to our old friend, the free spirit, who is now jauntier than ever.

> At home in many countries of the spirit, at least as guests; repeatedly slipping away from the musty, comfortable corners where preference and prejudice, youth, origin, accidents of people and books, and even the fatigue of traveling seem to have driven us; full of malice at the lures of dependency that lie hidden in honors, or money, or duties, or enthusiasms of the senses; . . . grateful to the god, devil, sheep, and maggot in us, curious to a fault, researchers to the point of cruelty, with unmindful fingers for the incomprehensible, with teeth and stomachs for the indigestible, . . . with front and back souls whose ultimate aim is clear to nobody, with fore- and backgrounds that no foot can fully traverse, hidden under the cloak of light . . . This is the type of people we are, we free spirits! (44)

What I have omitted is just as good as what I have included. The free spirit is on an even greater "high" here than in *HH*, which was the "*book for free spirits*" and even more eloquent, though perhaps not merrier, than *GS*. But where *D* had to clear the ground by its investigation of the "*prejudices of morality*," the path to the "free spirit" in *BGE* has to be cleared by getting rid of the "prejudices of the philosophers." They claim to be seekers of truth, but are they so in fact?[21] What is the value of the will to truth? Nietzsche thinks that he is the first to have asked such a question. "Most of a philosopher's conscious thought is secretly directed and forced into determinate channels by the instincts" (3). These instincts are basically physiological, driving logic itself. Life itself is not rooted in truth; indeed, "untruth" is "a condition of life" (4). The free spirit, then, is contrasted to the stereotype of the philosopher. A bona fide free spirit does not simply dance over morality in *BGE*; the free spirit is by now impelled deliberately and intelligently to deconstruct it. Free spirits are the authentic philosophers of the future, "those who attempt" (42) with contempt for certain views of truth about whose value they and only they are asking. If you ask why truth is worth more than appearance, you are already above the philosophical rabble. The focus of our philosophical truthfulness must be morality, but Nietzsche wants to focus first on the truthful philosopher.

The judgments and evaluations of this prospective new breed are and will be exciting. Possessor of a new and dangerous knowledge, enough to induce seasickness, one who believes what the true philosopher does

---

21. Here I am moving through selected portions of chaps. 1 and 2.

and should believe "suffers from such a train of thought as if from sea-sickness" (23). Free spirits, curious venturers, are far above the madding mediocre crowd. With the word "mediocrity" we come down to earth with that intense weariness of spirit that troubled Zarathustra. In fact, "mediocrity" is rather too fine a word for the crowd. Common people stink in virtue of their mediocrity. And where are you guaranteed to find them? "You should not go to church if you want to breathe *clean* air" (30). If we read in an earlier passage that the Bible offended Nietzsche's sense of *touch*, so that he had to put gloves on in order to read it, what Christians do to his sense of *smell* is just as bad. "Bad air! Bad air" (*OGM* 1.15). For Christians are not only mediocre; they also reckon themselves salt of the earth! As if mediocrity were not bad enough. The opposite of courage, the mark of the free spirit, is timidity. Nietzsche is eloquent on this point. But Mediocrity, the companion with which Timidity hangs out, is worse still. The European has become a herd creature, a mediocrity. This is the cultural crisis of our time. God, the prop of morality, has gone. Both a type of person (mediocre) and a corresponding type of morality (herd) characterize modernity in "aged Europe" (*AOM* 324).

> Now suppose that belief in God has vanished: the question presents itself anew: "who speaks?"—My answer, taken not from metaphysics but from animal physiology: *the herd instinct speaks*. It wants to be master: hence its "thou shalt!"—it will allow value to the individual only from the point of view of the whole, for the sake of the whole, it hates those who detach them-selves—it turns the hatred of all individuals against them. (*WP* 275)

Contemporary morality displays firmly cloying remnants of the di-vine. How does morality succeed in retaining its vitality now that it is apparently cut off from its divine source? Easily enough, unfortunately. The source was never truly divine in the first place; it was popular. *OGM* will later try to tell the story. In *GS*, Nietzsche had stated that morality "is herd-instinct in the individual" and had gone on to contrast the way conscience used to function in relation to the herd with the way that "today one feels responsible only for what one wants and does." He had concluded with an important observation: "There is no point on which we have learned to think and feel more differently."[22] We must weigh these words well; yet, in an unpublished note, Nietzsche makes another important observation: "My philosophy aims at an ordering of rank: not an individualistic morality. The ideas of the herd should rule in the herd—but not reach out beyond it: the leaders of the herd require a fundamentally different valuation for their own actions, as do the

---

22. *GS* 119. I am using Walter Kaufmann's rendering of this last phrase in *The Gay Science* (Vintage: New York, 1974); however indulgent it is, it brings out its force.

independent, or the 'beasts of prey,' etc." (*WP* 287). It is the individual-ism of rank that matters, when individualism is in question. The higher man is not just independent; he is superior.

Modernity presents us with a paradoxical as well as a dismaying spec-tacle. Standard European morality, against both nature and reason, is the product of long compulsion, a long training in obedience to law. But it looks as though precisely such conditions were needed to school the spirit. "The strange fact is that everything there is, or was, of freedom, subtlety, boldness, dance, or masterly assurance on earth . . . has only developed by virtue of the 'tyranny of such arbitrary laws'" as have prevailed, and all this over the widest range of human activity. How else could people survive, even flourish? Yet consider what morality actually looks like when one sees it aright: instinct, faith, and the herd have grounded it from Plato onward. In the name of reason Descartes made a break, but reason is itself a tool for something else, as "superficial" Descartes failed to see (*BGE* 191). To unlearn the way we think about morality is demanding, for these ways have infiltrated the marrow of our historically evolved souls. Preoccupied with the fate of Europe, the underlying question of *BT*, "What is man?" still haunts Nietzsche in *BGE*; in this light we see most clearly how *BGE* is *Z* in prose. Mediocrity—the mediocrity and, even worse than mediocrity, the bad odor of the herd person—is the problem.[23]

The crisis is deepening. The obedient, herd type is increasing in Europe. Even the commanders use language unfitting for themselves, though, unfortunately, fitting enough for the rabble. If that is how it is with those who command, small wonder that Timidity is mistress of the herd. Mediocrity is not just the general order of the day; it has enervated and demeaned the best. Nietzsche argues that the moral basis of the mediocre attitude is grounded in the failure to appreciate that "moral-ity" is the ingrainment in the herd of what is necessary for community. Here he not only takes us back to the primitive stages of society but also attacks contemporary democracy. "Democracy is Christianity made natural" (*WP* 215). With these words, Nietzsche opens before us visions of pastures green in which the herd grazes but that we cannot explore, thus unfortunately forgoing discussion of Nietzsche on Christianity and political morality. Socialism is a target for Nietzsche, with its concern for equal rights and the alleviation of suffering.

23. For a transatlantic echo, see the remark made by one of Walker Percy's characters in *The Moviegoer* (New York: Vintage, 1998): "Ours is the only civilization in history that has enshrined mediocrity as a national ideal" (223). A vicar in the semi-transatlantic Henry James story "The Third Person" confesses that we owe some brave criminal souls "in our shabby little shrunken present, the sense of a bustling background, a sort of undertone of romance"; in *The Turn of the Screw and Other Stories* (Harmondsworth, UK: Penguin, 1969), 185.

Is there hope? Perhaps. There is certainly an example for us in modern Europe, though he is not our contemporary: Napoleon. "The history of Napoleon's impact is practically the history of the higher happiness attained by this whole century in its most worthwhile people and moments" (199). In a later note, Nietzsche said: "One should recall what one owes to Napoleon: almost all of the higher hopes of this century" (*WP* 27). Nietzsche scorned the plebeian French Revolution, but "the Revolution made Napoleon possible: that is its justification. For the sake of a similar prize one would have to desire the anarchical collapse of our entire civilization."[24] Moving outside the confines of *BGE*, we find that Nietzsche was not altogether and unreservedly happy about Napoleon.[25] Nor is Napoleon absolutely incomparable.[26] Nor is Nietzsche doing anything distinctive in lauding Napoleon in the way that he does.[27] Beethoven's *Eroica* had celebrated him, and at this point, study of the pre-Nietzschean connection between music, heroes, and Napoleon helps us to contextualize Nietzsche.[28] Was Nietzsche consciously or subconsciously drawn to the paradoxicality of Napoleon's personality as well as to the form of heroism that he extols in the face of his feckless contemporaries in a febrile age?[29] Perhaps it is hard to be definitive, but whatever exactly drew Nietzsche to him, his Napoleon is principally and usually the shining exemplar of the values that philosophers and commanders need today.

We are examining a question where the stakes are fantastically high. The first of Nietzsche's three essays in *OGM* builds to its climax with an account of the fateful struggle in Europe over about two millennia, though the story goes back further than that. "The symbol of this fight, written in a script that has hitherto remained legible throughout human history, is 'Rome against Judea, Judea against Rome'" (16). Judea won. But then the Renaissance unfurled the banner of the classical ideal of aristocratic values rather than Jewish-Christian plebeian values. What happened? First, the Reformation and then, with the French Revolution,

24. *WP* 877, but the whole note has to be read.

25. See *WP* 1026.

26. On Goethe, see *WP* 104, 1017. On Byron and Napoleon, see *D* 109, 248, 549.

27. One thinks, for example, of Hegel's celebrated description of Napoleon as a "world-soul": Terry Pinkard, *Hegel: A Biography* (Cambridge: Cambridge University Press, 2000), 228. When Napoleon faced his nemesis in 1814, Hegel said that "the spectacle of an immense genius destroyed by mediocrity" was a tragic thing: Peter Singer, *Hegel* (Oxford: Oxford University Press, 1983), 2.

28. On heroes, see Daniel Chua, *Absolute Music and the Construction of Meaning* (Cambridge: Cambridge University Press, 1999), chap. 18; cf. chaps. 30 and 32.

29. For a snap description of this paradoxicality, see George Rudé, *Revolutionary Europe: 1789–1815* (London: Collins, 1964), 223–24. For an account of French paradoxicality, see Alexis de Tocqueville's classic *The Ancient Regime and the French Revolution* (London: Fontana, 1966), 227–28.

"the last political nobility of Europe, that of the *French* seventeenth and eighteenth centuries, collapsed under the *ressentiment*-instincts of the rabble." Now comes the comet, the portent.

> The most dreadful and unexpected thing happened in the middle: the ancient ideal itself appeared *bodily* and with unheard-of splendour before the eye and conscience of mankind, and once again, stronger, simpler and more penetrating than ever, in answer to the old, mendacious *ressentiment* slogan of *priority for the majority*, of man's will to baseness, abasement, levelling, decline and decay, there rang out the terrible and enchanting counter-slogan: *priority for the few!* Like a last signpost to the *other* path, Napoleon appeared as a man more unique and late-born for his times than ever a man had been before, and in him, the problem of the *noble ideal itself* was made flesh.[30]

Nietzsche enthuses; some of us, however, will feel distinctly chilly when we learn not only of what has been but of what Nietzsche expects will be.

> *"Our faith in the masculinization of Europe."*—We owe it to Napoleon . . . that a few warlike centuries, incomparable to any other in history, are likely to follow in succession—in short, that we have entered the *classic age of war*, of sophisticated yet popular war on the largest scale. . . . All coming ages will look back on this kind of war with envy and deep respect as something perfect, for the national movement out of which this war glory is growing is merely the counter-shock against Napoleon and would not exist without Napoleon. He should be credited one day for having enabled *man* in Europe to become the master over the businessman and the philistine—perhaps even over "woman," who has been spoiled by Christianity. (*GS* 362)

There is more in this passage, and we impoverish our account by not recording it, but here we clearly are on dangerous ground. What Nietzsche glorifies is not war per se. He knew from experience, at least as far back as the 1860s, that war can be a rabble affair. Connections that he makes between Napoleon and Bismarck are not designed as a strike in favor of German militarism (*WP* 128). The point is that action born of strength cannot be condemned as immoral. War is not intrinsically immoral. Nothing is. A note reads:

> To remain objective, hard, firm, severe in carrying through an idea—artists succeed best in this; but . . . with natures like Caesar and Napoleon, one

---

30. *OGM* 1.16. Calling this "a problem," Nietzsche remains quite subtle. He ends: "Just think *what* a problem that is: Napoleon, this synthesis of *monster* [*Unmensch*] and *Übermensch*" (the German is included in the English translation I am using).

gets some notion of "disinterested" work on their marble, whatever the cost in men. On this road lies the future of the highest men: to bear the *greatest responsibility* and *not* collapse under it. (*WP* 975)

The phrase "whatever the cost in men" reminds us of what Nietzsche has said about slavery. On his reckoning, even those who do not particularly like what Napoleon did ought at least to appreciate its true nobility.

If, then, we keep in mind the question of Nietzsche and Hitler in connection with Nietzsche's moral philosophy, it is not just because some insist that this is where the question of Nietzsche and morality comes to roost and why (among other reasons) Christians (among other people) must abjure and abhor Nietzsche's ideas. It is because mediocrity, herd, and Napoleon naturally open out into this question in the twentieth and twenty-first centuries, particularly when Nietzsche speaks of the future. Sir Herbert Butterfield once confessed: "When I ask myself why I dislike Napoleon so much less than Hitler, I find myself feeling that in the one case the redeeming features were due to an urbane and aristocratic education, while in the other case there is an uncouthness and barbarity of ideas. . . ."[31] This is both honest and significant. If the resolutely Christian Butterfield could feel like that, how much more Nietzsche, disdainful as he was of those who do not themselves disdain the rabble type? So we move on to a scene that is darker, for our own day, than the Napoleonic scene. Was Nietzsche's celebration of Napoleon as a man beyond good and evil a celebration of Hitler? Is that implicit in his moral thought?[32]

The Dark Question

The Jews—a people "born for slavery" as Tacitus and the entire ancient world say . . .—the Jews have achieved that miraculous thing, an inversion of values, thanks to which life on earth has had a new and dangerous charm for several millennia:—their prophets melted together "rich," "godless," "evil," "violent," "sensual" and for the first time coined an insult out of the word "world." The significance of the Jewish people lies in this inversion of values; . . . the *slave revolt in morality* begins with the Jews. (*BGE* 195)

31. The reader might want to read the whole sentence: see Herbert Butterfield, *Christianity and History* (London: Bell, 1949), 44. Bonhoeffer apparently believed that Hitler's credentials as antichrist fell short for much the same reason: see Georg Huntemann, *Dietrich Bonhoeffer: An Evangelical Reassessment* (Grand Rapids: Baker, 1996), 178.

32. I am aware that many who have suffered under Communism in the twentieth century are dismayed at the disproportionate amount of adverse attention paid to Hitler in comparison with Stalin and others. I sympathize with this reaction, but I retain reference to Hitler because of the national connections between Nietzsche and Hitler and the allegations of specific influence.

When Nietzsche pondered good and evil, he came to the conclusion that something extremely disquieting had happened in the history of the human race. There is a fairly succinct statement on the subject at the beginning of the first essay in *OGM* that is on "Good and Evil," "Good and Bad." Sound historical thinking—hitherto lacking in English self-styled experts in moral philosophy—denies that the judgment "good" originates among beneficiaries of altruism or bears some sort of utilitarian meaning. "Good" is originally language that expresses the evaluation of those who are in a powerful position, living naturally according to their egoistic instincts. The evolution of language helps us to see how valuations mutate. Across different languages there is evidence that what *becomes* morally "good" *originates* in the vocabulary used by men who are aristocrats of the spirit, in conformity with the nobility of their rank. Correspondingly, "bad" originally meant "plebeian" and "low" in a social sense. "Bad" is not "evil." "Good" and "evil," as moral evaluations, evolve out of "good" and "bad." But the hard fact of life is that moral language and moral sensibility have evolved away from origins and against the grain of nature. They have been hijacked and inverted.

What happened? In the first place, priests happened. Priests differ from the original aristocratic warrior type by virtue of their relative external inaction and their inwardness. The priest is the abstinent and teacher of abstinence, the self-refined opponent of the senses. And the God produced out of this misdirection of instinct is a kind of nothingness, the ultimate "Not-life." If one really wants nihilism, this is where to find it. "Not-life" is the Buddhist Nirvana, but it is Jews, not Buddhists, who have affected Europe. In connection with this point, Nietzsche proceeds to develop one of his most celebrated theories, to which I have already referred, concerning the notion of resentment, or *ressentiment*. Thus, some have significantly claimed that, for Nietzsche, "'morality,' strictly speaking (though he will use the term more loosely at times) is the mode of valuing rooted in *ressentiment* and the metaphysical faith in opposite values."[33] "The driving force [of Christianity] is: *ressentiment*" (*WP* 179). He was not the first to make moral use of this term.[34] The idea is that

33. Tyler T. Roberts, *Contesting Spirit: Nietzsche, Affirmation, Religion* (Princeton, NJ: Princeton University Press, 1998), 42.

34. Robin Small, *Nietzsche in Context* (Burlington, VT: Ashgate, 2001), xix. While granting that Nietzsche gives the term his own spin and use, Small remarks that the "area of value and morality is where Nietzsche has most often been credited with an originality which owes little or nothing to either familiarity or interaction with other philosophical thinkers." Small rectifies this picture. Cf. Lange, although he approaches the "social question" so differently from Nietzsche: "Amongst the attacks which have quite recently been directed not only against the mythical tradition of Christianity, but also against its morality, that is not the least prominent which characterizes Christianity as a religion of envy and hatred of the poor against the rich"; Friedrich A. Lange, *The History of Materialism*,

the powerless become resentful toward the powerful and then moralize their attitudes. The Jews flaunted a slave morality rooted in herd resentment and so achieved an inversion of values. They have truly inverted the natural order of valuation. How do we counter it? By a repristination of master morality. So we arrive at Hitler, to all appearances the anti-Semitic exemplar of Napoleonic master morality. Anti-Semitism and master morality are not the same thing, and we shall bear this in mind.

The questions that surround the alleged fact or nature of Nietzsche's anti-Semitism are quite complex. At one stage Nietzsche's anti-Semitism and celebration of the Aryan master race were hailed as the explicit progenitors of Nazism. Things changed in Nietzsche scholarship some time ago, though most who are not aware of the scholarship seem not to be aware of the change.[35] It is argued that, far from being a revisionary reading, the acquittal of Nietzsche on the above charges takes us back to the time before the Nazis, when Nietzsche was not regarded as racist and considered more philo- than anti-Semite.[36] Nor did he proclaim a particular master race, and if he had, it would certainly not be a German master race.[37] The argument is that the Nazification of Nietzsche is founded on a complete distortion of what Nietzsche said, a distortion that owes a lot to the seizure by Nietzsche's anti-Semitic sister, Elisabeth, of as many of his notes and as much of her brother's legacy as she could lay her hands on. Those hands of hers were soiled with anti-Semitism. Elisabeth had married a highly unstable proto-Fascist, who eventually tried to spread his propaganda in Paraguay. It is "one of the worst insults," Lampert avers, "that Nietzsche was tainted with German racial hatred."[38]

trans. Ernest Chester Thomas, 3rd ed., 3 vols. in 1 (London: Kegan Paul, 1925), 2.2:305. Nietzsche is less focused on the economic picture than this. While comparison is also sometimes made between Nietzsche and Kierkegaard here, Kierkegaard does not use the term *ressentiment* to characterize the resentment of envy; see Søren Kierkegaard, at least in *The Present Age* (New York and London: Oxford University Press, 1940), 23ff.

35. The general works by Kaufmann and Hollingdale make the point. For example, "Nietzsche's views are quite unequivocally opposed to those of the Nazis—more so than those of almost any other prominent German of his own time or before him": Walter Kaufmann, *Nietzsche: Philosopher, Psychologist, Antichrist*, 4th ed. (New York: Vintage, 1974), 393. Ansell-Pearson, *Introduction to Nietzsche*, chap. 2, is generally helpful here. Unfortunately, stereotypes are perpetuated in their stereotypical form by influential popular authors such as Ravi Zacharias, *A Shattered Visage: The Challenge of Atheism* (London: Hodder & Stoughton, 1996), 18.

36. Sander L. Gilman, "Nietzsche, Heine and the Otherness of the Jew," in *Studies in Nietzsche and the Judaeo-Christian Tradition*, ed. James C. O'Flaherty, Timothy F. Sellner, and Robert M. Helm (Chapel Hill: University of North Carolina Press, 1985), 206–25.

37. Reginald J. Hollingdale, *Nietzsche: The Man and His Philosophy*, rev. ed. (Cambridge: Cambridge University Press, 1999), 186.

38. Laurence Lampert, *Nietzsche and Modern Times: A Study of Bacon, Descartes, and Nietzsche* (New Haven: Yale University Press, 1993), 434.

Not all, however, see it quite that way. "Picture what one would say today in most circles about someone who announced, as did Nietzsche in 1888, that 'the priestly instinct of the Jew [had] committed the . . . great crime against history.'"[39] Jacques Derrida's doubts on this score have been quite well publicized, though those who would chase them down will immediately find that their form is dependent on Derrida's philosophical view of writing and of text.[40] Some of Nietzsche's defenders undoubtedly go much too far in their zeal to exculpate Nietzsche.[41] Johann Overbeck, who knew Nietzsche practically as well as did anyone, thought that the anti-Christianity of *A* was, at bottom, anti-Semitic, though we should remember that Overbeck had his own radical Christian ax to grind.

The word "complex" provides a safe refuge for us here. True, if we delved more deeply into the question, we might resolve that complexity to some extent. We recognize the need to distinguish, as did Nietzsche, between different elements in the history of the Jews and Judaism.[42] My own judgment in this matter is of nugatory weight, but it appears to me that injustice is done to Nietzsche if he is regarded as an anti-Semitic precursor of Hitler. He is more anti-anti-Semite. "What a blessing the Jew is among Germans" (*WP* 49). On encountering such a phrase, we need not as a reflex action fine-tune our antennae for Nietzschean irony. On the other hand, strong words said about the Jews do not help Nietzsche in this matter, though stronger words still are said about the Christians who perpetuated the Jewish inversion of values. There is much to be said for O'Flaherty's characterization: "Nietzsche saw the Jews in a favourable light when they were the object of anti-Semitism, and in an unfavourable light when he recognized in them many of the characteristics of German Christians."[43]

However, we must open the door to heed and briefly respond to a queue of protesters. First is Figgis: "Every teacher must be held responsible

39. Tracy B. Strong, "Nietzsche's Political Misappropriation," in *Cambridge Companion to Nietzsche*, ed. Magnus and Higgins, 132. Strong's essay shows that he is not illicitly reading "today" into "yesterday." The Jewish philosopher Emmanuel Levinas, whose work offers such a striking contrast to Nietzsche, was accused of being the latest in the long line of defenders of slave morality: see William Large, "The Difference between Genealogy and Phenomenology: The Example of Religion in Nietzsche and Levinas," *Journal of Nietzsche Studies* 19 (2000).

40. See Jacques Derrida, "Otobiographies," in *The Ear of the Other* (Lincoln: University of Nebraska Press, 1988), e.g., 31.

41. As when Walter Kaufmann quotes a passage from *A* as evidence that Nietzsche denounced nothing more vigorously than he did anti-Semitism (*Nietzsche*, 298).

42. See Weaver Santaniello, "Nietzsche's Hierarchy of Gods in the *Anti-Christ*," *Journal of Nietzsche Studies* 19 (2000). Although I have not studied the major monographs on the issue, I am aware that Nietzsche's negative stance toward Judaism in *A* is arguably consistent with his opposition to nineteenth-century Christian-German anti-Semitism.

43. O'Flaherty, in *Studies in Nietzsche*, ed. O'Flaherty, Sellner, and Helm, 9.

for the natural consequences of his teaching, however little he intended them. . . . In any case Nietzsche is guilty of them unless he took pains to avoid them."[44] For this, Nietzsche would have contempt: he says what he has to say, and it is not his problem if inferior readers put his words to their inferior ends. This is Nietzsche's aristocratism of authorship, as disdainful of moral consequence as are his portrayed aristocrats of rank. Yet, in a culturally anti-Semitic cauldron, what someone said unfavorably about Jews could have unfavorable consequences for the Jew in front of you. Then we hear Fraser: "Those who have sought to depict Nietzsche as mounting a sustained campaign against anti-Semitism often miss the sense in which his attack upon anti-Semitism is largely an attack upon vulgarity," against the mob.[45] True, and the most vulgar of people can fancy himself or herself above the mob. Now we hear Foot: "Nazi action and Nietzsche's reputation may be linked in the way suggested by Mann, that is, in the way his treatment of evil has to look to us in the light of what they did."[46] Yes: Nietzschean moral philosophy positively lacks any strong resource for combating what he might have wanted to oppose in anti-Semitism.[47] Then we meet Heller, writing of world history after Nietzsche, Lawrence, and Yeats: "It is impossible to be sure that its recent terrors have nothing whatever to do with the fascinations the dark river gods of the blood and the soil, Dionysus, Priapus, or Pan, have held for those minds."[48] Heller is no moral scaremonger. Nietzsche certainly does cry out that Dionysus is simply honest to things as they are and that dishonesty lies in speaking of things as they *ought* to be as though they *are*.

But perhaps it is the apt application of Pascal's dictum about Montaigne's authorship that is the most searching of all: "As his book was not written to encourage piety, he was under no obligation to do so, but we are always under an obligation not to discourage it."[49] Let the reader apply.

Connections between anti-Semitism and Hitler, on the one hand, and master morality and Napoleon, on the other, are implicit in some of the comments made above. Nietzsche discourages deployment of moral grounds against what have been widely deemed evils in our century or

44. John Neville Figgis, *The Will to Freedom, or The Gospel of Nietzsche and the Gospel of Christ* (London: Longmans, Green, 1917), 266; cf. 270.

45. Giles Fraser, *Redeeming Nietzsche: On the Piety of Unbelief* (New York: Routledge, 2002), 133.

46. Foot, "Nietzsche's Immoralism," in *Nietzsche, Genealogy, Morality*, ed. Schacht, 7.

47. It certainly might be argued that moral power does not automatically derive from moral theory. Still, deficiency in theory may result in deficiency in power.

48. Erich Heller, *The Importance of Nietzsche* (Chicago: University of Chicago Press, 1988), 138.

49. Blaise Pascal, *Pensées*, trans. A. J. Krailsheimer (London: Penguin, 1966), 680.

any other. If "Nietzsche never defined the value of an individual in terms of either biology or race, but always in terms of 'culture,' there is scant moral protection for most people."[50] What Nietzsche advances in *BGE* and *OGM* may be immoralism, rather than anti-Semitism, and Napoleonic master morality, rather than crude Teutonic racial supremacy. But suppose "immoralism" is directed *against* "God" in a way that is indifferent to whether it can be deployed *for* Hitler. Can this immoralism successfully accomplish an anti-Christian crusade, on Nietzsche's terms, without proportionately encouraging the attitudes of a Hitler? In the 1930s, Christianity was often viewed in Germany as being against the strong, the heroic, and the healthy.[51] There are apparently grounds for attributing to Hitler the observation that "the biggest evil for the German people was accepting Christian humility."[52] If so, he would have found no better ally than Nietzsche in such a cause.

Doubtless we should guard against pitting Nietzsche in relation to Christian morality just in light of accusations later made against Nietzsche at the expense of what we find in Nietzsche himself. On the other hand, if we are interested in the significance of Nietzsche's resistance to Christian morality, it is good to keep our feet on world-historical ground. As a matter of fact, light is shed on Nietzsche's thinking in its own right if we turn to another scene haunted by the Nazi specter, one that features the dying, decaying body. But I shall leave the Nazis out of it and just report the biomedical implications of Nietzsche's celebration of strength and contempt for weakness. Setting out a *"Morality for Physicians"* in *TI,* Nietzsche says:

> A sick person is a parasite on society. Once one has reached a certain state it is indecent to live any longer. Vegetating on in cowardly dependence on physicians and their methods, once the meaning of life, the *right* to life has been lost, should be greeted with society's profound contempt. The physicians, for their part, ought to convey this contempt—not prescriptions, but every day a fresh dose of *disgust* at their patient. (9.36)

Nietzsche proceeds to attack the Christian position on life and weakness, "the pitiful and ghastly comedy which Christianity has made of the hour of death." It is not always easy to figure out the boundaries between literal and metaphorical use of language in Nietzsche's literature when it comes to questions of sickness and health. On the face of it, Nietzsche

50. Ansell-Pearson, *Introduction to Nietzsche*, 31.
51. I do not mean to suggest that this was the case only in Germany, as though to distinguish Germany decisively from anywhere else.
52. Richard Weikart, "The Roots of Hitler's Evil," *Books & Culture* 7, no. 2 (2001): 19.

uses "sickness" and "health" principally as metaphors for speaking of culture, as in the following significant passage in *OGM*:

> The sick are the greatest danger for the healthy. . . . I speak, as is appropriate of man's cultural domains, of every kind of "Europe" which still exists on earth. The *sickly* are the greatest danger to man: *not* the wicked, *not* the "beasts of prey." Those who, from the start, are the unfortunate, the downtrodden, the broken—these are the ones, the *weakest*, who most undermine life amongst men. . . . We need good air! good air! At all events, well away from all madhouses and hospitals of culture. (3.14)

But the passage from *TI* and Nietzsche's consistent interest in physiology in *OGM* effect a significant fusion of literal and metaphorical reference. When Nietzsche comes to talk explicitly of early Christian care for the poor and the sick, it is hard to believe that he meant us to expel the literal sense of the passage from our minds.[53]

In the passage quoted from *TI*, Nietzsche effectively proposes that physicians collude with those who are undertaking suicidal projects. He had long since defended suicide. "There exists a right by which we take a man's life but none by which we take from him his death" (*HH* 88). "Why should it be more laudable for an old man who senses the decline of his powers to await his slow exhaustion and dissolution than in full consciousness to set himself a limit?" (*HH* 80). Christianity cut in here at just the right time. "When Christianity came into the world, the craving for suicide was immense—and Christianity turned it into a lever of its power."[54] Prior to this discussion in *TI*, Nietzsche had rejected the habit of consulting physicians to keep life going. Compared with the Greek and Roman advocacy of suicide, "the desire to carry on existing from day to day, anxiously consulting physicians and observing scrupulous rules of conduct, without the strength to get any closer to an actual goal of one's life, is much less respectworthy" (*HH* 80). It all adds up to a picture of human worthlessness unless the strong man determines to

53. *OGM* 3.18. Although I take care to recognize the metaphorical interpretation in my essay "Bioethics in the Shadow of Nietzsche," I am less sure now about the correctness of my emphasis in that account; see my essay in *Bioethics and the Future of Medicine: A Christian Appraisal*, ed. John F. Kilner, Nigel M. de S. Cameron, and David L. Schiedermayer (Grand Rapids: Eerdmans, 1995), 112–23. Solomon's essay "One Hundred Years of *Ressentiment*" (in *Nietzsche, Genealogy, Morality*, ed. Schacht) is cautious about the meaning of "health" in Nietzsche. For the whole health issue in the late nineteenth century, see Moore, *Nietzsche, Biology, and Metaphor*, esp. part 2. While I cannot cite him in support of any particular reading of the relevant passages in *OGM*, see Robert Gooding-Williams's observation that in late-nineteenth-century thought it was common to link "physical exhaustion with cultural decay," in *Zarathustra's Dionysian Modernism* (Stanford, CA: Stanford University Press, 2002), 129.

54. *GS* 131. Here I am following Kaufmann's translation in *The Gay Science*.

make something of himself. And physicians are increasingly culturally significant as the power of religion recedes.[55] Master morality is a mantle cast over all personal and social life—for him who dares. He who dares not is contemptible.

Drastic Revaluation

In Nietzsche's attack on Christian morality, perhaps nothing is more arresting than his attack on the notion of compassion, understood as pity, to which we have previously alluded. Schopenhauer regarded cruelty as the essence of immorality and compassion as the essence of morality. Nietzsche regarded morality as an extraneous imposition upon nature. Cruelty is not immoral, nor is compassion moral. Whereas cruelty is generally sanctioned, compassion is generally castigated. "Precisely here," Nietzsche instructs his readers in the preface to *OGM*,

> I saw the beginning of the end, standstill, mankind looking back wearily, turning its will *against* life, and the onset of the final sickness becoming gently, sadly manifest: I understood the morality of pity, casting around ever wider to catch even philosophers and make them ill, as the most uncanny symptom of our European culture which has itself become uncanny. (5)

The fact that Nietzsche alerts us to the novelty of this European situation should also alert us to be careful in the interpretation of what he means. He is struck by the fact that "up till now, philosophers were agreed as to the *worthlessness* of pity"—for example, Plato, Spinoza, La Rochefoucauld, and Kant. Schopenhauer is the fly in the ointment. There are a number of strata in Nietzsche's overall account of compassion. I am unable to do justice to much that is involved, nor am I sure that I have grasped the interrelationship of various strands in his account.

Nietzsche is clear that a certain kind of cruelty is natural, belonging to nature. But there also is an inculturated kind. "Our virtues?" asks Nietzsche. "We probably still have our virtues too. . . . We Europeans from the day after tomorrow, we firstborn of the twentieth century,—with all of our dangerous curiosity, our diversity and art of disguises, our worn-out and, as it were, saccharine cruelty in sense and spirit."[56] As Byron

55. As the dominantly influential social professionals, they are poised to replace "curers of souls." At this rate, the physician would stop being "a medicine-man and become a saviour" with this advantage: "He will require no miracles, nor will he need to have himself crucified" (*HH* 243).

56. *BGE* 214. Hollingdale nicely renders it in his translation: "our mellow and as it were sugared cruelty in spirit and senses"; Friedrich W. Nietzsche, *Beyond Good and Evil* (London: Penguin, 1990), ad loc.

put it: "We have progressively improved into a less spiritual species of tenderness."[57] This little worries Nietzsche. The problem is *ressentiment*. By the time Nietzsche comes to make some strong statements on cruelty, in the first essay in *OGM*, he has preemptively struck so hard at Christian resentment that we can barely catch our moral breath to express repudiation of or horror at what Nietzsche positively countenances. Christianity, or its epigones, is produced when one screws up morality and fails to understand its genealogy. Resentment is reactive; nobility is creative. Nobles might be resentful in their own way, but it is a noble way, a nobility of spirit that shrugs off the things that cling to and cloy weaker natures. Noble resentment just operates in short bursts. It is bounded by respect for the enemy. Go to the nobles if you want talk about love and learn something about the way the strong honors the strong. Meanwhile, as beasts of prey, nobles go on their spree. When they do, "they *return* to the innocent conscience of the wild beast, as exultant monsters, who perhaps go away having committed a hideous succession of murder, arson, rape and torture, in a mood of bravado and spiritual equilibrium as though they had simply played a student's prank" (11).

That is what Nietzsche countenances—a cruelty only improperly subject to moral condemnation. What exactly, he asks, is supposed to be wrong with such cruelty? Think of the confusions involved in condemnation. Imagine a lamb regarding a bird of prey as morally evil. It is no such thing, and it has absolutely nothing against lambs. The tenderer the better, in fact. We easily anticipate the retort of the moral person: humans are not birds of prey. Humans can *choose* whether to injure, and the ascription of good and evil to agent and to action makes sense only if choice is involved. But that is just where common moral reasoning goes wrong, Nietzsche has long told us. His basic convictions about human agency come to roost here—with a vengeance, one is tempted to say. In Nietzsche's treatment of the lamb versus the bird of prey, "we have a foundation of the paralogism of *ressentiment: the fiction of a force separated from what it can do*. It is thanks to this fiction that reactive forces triumph."[58] *Ressentiment* tries "to deprive active force of its material conditions of operation, to keep it strictly separate from what it can do."[59] But choice and obligation are fictions. "A man as he *ought* to be: that," says Nietzsche, "sounds as insipid as 'a tree as it ought to be'" (*WP* 332).

Nietzsche believes that the common moral retort to this position harbors a conceptual error generated by the grammar of the linguistic

57. Quoted in Leslie A. Marchand, *Byron: A Portrait* (London: John Murray, 1971), 153.

58. Deleuze, *Nietzsche and Philosophy*, 123.

59. Ibid., 127.

subject: "I." In truth, there is no "subject" behind the action. Grammar has become confused with metaphysics. Back, then, to the earlier scenario. If you *fear* the strong warrior, that is understandable. But there certainly are characters abroad who are much worse than noble predators, and we know who they are: the men of European mediocrity. "Pity" is the slogan under which they operate. Do we really want to erect culture on the reactive instincts of *ressentiment* that undergird such contranatural valuations? Is the domesticated household pet really Europe's finest product? Nietzsche sighs: "Grant me just one glimpse of something perfect, completely finished, happy, powerful, triumphant, which still leaves something to fear! A glimpse of a man who justifies man *himself*" (12). As it is, our European destiny is that "in losing the fear of man we have also lost our love for him, our respect for him, our hope in him and even our will to be man. . . . What is nihilism today if it is not *that*? . . . We are tired of *man*" (12).

If passion be expended on such a state of affairs, it should not be in the form of a moral or pitying disapproval of the natural exercise of power. Nietzsche expends his in another direction. The thirst that he must slake here is incredibly deep and incredibly strong; witness the messianic close of the second essay in *OGM*, which is extraordinarily vivid. We need a new redeemer, one who comes with the strength of an eagle, not coddling the lamb in his arms.

> But at some time, a time stronger than our effete, self-doubting present, the true Redeemer will come, whose surging creativity will not let him rest in any shelter or hiding place, whose solitude will be misinterpreted as a flight from reality, whereas it will in fact be a dwelling *on*, a dwelling *in* reality—so that when he comes forth into the light he may bring with him the redemption of that reality from the curse placed upon it by a lapsed ideal. This man of the future, who will deliver us both from a lapsed ideal and from all that this ideal has spawned—violent loathing, the will to extinction, nihilism—this great and decisive stroke of midday, who will make the will free once more and restore to the earth its aim, and to man his hope; this anti-Christ and anti-nihilist, conqueror of both God and Unbeing—*one day he must come*.

Thus spoke Nietzsche, longing for Zarathustra and Dionysus.[60] It is not Hitler, the "dark Messiah," that Nietzsche wants but Zarathustra, the "impious" Messiah (*OGM* 2.25).[61] This search for the proper man

60. For Dionysus as the coming redeemer god in literature prior to Nietzsche, see Jürgen Habermas, *The Philosophical Discourse of Modernity* (Cambridge, UK: Polity, 1987), 88–92.

61. I borrow the phrase "dark Messiah" from Thomas Wolfe, *You Can't Go Home Again* (New York: Harper Perennial, 1998), chap. 38.

and the prophecy of the "Overman" or "Superman" is the boldly defined context of the investigation into morality that takes place in *OGM*, which is one reason I have given so much space to *Z*. If anyone will trounce pity, now that Nietzsche has exposed it, it is he, the true redeemer. *BGE* placards before our eyes, for our inspection, morality and humanity. The first must submit its claims to harsh physiological reality. The second is described in terms of present mediocrity and longed-for overcoming. These two features are reflected respectively in the conclusions to the first two essays in *OGM*: the "Note" appended to the first essay and the cry for the redeemer that ends the second.

This is strong stuff, but is it horrific too? Is Nietzsche glorying in and glorifying rape and torture? If he is not emotionally happy about it, does he allow it untrammeled moral space; qua natural, is it unobjectionable? Is it "right"? In one respect, it is as "right" as anything can be, but Nietzsche insists that if such a word applies, we must strip it of moral denotation. Torture and rape are not immoral if we take the exemplifying instances that Nietzsche has in mind. For in such cases they are the efflux of innocent life. Life is valuation. Who can possibly pass moral judgment on or against it, and from what vantage point? At risk of anodyne interpretation, it seems to me that Nietzsche rather accepts cruelties than glories in them, considered strictly as actions, though he may glory in a noble agent such as Napoleon. But when they are considered under the aegis of the economy of the whole of life, Nietzsche reacts to them in Dionysiac style. Despite any developments and shifts in thought since *BT*, here is a positive connection with *OGM*. One cannot parcel out life; one affirms it tragically and joyfully, innocent cruelties included. Not all cruelties are innocent. Staten seems to me to be right: "Nietzsche's positive valuation of the concept of a healthy instinctual nobility is so strong that as his narrative unfolds this pole attracts all positive values and repels all negativity. Thus when cruelty is ascribed to the noble ones, it is validated as healthy release of impulse; when it is ascribed to the underclasses it is stigmatized as reactivity."[62] Reactivity and *ressentiment* are distasteful violations of nature. "Not the corruption of man but the extent to which he has become tender and moralized is his curse" (*WP* 98). We must cast a cold and noble eye on suffering rather than pity people (*WP* 119).[63] Safranski comments: "Nietzsche's analysis of morality is positively obsessed with revealing the primal cruelty that is masked in morality. Consequently, for him, open cruelty is the moment of truth."[64]

62. Henry Staten, *Nietzsche's Voice* (Ithaca, NY: Cornell University Press, 1990), 18.

63. The allusion is to Yeats's gravestone, which bids us "cast a cold eye on life, on death," words that come from his own poem "Under Ben Bulben."

64. Rüdiger Safranski, *Nietzsche: A Philosophical Biography* (New York: Norton, 2002), 187.

It has been claimed that Nietzsche admires barbarian nobles "primarily for their lack of absolutism, for their attitude that it is impossible for everyone to be bound by the same rules of conduct, for their 'pathos of distance.'"[65] Indeed, Nietzsche's "main objection to morality is its absolutism."[66] But is this so? Nietzsche's "primitive" nobles do not have a studied position on absolutism. While they are not indifferent to the question of whether everyone has the same rules of conduct—they can certainly catch a man in lèse-majesté—they really just get on with the job, practically pursuing what might amount to an "absolute," as far as they are concerned, but unconcerned about theoretical distances or their pathos. Is Nietzsche's main objection to morality its absolutism? Absolutism is grounded in Platonic and Christian realism, a conviction that there truly is a moral sphere, containing moral truth. Absolutism is rooted in transcendence. Under the putative guidance of "truth," the historical course of things has been fatal. What is taken as "truth" reverses life and denies actuality. What passes for absolute truth is really historical custom. The root problem is transcendence; absolutism is the offshoot.

When Nietzsche refers the readers of *OGM* back to his earlier writing, he cites passages that tackle the "morality of custom." While *OGM* purports to lay dramatically bare the sociolinguistic mechanism behind the emergence of the notions of "good" and "evil," a rather more mundane though significant set of considerations had long led Nietzsche to attack the way in which these polar notions were conceived. "To be moral," he told the would-be readers of *HH*, is "to act in accordance with custom, to be ethical means to practise obedience towards a law or tradition established from of old" (96). So if you do what is customary "as if by nature," you are called "good"; if you flout custom, you are called "evil." Custom and therefore goodness and therefore morality function to preserve community. Underlying this state of affairs is a predilection for permanence over the putative immediate advantages to the individual who breaks with custom (*AOM* 89). What Nietzsche does with this interestingly contrasts with what Hegel does. For Hegel, Greek morality of custom is "spontaneous unreflected Want," and unreflective morality cannot continue to hold its ground against the principle of Subjective Freedom, embodied in Christianity.[67]

65. Alexander Nehamas, *Nietzsche: Life as Literature* (Cambridge: Harvard University Press, 1985), 215.

66. Ibid., 223.

67. Georg W. F. Hegel, *Lectures in the Philosophy of History* (New York: Dover, 1956), 334. Hegel argued that the aim of the "German Spirit of the new World" was "the realization of absolute Truth as the unlimited self-determination of Freedom—that Freedom which has its own absolute form itself as its purport" (341). But he aligned this with the Christian

For his part, in *OGM* Nietzsche integrates his thinking about custom into a treatment of guilt and bad conscience, which is the theme of his second essay. Consider the breeding of humans as promise keepers. What is needed for that? Training in predictability; therefore, a morality of custom. What is needed for that? Memory. And what inculcates that? Punishment and pain. Naturally, this is a flat-footed rehearsal of Nietzsche's points, but what is important to him is that we clean up the errors involved in our thinking here. Consider the interconnection of custom and punishment. Punishment was not originally meted out on the basis of presuming freedom of the will, a belief in human agency that maintains that humans can do otherwise. No; punishment applied because of a wrong done to the perpetrator of punishment. It is the rationalization of anger and is fixed in a kind of equivalence between creditor and debtor. And debtors are creatures of promise. More than compensatory transaction in kind is going on here. There is or must be pleasure in the exaction of what is due, and that is where cruelty factors in. Cruelty was part of the festive joy of the ancients, and the history of culture, as pointed out in earlier work, is largely the tale of cruelty's "intellectualisation and 'definition'" (*OGM* 2.6). As the ages rolled on, people began to feel shame at cruelty; which is to feel shame at one's instincts; which is to feel shame about oneself; which is to feel shame at life. Now what happens is that instincts naturally turned outward become turned inward. Society develops, social justice develops, the state develops, and bad conscience develops as we progressively gnaw away at ourselves. We are becoming socially and culturally sick, Nietzsche opines, and we should be sick of our condition.

By now we certainly are familiar with this, and it is not surprising that the critique of religion kicks in. This critique already featured in his remarks on this theme in Nietzsche's earlier work, for example, on "The Desire to Be Just and the Desire to Be a Judge" in *AOM* (33). According to Schopenhauer, "the insight into the strict necessity of human actions is the boundary line which divides *philosophical* heads from *the others*." As far as Nietzsche is concerned, it is striking and truly a pity that Schopenhauer's metaphysics ruined his insight. Schopenhauer's error aside, one who consistently takes Nietzsche's line on this repudiates a religious or any other morality that ascribes accountability, and so guilt, to the self. More than that, one also rejects a religious doctrine teaching that someone has taken this guilt upon himself: Jesus, the Lamb of God. But as the priests set the Jewish people on a sordid continuation of its

---

principle, which the German people are destined to bear. See Hegel's whole chapter on "The Roman World." Stephen Houlgate's *Freedom, Truth and History: An Introduction to Hegel's Philosophy* (London: Routledge, 1991) provides a good point of entry into Hegel's idea of history.

history, so religion became deeply implicated in a guilt-and-conscience racket—which is where Nietzsche picks things up in the second essay in *OGM*. Bad conscience is guilt, and guilt is maximized in proportion to the object toward which one's guilt is directed. And what is bigger than the Christian God?

Genealogy traces antinatural developments in the history of morality. But there is hope for reversal. There is an "unstoppable decline in faith in the Christian God" that is leading to a decline in the consciousness of guilt. Atheism, in destroying belief in God, destroys guilt. "Atheism and a sort of *second innocence* go together" (*OGM* 2.20). Just as well, for the Christian-based developments that are occupying our genealogical attention need to be radically exposed for what they are: the highest form of cruelty. It is "a sort of madness of the will showing itself in mental cruelty which is absolutely unparalleled" (2.22), and the reason for this is obvious enough by now.

This phenomenon of imposing burdens on oneself by contradicting the actuality of nature fascinates Nietzsche, bent as he is on totally reversing the Christian worldview. No more fascinating case exists than the case of the ascetic ideal, the theme of Nietzsche's last essay in *OGM*. The ascetic case loomed large in Nietzsche's reckoning with Christianity in *HH*. If we read Nietzsche's treatment "The Religious Life" there, which contains so much of what is thenceforth central in his attack on Christianity, we are struck by the comparatively large proportion of space devoted to the phenomenon of asceticism, the figure of the saint. What, muses Nietzsche, drives such an unnatural practice? Well, a drive to exercise power can certainly be inwardly directed, so as to exercise a kind of tyrannical power over oneself. Remember that the errors of reason underlying Christianity can lead to a powerful discharge of emotion; thus, tension builds up and self-denial in turn relieves the tension. Again, "in many respects the ascetic too seeks to make life easier for himself: and he does so as a rule by complete subordination to the will of another or to a comprehensive law and ritual" (*HH* 139). There are other things to say as well, but the point is that the ascetic soul is composed of a number of familiar drives and elements whose confluence can be explained without positing a mighty moral mystery behind it all, traceable to the reality of a wonderful metaphysical being presiding over the world.

So says Nietzsche in *HH*, but a much more detailed analysis and more developed line is taken in *OGM*, where Nietzsche asks, in his third and last essay, "What Do Ascetic Ideals Mean?" The first answer is that they can mean many different things, and their plurality reveals something interesting and quite significant. The will needs to will something rather than not will, even to will *nothingness* rather than not will. Schopenhauer is again Nietzsche's point of reference. In the case of an artist, as long as our interest is in the actual person, ascetic ideals do not necessarily signify much that is interesting, because an artistic creation is not identical with the person himself. What of a philosopher? Take Schopenhauer: here the ascetic ideal, worked out in conjunction with his notions of aesthetic contemplation, was advanced in order to counteract sexual torment. Schopenhauer is not alone in that respect; philosophers frequently need to be negative about sensuality in order to enhance their intellectuality. In its way, asceticism thus serves the purpose of affirming existence. But nota bene: this asceticism is not a type of sainthood. Qua philosopher, the philosopher is self-serving. Poverty, humility, and chastity are not cultivated as virtues in their own right but are viewed as prerequisites for existence and productivity. Asceticism plays a role in this connection.

This is all relevant to Nietzsche's interpretation of Christianity in particular. Philosophers and priests alike espouse that ascetic ideal, which reverses the flow of life. The form of asceticism is similar: denial of the senses and denial of life. But how are we to understand the drive underneath the form, the "ascetic ideal" itself? "Only now that we have the *ascetic priest* in sight can we seriously get to grips with our problem: what does the ascetic ideal mean?" (*OGM* 3.11). The ascetic priest is a universal figure; it follows that *"life itself must have an interest* in preserving such a self-contradictory type. For an ascetic life is a self-contradiction."

Nietzsche finds this intriguing. We observed how, from the beginning of *HH*, he puzzled over how something could get twisted into its opposite. The puzzle is profound, bordering on, if not crossing into, the realms of profound ontological paradox. Schopenhauer's enterprise exemplifies it. If life presses on qua life, its force necessarily expressed and maximized, how is self-renunciation possible? How is it possible, not just psychologically but also ontologically, if we may risk slipping a foot inside the border of undefended metaphysical interpretation of Nietzsche? How can the river flow backward? Is it not an impossible possibility? It is more than just a puzzle about how anyone ever came into the position of identifying with error the instinct for life. That is explicable. The problem is that, physiologically, an ascetic life contra life is an impossibility. So Nietzsche's proposal is this: *"The ascetic ideal springs from the protective and healing instincts of a degenerating life"* just in order to maintain itself. It is the paradoxical effect of a positive life-force. From a physiological point of view, it is a struggle against exhaustion and disgust with life. The ascetic priest is self-conserving. So he exhibits a form of power. And through power, he leads others.

It is a religiously, morally, and culturally fatal leadership. We recall the roots and direction of *ressentiment*. The ascetic priests redirect it and then get people to blame themselves for their sickness. Guilt is the goal and issue of this classical priestly success in redirecting life-force. Having generated the guilt, they proceed to comfort the guilty. "We have every right to call Christianity in particular a large treasure-trove of the most ingenious means of consolation" (*OGM* 3.17). Nietzsche's interpretation of ascetic theology and practice in terms of a theory about the ascetic ideal is an excellent working illustration of the way he approaches morality; here he understands moral theology and practice on the basis of a theory about morality that interweaves history and psychology. Even more to the present point, the disease that festers at the root of Christianity comes to light with intellectual clarity upon an examination of asceticism. Underlying the professionally sympathetic orientation of the priest is intense antihumanity. The "two worst epidemics" of Nietzsche's day are *"great nausea at man"* and *"deep pity for man"* (3.14). The latter is the outward manifestation and product of the former inner reality.

Conclusion

Nietzsche believed that he lived in critical days. Michael Allen Gillespie's study *Nihilism before Nietzsche* captures the importance of much that was going on. In a sustained piece of historical argumentation, he traces the crisis caused by Ockham's view of God's omnipotence that led, by reaction, to the ascription of high powers to humans. At the end of the eighteenth and beginning of the nineteenth centuries, Fichte made a decisive move, postulating will as the creative ground of human life and thought. Thenceforth, the "history of nihilism is the history of the development of this notion of will."[68] Nietzsche redefines nihilism. Nihilism is not what happens when humans create values in a godless world. On the contrary, such creation is our salvation from nihilism, which is the state of resigned anomie signifying the enfeebled self-esteem of post-Christian humanity. Christian morality is intrinsically suited to this condition, which is why its strong presence in decaying Europe is perniciously foreboding. For the sake of the highest humans, it has to go.

As far as Nietzsche is concerned, the problem extends way beyond Germany.[69] Pessimism is poised to overwhelm humanity. Nietzsche targets the "romantic pessimism" of Schopenhauer. Nietzsche agrees that human life is such that some form of pessimism is in order, but let it be a "Dionysian pessimism" (*GS* 370). Melancholy is rife. In his revised edition of *Modernism as a Philosophical Problem*, which already had one

68. Michael Allen Gillespie, *Nihilism before Nietzsche* (Chicago: University of Chicago Press, 1996), 255.

69. Gillespie's account (ibid., 145–56) of Turgenev's Bazarov is particularly noteworthy. The connections between Russia and Germany are darkly interesting in this context.

chapter on Nietzsche, Robert Pippin added another: "The Death of God and Modern Melancholy."[70] The more that one ruminates on this and on its connection with Nietzsche's approach to morality, the more we see that delicacy is called for in the attempt to grapple with Nietzsche from a Christian point of view. On the one hand, Nietzsche exhibits exhilaration, sensitivity, sobriety, and authenticity; on the other, pathos, searching, demoralization, agony.[71] The task of balanced assessment is too big for the present volume but nonetheless important.

"In the helter-skelter of his irritable genius, Nietzsche jumbled together the ferocity of solitary beasts, the indifference and hauteur of patricians, and the antics of revellers, and out of that mixture he hoped to evoke the rulers of the coming age."[72] In the end, the consequences of Nietzsche's teaching are dire. Where the psalmist cries: "Why do the wicked prosper?" Nietzsche echoes: "Why do the weak triumph?" Just what influence Nietzsche's thought had on what happened after his day is impossible to gauge with precision. But whatever went into the keg, things exploded in Germany, in terms of "the rulers of the coming age." Dietrich Bonhoeffer was there when it happened, and he paid the ultimate earthly penalty.

70. Pippin, *Modernism*, chap. 6. The subtitle of Pippin's work is *On the Dissatisfactions of European High Culture*.

71. Back in 1830, Stendhal, in a French novel much admired by Nietzsche, was saying that the "end of paganism was accompanied by the same state of anxiety and doubt which afflicts the gloomy and bored mind in the nineteenth century"; *The Red and the Black* (Oxford: Oxford University Press, 1991), 217.

72. George Santayana, *Egotism in German Philosophy* (London: Dent, 1939), 120.

8

What We Hazard

This is convulsion, and no healthful life.

Byron, *Manfred*, act 2, scene 2

Bonhoeffer and Nietzsche

"A theological reception of Nietzsche appears as a dubious if not aberrant field of research."[1] This formulation is a little tortured, but just as we have reported the inception of Anglo-American philosophical interest in Nietzsche, so we record here twentieth-century theological interest. Since the "God is dead" movement in the 1960s, Nietzsche has received a fair amount of attention in the theology of the English-speaking world. Among those who wheeled into that debate was Dietrich Bonhoeffer. In the United Kingdom, considerable controversy attended Bishop John Robinson's *Honest to God*, and a deceased Bonhoeffer was embroiled in it, his ruminations feeding significantly into the radical current.[2] It was

1. Isabell Madelon-Wienand, discussing Peter Köster in "The Nietzschean Legacy in Drewermann's Critique of Christian Theology: A Disappointing Promise," *Journal of Nietzsche Studies* 15 (1998): 45.

2. For a lively account of the background to the controversies, see Keith Clements, *Lovers of Discord: Twentieth Century Theological Controversies in England* (London: SPCK, 1988), chap. 7. Though Robinson may be placed outside the "death of God" movement, see William Hamilton's essay "The Death of God Theologies Today," in *Radical Theology*

quite a controversial appeal to Bonhoeffer, but there he was.[3] Since those heady days, developments in theology that familiarly feature under such headings as postmodernism or feminism seem headier yet. Nevertheless, starting out with Bonhoeffer aids us in responding to Nietzsche's moral thought. Like Barth, who launched us into an earlier chapter, Bonhoeffer is an influential twentieth-century thinker who lived and wrote in the German-speaking world of the more-or-less immediate post-Nietzschean era. Their sensibilities were formed at a time closer to Nietzsche's than our own, which of itself is advantageous; because of the abiding value of their contributions, I am letting them have the first say in the sixth and now the present chapter. According to Eberhard Bethge, when Bonhoeffer was young, he "read all of Nietzsche very carefully, and Nietzsche's tremendous plea for the earth and for loyalty to its creatures never left his mind."[4] When Bonhoeffer was writing his *Ethics*, he was aware of Nietzsche as his antipode.[5] It is both understandable and justifiable, I believe, that Giles Fraser takes up an aspect of their relationship right at the beginning of his work.[6] His argument runs as follows.

"Bonhoeffer saw in Nietzsche's phrase 'beyond good and evil' an approach to ethics that he believed to be at the very heart of Protestant theology and central to a proper understanding of the Gospel." Thus, there is an affinity between Nietzsche and Jesus that Bonhoeffer picks up. Both are against "morality." Bonhoeffer follows suit: the Christian, like the *Übermensch*, is "able to operate beyond conventional morality because of his or her life in Christ." Divine grace is the foundation of Christian action, and divine freedom is its form. The knowledge of good and evil, as the biblical narrative of the fall tells us, is a sign of disunity and not a knowledge on which humanity is originally perched in authentic creatureliness before flight into action. Moving on to Bonhoeffer's "religionless Christianity," Fraser links, without completely identifying

---

and the Death of God, by Thomas J. J. Altizer and William Hamilton, new ed. (Harmondsworth, UK: Penguin, 1968), 36–37.

3. John A. T. Robinson in *Honest to God* (London: SCM, 1963) joined Bonhoeffer to Bultmann and Tillich, but in Robinson's article on the subject in *The Observer*, March, 17, 1963, where Bultmann was absent, Bonhoeffer was prominent. For an example of the resistance to this use of Bonhoeffer, see Heinrich Ott, *God* (Edinburgh: St. Andrew Press, 1974), 17ff. Ott's own detailed treatment of Bonhoeffer is found in *Reality and Faith: The Theological Legacy of Dietrich Bonhoeffer* (London: Lutterworth, 1971).

4. Eberhard Bethge, "The Challenge of Dietrich Bonhoeffer's Life and Theology," in *World Come of Age*, ed. Ronald Gregor Smith (London: Collins, 1967), 27.

5. See, for example, the most recent full-length study known to me of Bonhoeffer's "nonreligious interpretation" of the Bible: Ralf K. Wüstenberg, *A Theology of Life*, subtitled in English to suit its Anglo-Saxon readership *Dietrich Bonhoeffer's Religionless Christianity* (Grand Rapids: Eerdmans, 1998), 138–39.

6. For what follows, see Giles Fraser, *Redeeming Nietzsche: On the Piety of Unbelief* (New York: Routledge, 2002), 4–8.

them, Nietzsche's and Bonhoeffer's love of the earth. In their respective ways, both men regard denial of this as constitutive of *ressentiment*. Both want life and action to issue from strength.

There appear to me to be at least two difficulties with this account. The first is that Bonhoeffer's comments are taken out of context. With the exception of one reference to *Ethics*, Fraser uses just two sources: the *Letters and Papers from Prison* and Bonhoeffer's address: "What Is a Christian Ethic?" delivered in Barcelona in 1929.[7] But we need to place in their proper context two quotations from Bonhoeffer's Barcelona address. The first, given in its fuller form by Fraser, is this:

> The Christian gospel stands beyond good and evil. . . . It was by no means Fr. Nietzsche who first penetrated "beyond good and evil," even though it was on this basis that he denounced the "moral poison" of Christianity. But, however much it may have come to be obscured, this insight belongs to the patrimony of the gospel itself.

In this connection Fraser mentions Nietzsche's aphorism in *BGE*: "Jesus said to his Jews: 'The law was made for servants—love God as I love him, as his son! What do we sons of God have to do with morality?'" (164). This is one of a series of aphorisms, and we need to be on constant lookout for ironies in this kind of material. Still, for the moment we are interpreting Bonhoeffer rather than Nietzsche, and so we move on to the second quotation, which goes like this:

> The Christian himself creates his standards of good and evil for himself. Only he can justify his own actions, just as only he can bear the responsibility. The Christian creates new tables, new Decalogues, as Nietzsche said of the Superman. Nietzsche's Superman is not, as he supposed, the opposite of the Christian; without knowing it Nietzsche has introduced many traits of the Christian made free, as Paul and Luther know and describe him.[8]

But what exactly was Bonhoeffer saying here? In this address, he is affirming that there *are* concepts of good and evil, and it is valid to consider action under these rubrics, but "the concepts of 'good' and 'evil' exist only in the performance of an action, i.e. at any specific present, and hence any attempt to lay down principles is like trying to draw a bird in flight." So "there cannot be good and evil as general ideas, but only as qualities of a will making a decision. There can be only good and

7. The latter is found in Dietrich Bonhoeffer, *No Rusty Swords* (New York: Harper & Row; London: Collins, 1965), 35–44. I shall not specifically follow up the material from idem, *Letters and Papers from Prison* (London: SCM, 1971).

8. See Fraser, *Redeeming Nietzsche*, 167n12.

evil as done in freedom." Bonhoeffer understands ethics as the way from humans to God. Good and evil, as conventionally understood, belong to ethics. But there is no way from humans to God; to say otherwise is to deny grace. So "the Christian message stands beyond good and evil." Corresponding to ethics as a way from humankind to God is the control that I have in relation to God if I subsume my action under moral principles. It leads to "moral action without immediate relationship to God." Grace and freedom are denied. What is right about the Superman is his independent nonconformity.

However, in the course of saying all this, Bonhoeffer is emphatic: it is under God that the Christian creates one's standards of good and evil. It is surely a kind of subcreation, parasitic on the existence of good and evil. But if the Christian creates, what bearing does already existing good and evil have on it? Bonhoeffer puts matters too cryptically to permit a ready answer. The creation of which Bonhoeffer speaks is contrasted with life under moral principles and the avoidance of personal responsibility, but he does not deny the actuality of good and evil in the context of the practice of obeying God's personal command, his particular will. Discerning it can be a murky affair, and Bonhoeffer makes much of this. But we operate under our own judgment and under God's judgment. The accent lies on act: "There is ethics only in the performance of the act, not in the letter of the laws." Bonhoeffer's formulations and appeal to Nietzsche embrace the conviction that God is a judge who can reckon our actions good or evil and that actions can be so reckoned by ourselves, however uncertainly, as long as we undertake them according to the form of freedom, not the form of moral law. All this distances Bonhoeffer from Nietzsche more than Fraser allows, however infelicitously Bonhoeffer formulates his arguments in light of the point he is surely trying to make.

The second difficulty is greater and more significant. It lies in the range of sources on which Fraser draws. If we want to make the most of comparison between Nietzsche and Bonhoeffer, the unfinished *Ethics*, fruit of Bonhoeffer's relative maturity, must be our principal quarry.[9] If we read the work according to the order followed in the sixth German edition, Bonhoeffer opens his campaign thus: "The knowledge of good and evil seems to be the aim of all ethical reflection. The first task of Christian ethics is to invalidate this knowledge."[10] This is so because humankind

9. Andrew Shanks rightly observes that Bonhoeffer was more discriminating in later writing than when he was following a "fashionable vitalism" in the Barcelona lectures: "Bonhoeffer's Response to Nietzsche," *Studies in Christian Ethics* 10, no. 2 (1999): 82.

10. Dietrich Bonhoeffer, *Ethics* (London: Macmillan, 1965), 17. However, my point is unaffected by a critical decision about where in the *Ethics* this passage should be placed.

was created to know God and to know God as its good. Knowledge of good and evil is the sign of disunity and fall. Fraser rightly highlights the presence and importance of this line of thought in the Barcelona address. But some time after that address and quite a long time before *Ethics*, Bonhoeffer changed.[11] That was before the winter semester of 1932–33, when Bonhoeffer lectured in the University of Berlin on creation and the fall.[12] These lectures arguably constitute a significant turning point in Bonhoeffer's theological development.

Creation and Fall deliberately and frequently engages Nietzsche.[13] Bonhoeffer says that "Adam knows neither what good nor what evil is and lives in the strictest sense *beyond good and evil*; that is, Adam lives out of the life that comes from God, before whom a life lived in good, just like a life lived in evil, would mean an unthinkable falling away."[14] But here Bonhoeffer is denying to Adam the kind of moral goodness under which human life is subsumed after the fall; he is not denying the "good" pronounced by God in creation. The fall is drastic: "The fall *really* makes the creature—humankind-in-the-imago-dei—into a creator-sicut-deus."[15] Corrupt divinity has been substituted for uncorrupted humanity. Self-division is the consequence. Transgression issues in the "desperate, . . . unquenchable . . . eternal thirst that Adam feels for life," which is "essentially a thirst for death."[16] The *imago* proper, be it recognized, entails freedom for the other. This is all a far cry from Nietzsche. When Bonhoeffer summons us to life beyond good and evil, he is summoning us to creaturely life beyond the norms of fallen life but not outside the scope of divine commandment and what God establishes as our "good."

However, it is in the *Ethics* that the gulf between Bonhoeffer and Nietzsche appears most clearly. *Ethics*, *BGE*, and *OGM* are similar in this respect: what is said about ethics is said forcefully, and it is forceful because it is embedded in an analysis of contemporary times. For Bonhoeffer, these were days when Shakespeare's characters walked the earth again. "Today there are once more villains and saints, and they are not hidden from the public view. Instead of the uniform greyness of the rainy day we now have the black storm-cloud and the brilliant light-

11. Eberhard Bethge, *Dietrich Bonhoeffer: A Biography*, rev. ed. (Minneapolis: Fortress, 2000): "The Transition from Theologian to Christian," 202–6.

12. Dietrich Bonhoeffer, *Creation and Fall: A Theological Exposition of Genesis 1–3* (Minneapolis: Fortress, 1997).

13. See the editorial notes that accompany the critical text of Bonhoeffer's work. Dialogue with Nietzsche includes dialogue with *BGE* in particular.

14. Bonhoeffer, *Creation and Fall*, 87–88.

15. Ibid., 116.

16. Ibid., 143.

ning-flash. . . . Reality lays itself bare. Shakespeare's characters walk in our midst."[17] When naked reality parades itself in that way, we see that Bonhoeffer's statement is weighty: "One is distressed by the failure of reasonable people to perceive . . . the depths of evil."[18] In adumbrating a theological anthropology that positioned essential humanity beyond good and evil, Bonhoeffer did not abandon "reasonableness." "Reasonableness" is not a sign of benign moralism in the midst of dire days. It is a sign of sanity, of sanity in the shadow of the antichrist.

> In Soloviev's story of the Antichrist, in the last days before Christ's return the heads of the persecuted churches discuss the question of what is for each of them the most precious thing in Christianity; the decisive answer is that the most precious thing in Christianity is Jesus Christ Himself. . . . In the face of the Antichrist only one thing has force and permanence, and that is Christ Himself. . . . He is the centre and strength of the Bible, of the Church, and of theology, but also of humanity, of reason, of justice and of culture. Everything must return to Him; it is only under His protection that it can live.[19]

"Reason" is on that list. There is a desperate shortage of it, or it is in a desperately myopic condition. Where reason falters, evil flourishes. The contrast between Bonhoeffer's and Nietzsche's attitudes to their times is quite striking. In 1888, Nietzsche wrote as follows:

> *Culture contra civilization.*—The high points of culture and civilization do not coincide: one should not be deceived about the abysmal antagonism of culture and civilization. The great moments of culture were always, morally speaking, times of corruption; and conversely, the periods when the taming of the human animal ("civilization") was desired and enforced were times of intolerance against the boldest and most spiritual natures. Civilization has aims different from those of culture—perhaps they are even opposite. (*WP* 121)

Nihilism is Nietzsche's great enemy, threatening culture. Just over fifty years later, it is not post-Christian nihilism as Nietzsche understands it but the post-Nietzschean post-Christian "void" that troubles Bonhoeffer. It is the fate of civilization rather than of culture that is in the balance. In our times

> the western world is brought to the brink of the void. The forces unleashed exhaust their fury in mutual destruction. Everything established is threat-

17. Bonhoeffer, *Ethics*, 64.
18. Ibid., 65.
19. Ibid., 56. The reference to Vladimir Soloviev is the more interesting for us because, as a thinker, Soloviev was apparently on the track of both Dostoyevsky and Nietzsche.

ened with annihilation. This is not a crisis among other crises. It is a decisive struggle of the last days. . . . The void towards which the west is drifting is not the natural end, the dying away and decline of a once flourishing history of nations. . . . It is the supreme manifestation of all the powers which are opposed to God. It is the void made god. . . . Its dominion is absolute. It is a creative void, which blows its anti-god's breath into the nostrils of all that is established and awakens it to a false semblance of new life while sucking out from it its proper essence.[20]

Nietzsche and Bonhoeffer are poles apart, a fact that is not accounted for by the fact that they lived in and talked of different times. Both read human history as a collision of Christ and antichrist. They choose their allegiances differently.

The orientation of Bonhoeffer's later Christology is largely explicable in terms of his early christological question: "Who is Jesus Christ for us today?"[21] Given the refusal of many people in the churches and the willingness of some outside the churches to stand against Hitler, Bonhoeffer found himself puzzling about Christ's lordship over the religionless. What kind of Christ is this? The opposite of Nietzsche's kind. Bonhoeffer's Christ is a completely free man, the unparalleled exemplar of human freedom, a freedom expressed in action untrammeled by vacillation between innumerable possibilities, a freedom integrated in the will of God. "He lives and acts not by the knowledge of good and evil but by the will of God. . . . In it the origin is recovered; in it there is established the freedom and the simplicity of all action."[22] "Simplicity" picks up the kind of deep integration that James urges on his readers (James 1:8). Self-division, a sign and cause of shame, is banished in Jesus and in discipleship.[23] If inward adherence to God is the cause, confident action before fellow humanity is the sign of its banishment. Action, not talk, is the mark of the strong individual; determination to live by the will of God signifies individual strength, not craven conformity.[24] The context of the exposition is the insistence that ethics is not about the knowledge

20. Bonhoeffer, *Ethics*, 105–6. With both Nietzsche and Bonhoeffer, compare Hermann Hesse, *Demian* (London: Peter Owen, 2001), 163–64.

21. Dietrich Bonhoeffer, *Christology* (New York: Harper & Row; London: Collins, 1966).

22. Bonhoeffer, *Ethics*, 30. The "origin" is human action in accordance with the plan of creation, not the fallen condition.

23. For Bonhoeffer's brief remarks on shame in *Ethics*, see 20–26.

24. Bonhoeffer says, "Not in the flight of ideas but only in action is freedom" (*Letters and Papers*, 15). Compare Nietzsche on Christianity, guilt, and judgment (*AOM* 33) with Bonhoeffer on Christ against the Pharisees, a case of "action" over against "judgment" (*Ethics*, 26–37).

of good and evil but about conformity to the good.[25] In all things, Christ is exemplar.[26]

As far as I can judge, it is sometimes tacitly or practically taken for granted that a Christianity such as that exemplified by Bonhoeffer is not subject to the main lines of Nietzsche's critique.[27] The question, then, is whether or not Bonhoeffer exemplifies an authentic Christianity. The features that I have indicated stand as a testimony to a Christianity different from that portrayed by Nietzsche, and surely in their principle, as far as we have outlined them, they survive rigorous theological testing as a fair statement of Christian belief. If Bonhoeffer in his thought and life captured anything of the spirit and truth of Christ and if he exemplified anything of Christianity in his resolute and single-minded stand against Hitler in the name of Jesus, then Nietzsche's sketches of Christianity and Christian anthropology appear very inadequate. I have earlier suggested that Nietzsche's portrayal of Christian theological anthropology and of Christ succeed, for the most part, in missing Christ and Christianity altogether. When he contrasts his own version of humanity beyond good and evil with the conventional morality of the herd, Nietzsche misses the *tertium datur*. Bonhoeffer provides it. We can hardly take seriously Nietzsche's portrayal of Christ, Christianity, and Christian morality when we think about Bonhoeffer. Would Nietzsche have been repelled as much by Bonhoeffer as by Hitler? Figuring out the what, why, and wherefore of an answer would be quite revealing.[28]

Jesus as "man for others" is a well-known description by Bonhoeffer. Yet the *Ethics* cannot and does not try to conceal from us Jesus in his individuality. To the radical extent that Jesus is the man for others, he stands alone and lonely. We need to read some of the celebrated passages in the *Letters and Papers from Prison* against the background of the *Ethics*.[29] If we do not, we shall gather a wrong impression of what Bonhoeffer says about the strength and weakness of God on the cross, something that seems to play into the hands of a Nietzschean criticism of

25. I agree with James McClendon's comment that this thesis is argued "with perhaps typical German abruptness," though I find Bonhoeffer generally clearer in *Ethics* than in *Creation and Fall*: James W. McClendon Jr., *Systematic Theology*, vol. 1, *Ethics* (Nashville: Abingdon, 1986), 59.

26. This is not to ascribe to Bonhoeffer an "exemplarist" Christology.

27. In postmodern context, see, e.g., John D. Caputo, *The Prayers and Tears of Jacques Derrida: Religion without Religion* (Bloomington: Indiana University Press, 1997), 219.

28. I do not want to make too much of Bonhoeffer, as though we virtually had to await his arrival before an alternative to Nietzsche was expressed and exemplified. His historical context, however, makes him an especially rewarding figure to consider in connection with Nietzsche's critique of Christianity.

29. I am aware that a hermeneutical assumption is being made here. If some find it too controversially strong, let us just read the texts in tandem.

Christianity on weakness.[30] While Bonhoeffer's fragmentary treatments of strength and weakness should not be pressed into a consistent system, there appears to be a kind of dialectic at work. On the one hand, Bonhoeffer wants us as Christians to reckon with and encounter humanity in its strength. We are not to ferret out human guiltiness, fear, weakness, and anxiety but take humanity as it is, without insisting that the gospel effectively addresses only those who can be psychologically reduced to weakness.[31] On the other hand, as far as Christians are concerned,

> God lets himself be pushed out of the world on to the cross. He is weak and powerless in the world, and that is precisely the way, the only way, in which he is with us and helps us. . . . Christ helps us, not by virtue of his omnipotence, but by virtue of his weakness and suffering. . . . The Bible directs man to God's powerlessness and suffering; only the suffering God can help.[32]

This is not a particularly successful move. It derives from Matthew 8:17 (as the full letter shows) a one-sided axiom about divine weakness, but the Matthean text can and should also be connected with powerful signs and wonders. This move interprets what Bonhoeffer regards as in some respects a positive process (the process of secularization) in terms of what he would have to regard as in manifest respects an unjust or evil deed (the handing over of Christ to death). These "respects" seem to collide.[33] But where Nietzsche pits immoral or amoral strength against the pathos of the religious celebration of weakness, Bonhoeffer redefines the disciple's power not in order to create or sustain *ressentiment* but to meet, with a kind of acceptance, the natural religionlessness of his day. He does not complain about secular strength, but he can show a better way. To show a better way without complaint or *ressentiment* is a sign of strength. Bonhoeffer's attack on an escapist church harboring the compliant person is as heartfelt as anything Nietzsche said about and against

30. Bonhoeffer, *Letters and Papers*, 360–61.

31. I use "guiltiness" rather than "guilt" to denote subjective feelings rather than objective status *coram deo*. Nietzsche somewhere speaks of "the sinner" "in whom God has more joy than in the "just man." Bonhoeffer's is a counterblast to the kind of thing that Nietzsche thinks Christians have achieved with their "moral scepticism" (*GS* 122). Bonhoeffer's most striking remarks on this are in connection with justification and the "good man" in *Ethics*, 60–63 and 110–43. I agree with Clifford Green that we need to read Bonhoeffer on "religionless Christianity" against this background: "Human Sociality and Christian Community," in *The Cambridge Companion to Bonhoeffer*, ed. John W. de Gruchy (Cambridge: Cambridge University Press, 1999), 129.

32. Bonhoeffer, *Letters and Papers*, 360–61.

33. Perhaps this corresponds to an apparent tension between Bonhoeffer's pessimism about the West in *Ethics* and what he says about secularization in *Letters and Papers*. Whether or not the tension is merely superficial is a question beyond our scope.

the weak. Bonhoeffer's analysis gives credibility to his claim that Jesus wants to make "men" of us.[34] When it comes to true humanity, action, good, and evil, Bonhoeffer is Nietzsche's credible Christian antipode.

Good and Evil

I have lifted the title of this chapter from Socrates' remark in Plato's *Protagoras*: "If, therefore, you have understanding of what is good and evil, you may safely buy knowledge of Protagoras or of any one; but if not, then, O my friend, pause, and do not hazard your dearest interests at a game of chance."[35] We hazard a great deal if we approach Nietzsche without that knowledge. Arguments over the proper way to define or understand concepts will frustrate those on the coal face who summon us to attend urgently to phenomena conceived under such terms as "good" and "evil" or to action familiarly conceived under the rubric of "morality." Attempting tight definitions can direct attention away from the phenomena that evoke what we term "moral" reactions, diverting it to the business of sophisticated conceptualization. In the following, I just want to look at what we might make of these three notions—good, evil, and morality—from a theological point of view and in light of what Nietzsche says.

Let it be granted that "evil" is hard to define and that the proper application of that word is subject to some disagreement in many if not all cases. Even so, let us apply it to an identifiable phenomenon such as delight in inflicting pain by torture, what often goes under the description of "moral evil." Those who perceive something as morally evil probably normally and intuitively regard such a judgment about the phenomenon in question as significantly and profoundly objective. If they are uneasy about the suggestion that "objectivity" entails, connotes, or sanctions the idea of a transcendent moral source or extrinsic order independent of our judgment, they may grant that the judgment should be called "subjective" but maintain that it should be normative. Exposure to the extreme suffering that is caused and to the agency that causes surely generates the prima facie impression that when we identify a state of affairs as evil, we do so with all the objectivity that pertains to sense perception, even if we are making a value judgment.[36] It is

34. Bonhoeffer, *Letters and Papers*, 361.
35. Plato, *Protagoras*, in *The Dialogues of Plato*, trans. Benjamin Jowett (Oxford: Clarendon, 1875), 1:127.
36. I am making no specific philosophical assumptions about the sort of objectivity that might be predicated of sense perceptions. We are talking about (roughly) practical judgments.

not that exposure to evil generates a conscious epistemological stance. Rather, mind and emotion join in immediate or (perhaps we should say) intuitive response, containing the judgment that a given phenomenon is evil and morally horrifying. Indeed, "morally horrifying" may border on being an excessively weak characterization.[37] If we nevertheless retain the phrase, then the phenomena of evil, deliberate cruelty, and suffering will encourage us to regard the phenomenon of the "moral" in a light different from the one cast on it when we hear the word in a different context. For the word "morality," abstracted from the context of such things as torture or rape, can connote "law," "imposition," "heteronomy" (unless it is qualified as "personal morality") and thus incline us to regard its alleged objectivity as tyrannous.

Experience of what we are calling evil leads to grim and burdened reflection on its conceptual opposite, which is naturally designated the "good." Brought into conceptual play as the extreme opposite of evil, the "good" is thus shorn of any pejorative connotation associated with a heteronomous "morality." Indeed, if we regard "morally horrifying" as terminologically too weak to capture the phenomenon of evil, we might regard "morally admirable" as terminologically too weak to capture the phenomenon of the good.[38] However we use our language, when we order our vocabulary of good and evil to distressing phenomena such as those that I have instantiated, we best gain an orientation to morality in a Christian, as opposed to Nietzschean, perspective. "Morality" no longer sounds like an imposition.

The concept of the good, derived as the antithesis of evil, should profoundly, even proportionately, attract all those whom evil profoundly repels. "Evil" possesses an unsurpassable quality, naming something that evokes the ultimate "moral horror," and we may wonder if it can ever attain a theoretical point of dark perfection, than which no greater evil can be conceived. If it can, its conceptual opposite is the idea of perfect goodness. That is the idea of God or one governing aspect of the idea of God, albeit abstractly conceived. We can convert this into personal language by appropriately modifying it and saying, "God is perfectly good" rather than "God is the idea of perfect goodness." But here we certainly collide with Nietzsche: "Let us remove supreme goodness from

37. For "moral horror," see Robert M. Adams, *Finite and Infinite Goods: A Framework for Ethics* (Oxford: Oxford University Press, 1999), 104–7.

38. Perhaps this is too far-fetched, and it certainly is too complex to make anything depend on it, but I wonder if Bernard Williams's analysis encourages us to consider whether morality stands to goodness in a relationship analogous to that in which sincerity stands to authenticity: *Truth and Truthfulness: An Essay in Genealogy* (Princeton, NJ: Princeton University Press, 2002), 183.

the concept of God: it is unworthy of a god" (*WP* 1037).[39] The Christian claim is that goodness is instantiated as truly and as deeply as is evil. Whether or not that claim can be substantiated, the *idea* of God as perfectly good should attract as surely—even in proportion—as the idea of evil repels. Some will protest that other things that are unattractive go into the Christian idea of God and that the attraction of divine goodness is reduced by the copresence of other attributes or perfections. However, I am not offering an exposition or defense of the Christian understanding of God per se. I am trying to conceive of the beauty of goodness, understood as the purest antithesis to the ugliness of evil. We need to do so in order to be oriented aright to the Christian understanding of morality. If nothing evokes moral horror like evil, then nothing should evoke moral approbation like goodness, so that as long as our experience of evil is what guides us into reflection, the idea of God is the immediate cause of praise, as far as the perfection of goodness is concerned. It is in such a context that we should be inquiring about the divine establishment of morality or moral law. If you like, we should be talking about the good before talking about the right.

Bonhoeffer was surely right to tease out, as he did, what we find in the account in Genesis that opens the Hebrew and Christian Scriptures. "Good" is first introduced to us as a quality ascribed to the created order, including humanity. To know good and evil, as humans come to know it, following the primal transgression, is to know them under the aegis of failure and, especially, in the shadow of violence. To breach the divine prohibition is to become acquainted with violence; violence is the most striking manifestation of the presence of evil in the human heart.[40] Within such an order, humans distantly echo their created goodness most obviously by abstaining from violence. It may seem that I have quietly collapsed distinctions within cruelty and violence that Nietzsche implicitly retains: between innocent barbarian cruelty and the calculated sadism of a less innocent generation. Such a distinction between the two certainly may not appear very stark to those who have to endure it. But the cruelty of violence that Nietzsche at least sometimes finds innocent is the most significant manifestation of the presence of evil, after what happened in the garden, as far as the biblical record is concerned. Never

---

39. I do not, however, want to underestimate the importance of using "personal" rather than "abstract" language. This point is made forcefully by Emil Brunner, *The Christian Doctrine of God* (London: Lutterworth, 1949), chap. 13.

40. Gen. 6:9–13. What is going on in relation to sexuality is harder to fathom (Gen. 3:7). Implicitly, Noah's righteousness consists eminently in refraining from violence. John Milbank's critique of Nietzsche, especially in *OGM*, is embedded in the way he contrasts an ontology of peace to an ontology of violence: *Theology and Social Theory: Beyond Secular Reason* (Oxford: Blackwell, 1990), passim.

mind how blameworthy particular people, races, and cultures are for this or that violence. In theological perspective, human violence reflects an evil, not a natural, state of affairs. In "innocent" or "sadistic" form, we are dealing with a breach of goodness that is evil.

If, in the midst of this, Genesis at an early stage inducts us into what we might naturally call a moral worldview, there is a sense in which humans have brought "morality" on themselves. If we follow Bonhoeffer's lead, we must say that morality is not primal. It is a phenomenon of the fallen order, tied to the notion of (moral) law. Paul makes distinctions here in relation to earlier and later periods that might require us to nuance this claim (Rom. 5:13). But the humans who walk the pages of Genesis inhabit a world constituted under something like a moral order in a way that Adam primally does not.[41] The Adamic, primally human, relation with God is not usefully described as "moral" in the sense of living in the awareness of substantive right and wrong. That is the kind of knowledge it is better to avoid; it is a sign of the fall. As a bearer of substantive content, law does not obtain under the original Adamic regimen. There is just one prohibitive injunction, and its point is to prevent entanglement in "morality," to keep humanity away from a situation where disobedience to God becomes as natural as, indeed more natural than, obedience. If some of these statements seem too stark and too extreme, it suffices to say that the purpose of prohibition is to avoid implication in evil. God is not bent on immersing humans in the sphere of moral good and evil, but the exact contrary. If my account is deemed problematic and it is judged that the Adamic state is more felicitously described as a moral state, so be it, but it is moral in the extreme sense of absence of evil. It is the state of the "good," which those who hate evil must consistently love.

To live under the moral law and under what theologians call "fallen" conditions is therefore "unnatural," if "natural" describes a primal created order. On a theological account of humanity, moral law may be experienced by humans as extrinsic in two ways. It is experienced epistemically as revelation, the presumed declaration by a divine Other of what we are to do and not to do, to be and not to be. And it is experienced substantively as an imposition on us, an external law that constrains nature. Yet on the latter (substantive) score, the concrete content of moral law is meant to reconnect us with our primal humanity by a route originally as alien to God as it should have been to our own created being. And on the former (epistemological) score, Jeremiah looked forward to a time of internalization of law, where no Kantian

---

41. The question of the historicity of Adam is not immediately relevant to these observations.

could say that a theologically based moral imperative is a word from without that promises external reward; instead, it is a word spoken from within, by the Spirit, that causes the heart to desire goodness for its own intrinsic sake.[42] Moral law is the form in which we are reminded that to live humanly under God is no more an imposition on our nature, no more against its grain, than is its land speed an imposition on the cheetah. Communion, not antithesis, is the primal relationship between God and humanity; restoration of nature, not its destruction, is the ultimate objective of the moral law.[43] The design of morality is to prevent implication in evil. To the extent that we are convinced that opposition to evil is basic to—and not an imposition on—the dignity, reality, truth, and freedom of our humanity, we ought to regard the Christian idea of morality in terms of a "good" directive to rediscover the grain of original nature.

As already recognized, from Nietzsche's viewpoint the theology of creation and fall is palpably ridiculous. My objective is not to make the intellectual case for it but to ask what "good," "evil," and "moral" look like in its light. In a compressed way, I am trying to bring to light the theological framework within which the idea of morality has its place. What may appear to be less dramatic or more controversial examples of evil than the cruelties of rape and torture have their home in a worldview that unhesitatingly regards all cruelty as evil. The binding truth of such a moral perspective will be unquestionable to many a person sobered by encounter with the examples of evil that I have given, even if its theistic foundation is discounted. I am trying to give "morality" a hue, a feeling tone, quite different from what Nietzsche accords to it. He inveighs against the fundamental anthropology that undergirds and is brought to light in Christian moral teaching. If we restate that anthropology, we might find it intellectually unacceptable, but we should not find the ideas of good and evil abhorrent, if we find abhorrent the phenomena that I have tagged as "evil."

Nietzsche said:

> I regard Christianity as the most fatal lie that has yet existed, as the great unholy lie: I draw out the after-growth and sprouting of its ideal from beneath every form of disguise, I reject every compromise position with respect to it—I force a war against it. Petty people's morality as the measure of things: this is the most disgusting degeneration culture has yet exhibited. And this kind of ideal still hanging over mankind as "God"! (*WP* 200)

42. Jer. 31:33. I do not mean that the prophet is envisaging doing away with all external revelation or suggesting that we desire goodness rather than God.

43. This is not to deny that "law" can also function differently and dispensationally (Gal. 3:19–25).

Whatever has transpired in church life and church history, "petty people's morality" scarcely accounts for the principle of Christian morality. If we attend to Nietzsche's observations on cruelty, it must be in the light of this principle, not Nietzsche's speculations about popular *ressentiment*. It is not that Nietzsche himself was innately callous. In fact, the hypersensitive opposite is probably the case.[44] In the days of the Franco-Prussian War, Figgis writes of Nietzsche as "busied with the sick, driven nearly wild with sympathy."[45] Then he spied the splendor of the Prussian horse. "It was this power greater than pain which made pain irrelevant—that was the reality."[46] I am not sure just how strong a historical basis Figgis has for saying this.[47] But whatever is the case with that particular occasion, it is a plausible reading of the general evidence about Nietzsche. Figgis may even have been right to say that "no one had deeper feelings than Nietzsche. Much of his barbarity in philosophy is due to his fear of falling prey to them."[48] Apparently minor statements in Nietzsche's corpus hint at his sensitivity. "We are greatly distressed if we hear that a youth has already lost his teeth or has become blind; . . . we *suffer* over this" (*WS* 268).

There is testimony to the power of Schopenhauer's writing about suffering and sympathy.[49] Nietzsche may have been capable of feeling much the same as Schopenhauer apparently did. "I am one thing: my writings are another" (*EH*, "Why I Write Such Excellent Books," 1). Nietzsche was not personally indifferent to cruelty, but he regarded compassionate pity as a temptation, not an ennoblement. In a revealing letter written to Overbeck on Christmas Day of 1882, after his breakup with Lou Salomé, Nietzsche said: "Pity . . . is a kind of hell—whatever the Schopenhauerians may say."[50] Even more revealing is a comment in a letter less than a year later: "Schopenhauer's 'pity' has always been the *main* cause of trouble in my life—and therefore I have every reason to be well disposed towards moralities which attribute a few other motives

44. If we can be hypersensitive to suffering. Thomas Mann's essay "Nietzsche's Philosophy in the Light of Recent History," in *Last Essays* (London: Secker & Warburg, 1959), is effective on this point.

45. John Neville Figgis, *The Will to Freedom, or The Gospel of Nietzsche and the Gospel of Christ* (London: Longmans, Green, 1917), 20.

46. Ibid., 21.

47. Reading Figgis in conjunction with Walter Kaufmann, *Nietzsche: Philosopher, Psychologist, Antichrist*, 4th ed. (New York: Vintage, 1974), 179, makes us wonder whether Figgis was subscribing to the account offered by Elisabeth Förster-Nietzsche, Nietzsche's sister, who was not the most impeccably reliable of witnesses.

48. Figgis, *Will to Freedom*, 45.

49. So Richard Taylor, for example, in his introduction to Arthur Schopenhauer, *On the Basis of Morality* (Indianapolis: Bobbs-Merrill, 1965).

50. To Overbeck, *SL*, December 25, 1882.

to morality and do not try to reduce our whole human effectiveness to 'fellow-feelings.'"[51]

Despite the positive place that Christianity has for compassion, it cannot actually be identified with the essence of love. "Compassion" is an expression of love *sub specie temporalis*, but it is not applicable to the divine nature as such in this sense; it has no place within essential trinitarian relations apart from the divine relationship to humanity. But however we formulate our trinitarian theology—and it would obviously be a distraction if I try to defend myself here—we must certainly insist that *agapē* is not reducible to compassion. Compassion is one form of love exercised under specified conditions, but there are others, such as *philia*. Jörg Salaquarda is right: Nietzsche wrongly identifies love with *Mitleid*, "compassion . . . construed as pity."[52] We need many distinctions to analyze these things properly, such as that between weak pity and strong compassion, between sentiment without backbone and a turbulence stirred up within us by the world's evils. Interhuman compassion, however, had no obvious scope in Eden and cannot easily be projected onto the eschatological paradise regained. In identifying love with compassion, Schopenhauer did not fully grasp the nature of Christian *agapē* at this point either, even if he salvaged from Christianity something durable, solid, and true.

The principal difficulty in Nietzsche's account lies neither in what Nietzsche failed to understand nor in what he personally experienced. It lies in Nietzsche the philosopher and his statements about cruelty. The particular genealogical account of morality that he offers is not really essential to his fundamental argument; its scientific rejection would not affect the core of his philosophy.[53] It could be extensively revised or altered to preserve the basic conviction that does matter: that the "moral" is antithetical to the "natural." In theological terms, what Nietzsche means by the "natural" is composed of the natural and the nonnatural, the created and the fallen. Those who find such a theological scheme of things incredible might still mount against Nietzsche an argument in favor of the constitutive importance and governing role of morality in human affairs. We need to put to Nietzsche the question

---

51. *SL* 216, and see the rest of the letter.

52. Jörg Salaquarda, "Nietzsche and the Judaeo-Christian Tradition," in *The Cambridge Companion to Nietzsche*, ed. Bernd Magnus and Kathleen M. Higgins (Cambridge: Cambridge University Press, 1996), 107.

53. Daniel Conway is probably right on the reason why not; "Genealogy and Critical Method," in *Nietzsche, Genealogy, Morality: Essays on Nietzsche's "Genealogy of Morals,"* ed. Richard Schacht (Berkeley: University of California Press, 1994), 324–25. Also see Will Dudley, *Hegel, Nietzsche, and Philosophy: Thinking Freedom* (Cambridge: Cambridge University Press, 2002), 220.

he himself poses at the beginning of *BGE*, concerning the value of truth. Ivan Karamazov sought to show that the actuality of even the most exalted state of affairs—the existence of God—does not entail that we accept it in a glad embrace. So, it might be argued, it would have been far better for Nietzsche to insist that we live by the "fiction" of morality and to encourage us to adhere to what our minds have fashioned than to consign pity to unnaturalness. For Nietzsche, "suffering is the great objection to existence; in order to affirm existence, Nietzsche must affirm this suffering and all the dark forces that cause it. Pity stands in the way of affirmation."[54] So why not stand in the way of affirmation? It is possible: Schopenhauer allegedly did it. Alternatively, it might just be said that it would be better to confess philosophical ignorance about how to articulate grounds for "moral" care than to impugn those grounds in such a way that the phenomenon of caring is itself imperiled or expelled.

So a nonreligious moralist might argue, but from a Christian, and not merely Christian, point of view, the problem lies in Nietzsche's preference for the *Übermenschen*-in-waiting over the suffering mass. In Woody Allen's film *Interiors*, Pearl is rather contemptible by Nietzschean standards, unable to follow a discussion about meaning and morality, palpably lost at the mention of Schopenhauer at a dinner party, absolutely herdlike in her ruminations on right and wrong. Her stepson-in-law is intellectually in a different league, with a literary and artistic bent that enables him to think for himself and live for himself. It is he, however, who shabbily tries to force himself sexually on his sister-in-law while herdlike Pearl spontaneously plays her part in the prevention of a suicide. On Nietzschean principles, the stepson-in-law cannot particularly be faulted; his attempted indulgence in a little harmless rape need not count against him significantly, if at all. Pearl, on the other hand, has nothing whatsoever going for her. Her prospects for Nietzschean commendation are not in the least enhanced by collusion in saving the life of an insignificant member of the herd. But the fact of it is that, amid the stark realities of human life and human suffering, those at the receiving end of things will rightly prefer the bovine plebeian to the sophisticated artist in this scenario. The humdrum morality of the pathetic herd will do a lot more for those who suffer than do Nietzsche's heroes. A less privileged Pearl might have said that she had her work cut out for her in helping the needy and thus she had little time (and even less ability) for the luxury of value creation. But the "knowledge that life requires hostility, torture,

54. Henry Staten, *Nietzsche's Voice* (Ithaca, NY: Cornell University Press, 1990), 104.

and death causes Zarathustra less nausea than the knowledge that life requires the rabble."[55]

"Irresponsibility," pronounced Gilles Deleuze: "Nietzsche's most noble and beautiful secret."[56] It is not irresponsible to be scientific about the physiology of pain or to weigh carefully the conclusion that it is "an *intellectual* occurrence in which a definite judgment is expressed—the judgment '*harmful*,' in which long experience is summarized" (*WP* 699).[57] Neither is it irresponsible for psychological analysis to be soberly applied: "Pity is a squandering of feeling, a parasite harmful to moral health; 'it cannot possibly be our duty to increase the evil in the world.' If one does good merely out of pity, it is oneself one really does good to, and not the other. . . . The suffering of others infects us, pity is an infection" (*WP* 368). Physiology can illuminate and does not necessarily reduce; psychology can humanize and does not necessarily "demoralize."

But Nietzsche's whole outlook is fatally myopic. He either just does not see or does not allow that pity can be something different from what he takes it to be.[58] He believes that pity shames, and deep at the heart of the unlikely teaching on eternal recurrence is the need to overcome the associated phenomena of guilt and shame. If we do not redeem the past, we are not freed to create and evaluate for the future, because we are shackled by the alien conviction that something unredeemed and irredeemable clings to and so governs our persons. It was the genius of Christianity to capitalize on this state of affairs, which it had itself introduced into the European soul. If the past is not redeemed, we are subject to guilt and shame, remorse and regret. Nietzsche's endorsement of cruelty is part and parcel of his determination to follow through a relentlessly anti-Christian agenda, although it is also predicated on an independent attempt to follow through a relentlessly naturalistic philosophy.

In theological perspective, there is more than one way to distinguish between guilt and shame. "Guilt" is best regarded first in terms of objective adjudication, not as a matter of feelings but as a description of the status that attaches to humanity before God. It is not primarily a psychological notion. We can certainly talk about feeling guilty, but that is theologically healthy only when it is an inward emotional con-

55. Irving M. Zeitlin, *Nietzsche: A Re-examination* (Cambridge, UK: Polity, 1994), 25.

56. Gilles Deleuze, *Nietzsche and Philosophy* (New York: Columbia University Press, 1983), 21.

57. Lange's way of approaching the physiology of sympathy surely influenced Nietzsche; Friedrich A. Lange, *The History of Materialism*, trans. Ernest Chester Thomas, 3rd ed., 3 vols. in 1 (London: Kegan Paul, 1925), 2.2.122.

58. See Martha C. Nussbaum, "Pity and Mercy: Nietzsche's Stoicism," in *Nietzsche, Genealogy, and History*, ed. Schacht.

formity to our status or conscientious acquiescence in objective reality and divine judgment about our status.[59] It is not for nothing that Barth and Bonhoeffer, a generation or two after Nietzsche, fought against the psychologizing of the concept of guilt or other concepts that arise in theological soteriology. What of shame in relation to guilt?[60] Like guilt, shame can be regarded nonpsychologically, as when we bring shame, in the sense of dishonor, on our nation or institution. But it is characteristically inward and broadly psychological. It makes sense to speak of being guilty toward another, ashamed toward oneself. In yoking together love of God and love of neighbor, Jesus indirectly indicates that guilt has to do with God and neighbor; "as yourself" is a reality rather than a prescription. On the other hand, shame reflexively directed toward oneself is, as Nietzsche said, self-division.[61]

Within a Christian perspective, our concern should not be to induce directly a psychological state (shame) but to bring home the objectivity of the human condition before God (guilt). Correlatively, the reason for establishing guilt is to produce not primarily remorse but repentance. Remorse is emotion directed toward the past; repentance is action directed toward the future. Like shame, remorse has its important place, but as guilt is the proper foundation of shame, so repentance is the proper goal of remorse. Just as belief in humanity as God's good creation is the presupposition of regarding humanity as sinful, so also the affirmative goal of restoring the creature in Christ is the ground of the divine summons to repentance. Divine pity does not detract from human dignity; on the contrary, it presupposes it. Along some such lines Christians ought to regard the way in which Christianity plots the relations of pity and shame, and Nietzsche ought thus to have regarded those relations.

59. For a brilliant account of what happens when subjective guilt remains but its objective basis is obscured, see Franz Kafka, *The Trial* (London: Penguin, 1994), memorably filmed by Orson Welles. To describe matters like this is not to deny that Kafka draws on empirical, historical experience, as well as introducing symbolism, in his narrative.

60. See, e.g., David Wells, *Losing Our Virtue: Why the Church Must Recover Its Moral Vision* (Grand Rapids: Eerdmans, 1998), chap. 4. John Hare thinks that guilt is appropriately conceived of as a response to the voluntary doing of wrong; we may regard shame as "a response to the inadequacy or blemish of what one *is*, and the consciousness of lack of proper resources"; see his "Naturalism and Morality," in *Naturalism: A Critical Analysis*, ed. William L. Craig and J. P. Moreland (London: Routledge, 2000), 189–211. On the verge of taking up his appointment in Basel, Nietzsche wrote: "One is honest about oneself either with a sense of shame or with vanity" (*SL* 46). William Blake is better: "Shame is Prides cloke," in "Proverbs of Hell," in *The Marriage of Heaven and Hell* (Oxford: Oxford University Press, 1975), 81.20. It must be strongly emphasized that we are touching here on only one or two aspects of shame.

61. John Owen remarked that shame is "nature's shrinking from itself and the posture it would appear in": "A Practical Exposition upon Psalm CXXX," in *Works*, ed. William H. Goold, vol. 6 (Edinburgh: Banner of Truth, 1967), 373.

Nietzsche, having concluded that there was nothing credible in what Christians trumpeted as objective reality, turned to psychological interpretation.[62] But what was the result? The Zarathustran production of a world without guilt or shame, remorse or repentance, a world existing only if we cut ourselves off from authentic interhuman relationships. In point of fact, it is Nietzsche who creates an ideal world projected as the background to his genealogical moral investigations and his moral philosophy. For the Christian, the self-relatedness of shame and remorse is supposed to be rooted in the other-relatedness of guilt and repentance, but Nietzsche's determination to own, without remorse, whatever is past, present, and future logically drives him into isolation, quite apart from other factors that do the same. He has cut himself off from the possibility of living by the grace of another, whether divine or human, in forgiveness for anything done amiss, since forgiveness is radical pity and breeds radical shame.[63] There certainly are pathological attitudes to forgiveness, and Nietzsche is not to be blamed if he recoiled from them. So should Christians. But the expulsion of pity from the social realm in order to secure the permanent banishment of shame becomes a disastrous legacy of Nietzsche's social thought, to which we now briefly turn.[64]

Wider Aspects

The nature and effects of Nietzsche's way of thinking are as starkly illuminated in relation to matters of medicine, life, and death as they are in any area where questions of morality, compassion, and shame are intertwined. The question of euthanasia probably best illustrates this, and Nietzsche's remarks on physician euthanasia warrant our interest in it; nevertheless, we need not incur the accusation of fastening on to a particularly emotive topic in order to make our point, so I shall not pursue it. It is sufficient to note that we can detect Nietzsche's way of thinking more generally in biomedical ethics. Edwin DuBose, for instance, is partly inspired by Nietzsche in describing patient resentment

62. See John Lippitt, "Nietzsche, Kierkegaard and the Narratives of Faith," in *Nietzsche and the Divine*, ed. John Lippitt and Jim Urpeth (Manchester, UK: Clinamen, 2000), 88.

63. In Borges, "A Prayer," see the sincere connection between forgiveness as "the act of another, and only I myself can save me" and wanting "to die completely" (not recur eternally): Jorge Luis Borges, *Collected Fictions* (New York: Penguin, 1998), 339.

64. Although we must distinguish forms of and causes for pity, see the connection between pity, human degradation, and implicit shame in Thomas Wolfe, *The Web and the Rock* (Baton Rouge: Louisiana State University, 1999), 57–62. Pathological attitudes toward forgiveness can be intertwined with complex attitudes toward sexuality, as in the case of Rousseau, whom Nietzsche came to detest: Ronald Grimsley, *Jean-Jacques Rousseau* (Totowa, NJ: Barnes & Noble; Brighton, UK: Harvester, 1983), 52.

toward the physician, largely constituted by "envy, the counterpart of shame."[65] What is under consideration here is the way in which the patient's emotions of envy and shame are partly grounded in envy of the physician's health and allied security. The relation between patient and physician is unequal, and, according to Nietzsche, physician compassion creates patient shame. Sensitive to this, DuBose calls for a culture of medical interdependency, so that the physician as much needs to receive purpose and meaning from the patient as the patient needs the obvious help of the physician. From the theological standpoint that DuBose advocates, only a view of God that dispenses with him as the traditional theistic "Other" and alternatively depicts him as a self-giving being will do the trick.

The discussion nicely illustrates both the pertinence and shortcomings of Nietzsche's perspectives on morality in general and on morality as compassion, in one of the culturally most significant areas. It is significant both by his own standards, as he observes physicians replacing priests, and by ours, as we are caught up in perplexing questions about the ethics of the medical profession. Much of what DuBose says about interdependency is right, though Nietzsche insists both that Christian morality is in some respects riveted to asymmetrical compassion rather than equal respect and that its egalitarian spin-off substitutes and epigones, such as socialism, are wrong on equality and mutuality.[66] But in a measure, DuBose is forced to gloss over the sheer facts of the situation and to insist that a situation of asymmetrical medical dependence be understood as symmetric interdependence, in order to avoid something like a Nietzschean critique.

This move is unnecessary and unconvincing. We need greater confidence in the traditional ontological underpinnings for a Christian theology of compassion than DuBose possesses.[67] If physician *service* to the patient is born of compassionate *respect*, grounded in a conviction about the love of God that takes that *compassionate form* as need arises but is rooted in the *ontological joy* of love, then we do not need to protect the dignity

65. Edwin R. DuBose, *The Illusion of Trust: Toward a Medical Theological Ethics in the Postmodern Age* (Dordrecht: Kluwer Academic Publishers, 1995), 93.

66. "Respect for man—and not merely virtuous men—is perhaps what divides us most sharply from a Christian evaluation" (*WP* 747).

67. For an important account and application of these underpinnings, and one that makes much of the distinction between "pity-love" and "respect-love," see John Wyatt, *Matters of Life and Death* (Leicester, UK: Inter-Varsity, 1998). The despised Augustine, commenting on the Johannine Epistles, observed how easy it was to feel superior when we do good and that we should want our fellow humans to be equals and not unfortunates: John Burnaby, *Amor Dei* (London: Hodder & Stoughton, 1938), 131. Cf. Augustine on the importance of the will in compassion: Carol Harrison, *Augustine: Christian Truth and Fractured Humanity* (Oxford: Oxford University Press, 2000), 93–94.

of humanity by strained attempts to block a Nietzschean foot coming in at the door. Better than theoretical description, practice will reveal how the dynamics of compassion operate in relation to human dignity. These are things better shown than said, to modify Wittgenstein's terms; this is one reason Bonhoeffer saw "prayer and righteous action" as more potent forms of Christian witness in a "world come of age" than communication in traditional words. The wider need for something like a Wittgensteinian philosophical inspiration is constantly impressed on anyone who reads Nietzsche against the background of early-third-millennial life. Not only is the distinction between "showing" and "saying" apt, but the very concept of Christian compassion also cannot be limned except by describing how it shapes a form of life, to use Wittgenstein's celebrated formulation. Medical practice is as public an area as we can think of to express the conceptual interconnections that theology aspires to describe in an effort to dignify human beings.

On the broader social front, Nietzsche's teaching on justice—or at least its effect—has probably attracted as much adverse attention as any other feature. Philippa Foot, for instance, considering Nietzsche's "inspiring call to a kind of joyous paganism that would leave us with all that is best in morals," rejects it principally because it appears to have "a fatal implication for the teaching of justice."[68] It is obvious why. Nietzsche will not allow us to impose on the natural order a principle to which it must morally conform. Justice is what we are finding all around us, in the existing order; it is the job of the higher people to accept it and live with it in Dionysiac style. If we try to understand justice morally, Nietzsche exposes our attempt as the "development of the drive to revenge."[69] Stanley Rosen wants to separate a legitimate quest for justice from an anthropology that Nietzsche rightly rejects: "The decisive problem for the next philosophical generation is to separate justice from pity and shame."[70]

A critique of Nietzsche's moral thinking in relation to justice is indubitably important, and we can take a theological track in such a critique.[71] But in rightly concerning ourselves with the question of justice, we must not miss a deeper, more radical, and fundamentally valid criticism of the

68. Philippa Foot, "Nietzsche's Immoralism," in *Nietzsche, Genealogy, Morality,* ed. Schacht, 6–7. However, see Maudemarie Clark's important criticisms of Philippa Foot in the essay that follows in the same volume: "Nietzsche's Immoralism and the Concept of Morality."

69. *WP* 225, an unpublished formulation that nevertheless is reflected in his published work.

70. Stanley Rosen, *The Mask of Enlightenment: Nietzsche's Zarathustra* (Cambridge: Cambridge University Press, 1995), 250.

71. Zeitlin, *Nietzsche: A Re-examination,* especially the "Epilogue."

way Nietzsche sets about things, to which succinct expression is given in Virginia Held's study *Feminist Morality*.[72] While occupied with the matter of justice, she wishes to concentrate on an ethic of care. Such an ethic is grounded in the experience of mothering and in the mother-child relationship. Held is aware of the danger of taking one relationship as paradigmatic for other social relationships. And "mothering" is not necessarily done by a gendered mother. But mothering is clearly something that we understand on the basis of female experience, and the ramifications of the idea are considerable. "Perhaps we should think of such felt relationships as those expressed between mothering person and child as the fundamental fabric of society. . . . And we might think that experience of and in such relationships should be central to our development of morality and culture."[73]

This seems to me indisputably important. At issue between Schopenhauer and Nietzsche is the question of whether compassion is a natural and instinctive spring of morality or an imposition on nature invented by Christianity. In considering Nietzsche's asseverations on the unnaturalness of compassion, we must insist on attending to the biological roots of maternal care and compassion.[74] Attending to the moral and social significance of the mother-child relationship brings to light the waywardness of Nietzsche's thinking on morality.[75] The moral role of the emotions of compassion and sympathy discussed in Held's context must be brought into play in an effective theological critique of Nietzsche.[76]

The stakes in this discussion are high. In a rather poignant phrase, Richard Rorty commented: "Christianity did not know that its purpose was the alleviation of cruelty."[77] The poignancy is twofold. First, the words express the longing (reaching far back in Rorty's life and childhood experiences) that we rid the world of cruelty. If Nietzsche felt anything like the same longing, it is sad and ultimately damaging that he first constructed

72. Virginia Held, *Feminist Morality: Transforming Culture, Society, and Politics* (Chicago: University of Chicago Press, 1993).

73. Ibid., 93. The context of this remark is the discussion "Expression." For the discussion "Moral Theory from a Feminist Perspective," see chap. 4.

74. However, Held does not want to emphasize biological motherhood and argues against a stock way of understanding childbirth as "natural."

75. Nietzsche's discussion "Woman and Child" in *HH* must be integrated into his wider comments on women. E.g.: "Look into it; women's love and sympathy—is there anything more egoistic?" (*WP* 777).

76. Held, *Feminist Morality*, e.g., 30, 66. On religion, Held is studiously silent (214).

77. Richard Rorty, *Contingency, Irony, and Solidarity* (Cambridge: Cambridge University Press, 1989), 55. For an example of a moving commentary on this, embedded in a wide-ranging account of one strand of intellectual history, see David Lyle Jeffrey, *People of the Book: Christian Identity and Literary Culture* (Grand Rapids: Eerdmans, 1996), chap. 4.

a philosophy and then slanted his construct in a way that makes favorable commentators sweat to explain the meaning and alleviate the effects of a philosophy that will not call cruelty immoral, a philosophy that finds compassion unbearable in comparison with natural, even violent, self-expression.[78] Second, Rorty himself is sufficiently Nietzschean to try to combine the project of creating personal value and denying objective morality with an ironic rescue of the ethic of compassion. If a heartfelt and nonposturing distaste for cruelty, such as Rorty has, can nevertheless not find any basis in normative morality, then we are roughly back with Nietzsche's critique of the legacy of Schopenhauer, and the question arises whether the sustained experience of compassionate emotion can survive the disappearance of its moral grounds.[79]

We must resist Rorty's separations. "The desire to be autonomous is not relevant to the liberal desire to avoid cruelty and pain."[80] That is questionable. Here Schopenhauer has something to teach us. He experienced compassion as a sentiment that enabled him to feel profoundly the sufferings of another and yet feel them deeply in oneself.[81] Schopenhauer concluded that such an intense quality of empathy requires an explanation of the individual and individuation in terms provided in different ways by Kant and by Indian religious philosophy. Kant's contribution is the thought that space and time are forms of perception but are not the metaphysical objectivities *an sich* that we naively take them to be. Eastern religious thought rids us of confusion over the individual and the many: we are not fundamentally discrete individuals; we are one. That explains the ability to empathize, which is deep in human nature.

From a Christian point of view, while the metaphysical reasoning and conclusion may be alien, the instinct driving Schopenhauer's reasoning is to be affirmed in two respects. First, with him, we want to affirm compassion. This is where Held helps us. Second, we want to recognize that there is a puzzle about the relation of the one to the many that is presented to our thought when we ponder the depth of true compassion. In contrast to Schopenhauer, it is the fundamentally relational nature of human beings, grounded in the internally relational nature

78. The preface to and essays in *OGM* particularly demonstrate these traits. With respect, Kaufmann sometimes goes to absurd lengths to exonerate Nietzsche via the device of blunting criticism of him by constantly turning some aspect of it against others. E.g.: "In his keen appreciation of suffering and self-sacrifice as indispensable conditions of self-perfection, Nietzsche seems more 'Christian' than most philosophers" (*Nietzsche*, 271).

79. See Stephen N. Williams, "Bioethics in the Shadow of Nietzsche," in *Bioethics and the Future of Medicine: A Christian Appraisal*, ed. John F. Kilner, Nigel M. de S. Cameron, and David L. Schiedermayer (Grand Rapids: Eerdmans, 1995), 112–23.

80. Rorty, *Contingency, Irony, and Solidarity*, 65. Cf. Nietzsche: "'Autonomous' and 'ethical' are mutually exclusive" (*OGM* 2.2).

81. This contention is central to Schopenhauer's argument *On the Basis of Morality*.

of God as Trinity, that accounts for the way compassion works when it works properly. Schopenhauer shows how a keen concentration on the emotional reaction to cruelty leads us to consider the fundamentally interrelational character of human existence. In so doing, we should challenge the "autonomy" premise. The liberal's desire to avoid cruelty and pain ought to put under pressure the positive significance accorded to autonomy, as autonomy is understood by Rorty.

Of course, what we mean by "autonomy" and variations of autonomy have to be analyzed, and I have picked on Rorty's use of the word here without giving an account of it. However, Christians will want to press the issue of cruelty to the point where the test of the strength of our feelings of sadness and abhorrence lies in our willingness to consider autonomy in the light of compassion and cruelty, not in relative independence of them. The defense of autonomy is unsafe unless the fundamentally relational character of human existence, as brought to light in the phenomenon of compassion, is firmly secured. If autonomy remains precious, one important form that it will take is the voluntary renunciation of self for the sake of others. What that might mean can be illustrated in myriad ways, and we await the illustrations before the proposition can be truly luminous. But in such a context, imbued with such an ethos, the struggle for justice has the possibility of flourishing without prejudice to all that is good, right, important, and true in the now-traditional liberal endeavor to protect human freedoms and independence. Here I affirm this as an article of faith; we are on to an issue that is far more significant than the space allocated to it in this volume indicates. It is time to rejoin Nietzsche before the curtain falls.

The End

OGM was printed in 1887. In the following year, the last full year in his active life, Nietzsche produced no fewer than six works, though they did not all immediately see the published light of day. These included the two short volumes on Wagner and a book of *Dithyrambs of Dionysus*. *DD* is all too easily skated over in accounts of Nietzsche's authorship, but reading his poetry is in fact quite a good way into important elements in Nietzsche's thought.[82] This contained material written over an approximately five-year period before its collection in that volume. In 1888 Nietzsche also wrote *Twilight of the Idols*, which succinctly sums up so much of Nietzsche's

82. In the course of a relatively brief account, it is instructive to find Hans Küng making use of this poetry: see *Does God Exist?* (London: Collins, 1980), "Nihilism—Consequence of Atheism."

thought; *The Anti-christ*, his final shrill denouement of Christianity; and *Ecce Homo*, his intellectual biography, which ended with the words "— Have I been understood?—*Dionysos against the Crucified.*"[83]

Nietzsche's personal story over these years is a sad one. He seems to have had a good spring in 1888 and, to all appearances, was in sound form when he turned up in Turin late in the summer. Things were starting to happen for him. Georg Brandes, a professor at Copenhagen, had taken his appreciation of Nietzsche to the point of giving a series of lectures on him. Nietzsche knew of it and was delighted. But his mind was caving in. The signs were clearly there earlier, but the first days of the New Year were rolling in when the decisive event happened. There, in the Piazza Carlo Alberto, on the morning of January 3, Nietzsche witnessed a cab horse being beaten by its driver. It was too much for him. He collapsed, sobbing, arms around the neck of the horse.

It was reminiscent of a scene out of Dostoyevsky's *Crime and Punishment*. Was Nietzsche conscious of it at the time? In Dostoyevsky's novel, there is a dream about childhood, about being seven years old, walking with your father; there is a thin horse unable to pull the load of wood or hay; men jump on the cart, laughing; the vicious thrashing of the mare begins. "Papa, Papa, . . . look what they are doing, Papa. They are beating the poor horse!" "Thrash her, thrash her!" bellows the crowd. First the whips, then the crowbar. On it goes. Finally, the end.

> The poor little boy was quite beside himself. He pushed his way, shrieking, through the crowd to the mare, put his arms round the dead muzzle dabbled with blood and kissed the poor eyes and mouth. . . . Then he sprang up and rushed furiously at Mikolka with his fists clenched. At that moment his father, who had been looking for him for a long time, caught him up and carried him out of the crowd.[84]

"'Papa, why did they . . . kill . . . the poor horse?' the boy sobbed, catching his breath. The words forced themselves out of his choking throat in a scream." A moment later, Raskolnikov, the dreamer in Dostoyevsky's story, woke up. He recovered waking consciousness. Nietzsche knew the story, but he apparently never recovered sanity.

83. Nietzsche described *TI* as "a very stringent and subtle expression of my whole *philosophical heterodoxy*"; after it, and after *CW*, "to be a Christian" would be "improper": *SL*, September 14, 1888. In his biography, Hollingdale describes it as "an aphoristic summary of his entire thought": Reginald J. Hollingdale, *Nietzsche: The Man and His Philosophy*, rev. ed. (Cambridge: Cambridge University Press, 1999), 170. Nietzsche had also concurred in the designation of himself as "antichrist," the authentic Christian label to stick on him, as he saw it: see *SL*, letter of March 1883, 211.

84. Fyodor Dostoyevsky, *Crime and Punishment* (Oxford: Oxford University Press, 1998), 56.

"These things we know, but not those that he felt as he descended into his last darkness."[85] In the first chapter, I observed that some who were close to Nietzsche were not convinced that this was a genuine mental collapse, but whatever was really going on at the time, it was certainly a clinical turning point. Nietzsche was under care for the remaining eleven years of his life, first at a clinic in Jena, then back with his mother in Naumburg, finally under his sister's responsibility at Weimar after his mother's death in 1897. As the invalid languished, his fame grew. Apparently, of all the places receptive to Nietzsche in that last decade, Russia, the land of Dostoyevsky, held pride of place. Fame and legend became intertwined, all manipulated, as far as possible, by sister Elisabeth, who had returned permanently from Paraguay in 1893, some time after the suicide of her anti-Semitic husband. While her brother was still alive, Elisabeth set about being Nietzsche's literary executor, and by the time he died, she had made significant headway in propagating the image of a Nietzsche who would be hailed as the philosopher of Hitler. Death summoned Nietzsche in August 1900. Fourteen years later, German soldiers went to war carrying copies of the Bible and of *Thus Spoke Zarathustra*.[86]

The story of Nietzsche's reception in the twentieth century could be told at length.[87] There are the Nazi connection, the Heidegger lectures, the subsequent interest in the Heidegger lectures, and the contributions of such as Walter Kaufmann and Gilles Deleuze, to take two prominent fairly recent examples of those who generated a considerable amount of discussion in the United States and France. The tide of written interpretation became a flood, and the flood something like a cataclysm. Nietzsche has for some time ridden the crest of the wave of researches in intellectual history. At the time of writing, the wave still rolls with no sign of abatement. He predicted something like this.

We have reported that in *EH* Nietzsche ran through his own publications. He did it all the way from *BT* to two of the 1888 volumes, *TI* and *CW*. Before proceeding to the description of his literary corpus, he said: "Seeing that I must shortly approach mankind with the heaviest demand that has ever been made on it, it seems to me indispensable to say *who I am*."[88] And who was he? "A disciple of the philosopher Dionysos" (*EH* 33). One who overthrows idols. The author of *Z*, the world's greatest literary creation. Philosopher, prophet, and teacher, we might tamely

85. Borges, "The Maker," in *Collected Fictions*, 293.

86. As far as I can judge, this is well documented. I understand that Goethe's *Faust* was sometimes pocketed too.

87. See Magnus and Higgins, *Cambridge Companion to Nietzsche*, part 4; and Gianni Vattimo, *Nietzsche: An Introduction* (London: Athlone, 2002), part 5.

88. Number references in the following text are to pages in *EH*, not sections.

say. Why is he himself so wise? Nietzsche asks. Answer: His life and education, family and health, freedom from *ressentiment* but warlike nature—all this explains it. Intellectual cleanliness and the antithesis of Christianity explain it too. Why is he so clever? Because he has thought the right way about the right issues and maintained the correct diet for his purposes. He knows where and under what climatical conditions to think. He deploys his time well, such as by discriminating reading and listening to good music. He has kept faith with his task and sublimely executed it.

> Anyone who saw me during the seventy days of this autumn when I was uninterruptedly creating nothing but things of the first rank which no man will be able to do again or has done before, bearing a responsibility for all the coming millennia, will have noticed no trace of tension in me, but rather an overflowing freshness and cheerfulness. . . . My formula for greatness in a human being is *amor fati*; that one wants nothing to be other than it is, not in the future, not in the past, not in all eternity. (67–68)

Finally, why does he write "such excellent books," the ones that he proceeds to describe? It is because he is a stylist and psychologist. It is because "I come from heights no bird has ever soared to, I know abysses into which no foot has ever yet strayed" (73). *Z* is definitely center stage, in the center of what Nietzsche wrote, for "I am one thing, my writings are another" (69). What does Nietzsche mean? That is a matter for psychological interpretation. As for his authorship in general, most of the points that Nietzsche wants to make are made before he gets down to commenting on particular books in *EH*. But he returns to the "why" questions in one more final section, after the literature has been surveyed and he is now in a position to conclude on the matter of why he is a destiny. And why is he a destiny?

> I know my fate. One day there will be associated with my name the recollection of something frightful—of a crisis like no other before on earth, of the profoundest collision of conscience, of a decision evoked *against* everything that until then had been believed in, demanded, sanctified. I am not a man[;] I am dynamite. (126)

The key is the revaluation of values. Nietzsche describes himself as an immoralist in two respects. "I deny first a type of man who has hitherto counted as the highest. . . . I deny secondly a kind of morality which has come to be accepted and to dominate as morality in itself" (128). Nietzsche defines himself contra Christianity, and Christian morality is the essence of the Christianity that he attacks. Let us listen to him again: "The *unmasking* of Christian morality is an event without equal, a real catastrophe. He who exposes it is a *force majeure*, a destiny—he breaks the history of mankind into two parts. One lives *before* him, one lives *after* him" (133). This is the scene of the engagement, collision, and eternal antagonism between Dionysus and the Crucified.

But is Nietzsche's authorship definable principally in terms of the collision with Christianity? Nietzsche wrote to Brandes that *EH* is "a ruthless attack on the crucified Christ, and it ends by hurling such thunders and lightnings at everything Christian or infected by Christianity that one swoons." But in the same letter, he adds that the Germans "come off worst" in it.[89] In our first chapter, I reported the judgment that Germans feed particularly on ideas, and I subsequently recorded Nietzsche's horror at his compatriots' herdlike docility. One of Thomas Mann's characters bursts out climactically: "Damn, damn these corruptors who taught their lessons in evil to an originally honest, law-abiding, but all too docile people, a people too happy to live by theory."[90] More prosaically, we might cite Habermas's criticism of Heidegger's theoretical approach as having some affinity with this viewpoint.[91] But can anyone say it more authentically and effectively than a significant precursor of Nietzsche, Max Stirner?

> The Germans are first and foremost exponents of the historical vocation of radicalism; they alone are radical. . . . There are no others so relentless and ruthless; not only do they bring about the collapse of the existing world so that they themselves stand fast, they also bring about the collapse of themselves. When Germans demolish, a god must fall, a world must pass away. To Germans, destruction is creation, the pulverization of the temporal is eternity.[92]

Nothing said in this volume is meant to suggest either an indictment or praise of Germany or the Germans. At this point we are recording Germans on Germans. Nietzsche had plenty to say about his fellow countrymen. Along with Hölderlin, Heine, Stirner, and others, he is a witness to and embodiment of the mighty, passionate, and dynamic vitality of a singular people or assembly of peoples. In the nineteenth century, in the land and language of Luther, the collision and collusion of pagan and Christian came to perfervidly heightened and supreme expression. Nietzsche is the epitome and perhaps the summit of the collision.

89. *SL*, November 20, 1888.

90. Thomas Mann, *Doktor Faustus* (New York: Viking, 1999), 506.

91. Jürgen Habermas, *The Philosophical Discourse of Modernity* (Cambridge, UK: Polity, 1987), 159.

92. Karl Lowith, *From Hegel to Nietzsche: The Revolution in Nineteenth Century Thought* (London: Constable, 1965), 355.

9

POSTSCRIPT: OF TRUTH

Philosophical Fragments

In *A*, Nietzsche asked:

> Do I still have to add that in the entire New Testament there is only *one* solitary figure one is obliged to respect? Pilate, the Roman governor. To take a Jewish affair *seriously*—he cannot persuade himself to do that. One Jew more or less—what does it matter? . . . The noble scorn of a Roman before whom an impudent misuse of the word "truth" was carried on has enriched the New Testament with the only expression *which possesses value*—which is its criticism, its *annihilation* even: "What is truth?" (46)

Presumably, impudence is ascribed to Jesus; certainly, nobility to Pilate.[1] At all events, Nietzsche puts a premium on this question. It is the alpha and omega of all the questions that he would have us ask. Rightly so. There is no doubt that, in Scott Fitzgerald's phrase, we are all too prone "to continue with the cracked echo of an old truth in the ears."[2] If Nietzsche exaggerated his own importance, reckoning that the better part of wisdom

---

1. Perhaps Nietzsche did not believe that the exchange had taken place as recorded but that the canonical writers pitted their own understanding about truth against the questioning Pilate. As far as Nietzsche is concerned, Pilate, unlike them, knew what he was talking about.

2. Scott Fitzgerald, *Tender Is the Night* (New York and London: Penguin, 2000), 276.

was to heed Zarathustra rather than Jesus, that fact should not distract us from adverting to the question of truth in the train of an encounter with Nietzsche. Early in the twentieth century, Figgis averred that "Nietzsche's call to reality is a lesson to all Christians."[3] There is much to be said for Jaspers's conclusion: "Taken as a whole, . . . his vast work has come to be a means of teaching veracity to ourselves."[4] Stern echoes Jaspers in his conviction that "Nietzsche is a Protestant philosopher. Beyond truth there is, for him, truthfulness."[5] Doubtless, along with an appropriate explanation of how they are using the words, Christians will be ready to agree with Nietzsche that a serious interest in truth and disposition to truthfulness are infrequent enough; Nietzsche, as we have seen, denies to Christianity such an interest or to Christians such a disposition, excepting the few like Pascal. I am not going to try to work out what Nietzsche said or thought on the question of truth. It is a rather forbiddingly complex task at the best of times and an absolutely impossible one here.[6] But I shall poke around one or two aspects briefly in this concluding chapter, without attending either to Nietzsche's corpus as a whole or to any germane distinctions between his earlier and later thought.

In *BGE*, Nietzsche wrote:

> It has gradually become clear to me what every great philosophy has hitherto been: a confession on the part of its author and a kind of involuntary and unconscious memoir . . . that the moral (or immoral) intentions in every philosophy have . . . constituted the real germ of life out of which the entire plant has grown. To explain how a philosopher's most remote metaphysical assertions have actually been arrived at, it is always well . . . to ask oneself first: what morality does this (does *he*—) aim at? I accordingly do not believe a "drive to knowledge" to be the father of philosophy, but that another drive has, here as elsewhere, only employed knowledge (and false knowledge!) as a tool. (6)

3. John Neville Figgis, *The Will to Freedom, or The Gospel of Nietzsche and the Gospel of Christ* (London: Longmans, Green, 1917), 306.

4. Karl Jaspers, *Nietzsche and Christianity* (Chicago: Gateway, 1961), ix. "Truth," he later says, "is only what Nietzsche brings out of ourselves" (107).

5. Joseph P. Stern, *Nietzsche* (London: Fontana, 1985), 70. In context, Stern is concerned with how Nietzsche establishes perspectivism. He also says that Nietzsche's is "essentially a modern kind of truthfulness. Experiencing the world as a fragmented thing . . ." (29).

6. An idea of the complexity can be gained from Maudemarie Clark's careful study, *Nietzsche on Truth and Philosophy* (Cambridge: Cambridge University Press, 1991). See too, e.g., Tim Murphy, who differs from Clark, in Murphy's *Nietzsche, Metaphor, Religion* (Albany: State University of New York Press, 2001); and Brian Leiter, "Perspectivism in Nietzsche's *Genealogy of Morals*," in *Nietzsche, Genealogy, Morality: Essays on Nietzsche's "Genealogy of Morals,"* ed. Richard Schacht (Berkeley: University of California Press, 1994), 334–57.

Here we are in the neighborhood, if not on the very territory, of knowledge as power and the hermeneutics of suspicion. The line Nietzsche takes here is paralleled in Christian thought.[7] In his lengthy study of Protestant theology in the eighteenth and nineteenth centuries, Barth wrote:

> The new picture of the world, mathematically scientific thought, anthropocentric, autonomous philosophy, the virtue of "historical truthfulness," and with this the distaste for miracle . . . —all this is not a foundation and a cause, but an instrument, indeed one might go so far as to say a garb, for the criticism. . . . Man makes the opposition to older Christianity which had come about through his new moralism into a contrast between the modern and the obsolete presuppositions for cosmology and epistemology—in order to justify himself.[8]

We give no hostages to Barthian theology if we take these words as indicative of an affinity not just between the substance of Nietzschean and Christian thought on this point, but also between a Nietzschean and a (defensibly) Christian way of reading intellectual history, even though the differences are also undeniable. One way or another, it is theologically plausible to propose that moral or immoral intention undergirds thought. If it is possible to formalize the elements in the biblical account of the original human transgression, action is rooted in desire that sways and clouds the intellect; if the intellect proceeds to direct the will to action, it is itself driven by some form of volition.[9] I am less concerned with the precision of this formulation, and less still with its adequacy, than with the point of contact between a Nietzschean and a Christian view of intellectual machinations, which is roughly the view that some "spirituality" informs and drives them.

The desire to pronounce something good or evil is, in Nietzschean terms, the intellectual product of a "moral" impulse; whether or not Christianity wants to use exactly those categories in relation to its own story (and whether or not Nietzsche would refine my rather crude conceptualization of his position), his account is commensurable with the idea that transgression in Eden was the product of desire rather than being simple intellectual failure. Christianity may or may not encourage our deducing from this some universal and unexceptionable judgments about human motivation and action. But there is a marked compatibility between Nietzsche's claim that moral or immoral intentions underlie

7. See Merold Westphal, "Nietzsche as a Theological Resource," in *Nietzsche and the Divine*, ed. John Lippitt and Jim Urpeth (Manchester, UK: Clinamen, 2000), chap. 2.
8. Karl Barth, *Protestant Theology in the Nineteenth Century* (London: SCM, 1972), 108.
9. Cf. James 1:14.

the drive to knowledge and a theological claim that intellect does not function in a moral vacuum.[10]

This consideration challenges the bona fides of many discussions that go on about truth, whether in life or in literature, if discussion pretends to be dispassionate, an ambition rather less common since the advent of postmodernity. It also diverts discussion into an investigation of life, body, morality, and desire. But what are we to make of the widespread view emerging from a morass of considerations, that the drive to knowledge and, putatively, to truth is in fact a drive to power? Is Nietzsche's identification of a "moral" basis for thought rightly developed and refined in terms of intentions rooted in concealed will-to-power? Can Christianity be hospitable to this claim about the association of truth and power, even if Nietzsche lauds, while others lament, the fundamental "power" drive behind thought? The kind of claim that we encounter here comes in more versions than one, and Nehamas points out that Nietzsche "does not ever analyze truth as . . . power."[11] The proposition that has been going the familiar rounds for some time now, whether or not it is extracted from Nietzsche, is to the effect that humans and societies can be regarded as power systems whose essential form is frequently masked by apparently direct interest in knowledge and truth. From Nietzsche's point of view, maximization of power might be unobjectionable, but the uses of power may be objectionable, especially as long as they lay specious claim to a primary interest in truth. The figure who looms large in modern, post-Nietzschean discussion is Michel Foucault.[12]

I shall not rehearse the main lines of a theological response to Foucault.[13] Foucault asks, Where is power best studied? and answers, Where it is most naked, least legal, at extremities. Christians must also ask where and reciprocally trade in the same semantic coin, answering with reference to nakedness, legality, and extremity.[14] That reference is certainly not to

10. See Charles Taylor, *Sources of the Self: The Making of Modern Identity* (Cambridge: Cambridge University Press, 1989), part 1, though his discussion is general and not specifically about Nietzsche.

11. Alexander Nehamas, *Nietzsche: Life as Literature* (Cambridge: Harvard University Press, 1985), 54. This is not to say that he never makes connections. "Knowledge works as a tool of power. Hence it is plain that it increases with every increase of power" (*WP* 480).

12. For a helpful essay on Foucault's interaction with Nietzsche on power, see Keith Ansell-Pearson, "The Significance of Michel Foucault's Reading of Nietzsche: Power, the Subject, and Political Theory," in *Nietzsche: A Critical Reader*, ed. Peter R. Sedgwick (Oxford: Blackwell, 1995).

13. For a start, see Miroslav Volf, *Exclusion and Embrace: A Theological Exploration of Identity, Otherness, and Reconciliation* (Nashville: Abingdon, 1996). Chapter 6, in particular, contains a discussion of Foucault, but the whole work should be consulted.

14. Michel Foucault, "Two Lectures," in *Power/Knowledge: Selected Interviews and Other Writings, 1972–1977*, ed. Colin Gordon (New York and London: Pantheon, 1980), 81.

an ecclesiastical institution but to Jesus and the cross. Foucault analyzed the question of power in relation to *discourse* about truth: Who is served by it? His intellectual oeuvre was deeply occupied with the question of language and with the significance of Nietzsche's reflections on language.[15] Quarrying Nietzsche's literature in relation to the question of language is a demanding undertaking, and it is often not what he said about language but what he did with it, with play and aphorism and other things besides, that caught the attention of thinkers such as Derrida and those who delved into Nietzsche from the 1960s onward. Nietzsche's most frequently quoted words about language come from a sustained piece that he wrote on the nature of language, his early and unpublished essay "On the Truth and Lies in a Non-moral Sense."[16] The oft-quoted paragraph reads:

> What then is truth? A movable host of metaphors, metonymies, and anthropomorphisms: in short, a sum of human relations which have been poetically and rhetorically intensified, transferred, and embellished, and which, after long usage, seem to a people to be fixed, canonical, and binding. Truths are illusions which we have forgotten are illusions; they are metaphors that have become worn out and have been drained of sensuous force, coins which have lost their embossing and are now considered as metal and no longer as coins.[17]

These words of Nietzsche conjure up at least two worlds. One world beckons us to revelry, to pulsating exploration of the nooks and crannies of language, entered—though perhaps not exited—in a spirit of good cheer. The other world is the sober site of a philosophical labyrinth that, once you enter, you may indeed exit, but only after laboring over the hardest of problems in the lengthiest of volumes and promising to revisit the maze.[18] Does not the very word "language," for a good many pundits, connote both the end of a world where truth was objective and the proximity of a task—relating language to truth—that is demanding, daunting, or playful fun?

15. See, e.g., Michel Foucault, *The Order of Things: An Archaeology of the Human Sciences* (London: Tavistock, 1970). Nietzsche is the "first to connect the philosophical task with a radical reflection upon language" (305). Nietzsche makes a dramatic and crashing entry into this work (263). There is much in it that is rewarding for a study of Nietzsche, especially in connection with the "death of man" (e.g., 342).

16. Friedrich W. Nietzsche, *Philosophy and Truth: Selections from Nietzsche's Notebooks of the Early 1870's*, ed. Daniel Breazeale (Atlantic Highlands, NJ: Humanities, 1990). I am citing page references for this essay.

17. Ibid., 84.

18. "Language is a labyrinth of paths. You approach from *one* side and know your way about; you approach the same place from another side and no longer know your way about," writes Ludwig Wittgenstein, *Philosophical Investigations* (London: Blackwell, 1958), 203.

I draw attention to Nietzsche's essay in order to pick out its underlying concern with truth. I shall neither plot it in relation to Nietzsche's overall or final outlook nor proffer interpretation of its detail. But it is useful to obtain a rudimentary grasp of how the question of language appeared to him in that essay. Nietzsche's initial move is to put humans in their place by exposing their vaunted drive to knowledge for what it is. Humans have a propensity to confuse their perspectival self-centeredness with the essence of things. Pride and self-deception so dominate that one wonders how the drive for truth could have arisen in the human race. In fact, it comes from the need for social coexistence. In a social framework, conventions are established about what counts as truth. These are linguistic conventions, denominative designations for things. To lie is to misplace the designation. Socially, what is wrong with the lie is its consequences, and the drive for truth is actually the drive for pleasant consequences. Language does not originate in a truth about the world that is first derived from the world and then given linguistic expression. Language primally designates the relation in which things stand to us, not things in themselves. At the heart of its creative process is the deployment of metaphor.

Concept formation is equally a matter of construction. Discrete things that we encounter are not absolutely identical, so we unite them under a common conceptual framework. There is no such thing as a leaf and no such thing as honesty, just their constructed concepts. "Nature is acquainted with no forms and no concepts, and likewise with no species, but only with an *X* which remains inaccessible and undefinable for us."[19] Nor is there a transcendent realm ensuring that the formation of moral ideas are not subject to the same rules. What then is truth? The passage about the mobile army of metaphors is Nietzsche's answer. Proceeding from that point, he alleges that truthfulness consists in the apt employment of metaphor. A world now becomes built up, a world of lies in the nonmoral sense, a construct that nevertheless includes a notion of truthfulness. With that notion, a moral impulse is born. Throughout the essay, Nietzsche doggedly persists in the conviction that we construct rational schemata replacing the real world, which means that the ideal world and the moral drive are both constructs, however necessary they may be. Concepts are seductive: the concept is "merely the *residue of a metaphor*. . . . The artistic transference of a nerve stimulus into images is, if not the mother, then the grandmother of every single concept."[20] The enterprise of concept formation and worldview construction is great and admirable, but it certainly does not originate in or represent

19. Nietzsche, *Philosophy and Truth*, 83.
20. Ibid., 85.

a knowledge of—or even a drive for—truth. "Man" is his own measure and has forgotten that what he takes to be things in themselves are, in fact, metaphors. This brings us back, more or less, to what Nietzsche said at the beginning of the essay. There is the human eye's view of the world, but it is not *the* way of viewing the world; it is a perspective, and it is meaningless to ask which of different perspectives, human or insect, for example, is correct.

The conclusion of Nietzsche's essay discloses the interest in culture that underlies and animates this set of ruminations. "We have seen how it is originally *language* which works on the construction of concepts, a labor taken over in later ages by *science*," but the "drive toward the formation of metaphors is the fundamental human drive."[21] Nietzsche then proceeds to remark on the impetus underlying the production of art and myth, which is rooted in the love of illusion and in self-deception—which, on Nietzsche's reckoning, are not the moral categories we usually take them to be. Thus arises the question of contrasting human and cultural types, the intuitive thinker in contrast to the abstractive one. Underlying the question: "What is truth?" is the question: "What is 'man'?" These questions are inseparable for Nietzsche. Consequently, the linguistic question is always tied to the anthropological one, as far as I can see, even in the marrow of its principle.

Brief reference was made to Derrida earlier: does he not exemplify the same anthropological concern? The case for answering in the affirmative is elaborated in John Caputo's volume on Derrida, whose very title is eloquent.[22] Caputo will be the first to admit that, if Nietzsche's essay on language might drive a hard-nosed analytic philosopher a little way up the wall, his own exposition of Derrida will lead one to scale undreamed-of heights in the same upward trajectory. It is not my business to comment here on whether philosophers are better off with wax noses or whether such frustration is warranted.[23] But, one way or another, the volume is instructive. Its study of Derrida's later writing succeeds in showing tolerably clearly how questions of the philosophy of language that have

21. Ibid., 88.

22. John D. Caputo, *The Prayers and Tears of Jacques Derrida: Religion without Religion* (Bloomington: Indiana University Press, 1997).

23. "Frustration" only mildly describes the reaction of many of those who would dismiss Derrida's work. In relation to Nietzsche, try Jacques Derrida's *Spurs: Nietzsche's Styles* (Chicago: University of Chicago Press, 1979). But one might be reconciled to Derrida via Christopher Norris's exposition and partial advocacy in *Derrida* (London: Fontana, 1987); and via Derrida's own response to J. L. Austin, a discussion Norris treats in chap. 7. Kevin J. Vanhoozer, *Is There a Meaning in This Text? The Bible, the Reader, and the Morality of Literary Knowledge* (Grand Rapids: Zondervan; Leicester, UK: Apollos, 1998), takes Derrida quite seriously and massively supports the contention that the question about humanity underlies the question about language.

occupied Derrida are rooted in fundamental religious and anthropological questions of existence. Here, Nietzsche and Derrida join hands.[24]

The notion of truth as action, truth as something humanly embodied, brings Derrida into positive connection not only with Nietzsche but also with biblical theology (if that expression be permitted to stand undefended for a moment). In his account "Of Truth and Lies," Nietzsche refers to Plato. In *TI*, he glosses Plato's position by declaring: "I *am* the Truth."[25] From a Christian viewpoint, thinking about language, text, and truth in relation to Scripture spirals away into relative abstraction when it is cut off from the root of the theological notion of truth uncovered in the self-designation of Jesus.[26] Borges has declared that the "concept of a 'definitive text' is appealed to only by religion or by weariness."[27] But what of a definitive person? "Nothing can serve as a criticism of a person save another person, or of a culture save an alternative culture—for persons and cultures are, for us, incarnated vocabularies," as Rorty puts it somewhere.

Years on, Emil Brunner's contribution to this question still helps us find our theological orientation to the question of truth in the form that we are encountering it.[28] He argued that access to the biblical notion of truth is gained by attending to the ideas of lordship and fellowship that course through Scripture. Applied as they are to God and humanity, they disable the notion that truth can be possessed by cognition. The truth is personal reality and correspondingly known by personal contact. It is known in encounter—the "Bible conception of truth is: truth as encounter"—and so known in an existential relation, not in noetic objectivity. So we need to speak of the "fundamental Biblical category of personal correspondence, which lies at the heart of the Biblical concept of truth" (56). The sole analogy to this is the "encounter between human beings, the meeting of person with person" ("The Word unlocks person to person," 47). Brunner insists that its paradigm is drawn from the

24. Theologically, one line that can be taken in relation to Derrida is to think with Harold Coward and Toby Foshay, eds., about *Derrida and Negative Theology* (Albany: State University of New York, 1992). Taken in conjunction with Caputo's work (*Prayers and Tears*), it looks as though we are exploring a kind of messianic Zen here (e.g., 195).

25. *TI* 4. The "virtuous man" seems to think himself to be "the truth." "Nietzsche wants not only to stress the personal nature of truth, but also to portray (as Hölderlin had done) an age whose religious 'ideals' are not remote and 'transcendent,' but inherent in men's world" (Stern, *Nietzsche*, 53).

26. Those who, on critical grounds, maintain that Jesus did not designate himself as Truth can still read John 14:6 in the way that I take it here, as an important indication of the necessity of a personalist theology.

27. Jorge Luis Borges, *Collected Fictions* (New York: Penguin, 1998), 519.

28. Emil Brunner, *The Divine-Human Encounter* (London: SCM, 1944). Page references are generally given in the text.

realm of love. We have failed to achieve the right perspective on truth in the past; historical fatalities crowd the scene. "This confusion, this replacing of personal understanding of faith by the intellect, is probably the most fatal occurrence within the entire history of the Church. It has been the cause of the too rapid expansion of Christianity and Ecclesiasticism" (112). Brunner's claim is that "the truth acting . . . is the characteristic unphilosophical, non-Greek way in which the Bible speaks of truth" (147).

On Brunner's summary account of the history of Western thought, the perishing of Christianity presumably has more to do with its own misunderstanding of truth than its own will-to-truth, as Nietzsche proposes in a thesis that we shall take up shortly. Be that as it may, Brunner is theologically convincing up to an important point. The Word mediates between person and person because the Word is Person at heart, and human persons were created through that Word. What constitutes truth in relationship therefore guides us toward the biblical understanding of truth, interpersonal relationships providing at least a partial analogy for our understanding. Yet Brunner's argument has two limits. One, important enough in its place, will not detain us here, but the fact is that the word "truth" in Scripture can also be used in a way approximate to what is commonly called the "correspondence" sense, and this happens not just in ordinary-language, nontheological cases.[29] The other limitation needs more attention in the present context, and it comes to our attention when we return to the scene before Pilate, of which Nietzsche reminds us. This is a scene of encounter, and the "truth" is certainly about a profoundly existential relationship. But these are not the first words to be said on the matter of truth. Jesus is portrayed as peculiarly isolated, a portrayal captured in this climactic account but obviously not confined to it. His isolation indicates the direction in which we are to look to uncover the heart of discourse about truth. The most dramatic Old Testament incidents where individuals somehow encounter God himself are awesome affairs, leaving those who experience them in trembling gratitude that they were not annihilated. There was certainly encounter. However, imagine that those who experienced such encounters, which doubtless marked them for life, had lapsed into a Western philosophical moment and had occasion to ponder philosophical accounts of truth. We may venture to think that it is what or who they encountered, not the encounter itself, that engaged their attention. So it is in the case of Jesus. There is a quality to what is encountered in him that leaves us considering the putative truth encountered more than the truth as encounter.

29. An exegetical trawl through the Johannine usage reveals this.

While John's narrative highlights Jesus's impact on Pilate, it forces the eyes of the imagination to rest less on the relational impact than on the solitary figure hauled up before the governor, or more cautiously, it impresses on us that talk of truth proceeds from the heart of Christ rather than the heart of this relationship (John 18–19). In the account of Pilate, Nietzsche recognizes an issue deeper than the issue of language clamoring for our attention, an issue that lies behind it. What is "man"? Where is "man"? *Ecce homo*? (John 19:5 Latin Vulgate). Nietzsche warns us about traps in the domain of language. We are prone to jump into error over the "I," and in his eyes the general observation that I have mentioned previously would be applicable to the sentence "I am the Truth": "I am afraid we are not getting rid of God because we still believe in grammar" (*TI* 3.5). We cannot overlook his charge that we confuse grammatical subjects with unitary metaphysical subjects such as we think ourselves to be, and falsely ascribe personhood to God on the basis of that mistake. But whatever merit Nietzsche's point has, it is not christological merit. When the "I" that is the phenomenon of Jesus confronts us in the claim "I am the Truth," the grammatical nominative of linguistic syntax directs us to ponder something other than language, even if we do our pondering in language and in innocence of theories about language. "Truth" is the state of affairs that is embodied and expressed in Jesus Christ. Any metaphorical use of language, anything constructive and perspectival in our intellectual motions—all these are religiously embedded in the claim that there is a Creator.[30] Hence, there is a possibility of communication from the ultimate Creator of language that grounds our notions of truth and truthfulness. We might debate how tightly a theistic framework constrains a philosophy of language and what is entailed by theological notions of creation and revelation. But no amount of sophistication in discussions about language frees us from presuppositional questions about the world as created. Nor do they obviate the need for reckoning personally with Jesus. Nietzsche himself would not have thought otherwise.[31]

30. This is a thesis argued diligently in Vanhoozer, *Is There a Meaning in This Text?*

31. I do not doubt the significance of the questions that surround perspective and perspectivism either in their own right or in Nietzsche's work (e.g., *WP* 616). In relation to Nietzsche, we would need to pursue the question of Heraclitus. Is authentic Christianity bound to "Heraclitophobia," as Merold Westphal puts it? See his "Deconstruction and Christian Cultural Theory," in *Pledges of Jubilee: Essays on the Arts and Culture in Honor of Calvin G. Seerveld*, ed. Lambert Zuidervaart and Henry Luttikhuizen (Grand Rapids: Eerdmans, 1995), 119. This is a historically deep question. Petrarch, one of the three figures under whose banner Nietzsche launched his crusade in *HH*, was called a disciple of Heraclitus and experienced an all-too-typical "morass of psychological torment," whose connection with competing Heraclitean and Christian viewpoints rewards exploration. See Charles Trinkhaus, *In Our Image and Likeness*:

Will-to-Truth

In the whole of Nietzsche's corpus, one of the most interesting theses about Christianity and truth is that the advent of a religiously subversive will-to-truth in Europe is positively connected with the ethic of truthfulness that Christianity publicly promoted. This is stated at the end of *OGM*, but its discussion goes back particularly to book 5 of *GS*. Throughout the present volume, I have portrayed Nietzsche as being more or less uniformly negative about Christianity, but this does not give us the whole picture. Indeed, some readers familiar with Nietzsche may protest that I have been guilty of a serious distortion of his thought in this respect, thus making mockery of my pious interest in truth.

But just what Nietzsche's more positive comments on Christianity add up to is a moot question. "One must have loved religion and art like mother and nurse—otherwise one cannot grow wise"; religious, including Christian, formation is something for which to be grateful (*HH* 292). We need to outgrow religion, he claims.[32] Religion and religious feelings produced specific conditions for the emergence of admirable types (*HH* 234). "Every season has its own particular charm and excellencies and excludes those of other seasons. That which grew up out of religion and in proximity to it cannot grow again if this is destroyed" (*HH* 239). Additionally, there is the matter of music. Nietzsche puts Bach in context to show "how profoundly indebted we are to the religious life" (*HH* 219).[33] We can go beyond this: Christianity "has *chiselled out* perhaps the most refined figures in human society that have ever yet existed," and the French nation in particular came up with some really worthwhile Christian products in the shape of Pascal, for example (*D* 60, 192). If we reckon soberly with Jesus, at least elements of a Christian lifestyle apparently remain tolerable as long as the dogmas are gone (*WP* 239).[34]

Humanity and Divinity in Italian Humanist Thought, vol. 1 (London: Constable, 1970), esp. 40ff. From early on, Heraclitus could be regarded as a Christian before Christ; see Charles N. Cochrane, *Christianity and Classical Culture: A Study in Thought and Action from Augustus to Augustine* (New York: Oxford University Press, 1957), 230. The "superman" motif runs through this important study: see 113n1 and 30, 77, 372, 512; cf. 490 on the "oversoul."

32. It is obviously outside my remit to trace the implications of Nietzsche's reference to "art."

33. On Handel and Luther, see *AOM* 171. Bach and Handel are briefly linked in *AOM* 298, but Nietzsche also has reservations about Bach (*WS* 149).

34. Because of his clearly expressed revulsion toward Christian dogmas and his reference to Buddhism, I take Nietzsche to be doing more here than merely affirming the factual possibility of a Christian lifestyle, although he does not go so far as to commend it. A self-controlled ethic of nonresistance seems to be the most significant possibility.

According to an unpublished observation, we might even make room for the concept of "God," but only "as a maximal state, as an epoch—a point in the evolution of the will to power" (*WP* 639). Quite generally, Nietzsche's positive indebtedness to Christianity, to the extent it is there, is perhaps discerned less by reading his comments on Christianity than by considering his spiritual and intellectual formation. Nietzsche "knew and admitted the Christian basis of his real motivating force: his seriousness, truthfulness, and his radically uncompromising approach."[35]

I have no wish to conceal any of this, but I do not think that it adds up to anything that modifies the account thus far. However, I deliberately introduce these considerations here because I want to take the account further. That is why we must attend to Nietzsche's proposal about the development of the will-to-truth. In *GS* 5, just as at the beginning of book 4, Nietzsche is in the mood for rejoicing—or at least he is cheerful. God is dead, and the sea of knowledge lies open before us. What winds propel us on our voyage? "Science" and "truth" have played their crucial role in undermining the old religious worldview. How did that happen? "Where might science get the unconditional belief or conviction on which it rests, that truth is more important than anything else, than every other conviction?" (344). It cannot be from the idea that truth is useful, for untruth might be equally useful. A sheer will-to-truth has come from somewhere. That sort of will looks like a moral will. So where did the moral impulse come from, "if life, nature and history are 'immoral'" (344)? Nietzsche's reply is from Plato and from Christianity. Ultimately, they have generated the will-to-truth.

Nietzsche proceeds along a track now familiar to us by stating how morality is a problem and how faith is a psychological necessity. Weakness of will is the root of all kinds of evil. After probing the origins of religion and knowledge, Nietzsche arrives in Germany. He praises Leibniz, Kant, and Hegel for specific philosophical advances, but "the decline of the faith in the Christian god, the triumph of scientific atheism" was delayed by Hegel in particular (357). Schopenhauer took the atheistic plunge.

> This is the locus of his whole integrity; unconditional and honest atheism is simply the *presupposition* of his way of putting the problem, as a victory of the European conscience won finally and with great difficulty; as the most fateful act of two thousand years of discipline for truth that in the end forbids itself the *lie* of faith in God. . . . One can see *what* it was that actually triumphed over the Christian god: Christian morality itself, the concept of truthfulness that was taken ever more rigorously; the father confessor's refinement of the Christian conscience, sublimated into a scientific conscience, into intellectual cleanliness at any price. (357)

35. Jaspers, *Nietzsche and Christianity*, vii–viii.

Nietzsche proceeds to instantiate the things that are no longer credible: a benevolent providence, purpose in history, a moral world order, the veridical nature of religious experience. At the end of the last essay in *OGM*, Nietzsche interestingly picks up a point from the section just quoted: the attribution to Christianity of the will-to-truth that finally overcame it. "In this way, Christianity *as a dogma* was destroyed by its own morality," says Nietzsche in *OGM*, and "in the same way, Christianity *as a morality* must also be destroyed,—we stand on the threshold of this occurrence" (3.27). "Morality itself, in the form of honesty, compels us to deny it to be morality" (*WP* 404). "Among the forces cultivated by morality was *truthfulness*: this eventually turned against morality" (*WP* 5).

Bracketing the historical thesis, we can yet again keep theological company with Nietzsche to some extent. Of course, Christians will not concede the philosophical claim that faith and truth are incompatible bedfellows or the historical claim that the will-to-truth, fostered by faith, self-consistently expelled its own ancestor. Dostoyevsky said: "If anyone should prove to me that Christ was outside the Truth, and if it *really* was the case that the Truth was outside Christ, then I'd rather remain with Christ than with the Truth."[36] Presumably, the point is that if atheism turns out to be correct, we still ought to live (or Dostoyevsky himself will still live) as if it were not, as if Christ were the truth. We cannot explain this in terms of an attempt by Dostoyevsky to protect a notion of "truth" governed by its internal religious grammar from confused identification with, for example, a scientific notion of truth. He prefers faith, or Christ, to truth where or if they actually do collide. Dostoyevsky is choosing for and against.

But he must be resisted. The lines of a defense of Dostoyevsky's kind of approach (as I grasp it—I cannot be sure that I understand him right) are not difficult to sketch. We might adopt a philosophy of "as-if," deeming it right to live by a kind of illusion. We might argue that atheism does not prescribe a particular way of life and consistently permits a practical Christian "as-if," even while it denies the strict truth of Christianity. However, the Gospel narratives that attracted Dostoyevsky to Christ direct us away from those routes. Coleridge was right: "He who begins by loving Christianity better than Truth, will proceed by loving his own Sect or Church better than Christianity and end in loving himself better than all."[37] The battle in which Jesus is engaged is a battle over truth understood in a way that resists Dostoyevsky's dichotomy and is sympathetic

36. Quoted in Ronald Hingley, *Dostoyevsky: His Life and Work* (London: Paul Elek, 1978), 88. See Fyodor Dostoyevsky, *Devils* (Oxford: Oxford University Press, 1992), 263.

37. Samuel T. Coleridge, *Aids to Reflection* (London: Pickering, 1836), Aphorism 25.

toward Nietzsche's opposition to it.[38] The question facing Israel in the first century of the common era was whether Jesus was the executive of God's purposes for that nation and so for the cosmos. The terms on which the dispute over Christ is conducted in the New Testament give us a clear enough idea of what it is like for his claims to be true or to be false. Christ does not will that he be preferred over truth. The language of "truth" in the New Testament furnishes us with plenty of examples of how he might not be truthful, and therefore not the truth, and therefore not to be followed, as a false prophet is not to be followed. Logically, it might be urged, it does not follow from this that the disciple should follow Christ's preference and privilege truth over Christ. But it follows theologically. Christ is presented as a witness to the truth, a witness to God, summoning us to discipleship on the strength of the witness.

When all is said and done, it appears to me that one of the greatest religious thinkers of all time, author of the most interesting of all Christian counterpositions to Nietzsche, is vulnerable to Nietzsche's critical thesis about faith and truth. I have in mind Kierkegaard. Nietzsche and Kierkegaard speak the same language, as when Nietzsche says, in *GS* 5:

> It makes the most telling difference whether a thinker has a personal relationship to his problems and finds in them his destiny, his distress, and his greatest happiness, or an "impersonal" one, meaning he is only able to touch and grasp them with the antennae of cold, curious thought. (345)

The point is stated more powerfully by Kierkegaard himself, but he identifies faith as the passion in question, whereas Nietzsche goes on to speak of faith as, inter alia, "always most desired and most urgently needed where will is lacking; for will, as the affect of command, is the decisive mark of sovereignty and strength" (347). If one replies that Kierkegaard also makes faith a matter of the will, Nietzsche's rejoinder is that it is a weak and not a strong will; if one further replies that Kierkegaardian will is certainly not lacking in strength, Nietzsche will stipulate that the real test of that is its relation to truth. Kierkegaard's *Concluding Unscientific Postscript* particularly illuminates the issue at stake.[39] To serious faith and suffering, Kierkegaard attaches broadly, if

38. See Andrew T. Lincoln's thorough study *Truth on Trial: The Lawsuit Motif in the Fourth Gospel* (Peabody, MA: Hendrickson, 2000).

39. Søren Kierkegaard, *Concluding Unscientific Postscript* (Princeton, NJ: Princeton University Press, 1968). Page references are usually in the text. I refer to "Kierkegaard" as author, despite the pseudonymity under which he penned it. Despite all the similarities between Kierkegaard and Nietzsche, Kaufmann plausibly suggests how Nietzsche would have reacted to Kierkegaard, had he read him, by quoting *Z* 1.3, "Of the Afterworldsmen": "Weariness, which wills to reach the ultimate with a single leap, . . . created all gods and afterworlds."

not exactly, the qualities that Nietzsche ascribes to philosophical rigor and suffering. "The Socratic existential inwardness is as Greek light-heartedness in comparison with the grave strenuosity of faith" (188). After talking of faith as hovering over depths, Kierkegaard avers that "the suffering is . . . the seventy thousand fathom deeps on which the religious man constantly lies" (256). Where Nietzsche discerned three types of human being in his day—the man of action (Rousseau), contemplation (Goethe), and suffering (Schopenhauer), Kierkegaard describes the aesthetic, ethical, and religious stages of existence in terms of the existential determinations: "enjoyment-perdition; action-victory; suffering."[40] Nietzsche and Kierkegaard are united in the passionate conviction that individual suffering and existential depth are the requirements of the day.[41] Kierkegaard expresses the sentiments to which I have referred in his analysis of inwardness and passion, subjectivity and truth. Nietzsche is no stranger to that neighborhood. But how can Kierkegaard make faith simultaneously the pivot of religious subjectivity, solid, integrated, and fused with truth, where Nietzsche holds that never the twain (faith and truth) shall meet?

"I scarcely suppose that anyone will deny that it is the Christian teaching in the New Testament that the eternal happiness of the individual is decided in time, and is decided through the relationship to Christianity as something historical" (330). Here Kierkegaard takes up the problem posed in his *Philosophical Fragments*. The first part of *Concluding Unscientific Postscript* has already taken up the problem under the aspect of "The Objective Problem concerning the Truth of Christianity." Christianity rivets eternal happiness to a historical occurrence. Matters of infinite interest are at stake, and faith is the expression of inwardness, passion, and authentic subjectivity when they are oriented to what infinitely matters. According to Christian witness as recorded in the Gospels, God in Christ entered time, invoking faith. Faith is directed to God and to Christ, but it does not bypass history. To the contrary, the historical is the scene of the visiting eternal. This is intrinsically paradoxical. Furthermore, our knowledge of the historical is, at best, an approximation. That such and such happened might be more or less probable, but faith is infinitely interested and can neither rest on nor trade in probabilities. It is held fast by an objective uncertainty. Yet by its nature it is the antithesis of all that is tentative.

Kierkegaard operates along the front of a decisive boundary, demarcation, contrast, and hostility between the territories of objective cer-

40. Kierkegaard, *Postscript*, 261. For Nietzsche, see "Schopenhauer as Educator," in *UO*.

41. See Karl Jaspers, *Reason and Existence* (London: Routledge & Kegan Paul, 1956), preface.

tainty and of faith. To aim at and celebrate the attainment of knowledge, which is the speculative task, is to evacuate any resultant "religious" accomplishment of any vestige of faith (hence, the scandal of Hegel and Hegelianism). "Christianity does not lend itself to objective observation, precisely because it proposes to intensify subjectivity to the utmost; and when the subject has thus put himself in the right attitude, he cannot attach his eternal happiness to speculative philosophy," to say the least (55). The lengthy second book of *Concluding Unscientific Postscript* addresses the subjective, in contrast to the objective, aspect of the problem of Christianity, most famously under the slogan that "subjectivity is truth." Kierkegaard first occupies himself with Lessing's way of setting up the question of truth and history. Lessing is right to oppose, inter alia, a "simple and direct transition, from the reliability of an historical account to an eternal decision"; but the question thus arises, as far as Kierkegaard is concerned, of how to understand the subjectivity of the individual correctly (85). His preoccupation with this question makes up the bulk of the volume, which is the second part of book 2. My questions to Kierkegaard pivot on the important second chapter of this part.

"Let me say that Christianity wishes to intensify passion to its highest pitch; but passion is subjectivity, and does not exist objectively" (117). This is a programmatic remark. It leads to Kierkegaard's conclusion that the truth is paradoxical. Why? The category of "paradox," as with "dialectic," is quite complex, but clearly the paradoxical arises from the relationship between truth and the existing individual.[42] If we could abstract from existence, truth might be speculatively attained in its objective, nonparadoxical rationality. But the passion of existence, when infinite happiness is at stake, conscripts truth into essential relationship to it; truth is not allowed its own dispassionate existence and is in one respect a determination of the subject. This is paradoxical. Reflection on truth can really be that only if it is reflection on the relationship of the existing subject to purported truth. *The objective accent falls on WHAT is said, the subjective accent on HOW it is said. . . .* The truth is precisely the venture which chooses an objective uncertainty with the passion of the infinite." More: "Faith is precisely the contradiction between the infinite passion of the individual's inwardness and the objective uncertainty" (181–82). This is paradoxical, for we are entertaining and not expelling contradiction, positively appropriating the "absurd" from the standpoint of faith. The Christian doctrines of incarnation and forgiveness of sins, defying speculative understanding and appropriated with the right subjectivity, thus constitute paradoxes, and Kierkegaard is happy so to expound them.

42. David Gouwens is a safe pair of hands when it comes to treating *Kierkegaard as a Religious Thinker* (Cambridge: Cambridge University Press, 1996).

Nietzsche basically opposed faith and truth. We have seen his claim that the will-to-truth arose from the ethical virtue of truthfulness publicly paraded by Christianity and that its historical exercise led to the abandonment of Christianity. Religious faith does not properly conform to the ethical standards of Christianity, which therefore undoes itself. For Nietzscheans who strictly follow Nietzsche at this point, Kierkegaard may be credited with a passionate gallantry, even praised for an admirable quixotry, but that is as far as they can go and is concession enough. From Nietzsche's standpoint, let us run the argument like this. The virtue of faith is acquired by dint of the failure of objective certainty. Its passion is that of an infinite interest, and its aspiration is seemingly for the acquisition of truth and eternal happiness. But the celebration of paradox, contradiction, and absurdity is a desperate attempt to transform the necessity of uncertainty into the virtue of faith. Indeed, with his brand of uncertainty, Kierkegaard has stripped himself of all but a somewhat idiosyncratic notion of truth, from the standpoint of ethical truthfulness. His uncertainty is not of the kind that we get when high probability falls short of absolute certainty. Kierkegaard trades on the radical absence or impermissibility of a standard of rationality generated from anywhere but from within the life of faith. Now it just *might* be acceptable to allow the Christian concept of "truth" to keep to the comfort of its own home here—to allow that what counts for us as "truth" should be dictated by the internal constraints of the language of faith. But this is not the truth that the religious and ethical virtue of *truthfulness* requires, as conceitedly trumpeted by Christianity. *That* virtue requires the possibility, which has been actualized in intellectual history, that my Christian "truth" should be undermined. Kierkegaard does not finally succeed in separating faith from wish, and thus truthful from wishful thinking.

What are we to make of criticism along these lines, on Nietzsche's behalf? Whatever the strengths of Kierkegaard's contentions—and these are always significant—I think that this imagined response on Nietzsche's behalf exposes the difficulties in Kierkegaard's analysis, though I shall formulate them differently and more mundanely. More than once Kierkegaard tells us that there is nothing remarkable about Jesus. He does not put it so flat-footedly, but he employs the mode of the logical analysis of categories: for God to reveal himself in history, it is required that there should be nothing remarkable about the humanity in which he is revealed. Faith must be riveted to, and actually partake of, the paradoxical and the absurd, something that cannot happen if the speculative standpoint, which lauds objectivity, is able to get a foothold on the object of faith. Take a speculative approach, and Christology runs the risk of being a foundation for a religious proof, or something along those lines. And that, for Kierkegaard, is the problem. Speaking of the attempt to "obtain a proof of the resurrection," Kierkegaard avers that "the very existence of this proof constitutes the greatest difficulty of all" (384). The conclusion of Kierkegaard's first discussion of "Existential Pathos" shows us that Bultmann was by no means novel or alone in reading the search for historical proof as a version of works-righteousness.[43]

From a biblical viewpoint, this is surely suspect—and just how seriously Kierkegaard is prepared to accept that viewpoint as a criterion emerges in his underdiscussed book on Adolf Adler.[44] In Scripture, Jesus is portrayed as remarkable by almost any standards. It is true that he is depicted not primarily as a grand human exemplar but especially as the Messiah of Israel, and we might want to put an infinite qualitative Kierkegaardian distance between the Son of God and a good man.[45] Nevertheless, for many of those who do not believe, he remains a grand human exemplar. While highlighting this description of Jesus doubtless threatens to turn robust faith into an inaudible whimper, its stubborn truth must neither be obscured nor theologically disallowed. Kierkegaard goes too far.

It profits us to ask how Kierkegaard got there. What appears to have happened is that, in this extremely clever and edifying venture of transposing Christianity into the mode of possibility, in order to communicate its actuality indirectly, Kierkegaard allowed the logic of the relationship of history, faith, and certainty to be excessively dictated by dialectical categories forged out of logical abstractions. In prescribing for "the historical," Kierkegaard too much abstracted from *the* history. This line could certainly be developed into the thesis that Kierkegaard is more on Hegelian turf than first appears, has something in common with Hegel that weakens his own polemic, and occupies common ground just so that he can criticize Hegel and establish an infinite qualitative distance from him. But there is an "existential" question that we can ask Kierkegaard as well. "In the time of courtship, to be absolutely certain that one is loved is the certain sign that one is not in love" (407). It is all rather subtle.[46] Yet many of us will believe that this claim indicates more about Kierkegaardian (or his pseudonymous) pathos than about love or the

43. In its wider context, see Rudolf Bultmann's celebrated comment, "Demythologizing is the radical application of the doctrine of justification by faith to the sphere of knowledge and thought," in *Jesus Christ and Mythology* (London: SCM, 1960), 84.

44. Søren Kierkegaard, *On Authority and Revelation* (New York: Harper & Row, 1966). It is my impression that it is underdiscussed in nonspecialist accounts of Kierkegaard's philosophy of religion.

45. I am not assuming that "Son of God" in a messianic sense is the same as "Son of God incarnate," but if "infinite qualitative distance" is exaggerated when applied to the messianic notion, the language can be suitably modified.

46. In Kierkegaard, *Postscript*, see the asterisked remark at the bottom of 407.

richly existential phenomenon of Christian faith. Existentially, it appears that Kierkegaard cannot savor faith that lacks objective uncertainty at its constitutional heart, but that is a remark about Kierkegaard (or his authorship) rather than the logic of the Christian approach to truth.

The upshot is that, in Kierkegaard, historical knowledge is categorically too flattened out, as it were, in terms of its epistemic weight in relation to faith. He believes that historical knowledge per se can never be more than approximate. Therefore, it cannot satisfy infinite interest, which requires certainty. Worse, historical probabilities are seductive. They lure us toward the speculative point of view. But Kierkegaard surely exaggerates this temptation. A judgment of historical probability might be a link in the chain that connects faith to history without substituting speculation for passion. Faith is a refined passion, but a variety of ingredients can go into it. When Kierkegaard says that no one has come close to faith after critical inquiry, he appears to be confusing personal stories with logical categories. To acquire *fides historica* is not to acquire *fides salvifica*. But acquisition of *fides historica* may help someone to acquire *fides salvifica*.[47] Without being naive or reductionist in the matter, why did Luke, John, and Paul write as they did if Kierkegaard was right?[48] For these reasons, it appears to me that Kierkegaard's account of faith would not encourage Nietzsche to shrug off the sense that it is purchased at too high a price in relation to truth.[49]

Where does this leave us? Where it is quite unfashionable to be, but where Christianity is, nevertheless, and where Nietzsche and his sympathizers must face that it is. Christianity is irreducibly implicated in the empirical question of testimony to historical event. There is no other way of reading the biblical account, and any other reading is an accommodation that strays from the inner logic of Christian faith. That an empirical approach to the truth of Christianity is riddled with intellectual difficulties, or that it courts accusations of being everything from naive to boring, from being prepostmodern to tasteless—such argument is no objection to addressing the question of truth from the standpoint of

47. The question of "justifying" one's own faith, as opposed to helping someone else to acquire it, is too complex to consider here.

48. I am thinking of Luke 1:1–4; 1 Cor. 15:1–7; and the consistent Johannine emphasis on eyewitnesses.

49. Kierkegaard's story about the man and the boy, set in the middle of *Postscript* (212ff.), would with some justification clinch Nietzsche's conviction that faith is too closely allied to wishing at the expense of truth. We cannot follow many interesting trails in connection with Nietzsche and Kierkegaard. See Jaspers's telling first lecture in *Reason and Existence*; Michael Weston, *Kierkegaard and Modern Continental Philosophy* (London: Routledge, 1994), chap. 3; Gerd-Günther Grau, "Nietzsche and Kierkegaard," in *Studies in Nietzsche and the Judaeo-Christian Tradition*, ed. James C. O'Flaherty, Timothy F. Sellner, and Robert M. Helm (Chapel Hill: University of North Carolina Press, 1985), 226–51.

the biblical stake in history. If what Nietzsche or anyone else requires of us is *honesty*, then that is our confession. The ground of the Christian assertion about the truth of God and of Christ, a truth riveted to the project of deliverance from sin by God's action, is that there are documents testifying that Jesus walked the earth and was believed in as the Messiah of Israel on the grounds of his resurrection from the dead. Christians must explain why they believe that testimony. And they must, with equal insistence, keep asking how a disbelieving account of the emergence of this testimony is credible. The proper requirements of a will-to-truth force us to pay attention to why a few despised, herdlike, ignorant females became hysterical on the third day after Jesus's death. In fact, there is rather a lot to be said for them.[50]

Conclusion

> For it never seems to fail that when God becomes man among us, right here in Greco-Christian Europe, even in Prussia or, God forbid, in California, . . . whenever he speaks, he speaks to us, in our language, in Greek or Hebrew or Arabic, which endangers everybody else. Then the world is divided into those who happened to be standing in the right place, or living in the right time, or speaking the right language, when the God came, when the divine thunder struck—and those poor chaps who were not so lucky. The world divides into the "faithful," who are blessed by luck or providence, *O felix culpa*, and the *gentiles*, the *goyim*, everybody else, the unlucky and unblessed, those against whom the community fortifies itself.[51]

John Caputo's words occur in a volume whose treatment of religion is as postmodern as you will find, if postmodernity is the kind of thing of which this kind of thing can be said. But they pick up a perennial problem in the exposition of and apologia for Christian faith. In its traditional form, Christianity shares with some other faith traditions the belief that the universe neither came into existence with the beginning of time nor has endured as a self-sustaining material reality without beginning. Many Christians go beyond an affirmation of faith to an affirmation of the intellectual incredibility or incoherence of denying the reality of a personal Creator. Belief in God as Creator obviously underlies

---

50. The most important and compelling contemporary treatment I know of that advances along this line is that of N. T. Wright, the three volumes of whose projected five- or six-volume New Testament theology have now been published: *The New Testament and the People of God* (London: SPCK, 1992); *Jesus and the Victory of God* (London: SPCK, 1996); and *The Resurrection of the Son of God* (London: SPCK, 2003).

51. Caputo, *Prayers and Tears*, 245.

and is presupposed by belief in the resurrection of Jesus from the dead. It is the latter belief that both distinguishes Christianity and appears to give it its stamp as a religion that makes exclusive truth claims for itself. Indeed, it is possible to believe in the resurrection of Jesus without embracing Christianity, and affirmations other than the affirmation of resurrection cause the scandal of exclusiveness. But in referring to the resurrection and alluding to its "exclusiveness," I am assuming the wider context for its declaration by evangelists and apostles. In conclusion, I want to make some brief observations on the logic of the "exclusive" mentality that appears to follow if we insist on riveting Christianity to belief in a world-historical resurrection from the dead on Palestinian soil two millennia ago.

The problem of religious exclusivism that arises from confessing the resurrection of Christ and the Christ of the resurrection typically arises when we do not allow the Christian viewpoint to come into its own. It is a matter of perspective. On the Christian view of humanity, humans live only once on this earth as we know it, living as embodied beings in a particular space and time, cultural and linguistic environment. To almost all the nonreligious, that is a truism. This being the case, the Creator of heaven and earth can come no closer to humans, if he has a mind to do this, than by assuming human nature, thereby living once and dying once, because such is the human condition. The possibility of multiple divine incarnations is immediately problematic for this reason, quite apart from any others. But if it could be accomplished, it would not solve the problem of alleged exclusivism, since at any one time only one space could be privileged. Lest the discussion seem to spin off in a direction that will confirm Nietzsche's supposition that no one should be listening to theologians anyway, let me just make this bald point: the privileging of a particular space, time, and culture by the special presence of God is not a sign of exclusion or exclusivism. In fact, the boot is on the other foot. If there is a profound divine interest in humanity, the high point of revelation and identification is attained in the assumption of human nature in the only possible way—in one space, time, and culture.

Humans have to be somewhere; a truly *incarnate* personal deity has to be somewhere. The logic of possessing a scriptural record and promoting scriptural translation and the logic of Christian mission show precisely that exclusivism is *alien* to the Christian faith. The Scriptures of the Old and New Testaments are written in known languages that are not sacred; translation is mandated so that Jew and Gentile, churchgoer and Buddhist monk—all can read the same words. Mission is the announcement of the place and time of God's coming into the world so that no peoples or nations are excluded from knowledge or privilege. God is neither impersonal to the extent of being unable to share the human condition, nor remote to the extent of not wanting to do so. If that is indeed the case, what would *really* make Christianity exclusivist in spirit would be the *failure* to produce any verbal or written witness to divine action, and the *refusal* to engage in any missionary activity to the same end.

What initially looks like a becoming modesty about the claim that God has acted and revealed himself turns out, on analysis, to be not so modest. Supposing we say that no one can know or is justified in being confident that God became incarnate in Christ or that God is a personal, communicating being. Suppose such a belief takes its place among an array of other religious and nonreligious positions as just one more possibility. What are the implications of denying that anyone can be justifiably confident of its truth? Let us explore them: If we deny the right to justifiable confidence, we do not just deny the confidence; we also deny even the possibility that what is believed has any truth in it, or at least, we make the belief highly implausible. Why so? Imagine that God has purposefully acted and revealed himself in order to impart knowledge of himself. Then someone somewhere might be justified in being confident that God has done so. But it is objected that no one has the right to be confident. If that is indeed the case, we must assume that no such divine action or revelation has taken place. Why would it not have taken place? For one of two reasons: either there is no personal being around who can act and reveal in this way, or there is such a being, but he is unwilling to do so. In both cases, the Christian view of God is denied. So the denial that anyone can have justifiable confidence in the occurrence of revelation or incarnation amounts to the denial that there is a God such as Christians believe in. The religious option labeled "Christianity" is not really an option at all. It is dogmatically excluded.

I believe that the big steps that I have taken in this argument can be broken up into a suitably rigorous presentation, but my objective here is merely to depict in bold relief how the logic of Christianity looks from within Christianity. A consistently Christian will-to-truth will insist that faith stands or falls on the basis of the testimony to the resurrection of Jesus of Nazareth recorded in the Christian Scriptures. The logic of the theological convictions that surround this claim can be delineated along the lines above, so as to show why and in what sense Christian faith is "exclusivist." Such a conclusion to a book on Nietzsche sounds entirely humdrum. But the will-to-truth is not at the service of intellectual excitement. There is every indication that Nietzsche knew that. We therefore take our leave of him, as he leaves us—in a state of reflective sobriety.

CHRONOLOGICAL LIST
OF NIETZSCHE'S WORKS

ALL THE WORKS dated 1888 were completed in 1888, prior to Nietzsche's mental collapse, but were published at various times either during that year or later.

The Birth of Tragedy (1872)

Unfashionable Observations (1876; combining essays published at various times)

Human, All Too Human (1878)

Assorted Opinions and Maxims (1879)

The Wanderer and His Shadow (1880; *Assorted Opinions and Maxims* and *The Wanderer and His Shadow* became part 2 of *Human, All Too Human*)

Daybreak (1881)

The Gay Science (1882; a fifth book was added later)

Thus Spoke Zarathustra (1884; a fourth part was added later)

Beyond Good and Evil (1886)

On the Genealogy of Morality (1887)

The Case of Wagner (1888)

Dithyrambs of Dionysus (1888)

Twilight of the Idols (1888)

The Anti-christ (1888)

Ecce Homo (1888)

Nietzsche contra Wagner (1888)

BIBLIOGRAPHICAL NOTE

OF THE GENERAL introductions to Friedrich Wilhelm Nietzsche's thought, Joseph P. Stern's *Nietzsche* (London: Fontana, 1985) is one place to start. Another introductory volume by Stern, *A Study of Nietzsche* (Cambridge: Cambridge University Press, 1979), considerably overlaps with it. Stern was the writer chosen by Bryan Magee to introduce Nietzsche in the interesting and helpful volume *The Great Philosophers* (Oxford: Oxford University Press, 1987). One worry that some people have about Stern's two book-length introductions is that they make too much concession to those who want to associate Nietzsche with Nazism. Stern addresses this point succinctly at the end of his interview with Magee.

Stern is a better place to start than is Michael Tanner, whose *Nietzsche* (Oxford: Oxford University Press, 1994) was his contribution to the generally helpful Past Masters series. Tanner jumps into the account without providing a biographical framework, whereas Stern deliberately and rightly exceeded the space usually allowed in the Fontana Modern Masters series for a such an account. More important, Tanner is engaged in a running debate with alternative interpretations of Nietzsche, an engagement that is obtrusive in a short introduction; hence, one is almost as conscious of the phenomenon of Nietzschean interpretation as of Nietzsche's own thought. This is not to devalue Tanner's work as such; it is just to recommend that it not be taken as a way into Nietzsche.

Reginald J. Hollingdale provides a biographical approach to Nietzsche in a recent second edition of his *Nietzsche: The Man and His Philosophy* (Cambridge: Cambridge University Press, 1999). Hollingdale was a veteran translator of Nietzsche's work, and the biography is both accessible and solid; yet some prefer Ronald Hayman's longer *Nietzsche: A Critical Life* (London: Weidenfeld & Nicolson, 1980). This latter volume is certainly lively and readable, impressing on its reader Nietzsche's daily routines and struggles with ill health.[1]

The Cambridge Companion series is generally useful, and an overview of themes in Nietzsche is well provided by Bernd Magnus and Kathleen M. Higgins in *The Cambridge Companion to Nietzsche* (Cambridge: Cambridge University Press, 1996). This volume also provides bibliographical guidance. Since its appearance, the flood of studies on Nietzsche has continued to rise. One particularly elegantly written contribution may be mentioned: Rüdiger Safranski's *Nietzsche: A Philosophical Biography* (New York and London: Norton, 2002), which the reader is well advised to tackle as quickly as possible after securing an initial orientation in Nietzsche.

Regarding where to start in reading Nietzsche himself, that is a difficult matter. His works differ, and hardly any work will really give a good idea of what happens in the others. *The Twilight of the Idols* is an obvious candidate, and Nietzsche himself gives some encouragement to those who advocate starting there. Much of what is central in Nietzsche's thinking is certainly distilled into this slim volume, if readers are interested in a "systematic" approach to Nietzschean themes. Yet in *TI* we miss some quintessential Nietzsche of the kind encountered in a work that might alternatively, if controversially, be recommended for beginners (given my earlier caveat): *Beyond Good and Evil*. Nietzsche's major effort, *Thus Spoke Zarathustra*, should be read at an early stage only if the reader wants to absorb spirit, mood, and atmosphere rather than worry about exactly what Nietzsche taught and why he taught it; on that basis, *Z* can be recommended, and I do not want to underestimate the grasp someone might have of major components of Nietzsche's teaching on the basis of reading *Z* even before other works.

What of Nietzsche and Christianity? The late Jörg Salaquarda provides a solid account of "Nietzsche and the Judaeo-Christian Tradition" in *The Cambridge Companion to Nietzsche*. Hans Küng's easy style and wide range often conceals some careful and exact underlying scholarship; his account of Nietzsche in *Does God Exist?* (London: Collins, 1980) under "Nihilism—Consequence of Atheism" can be recommended. He is, however, somewhat overconfident on Darwin as "godfather" to the ideas on self-overcoming (the *Übermensch*). Carl-Heinz Ratschow gives a useful, readable, and interesting summary in his chapter on Nietzsche in *Nineteenth Century Religious Thought in the West*, edited by Ninian Smart et al., volume 3 (Cambridge: Cambridge University Press, 1988). The chronological framework of his account is generally helpful, but he underestimates the significance of *The Genealogy of Morality* and effec-

---

1. Curtis Cate, *Friedrich Nietzsche* (London: Hutchinson, 2002) is a longer biography.

tively cuts off his essay before getting to that volume. This contribution is also witness to both the necessity and the well-nigh impossibility of saying anything clearly and accurately about Nietzsche's teaching on eternal recurrence in short compass. And the interpretation of Nietzsche's family piety, which frames his account, is controversial.

For more detailed studies, one can turn to Karl Jaspers's *Nietzsche and Christianity* (Chicago: H. Regnery, 1961). This was an expansion of his 1938 lecture and used the older, by now inferior, German edition of Nietzsche's work. By the time Jaspers wrote this, he had already published the substantial and enduringly valuable *Nietzsche: An Introduction to the Understanding of His Philosophical Activity* (Tucson: University of Arizona Press, 1965), which displays all the advantages of having one philosopher engaging with another. This latter made some, but not detailed or systematic, reference to Christianity. The strength of the short study *Nietzsche and Christianity* is the way Jaspers places Nietzsche's views on Christianity in their wider context, especially the question of world history, thus bringing out its comprehensive dimension much more than the plan of my own study has admitted. Jaspers wanted to drive home the fact that Nietzsche "knew and admitted the Christian basis of his real motivating forces: his seriousness, truthfulness, and his radically uncompromising approach" (vii). But he verges on misleading us: given what Nietzsche said about Christianity as a force in history, let alone its presence in his own background, we need to be reminded more than Jaspers does that this kind of Christian basis, if not culturally ubiquitous, was at least culturally common. Nevertheless, the study remains useful.

Jaspers's interpretation was one important source for an interpretation of Nietzsche offered in a recent study by Alistair Kee, *Nietzsche against the Crucified* (London: SCM, 1999). It is racy and readable but not grounded in sufficiently detailed scholarship to give the interpretation the weight the author wants to give it. By contrast, see the helpful study by Tyler T. Roberts, *Contesting Spirit: Nietzsche, Affirmation, Religion* (Princeton, NJ: Princeton University Press, 1998), often traversing similar terrain. Tim Murphy's study *Nietzsche, Metaphor, Religion* (Albany: State University of New York Press, 2001) is also helpful and shows how difficult it is to describe Nietzsche on Christianity without describing Nietzsche on a host of other things, especially metaphor. Giles Fraser's *Redeeming Nietzsche: On the Piety of Unbelief* (New York and London: Routledge, 2001) is strong on the soteriological track in Nietzsche's thought and in its critique of Nietzsche on suffering and evil. Over the years, he and I have come to read Nietzsche in a quite similar fashion on many points; though I have taken occasional issue with him in this present volume, I have considerably benefited both from his study and from conversations in the past.

Several collections treat in detail this or that aspect of Nietzsche's relationship to Christianity. Two good collections are the older one by James C. O'Flaherty, Timothy F. Sellner, and Robert M. Helm, editors, *Studies in Nietzsche and the Judaeo-Christian Tradition* (Chapel Hill: University of North Carolina Press, 1985) and the recent one edited by John Lippitt and Jim Urpeth, *Nietzsche and the Divine* (Manchester, UK: Clinamen, 2000).[2] Anyone who reads these through will see just how much has been omitted in an account such as mine. One important feature in the latter collection is that essayists sometimes engage with non-Christian religion as well as with Christianity, which is also true of Weaver Santaniello's edition of essays *Nietzsche and the Gods* (Albany: State University of New York Press, 2001). This is a slighter volume than the other two mentioned, with essays uneven and sometimes indifferent in quality, which is not to deny the presence of several useful contributions. The same is true of a collection of essays published over twenty years ago by *Concilium*, breathing a quite different air, edited by Claude Geffré and Jean-Pierre Jossua, *Nietzsche and Christianity* (New York: Seabury; Edinburgh: T&T Clark, 1981). To this volume, Jean Granier, author of a detailed study on Nietzsche many years before that, contributed an epilogue, in which he remarked that while "the articles of this issue have contributed many truly pertinent observations, . . . they occasionally seem to be a little trivial because they are too anxious to make Nietzsche sound *closer* to the gospel than he is" (102). Where contributors to the more recent collections seek not to interpret Nietzsche's relationship to Christianity as one of entire hostility, they nuance their accounts more carefully.

Some of the most illuminating material on Nietzsche's attitude to Christianity emerges in works that do not concentrate on that question but include some discussion of it. To give one example: in a fine and illuminating study that repays careful reading, Gregory Moore, *Nietzsche, Biology, and Metaphor* (Cambridge: Cambridge University Press, 2002), has the chapter "Christianity and Degeneration." By carefully researching what was being written before and in Nietzsche's day and what Nietzsche was reading, works such as this are refining or revising our understanding of Nietzsche's thought in general and of his response to Christianity in particular.

2. Some papers from the same conference as the proceedings published in *Nietzsche and the Divine* are printed in the *Journal of Nietzsche Studies* 19 (2000).

Author Index

Adams, Robert M. 42n89, 251n37
Allen, R. E. 36n68
Allen, Woody 257
Alter, Robert 214n12
Ansell-Pearson, Keith 41n88, 159n24, 210n4, 225n35, 228n50, 274n12
Auden, Wystan H. 83n1
Austin, J. L. 277n23

Bacon, Francis 105, 105n47, 106n50
Baillie, John 181n5
Ballanche, Pierre-Simon 114
Barth, Karl 66, 66n33, 67, 67n36, 67n37, 67n38, 75n65, 131, 179n2, 180, 180n3, 181, 181n5, 181n6, 182, 187, 193n55, 207, 273, 273n8
Begbie, Jeremy 80n76, 81n77
Berkouwer, G. C. 67n37
Berkowitz, Peter 88n13, 99n34, 172n60, 189, 189n39, 195n61, 216n15
Bertonneau, Thomas F. 125n18, 125n19, 125n20
Bethge, Eberhard 242, 242n4, 245n11
Biser, Eugen 15, 15n5, 188n33
Blake, William 18, 18n16, 259n60
Blocher, Henri 70, 70n43
Blumenberg, Hans 105, 105n45, 105n48
Bonafoux, Pascal 190n43
Bonhoeffer, Dietrich 186, 186n26, 205n80, 223n31, 243, 243n7, 244, 244n10, 245, 245n12, 245n14, 246, 246n17, 247, 247n20, 247n21, 247n22,

247n23, 247n24, 248, 249, 249n30, 249n31, 249n32, 249n33, 250n34, 262
Borges, Jorge Luis 177n71, 178, 178n76, 195n60, 260n63, 267n85, 278, 278n27
Bowen, Elizabeth 112
Bradley, William L. 79n72
Brand, Hilary 78n69
Brobjer, Thomas H. 24n18, 26n24, 33n50, 36n67, 43n91, 58n23, 84n5
Brontë, Emily 44
Brown, Terence 18n16
Brunner, Emil 252n39, 278, 278n28, 279
Bultmann, Rudolf 97n31, 288, 288n43
Burnaby, John 261n67
Busch, Eberhard 131n28, 179n1, 186n24
Butler, Eliza Marian 29–30, 30n39, 30n41, 31, 31n44, 117
Butler, Joseph 136n41
Butterfield, Herbert 223, 223n31
Byron, George Gordon 16, 18, 19, 51, 83, 117, 147, 179, 209, 230, 241

Calvin, John 41
Caputo, John D. 248n27, 277, 277n22, 278n24, 290, 290n51
Cate, Curtis 20n2
Chadwick, Henry 125n19
Chaplin, Adrienne 78n69, 81n77
Chua, Daniel 52n6, 221n28
Clark, Maudemarie 211n8, 262n68, 272n6
Clark, Robert T. 33n50
Clarke, Graham 161n31

299

SUBJECT INDEX

Aaron 76
Absolute, Hegelian 37
absolutism 234
Adam 128, 245, 253
Aeschylus 42
agapē 46, 64, 256
anthropology
    Christian 97, 125–28, 142–43, 180, 246, 248, 254
    moral 209
    philosophical 179, 183
Antichrist 17, 176–77, 246–47
Anti-christ, The (Nietzsche) 90–91, 126–27, 189–91
anti-Semitism 71, 225–28
Apollo 58, 60–61, 76
Aquinas, Thomas. *See* Thomas Aquinas
art 40–42, 64, 73–78, 80–81, 89
    Nietzsche's enthronement of 71, 80–81
    Schopenhauer's view of 44, 46, 49
    Wagner's philosophy of 54
asceticism 44, 49, 236–37
"as if " 73, 75–77, 283
Aslan 68, 204–5
atheism 24, 26–27, 97–98, 236
Augustine 105, 109, 136, 141

Bach, Johann Sebastian 281
Bacon, Francis 105–6
Ballanche, Pierre-Simon 114
Barth, Fritz 179
Barth, Karl 66–70, 131, 179–87, 193, 199–200, 206–7, 259, 273

Bayreuth Festival 53, 56, 60, 71, 79, 85–87
Beethoven, Ludwig van 73, 88, 221
Beyond Good and Evil (Nietzsche) 128–29, 189, 216–18, 272
Bible 129–31, 278–79
Bible cited
    Genesis 252–53
    Job 201–4
    Revelation 169
Birth of Tragedy from the Spirit of Music, The (Nietzsche) 56–64
Bismarck, Otto von 19, 222
Bizet, Georges 143
Blake, William 18
Bonhoeffer, Dietrich 186, 241–53, 262
Bowen, Elizabeth 112
Brahms, Johannes 73, 85
Brandes, Georg 266, 269
British moral philosophy 214
Brontë, Emily 44
Browning, Robert 80
Brunner, Emil 278
Buddhism 46, 121, 141, 224, 281n34
Byron, Lord 16, 230–31

Calvin, John 41
Calvinism 107
Case of Wagner, The (Nietzsche) 86, 88–90
Celsus 125
child labor 42n89
choice, Nietzsche's view of 231
Christ. *See* Jesus

305